AGE OF INDUSTRIAL VIOLENCE
1910–15

AGE OF
INDUSTRIAL VIOLENCE
1910-15

THE ACTIVITIES AND FINDINGS OF THE
UNITED STATES COMMISSION ON
INDUSTRIAL RELATIONS

GRAHAM ADAMS, JR.

COLUMBIA UNIVERSITY PRESS
NEW YORK AND LONDON

First published in book form 1966
Second printing 1971

ISBN 0-231-02801-6
Library of Congress Catalog Card Number: 66-17857
Printed in the United States of America

To My Mother
and the Memory of My Father

ACKNOWLEDGMENTS

I EXPRESS my deep appreciation to Professor William E. Leuchtenburg of Columbia University for his friendly, careful, and perceptive guidance all during my research and writing of the manuscript for this book. My gratitude also extends to Professors Robert D. Cross and Richard Hofstadter of Columbia for their valuable criticisms of the work as it neared completion.

I owe a considerable debt to numerous librarians and archivists especially those of the AFL-CIO Archives, Catholic University, Columbia University, the Library of Congress, the National Archives, the New York Public Library, and the State Historical Society of Wisconsin. In different ways several people aided my research, including Mrs. Harold S. Bradley, Miss Sandra L. Carroll, Miss Fola La Follette, William E. Pemberton, Leonard Rapport, and Sister Frances Marie Walsh. Finally, I convey my thanks to Professors Basil Rauch and Chilton Williamson of Barnard College for their many kindnesses, advice, and encouragement. Grants from the Barnard College Committee on Research and Travel and from the Research Council of the University of Missouri greatly helped me to prepare the manuscript for publication.

GRAHAM ADAMS, JR.

January, 1966

A NOTE ON SOURCES

NEWSPAPERS and magazines formed a part of the necessary source material for the strikes covered in this book. Journalists may over-emphasize certain details to make a story colorful. Wherever possible, I have compared accounts and used, with equal distribution, a wide variety of publications of diverse ideological standards. Real and great violence did erupt during this era; reporters neither imagined it nor necessarily exaggerated it.

For the sake of fairness, all persons directly quoted from testimony given at the Commission's hearings were identified by name and/or position. Indirect citations of a longer and more general nature were also selected with an eye toward balance. Considerations of style and space did not permit long detailed reproductions of "question-answer" colloquies. Generally, commissioners phrased their queries judiciously and refrained from deliberate attempts to lead or trap witnesses. Since representatives of labor, capital, and the public all sat on the panel, few witnesses complained of unfair treatment. Frank Walsh's interrogation of John D. Rockefeller, Jr., however, did provoke considerable controversy. (See Chapter VII.)

INTRODUCTION

FROM THE close of the Civil War until the early twentieth century industrialization swept through America with startling rapidity. Huge corporations rose to dominate the economy, while masses of workmen found themselves permanently dependent upon the wage system. Severe tensions emerged, particularly in the field of industrial relations.

American society assumed that people could resolve their disputes pacifically. It presupposed a willingness on the part of its citizens to compromise, to abide by civil authority, and to seek desired reforms by peaceful means. If men, regardless of justification, rejected these postulates and resorted to violence, they attacked the basis of civilized order.

During the Progressive era, the United States Commission on Industrial Relations, by public hearings and research, traversed the continent to discover the underlying causes of industrial strife. Congress had charged these commissioners to investigate a sweeping range of topics and armed them with extensive power. Concerned chiefly with events in the years 1910 to 1915, these investigators questioned over 700 witnesses and collected about 6½ million words of testimony. Into their presence came men of international fame: John D. Rockefeller, Jr., Andrew Carnegie, Samuel Gompers, William D. ("Big Bill") Haywood, Louis D. Brandeis, and Clarence Darrow. Equally the probers paid attention to humble people known scarcely beyond their own neighborhoods: miners and farmers, garment workers and lumberjacks, silk weavers and mechanics. Human warmth, deep hatred, intense drama, and occasional comedy highlighted these sessions.

Several chapters depict important strikes probed by the federal body, but they do not approach these encounters as studies in economic history (business cycles, immigration, environment as among the sources of industrial discord). These sections simply portray representative examples of some of the major clashes which the Commission publicized through its hearings and research. A common unifying theme emerged from the inquiries, which sheds light on the Progressive period. Almost every strike, irrespective of origin, appeared to have erupted into violence which threatened the structure of society.*

In breadth and in depth the Commission presented a panoramic survey of America in turmoil. This book examines the origins, operations, and findings of the Commission, describes the image of violence which the investigations projected, and analyzes the impact of the Commission's work on American history.

* In the book the term "social conflict" is used chiefly in this broad sense rather than in reference to a study of the origins of some specific social movement (e.g., socialism, progressivism).

CONTENTS

AGE OF INDUSTRIAL VIOLENCE
1910-15

I

"THE CRIME OF THE CENTURY"

1

ON OCTOBER 1, 1910, AT 1:00 A.M., a thunderous blast rocked the entire downtown area of Los Angeles. The Los Angeles *Times* building exploded. An initial detonation in a passageway blew out one side of the first floor. Tons of ink stored in this alley then erupted. One powerful discharge hurled men and heavy linotype machines into the air and slammed them against walls. "Frames and timbers flew in all directions," a survivor recalled. "The force of the thing was indescribable." Within seconds the whole structure was roaring up like a gigantic torch.[1]

A hundred or more employees frantically rushed to escape. Some dashed to the upper windows, but firemen could not reach them with ladders. A few jumped, but others fell back into the flames. Not all who leaped landed in safety nets; many smashed against the concrete pavement. Hours later, nothing remained but a few steel girders. Beneath smoldering debris lay the charred bodies of twenty victims.

Harrison Gray Otis, anti-union publisher of the *Times*, promptly accused organized labor of what he called "The Crime of the Century." Repercussions from this Los Angeles tragedy soon spread beyond the borders of California. It set off a chain of events that affected American life far into the twentieth century.[2]

2

Two decades of industrial warfare had preceded this dramatic incident. In 1890 four Los Angeles newspapers, the *Times, Herald,*

Express, and *Tribune,* opened negotiations with the local branch of the International Typographical Union to reduce wages. The union refused and threatened a walkout. By August, however, three of the publications had agreed to compromise their differences with the printers and end the dispute. Only the *Times* held out. Otis imported strikebreakers, locked out his own workers, and through his editorials inaugurated an attack of unparalleled bitterness against organized labor.[3]

Otis always commanded attention in Los Angeles. A veteran of fifteen Civil War engagements, he had also fought in the Philippines during the Spanish-American hostilities. He gloried in his title of General and saw to it that the architecture of his Los Angeles *Times* building resembled that of a medieval fortress. At his home, "The Bivouac," he read the works of Friedrich Neitzsche with approval.[4]

But Harrison Gray Otis was more than a colorful eccentric. His paper developed into the most powerful editorial force in Los Angeles. General Otis and his cohorts gained control of the Los Angeles Merchants and Manufacturers' Association (M and M) and turned it into a vehicle for promotion of the open-shop policy toward labor. Ostensibly, this philosophy maintained that a company should have complete freedom to hire either union or nonunion employees. In reality, Otis and the M and M fought against any kind of independent labor organization. For twenty years Los Angeles unions strove for recognition. For twenty years Otis and his legions beat them back.[5]

Events on the national scene paralleled these developments on the West Coast. In 1903 employers throughout the country embarked on a counterattack against organized labor. First the National Association of Manufacturers opposed the recognition of any national union. Soon afterward the Citizens' Industrial Association, another vehemently anti-union organization, formed local Alliances in every major city in the United States. The Los Angeles Alliance, with 6,000 members and liberally backed by millionaire Henry E. Huntington, became the strongest in the nation. When Otis' M and M absorbed the Alliance, the new enrollment of the M and M included 85 percent of the city's businessmen. As the first decade of the new century ended, Los Angeles labor faced a wealthy, powerful, and articulate foe.[6]

Workers in Los Angeles realized that survival demanded consolidation. In 1904 eighty unions in the city united in a new Central Labor Council, which quickly received recognition from the American Federation of Labor. Three years later, the AFL, now thoroughly alarmed by the furious anti-unionism rampant in Los Angeles, singled out the California city for special consideration. At its national convention the Federation endorsed a resolution that damned the Los Angeles *Times* as "the most unfair, unscrupulous, and malignant enemy of organized labor in America." In an unprecedented move, the delegates then spotlighted the West Coast community for an intensive organization drive. They created a "Los Angeles Fund" and entreated all their members throughout the nation to contribute toward its growth.[7]

San Francisco, however, played the most vital role in the buildup of Los Angeles labor. In stark contrast to its southern neighbor, the northern city stood out as a labor-dominated community. San Francisco's building trades unions had taken advantage of the destruction caused by the great earthquake of 1906 to fasten closed-shop conditions on every phase of construction work. Their power waxed so great that in 1909 they elected the president of the Building Trades Council as mayor of the city. Hard, competent, pro-capitalist, and corrupt, these labor barons ruled their domain with an iron fist.[8]

Labor costs in the Bay City rose to 30 percent above those in Los Angeles. San Francisco employers, their backs to the wall because of the competition, told their unions that unless they equalized conditions by organizing Los Angeles labor, business in San Francisco faced collapse. As a result, San Francisco unions sent many of their crack organizers southward. Leaders from the rest of California then joined the march on Los Angeles. The spectacle of San Francisco's labor barony frightened Los Angeles businessmen; they braced themselves for a collision.[9]

3

This acceleration of labor activity led directly to the climactic year of 1910, when the Los Angeles unions struck the mightiest blow in their history. First they battled over beer. Through a series of boycotts over the years, when workingmen temporarily abstained from their favorite beverage, the International Brewery Workers' Union had achieved closed-shop agreements with the entire industry. In May, 1910, however, when contracts came up for renewal, the employers refused to grant any additional wage increases and declared an open shop. All Los Angeles brewery workers then walked out and initiated a strike that affected the whole industry.

The M and M prepared for war. If it smashed the Brewery Union, it would destroy organized labor's only real foothold in Los Angeles. Felix J. Zeehandelaar, secretary of the M and M and a close friend of General Otis, pledged the active support of his group to the Southern California Brewers' Association. Brewery owners then posted notices which invited former employees to return if they would accept open-shop conditions. The unions boycotted all saloons, established picket lines throughout the city, and arranged to pay strike benefits to their needy members. Neither side budged for almost a year.[10]

An even more important strike followed. For years the Founders' and Employers' Association had held the metal trades workers in total subjugation. Low wages, bad working conditions, and long and unequal hours characterized the industry. Workmen obtained posts only through an employment agency run by the owners. All laborers had to renounce and abstain from union membership. Detectives hired by the Founders' Association ferreted out employees suspected of pro-union sympathies; the companies dismissed such "agitators" immediately.[11]

In May, 1910, the Los Angeles Metal Trades Council presented a list of demands to their employers; it requested an eight-hour day and a minimum wage of $4 a day. In addition, the union mailed circulars proposing a joint conference to all the companies, the M and M, and the Founders' Association. The unions did not receive a single reply, but an industry spokesman informally admitted that many recipients had tossed the communication into the wastebasket. Some firms locked out their employees; by the first week in June 1,500 laborers had quit their jobs.[12]

Strike fever now spread through the city; labor organizations throughout the state responded with enthusiasm. From the spring of 1910 until December, strikes erupted among leather workers, laundry workers, railroad electricians, telegraph employees, construction workers on public works, photoengravers, carpenters, bakers, and tailors. In June labor federations and councils from all over California dispatched delegates to form a General Strike Committee in Los Angeles. Every participating group levied a weekly assessment of 25 cents per capita on its membership; San Francisco alone contributed $50,000.[13]

Now this General Strike Committee swung into action. It paid stipends of $7 a week to those in want and established a grocery store at the Labor Temple stocked with food purchased at cost in San Francisco. In addition, the Committee formed workers into squads of ten and insisted that all strikers perform picket duty on pain of losing their benefits. By September the Los Angeles Central Labor Council had expanded from sixty-two unions with 6,000 members to eighty-five unions with 9,500 members. Seventeen unions not directly associated with the Council brought the grand total of organized workers in the city to approximately 12,000. As Olaf A. Tveitmoe, chairman of the Strike Committee, remarked, "Not even the most sanguine organizer would have dared to dream a year ago that such a state of affairs could come to pass in Los Angeles." [14]

4

Labor's strenuous exertions in Los Angeles stimulated the M and M to an equal effort. Before long the conflict entered the law courts, affected city politics, and broke into violence. What began as a labor-management dispute evolved into a massive contest for control of a city.

The M and M struck its first major blow at labor when it prepared and presented to the City Council an ordinance to outlaw picketing. Spokesmen for the Founders' Association praised the measure as a deterrent to violence. Labor's representatives denied the necessity for such a law; they challenged its proponents to cite a single important example of violence perpetrated by a union man.

The unions tendered a petition, signed by several thousand, which asked the lawmakers to submit the legislation to a vote by the people. On July 16, 1910, the Council ignored this request and approved the act unanimously.[15]

Instead of insuring peace, the ordinance produced discord. Over the next few months police arrested men in so wholesale a fashion that the number apprehended soon exceeded 400. Demands for trial by jury filled the court calendar far into the ensuing year. General Otis' *Times* accused the strikers of purposely inviting arrest in order to arouse public sympathy. An affidavit signed by three men described a visit to the prison by a councilman. They quoted him as stating: "If we give you fellows an inch, you will take a mile, and the first thing we know you will be down there with clubs. That is why we passed this ordinance." Job Harriman, Socialist politician and chief attorney for the strikers, interpreted this remark as evidence that the ordinance "was a war measure on the part of those who had sufficient influence over the city council to control their election." [16]

Passage of the Anti-Picketing Ordinance and the apparent anti-labor attitude of the police and the courts drove the unions into full-scale political action. Union labor and the Socialist Party formed an alliance when Harriman, vice-presidential running mate of Eugene Debs in 1900, accepted nomination as Socialist candidate for mayor. He promised to repeal the Anti-Picketing Ordinance as the first act of his administration.

Organized labor plunged boldly into the campaign. Throughout the city, Socialists and unionists joined in exhaustive speechmaking and fund-raising activities; many unions formed their own independent Harriman clubs. Finally, during a visit to Los Angeles, the cautious and non-Socialist Samuel Gompers, president of the AFL, openly endorsed Harriman's candidacy. In his first test of strength, the primary of October 31, 1911, Harriman opposed incumbent mayor George Alexander of the Good Government League and Republican W. C. Mushet. Although a bit apprehensive about the Socialists, the League confidently expected Alexander to win by a substantial majority. In a startling upset, however, the Socialist Party scored a clear victory. Harriman garnered slightly over 20,000 of the approximately 45,000 votes cast, Alexander about 16,800, and Mushet about 7,500.

Labor had hardly finished cheering this political conquest when the Brewery Union achieved a settlement. Although only a few of the workers gained an increase in wages, the union maintained its closed-shop conditions. Despite all efforts of the powerful M and M to obliterate this one significant sanctuary of unionism, the brewers triumphed. Crowned with success on two fronts, organized labor looked forward to what seemed inevitable final victory.[17]

5

Unionists' high hopes for political triumph were not dampened when General Otis accused them of dynamiting the *Times* building. Such an unsubstantiated charge could not reverse the trend toward socialism. If, however, responsibility for this disaster could be placed on labor, all its gains would vanish. A twenty-year fight for economic justice by Los Angeles workers and the election itself hinged on the solution of this mystery and on the capture of the real culprits.

Superficial evidence indicated a labor conspiracy. On the same day that the *Times* building was blasted, an investigator discovered fifteen sticks of dynamite, attached by electric wires to a clock, at the home of Felix Zeehandelaar, M and M secretary. These explosives failed to detonate only because the clock was wound too tight. Forty-five minutes later, a caretaker at Otis' home located a suspicious-looking suitcase directly outside the General's rooms. Police barely managed to escape injury when the device went off a few minutes later.[18]

Exactly a month before these events, information supplied by a hotel employee had led police to the discovery of a small package of dynamite deposited near the annex of the Alexandria Hotel, then under construction by nonunion workers. Eight days later, officers had unearthed some explosives with fuses attached near the Hall of Records, which the anti-union Llewellyn Iron Works was building. A few weeks after the *Times* disaster, an explosion that could be heard fourteen miles away partially wrecked the Llewellyn plant itself. Nervous fear gripped the city. Was Los Angeles the target for a fantastic dynamite plot? The investigation of these incidents merged with that of the *Times* bombing.[19]

Anti-union forces shouted, *"J'accuse!"* "There is no doubt," cried the Assistant General Manager of the *Times*, "that this outrage can be laid at the doors of the labor unions." The president of the Founders' and Employers' Association telegraphed the White House to demand a federal probe of labor abuses such as this assault on the *Times*.[20]

Members of the M and M willingly accepted Otis' theory. They appropriated $50,000 to use, in part, to hunt down the guilty "Unionite murderers." In addition, the Founders' Association planned to raise a million dollars as a "defense fund" for industry. "Now is the time," thundered Felix Zeehandelaar, "to concentrate on the defense of Los Angeles from any and all encroachments by labor unionism." Manufacturing plants immediately increased the number of guards on night duty. Pressure from the M and M and the Chamber of Commerce forced the City Council to augment the police force.[21]

Organized labor retorted with angry denials and counteraccusations. The General Strike Committee issued an immediate and unequivocal disavowal of union guilt. Other labor sympathizers raised intriguing questions as to the possible implication of Otis himself. Had not the General admitted that he anticipated such a calamity? "What led him to expect it?" queried the *International Socialist Review*, "ARE HIS OWN HANDS CLEAN?" Investigators, this magazine observed, had conveniently discovered the devices at the homes of Otis and Zeehandelaar before they went off. Enemies had planted evidence to embarrass labor unions on previous occasions.[22] Eugene Debs forthrightly asserted, "THE TIMES AND ITS CROWD OF UNION-HATERS ARE THEMSELVES THE INSTIGATORS, IF NOT THE ACTUAL PERPETRATORS OF THAT CRIME AND THE MURDERERS OF THE TWENTY HUMAN BEINGS WHO PERISHED AS ITS VICTIMS." Finally, Samuel Gompers expressed his confidence in the innocence of the unions: "The greatest enemies of our movement could not administer a blow so hurtful to our cause as would be such a stigma if the men of organized labor were responsible for it." [23]

Two investigating committees now entered the field. A task force of experts in engineering, chemistry, and explosives appointed by the Mayor issued the first report. They declared that some form of nitroglycerin had set off the explosion at the *Times* building. A second body from the California State Federation of Labor concluded an exhaustive three-week inquiry, during which they examined witnesses and searched the wreckage of a building adjacent to the *Times'* lot. The Mayor's committee refused to allow them to inspect the actual property of the newspaper. Nevertheless, these analysts announced that a detonation of leaking gas had wrecked the structure. Many groups, in addition to M and M, offered rewards toward the capture and conviction of the guilty parties; the City Council, the California Building Trades Council, and the General Strike Committee soon raised the total to almost $100,000.[24]

6

The prospect of big rewards spurred a nationwide hunt for the criminals. The Los Angeles District Attorney's office and the M and M placed separate teams on the search. In addition, the Mayor hired famous detective William J. Burns to conduct his own probe. An analysis of the type of powder bought for the unexploded bomb at Zeehandelaar's home swiftly led to a description of the three purchasers. Detectives identified two of the suspects as men who at one time lived in an anarchist free-love colony near Tacoma. Their companion, known only as J. B. Bryce, remained a mystery. Early in January a special grand jury returned twenty-three indictments against the alleged culprits. Within a few days the District Attorney distributed 50,000 posters describing the wanted trio to all police chiefs, sheriffs, and postmasters in the United States. Then the manhunt stalled. A pursuit of the two reputed anarchists in Tacoma failed; J. B. Bryce remained an enigma.[25]

Detective Burns, however, played a hunch. He believed that the Los Angeles explosion had been planned in Indiana. Burns' agency had recently investigated the International Association of Bridge and Structural Iron Workers (BSIW), an AFL union located in Indianapolis. In the last few years this organization had encountered bitter and ruthless opposition from the United States Steel Corporation. U.S. Steel, with the belligerent National Erectors' Association, had beaten back the union and established open-shop conditions in almost every city in the country. In retaliation, Burns suspected, the BSIW had secretly resorted to dynamite.[26]

During a four-year period someone had unleashed seventy dynamite attacks, all directed against companies which employed nonunion labor. Had John J. McNamara, as secretary of the union, directed these onsets? The detective guessed that a monthly union appropriation of $1,000 earmarked for "organization purposes" had provided a war chest for these assaults. As accomplices, Burns surmised, John McNamara had frequently employed his brother, James B., and Ortie E. McManigal, a union member. Burns built his hypothesis on the fact that the device discovered at Zeehandelaar's home exactly resembled one used in a recent BSIW-directed bombing in Peoria, Illinois.[27]

To prove his theory, Burns had to find the link between California and Indiana. He felt that the answer to his puzzle might reside in the identity of the mysterious J. B. Bryce. But who and where was Bryce? For the next few months Burns' agents traced a winding trail that covered half the nation. They scrutinized hundreds of hotel registers, interviewed dozens of railroad conductors and gunpowder salesmen, poured over letters that soon filled entire vaults, and examined the records of express companies and telegraph offices. Slowly, painstakingly, they fitted the bits and pieces together. Then Burns received his first important break. Detectives spotted Ortie McManigal talking to a man whose description fitted that of J. B. Bryce. From that moment on, the sleuths never let Bryce out of their sight. When their newly found quarry visited John J. McNamara, Burns knew that he had scored a bull's-eye.

For the first time, the detectives realized that J. B. Bryce and James B. McNamara, John's brother, were one and the same.

Burns waited to spring his trap. He chose April 12, 1912, when McManigal and James McNamara registered at a Detroit hotel under assumed names. Ten minutes later police broke into their room, arrested both men, and seized their luggage. In the suitcases, officers found guns and six clock mechanisms similar to those used in Los Angeles and Peoria. After six months of one of the most dramatic manhunts in history, Detective Burns got his men.[28]

But the investigator still needed direct evidence against John McNamara, and to obtain it he resorted to subterfuge. Police told James McNamara and Ortie McManigal that they were wanted for robbery in Chicago. Since both men possessed alibis for that crime, they waived extradition and voluntarily accompanied the officers to Illinois. On the train James deduced that the lawmen had really arrested them as suspects in the Los Angeles case. He tried desperately to bribe his captors, offering as much as $30,000. Burns took his prisoners to the home of a Chicago police sergeant in order to keep their apprehension secret until he had extracted a confession from McManigal. Ortie proved a compliant witness. Told by McNamara that it was now every man for himself, McManigal dictated a detailed confession of the dynamite plot. He deeply implicated the McNamara brothers as the chief instigators of both the *Times* explosion and the destruction of the Llewellyn factory.[29]

Now the net closed on John McNamara. First Burns persuaded the Governor of Indiana to sign the papers necessary to extradite McNamara to California. On the following day Burns and Indianapolis police arrested the union secretary on charges of murder in the *Times* incident and for implication in the Llewellyn explosion. They rushed him to a police court, where the judge denied his request for counsel and granted a requisition for his transference. Within half an hour after the original apprehension, Burns and the police spirited their captive away in an automobile. The detective plotted this move in order to transport the labor chief out of the state before his friends could muster their resources to fight the extradition.* Los Angeles authorities imprisoned McManigal and the two brothers on April 26, 1911.[30]

7

Organized labor, particularly infuriated by the circumstances surrounding the arrest of John McNamara, a high union official, raised an angry clamor. "A frame-up and a plot," cried Samuel Gompers. "Burns has lied through the entire case." "Sound the alarm," Eugene Debs demanded. "The secret arrest of John McNamara . . . by a corporation detective agency has all the earmarks of another conspiracy . . . to discredit and destroy organized labor in the United States." Union spokesmen accused Burns of kidnapping McNamara from Indiana. They further charged that the police court before which John was arraigned did not possess proper jurisdiction, that officers had illegally extradited a man who was not a fugitive from justice, that the captors had not informed the prosecuting attorney of these court proceedings, and that the court had violated John McNamara's basic rights when it denied him opportunity to secure legal counsel. Burns' use of these dubious methods convinced many that a ruthless anti-union cabal had victimized two innocent men.[31]

Many labor leaders saw a parallel between the McNamara affair and the famous Steunenberg murder case. In 1905 a bomb had killed Frank Steunenberg, the former Governor of Idaho, whose administration was scarred by tempestuous labor conflicts, shortly after he had retired from office. Using secret and highly irregular methods, Idaho and Denver authorities had connived to extradite and jail three leaders of the Western Federation of Miners—Charles Moyer, William D. ("Big Bill") Haywood, and George Pettibone. Only attorney Clarence Darrow's defense rescued them from possible death sentences and won their acquittal. Unionists now strongly suspected that the Los Angeles incident smacked of these same devious tactics.[32]

* The story of Burns and the McNamaras went through a number of more detailed stages, which are omitted here for the sake of brevity. (See Stimson, *Rise of the Labor Movement in Los Angeles,* Chap. XXI, and other major sources cited.)

The AFL prepared for action. In May its national Executive Council issued a "Call to Labor" to provide funds for the defense of the accused. In June the Federation created a permanent McNamara Ways and Means Committee, which appealed to all local, national, and international unions to assess all members. Unions throughout the country responded generously. The Ways and Means Committee also sold McNamara buttons and stamps and distributed a motion picture which related the story of the "kidnapping." In San Francisco, the Building Trades Council pledged $100,000, and the National Committee of the Socialist Party offered aid to the defendants. Samuel Gompers then campaigned up and down the West Coast on behalf of the McNamaras. He damned the entire case as a "capitalist conspiracy in league with the corrupting influences of detective agencies." When Gompers visited Los Angeles, the brothers gave him fresh assurances of their innocence.[33]

Darrow assumed the task of defending the McNamaras. Long an advocate of lost causes, the lawyer nevertheless accepted this assignment with great reluctance; he feared that the prosecution had an airtight case. Only his own sympathy with labor and the pleas of Gompers persuaded him to take command. Job Harriman served as assistant to Darrow; the mayoralty election therefore hinged on the outcome of the trial. Indeed, organized labor itself stood at the bar of public opinion.[34]

As attention focused on Los Angeles, some observers worried about the courtroom's circuslike atmosphere. On July 12 both brothers pleaded not guilty to all indictments and the judge set October 11 for their trial. On that day both arrived at the court house handcuffed. John looked confident; his eyes, wrote a reporter, "moved fearlessly from face to face," his mouth a firm sharp line. James, the smaller, with a curiously shaped head and a ragged mustache, seemed to follow his brother like a faithful dog. But if the spectators in the packed courtroom expected fast-moving sensational developments, they were soon disappointed. More than a month after the trial opened, the attorneys had selected only eight jurors out of almost 600 talesmen.[35]

Week after week this procedure dragged on monotonously. Then abrupt dramatic news jolted observers out of their drowsiness. A detective from the District Attorney's office accused Darrow's chief aide of bribery. He had caught the investigator in the act of slipping $500 to a member of the jury in payment for a vote for acquittal. Had Darrow known about this scheme? Had the District Attorney planted the bribe-giver on Darrow's staff in order to embarrass the defense? Vituperative charges and bitter counteraccusations reverberated through Los Angeles.

Even before anyone could answer these questions, a second shock hit the public with even greater impact. On Friday morning, December 1, the District Attorney, on the grounds that he had "grave matters" to consider, asked the judge to grant a recess until afternoon. The court complied with this request. For the next few hours tension shot through the excited crowd of onlookers. When court reconvened, a few words uttered in a low voice by one of Darrow's assistants broke like a thunderclap over all Los Angeles. The defendants had reversed their pleas—James McNamara answered guilty to the charge of murder in the *Times* explosion; John McNamara pleaded guilty to conspiracy in the dynamiting of the Llewellyn Works. Both prisoners were ordered to appear on December 5 to receive sentence.[36]

"All over the city that sunny, warm afternoon," wrote one correspondent, "the eyes of men blinked and winked in vain efforts to repress the scalding tears that would well up. The shock was too great, the release of the pent-up strain too sudden. So they wept, shaken by emotions beyond their control." Those in the press section were amazed. They ranked among the nation's most seasoned reporters, and almost all of them believed implicitly in the innocence of the McNamaras. They clustered around Darrow. This trial, he said, was "the greatest strain of my life." He had grown convinced that the prosecution possessed an unassailable case. "It was our only chance. . . . It was in an effort to save J. B. McNamara's life that we took the action." Darrow denied that either the bribery imputation or the forthcoming election had influenced his decision. James McNamara avowed that he had resolved to risk the death penalty in order to uphold his principles and save his brother's life. Darrow predicted that because of the altered pleas

James would receive life imprisonment and John a shorter sentence.[37]

But the story behind the switch in pleas went far deeper. During the course of the trial Darrow had turned increasingly pessimistic. The prosecution seemed to learn the most intimate plan of the defense almost instantaneously. Darrow suspected and later confirmed that the District Attorney had lodged spies among his staff. The Chicago lawyer, of course, had placed his own informers in the prosecutor's office, but they only strengthened his opinion that the opposition held an exceptionally strong hand.[38]

Gloomily, Darrow began to consider a settlement out of court. He first expressed his idea during the weekend of November 18-19, when he and journalist Lincoln Steffens visited newspaper publisher E. W. Scripps. Steffens suggested application of the Christian principle of the Golden Rule as a means toward the solution of both Darrow's problems and the difficulties of Los Angeles labor relations. Hate breeds hate, Steffens argued, why not try the opposite? As a first step he proposed that they persuade the prosecution to drop its suit against the McNamaras and allow both brothers to go unpunished. This would end the McNamara affair, which if continued would only intensify class warfare. As a second move, Steffens recommended a conference between the leaders of labor and business to work out plans for future industrial harmony. Los Angeles would then become the best instead of the worst city for labor in the United States.[39]

Scripps, a Progressive and an old associate of Steffens, enthusiastically supported this plan; Darrow sanctioned it tentatively. Much to his surprise and delight, Steffens obtained endorsement from some of Los Angeles' leading businessmen and politicians. Darrow agreed to ask the AFL to dispatch representatives to the city to participate in the conferences. Only the District Attorney objected. He consented to settle out of court but refused to acquiesce in any proposition that involved eliminating punishment for the McNamaras. In addition, the National Erectors' Association learned of the negotiations and insisted on uncompromising terms. The District Attorney designated that the McNamaras plead guilty, James to obtain a sentence of life imprisonment and John a lighter punishment.[40]

By the end of November all parties reached accord. Darrow persuaded the defendants to change their pleas in order to avoid execution. An AFL representative, Edward C. Nockels,* arrived in Los Angeles and signified his agreement. The presiding judge, Walter Bordwell, indicated that he would not interfere with the arrangement. Steffens also procured wide acceptance of his project for a labor-management parley. The final stipulations included pleas of guilty but no confessions, life imprisonment for James, a ten-year sentence for John, abandoning pursuit of other suspects, and a local industrial relations conference.[41]

When Steffens filed his story on December 2, he interpreted the outcome of the trial as an admission of guilt by both sides. He emphasized the point that the McNamaras had not confessed but merely entered into a compact in order to pave the way for better labor relations. The journalist did not stress Christianity nor the principle of the Golden Rule, which, of course, underlay his entire solution; but reporters on other newspapers sensed this idea and publicized it throughout the country. Then on Sunday, December 3, according to Steffens, a cry for revenge arose from the pulpits. Clergymen censured organized labor, the McNamaras, and all those who had negotiated the compromise. "The Christian churches," wrote the journalist, "would not recognize Christianity if they saw it. . . . The sermons of that black Sunday turned the tide against us." [42]

Steffens believed that this outcry compelled the judge to inflict a harsher penalty than had been anticipated. Bordwell sentenced James to life imprisonment and John to fifteen years at hard labor. Instead of the humane statement which Steffens had expected, the judge vilified both prisoners. James McNamara manifested no surprise at the decision. He had never trusted Steffens' idealism; he held that men believe only in force, never in mercy or reason. Now, according to the newspaperman, he turned to Steffens and looked at him with "a smiling, cynical stare." "You see?" he said. "You

---

* Darrow, who assumed that Nockels acted for the AFL, did not know if he had reported the details of the negotiations to Gompers. The AFL President later stated that he first learned of the change in pleas from newspapermen. (New York *Times,* Dec. 4, 1911; Gompers, *Seventy Years,* II, 188.)

were wrong, and I was right. The whole damn world believes in dynamite."[43]

8

Imprisonment ended the careers of the McNamaras,* but for a time Steffens' labor-management rapprochement seemed possible. In December a group of prominent citizens assembled at the behest of the Chamber of Commerce to discuss arrangements for a peace conference. Soon afterward the Central Labor Council appointed its committee to represent them. Delegates from both groups convened in February, and the union men believed that all present made a sincere effort toward settling their differences. But they held no further meetings. Steffens' grand scheme for an industrial utopia turned to ashes.[44]

The McNamara case stopped the Los Angeles labor movement dead. All during the unrest, the metalworkers' unions had functioned as the hard core of the entire citywide strike. In February, 1912, most of the unions surrendered. They had picked up only a few scraps from the bargaining table and completely failed to win their major objectives—the eight-hour day and a union wage for all Los Angeles metal trade unions. In the next few months, catastrophe struck the metal unions as well as most of the other labor groups in the city. Leather workers', carpenters', teamsters', and retail clerks' unions all reported heavy financial losses and severe de-

* On December 10, 1911, the doors of San Quentin prison closed behind the McNamaras. John obtained his release in May, 1921, but James stayed on to become, by the 1930s, the oldest inmate in point of servitude.

All during his imprisonment James McNamara corresponded with Lincoln Steffens and Fremont Older. He never lost hope for release, nor did his attitude ever mellow toward the established order or the more orthodox labor chiefs: "I would not waste a scratch of a pen on ninety-eight percent of them, they have no vision." By the middle of the 1930s he still expected the workers of the world to arise: "The sword and pen is mighty, but the hammer and sickle is mightier."

(Mayo, p. 185; McNamara-Older correspondence, November, 1926–December, 1927, McNamara-Steffens correspondence, March, 1928–June, 1934, Steffens Papers. McNamara to Steffens, February 6, 1928, contains first quotation, McNamara to Ella Winters [Mrs. Steffens], June 8, 1934, contains second quotation, Steffens Papers.)

clines in membership. Only a few, such as the printers and the well-established brewers, managed to hold on to their previous status. These reversals badly crippled the Central Labor Council as well as the Councils of the Metal Trades and the Building Trades. With bewildering speed a promising field for labor cultivation once more turned into a desolate wasteland.[45]

The McNamara crime also smashed labor's political hopes. In November most observers had credited Socialist Job Harriman with an even chance to win the mayorality; some thought he held the lead. During their negotiations Darrow and Steffens had deliberately failed to inform him of their plans, for they believed that an admission of guilt by the McNamaras meant Harriman's political defeat. Nevertheless, although he played no role in the McNamara compromise, Harriman defended it before his constituents and consequently suffered grievously at the hands of the electorate. For days after the end of the case, "Vote for Harriman" buttons littered the gutters of Los Angeles. One Socialist periodical claimed that Harriman's "traitorous attorney associates shoved the dagger in his heart and at least *tried* to stab to death the whole working class of the Pacific Coast." In the election Good Government candidate Alexander easily triumphed over his Socialist opponent. What had Los Angeles labor to show for the most strenuous economic and political struggle of its history? As one labor official put it, "There is probably no city in America where such unfriendly sentiment obtains against organized labor as in this beautiful city of Los Angeles." [46]

Socialists in every part of the nation felt the effects of the Los Angeles trial. It tarred the Socialist Party of California with the brush of violence and killed its bright hopes throughout the state. On the national level, Eugene Debs had multiplied his popular vote almost ten times from 1900 to 1912, in only four presidential elections, and the Socialists promised to emerge as a major factor in American politics. But the McNamara debacle touched off a bitter public quarrel within the party over the use of violence. After 1912 the Socialists split into factions, and their power disintegrated.[47]

In addition, the shock of the McNamara crime sent tremors all through the American labor movement. "Organized labor, and more particularly trades unionism," declared one commentator, "is now thoroughly at sea. It is still staggering blindly under the sudden blow delivered full in its face by its own leaders. It is down, gasping for breath." From the beginning, union leaders had believed completely in the innocence of the two brothers. On the strength of this conviction, they had raised large sums of money, chiefly from the pockets of working men. Now many of these leaders felt humiliated and wrathful.[48]

The blow hit the AFL especially hard. "The McNamaras have betrayed labor," cried Samuel Gompers. "We have been deceived, we have been put upon." Federation vice-president John Mitchell found it difficult to renounce his belief in the innocence of the brothers, a view to which he clung as to an article of faith. Both the national AFL and the McNamara Ways and Means Committee condemned the brothers and denounced violence as a labor policy. Since the original arrest, the Committee had collected $236,000 and spent all but $10,000. It now discontinued further payments to Clarence Darrow.[49]

Eventually the AFL and other labor sympathizers assumed a more aggressive stance. They justified their defense of the McNamaras on the principle that every man is innocent until proven guilty. AFL leaders then accused the civilization that had spawned such a crime. A hostile and oppressive social system, they believed, had driven these otherwise decent and law-abiding men to desperate enterprises. "It is an awful commentary upon existing conditions," Gompers declared, "when men think they can obtain justice for labor only through violence, outrage and murder." A writer in the progressive *Survey* considered the Los Angeles case as an example of "how much too far the class struggle has been carried there and to what further lengths it may go." [50]

Debs accepted the McNamaras' actions as the answer to "government by injunction, anti-picketing ordinances and other capitalist devices to stay the march of labor." "You cannot view the class struggle through the stained glass windows of a cathedral or through the eyes of capitalist made laws," Big Bill Haywood of the IWW asserted. "I am with the McNamaras and always will be." [51]

Those on the other side interpreted the McNamara debacle in a variety of ways, most of them critical of the AFL and of Gompers.

"The question now to be asked—and labor must answer it—is whether the federation and the unions are going to persist in these lawless courses or whether, after the terrible warning of Los Angeles, they will mend their ways," said the New York *Times*. Both the conservative *Wall Street Journal* and the liberal *Nation* assailed Gompers: "No one short of a congenital idiot," the *Journal* contended, "could have ascribed [the dynamite attacks of 1905-10], to anything but a *deliberate* policy of violence pursued by this particular union; and we do not believe for a moment that Mr. Gompers is a fool, whatever else he may be." Equally, the *Nation* castigated the AFL chief because he had "committed the workingmen of America to the championship of these murderers." [52]

Inveterate anti-union forces, of course, tasted the fruit of complete victory. John Kirby, Jr., president of the NAM, even cast a questioning eye on the out-of-court settlement. He suspected a conspiracy to suppress the facts about the higher-ups in the labor movement. General Otis triumphantly declared, "It is proof of what we suspected from the outset—that this unexampled crime was either inspired by organized labor, or was done by desperate members of organized labor. . . . As to me and mine, we stand vindicated in our quarter of a century stand for industrial freedom." [53]

9

This bitter labor war attracted the attention of the U.S. Commission on Industrial Relations, which arrived in 1914 to study the Los Angeles situation. Leaders in the city greeted them with gravity. Both the M and M and the Labor Council requested that the federal body double the number of days originally allotted for the investigation. The Commission subsequently took testimony beyond the initially scheduled time.

The Los Angeles *Times* hailed the probe as a study of how "the city won and is maintaining industrial freedom." It criticized the commissioners for not calling representatives of unorganized labor. Did not these officials realize, asked the *Times*, that "so-called organized labor does not justly or fully represent the laboring men and women of this or any other nation?" The Los Angeles *Tribune*, however, looked forward to salutary results: Commission Chairman Frank P. Walsh's career "is a sure guaranty of the fairness and thoroughness with which the inquiry will be conducted." [54]

Tension spread through the 200 spectators at the hearings. During the first few days, some labor leaders, annoyed at the bursts of applause that greeted the testimony of certain businessmen, charged that the audience was packed. But toward the end, unionists cheered the investigation. "The probe might almost be termed theatrical," noted the Los Angeles *Record*. "This is due to the earnest effort made to have the proceedings absolutely public [and] open and above board."

Commission members searched the minds of some of the men who had played major roles in the drama of 1910–12. General Otis remained calm all through his extensive testimony except when someone in the audience tittered at one of his replies. Then he scowled and angrily stroked his white goatee. Felix Zeehandelaar, a staunch advocate of the M and M, appeared. A bit pompous in manner, noted one reporter, Zeehandelaar vigorously slapped the table and "pursed his lips impressively." Job Harriman, joined by many union chiefs, promoted the interests of labor. [55]

Los Angeles businessmen expressed their ideas through the various employer organizations, particularly the M and M and the Founders' Association. Members of these groups based their social outlook squarely on the concept of the open shop, which they defined as a situation in which the employer hired whomever he wished, union or nonunion. In their minds, the closed shop, in which all the employees joined a single union, represented an evil labor monopoly harmful to both workers and management.

Did these employers accept the concept of unionism at all? They claimed that they recognized the right of labor to organize only if the workers formed "good" unions. Such a union believed that employer and employee had complete identity of interest. Zeehandelaar echoed the views of most Los Angeles businessmen when he declared that he could not conceive of a situation wherein an "employer [who] is prosperous through the efforts of his employees [would] turn a deaf ear for an increase of wages if it was just and fair and equitable."

A "bad" union, according to these men, used those weapons generally associated with labor's actions against capital. General Otis granted that any *individual* worker possessed the right to strike, but "when the strike is undertaken by masses of workmen acting in conspiracy and accompanied by violence, coercion, picketing, assaults, and the boycott, it becomes organized crime." Nor did the M and M give its assent to peaceful collective bargaining. "I don't believe collective bargaining is in the interest of either the employee or the employer," Zeehandelaar declared, "because it does not take into consideration the personal efforts, the personal efficiency, of every man in the bargaining." [56]

While these employers delivered lip service to their creed of the open shop and a vaguely defined "good" unionism, in reality they actively fought any kind of labor organization. All the members of the Founders' Association, attested a leading manufacturer, tried every possible means to discover if an employee belonged to a union. Management found it easy to spot union men because these "agitators" always started to "worm into" the rest of the workers. When the first layoff occurred, management always fired the union men first. General Otis, although he still insisted he approved of his emasculated "good" unions and the open shop, broke down under close questioning and admitted that if an "organization is not accompanied by the closed shop and by violence and proscription, it goes to pieces. . . . Organized labor is not essential to the industries."

The most influential newspaper in the city, the Los Angeles *Times*, spoke for the M and M and for Los Angeles businessmen in general. Some of its pronouncements revealed a virulent antiunionism. On June 11, 1911, the paper called for vigilant action in the form of a "plain citizens' combine" for "the suppression of sedition and anarchy in the persons of the professional agitator." Within an hour, predicted the *Times*, "a brigade could be organized and armed with pick handles that would drive the lawless union laborites, closed-shop, murderous vermin into the sea." If the police failed, the *Times* declared in another editorial, the merchants, manufacturers, lawyers, and others would take the offensive until "the carcasses of some of the labor leaders who instigated disorder and dynamiting and murder might possibly be seen dangling from telegraph poles."[57]

Violence bred violence. Labor supporters who testified before the Commission demonstrated an equal obstinacy. Frank E. Wolfe, editor of *Western Comrade*, a pro-labor Socialist newspaper, claimed that *Times* editorials indicated that "these men intend to declare war, and that it means death to everyone who is foolish enough to stand in the streets at the time they do declare war." For troops the M and M preferred deputy sheriffs, this journalist continued, because that was "the simplest way of putting a Burns murderer on a legal basis." Then came one of the most dramatic moments in the hearing. The editor leaped from his seat and onto the stage where the commissioners sat. He flourished a sawed-off shotgun, one of a number purchased by the City Council.

MR. WOLFE: The operation of this gun is very simple. . . . I would assume that within one second a good handy Burns thug could kill or wound 25 or 30, at least, men and women and babies, because these people don't draw the line.

With your permission I will show you how rapidly it may be operated. [The witness goes through the motions of rapidly firing and reloading and firing the gun, operating the reloading mechanism many times, all in the space of a few seconds.] It will make 25 widows within that time. This end of the gun [indicating the muzzle] is designed for the working class; this [indicating the stock] for the capitalist class. [Applause.]

CHAIRMAN WALSH: Let us have perfect order . . . [hisses]—I will have to ask you to retire if you can't hold in your feelings.[58]

Job Harriman fought an unending battle against capital; he possessed few illusions. In Los Angeles, labor's drive for control had taken the form of a political party, he stated, while in Colorado it had led to a clash of arms. Harriman viewed both cases as skirmishes in the class war. "If that [the class war] were pressed to a further degree [in Los Angeles] it might take the same shape it took in Colorado. . . . But in all of it it is an exercise of power. . . . That is the fundamental proposition, and it is to preserve the interests of the class that has the power, and it is the world over true. It is inevitable." Economic interests wholly determined ideas of morality and law, the lawyer insisted. Men would achieve a harmony of interests only when large properties became "a social power instead of a class power." [59]

Women who appeared before the Commission expressed no gentler opinions. Frances Noel, chairman of the National Women's Trade Union League in Los Angeles, blasted the M and M as a bullying organization of big capitalists who deliberately set out "to cow not only the workers, but the small business man who had to depend on the banks and bigger financiers to maintain their business." The Association extended its rule of fear in Los Angeles so effectively that "to-day we have in all classes of this community a set of moral and intellectual cowards, even physical cowards, I dare say, because they wouldn't dare to defend themselves in any way." Her suspicions of the Los Angeles business leaders ran deep; she doubted the validity of the McNamaras' conviction and implied that it might have been a capitalist conspiracy.

A woman member of the Los Angeles Bureau of Labor, Mrs. Katherine P. Edson, concluded that the "Los Angeles *Times* poison has permeated clear into the working class itself against organization." When she tried to gather information for the Bureau from some of the workers, "I find that they look upon me with a great deal of suspicion, they think that I am a walking delegate." Since this woman had no direct connection with either labor or capital, Chairman Walsh solicited her suggestions as to how to improve industrial relations in the city. Her reply perhaps summarized the plight of Los Angeles: "I know of nothing that can remove this friction between employers and employees except a better understanding. And I don't know how you are going to get that. . . . it seems to me a very hopeless situation." [60]

These hearings revealed that after almost 25 years of ceaseless labor agitation Los Angeles remained an open-shop city. The McNamaras had destroyed more than a building; they had dynamited organized labor's best chance for economic and political progress in Los Angeles. Many witnesses before the Commission spoke with hatred. Capital gave no quarter and labor asked none. Yet Los Angeles with its history of violence, the Commission discovered, represented but one example of a community bitterly divided against itself.

II

TAFT PROPOSES, THE SENATE DISPOSES

1

"WHAT ARE WE AMERICANS GOING TO DO," asked Lincoln Steffens, "about conditions which are bringing up healthy, good-tempered boys like these McNamara boys to really believe, as they most sincerely do—they and a growing group of labor that the only re course they have for improving the conditions of the wage earner is to use dynamite against property and life?" Steffens' question with its ominous implications disturbed many thoughtful people. Weeks after the trial, newspapers and periodicals expressed concern over the class conflict in American society and its ever-mounting violence.[1]

In New York, a group of distinguished educators, social workers, and scholars accepted the challenge. They suggested that the President create a federal commission to investigate every phase of industrial relations. In effect their proposal demanded a searching examination of the most explosive social issues in America; it touched many special interests and millions of human beings. Would the Chief Executive and Congress dare proceed with so politically dangerous a venture? "It is somewhat as if, in the period prior to the Civil War, a President had appointed a Commission on Slavery," Outlook observed. "It may affect for untold good the future history of the United States, and the lives of innumerable men, women, and children."[2]

2

Alarmed by the perils intrinsic in the McNamara case, Survey magazine in New York started the drive for specific measures. Originally an organ of the New York Charity Organization Society* and financed by the Russell Sage and Carnegie Foundations, Survey by 1912 had grown into an independent, self-supporting publication. Its policy had broadened to include a critical examination of socioeconomic problems throughout the United States. Among its contributors the periodical boasted such notable reformers as Jane Addams, Jacob Riis, and Lillian Wald. Survey also maintained a nationwide press service and acted as publisher for the Russell Sage Foundation. Articulate and progressive, this monthly magazine exerted an influence far out of proportion to its relatively modest circulation. It could not compete with "battle, murder and sudden death for the attention of the masses," one editor, Edward T. Devine, explained, "but we gave facts to the key people who did the searching for us—the lawyers, scientists, economists and doctors." [3]

Survey's special concern for industrial relations stemmed from two of its chief editors, Devine and John A. Fitch. Longtime general secretary of the New York Charity Organization Society, Professor of Social Economics at Columbia, and founder of Survey, Devine had earned the epithet "dean of social welfare" in America. He ranked with Jane Addams and Julia Lathrop as a trail-blazer in the war against poverty. "Misery, as we say of tuberculosis," the Professor declared, "is communicable, curable, and preventable. It lies not in the unalterable nature of things but in our particular human institutions." Economist John Fitch had served in New York's Department of Labor and presently began a thirty-year career on the faculty of the New York School of Social Work. His three major books convey, by title alone, the scope of his interests—The Steel Workers, The Causes of Industrial Unrest, and Capital and Labor. He had also participated as a member of the Pittsburgh survey staff. This project, the first of its kind, produced an exhaustive analysis of the effects of industrialization on a major American city.[4]

A third editor, Paul U. Kellogg, injected youthful energy into the magazine's missionary efforts. When only twenty-three, Michigan-born Kellogg had reversed Horace Greeley's old adage and journeyed eastward. "The old frontiers of my grandfathers were gone," he asserted. "The new frontiers were the cities. So I came to New

* Until 1909, Survey bore the title of Charities.

York." Like Fitch, Kellogg joined the Pittsburgh survey. He also edited its multivolume report. "I stirred up trouble aplenty for the steel masters," he declared, but his findings received credit as the primary factor in abolishing the seven-day week in the steel industry. "For eighty-five years," this journalist proclaimed, "we have suffered from the overhang of institutions and patterns out of gear with American ideals of freedom and equality." A humanitarian with a passion for accuracy, Kellogg personified *Survey's* drive for social reform.[5]

In December, 1911, *Survey* devoted almost its entire issue to "The Larger Aspects of the McNamara Case." Outstanding intellectuals, businessmen, and labor leaders contributed their ideas to this symposium. *Survey* requested each participant to suggest means of improving labor conditions and to comment on the needs, if any, for changes in law and government relative to industrial relations. In a broader sense, the magazine had invited its contributors to analyze the state of American society as the nation entered the second decade of the twentieth century.[6]

Survey's correspondents appeared convinced that America was verging dangerously on a violent social upheaval. Over and over again they used the word "war" to describe the country's plight. "The American people must awake," charged labor attorney Meyer London, "to the fact that a bitter, merciless war divides society. . . . It is a war with all war's fury, with all its injustice, with all its crime breeding hatreds." Our nation has moved too rapidly into an industrial civilization, declared H. F. J. Porter, secretary of the National Society for the Promotion of Efficiency. "Out of this situation has arisen a type of leader who thrives through the existence of acute warfare. . . . This is true in the armies of both antagonists." "The vital and arresting point in this affair," attested author Bouck White, "is its disclosure of a state of internecine war in our civilization." "The issue is not capital or labor," cried Chicago social work leader Anita McCormick Blaine, "the issue is murder for greed and domination." [7]

Some writers indicted labor as the chief perpetrator of this violence. A former vice-president of the Baldwin Locomotive Company, George Burnham, Jr., maintained that "organized labor should

put its house in order" and rid itself of "unscrupulous leaders."
"We so believe in labor organizations," claimed H. E. Miles, an official of the NAM, "that we have coddled them, coddled them even
in their crimes, as a foolish parent coddles a naughty child." A professor of political economy, Henry R. Seager, warned unions that
they could not afford to make light of the nationwide demand for an
end to violence: "Lawlessness of this kind must be suppressed." Labor will never advance, contended W. B. Dickson, former vice-
president of U. S. Steel, until it abandons a number of fallacious
economic theories, "to say nothing of their crowning shame, i.e.
their readiness to resort to violence on the slightest provocation." [8]

Partisans of labor quite readily admitted that violence stalked
the land. "The workers have been driven until at last they are
turned," announced Paul Kennaday, Secretary of the New York
Association for Labor Legislation, "and now that they have been
shown how easy it is after all, to avenge their wrongs . . . we shall
have more murder and arson before we have less." "There are signs,"
he warned, "seeming to show that the forces are getting ready; that
the workers of this country . . . will not be afraid to take up arms if
driven much longer." E. R. A. Seligman, economist from Columbia
University, stated that the crime of the McNamaras indicated "a
type of mind that has begun in this country to despair of equality
and economic opportunity, and is being driven into violence because
of the conviction that no other kind of action is possible." Men
commit desperate acts, Florence Kelley, Secretary of the National
Consumers' League, declared, "as the cornered rat bites—not according to reasoned theories, but in the wrath and despair of baffled
effort and vain struggle." [9]

Survey's experts volunteered a multitude of remedies. Except for
the views of some businessmen, one consistent theme ran through
this bewildering array of ideas—the need for political and governmental action. Why, asked a Philadelphia rabbi, could not "a nation
that protects birds, fishes, forests, and wild animals" also "stretch its
paternal hand to safeguard its citizens?" "What this country needs,"
economist Robert Hoxie affirmed, "is a real and strong labor party."
Congressman Victor Berger, Wisconsin Socialist, wanted such a labor
party to advocate socialism. He pointed out that the McNamaras be-

longed to the "ultra-conservative wing of the trade union movement and have been devout followers of these labor leaders." Such "pure and simple" unionism, argued Berger, came but a step before "syndicalism, sabotage, slugging and violence." Boycotts and strikes, when they failed, he insisted, tempted men to desperate expedients, but socialist political action obviated this drive toward anarchy. Others stopped short of socialism but advanced a number of remedial measures—minimum wage-and-hour laws, abolition of child labor, and compulsory arbitration.[10]

Many felt that a thorough investigation of the crisis should precede any program of reform. "Should not our statesmen and thinkers," Louis Brandeis inquired, "seek to ascertain the underlying causes of this widespread deliberate outburst of crimes and violence?" This attack on the Los Angeles *Times*, asserted Hoxie, "was not merely the isolated act of an irresponsible pervert," but rather an outcome of conditions inherent in American society. Hoxie, joined by Boston merchant and reformer Edward A. Filene and efficiency expert H. F. J. Porter, called for a campaign to educate both employers and workers. "Has the violence of the McNamaras and perhaps of others been the blind striking back of labor against the provocation of capital?" queried writer James Bronson Reynolds. "Have private detectives and strike-breakers also their death-roll of blood-guiltiness?" If so, he urged, "let us have the whole truth about both sides in this struggle before we pass final judgment upon either." "Only the government can get at the whole truth," John M. Glenn, director of the Russell Sage Foundation, declared, "through its power to compel testimony and enter private premises." He pointed out that Progressive Wisconsin had already blazed a trail by the creation of its own fact-finding industrial commission. "Only by commissions," said Glenn, "shall we learn comprehensively the real truth." [11]

Some notable social reformers, including Jane Addams, Rabbi Stephen Wise, the Reverend John Haynes Holmes, Lillian Wald, and the Reverend John Howard Melish, soon met with *Survey*'s editors. Their conferences produced a petition to President William Howard Taft, which eventually contained twenty-eight signatures. The issues which derived from the McNamara affair, their document announced, have struck "the social conscience of the nation." In the last decades, it continued, America's industrial growth had far outdistanced her legal institutions; in those areas where the law had changed, capital exercised the most formative influence. "A profound restlessness" had permeated large groups of workers who felt that society had denied them any avenue to pursue their own legitimate interests. Injunctions, evictions, and spy systems spurred this "economic disenfranchisement." "The American people must think these things through," the reformers demanded. "We need more light. . . . We want light on that larger lawlessness which is beyond the view of the criminal court. This is a matter of public defense." 12

Specifically, the petitioners urged formation of a federal commission on industrial relations invested with vast authority. This body, the reformers advised, should conduct a searching inquiry into trade unions, trade associations, federal and state bureaus, and particularly the economic and social costs of strikes. "Today as fifty years ago," they concluded, "a house divided against itself cannot stand. We have to solve the problems of democracy in its industrial relationships and to solve them along democratic lines." 13

3

In Christmas week of 1911, the reformers presented their statement to President Taft. They could not have chosen a better occasion. At the same time, the capital witnessed the largest assemblage of scholars in the nation's history. Members of some thirty professional societies in both the social and physical sciences were meeting in Washington for a convention of the American Association for the Advancement of Science. Taft, along with a number of cabinet officers and high administrators, had addressed two of its meetings. Seldom had so many men of thought found themselves in such amiable contact with government.14

In one of his talks, at a luncheon of the American Economic Association, President Taft stressed the need for the expert in government. He asked for the aid of sociologists and economists for scientific analyses of public problems. With pride the Chief Executive pointed to his employment of learned specialists on several commissions, including the Efficiency and Economy Commission, which had just issued a preliminary report prescribing changes intended to cut millions of dollars off the national budget. Taft exhorted his audience to stir up popular support for this and similar endeavors.[15]

On the next day a delegation headed by Rabbi Stephen Wise and Jane Addams arrived at the White House to present their petition. Taft greeted them warmly. He even hinted that he might incorporate just such a plan in one of his next messages to Congress. In a front-page story, the Washington *Times* reported that ever since the McNamara confessions the Chief Executive had been considering the creation of some sort of commission to study labor-management affairs. It predicted favorable action by both the President and Congress.[16]

William Howard Taft may have promoted this plan for many reasons. In 1902 a previous industrial commission appointed by President McKinley had published nineteen large volumes of testimony, and the Republican Party had survived. Moreover, the Chief Executive's own experience with commissions had proved most salutary. Taft knew that in Congress the Democrats, who controlled the House, had already considered sweeping investigations into the shipping, money, and harvester trusts. A congressional probe of industrial relations might also tempt them. Far better for a Republican president to appoint such a task force and thereby control it than to allow a hostile Congress to do the job.[17]

With a presidential election in the offing, Taft's assistance may have stemmed from a last-minute attempt to garner some labor and Progressive votes. In addition, he badly needed financial aid, and some of those who had signed the petition commanded great wealth. But these political considerations probably played a minor role in the Chief Executive's thinking. He knew that Theodore Roosevelt planned to fight him for the Republican nomination and undoubtedly realized that most reform and labor ballots would flow either to T.R. or to the Democrats. At times Taft doubted his chances to gain renomination, much less re-election. In all likelihood, the President's major reason arose from his awareness of the

bitter tension that gripped labor-management relations. A conservative, Taft no doubt hoped that his commission would assuage
class conflict and thereby avert more radical legislation.[18]

President Taft kept his word. In his State-of-the-Union message on
February 2, 1912, he formally requested Congress to establish a
Commission on Industrial Relations.* Vast industrial expansion, the
Chief Executive stated, had produced revolutionary changes in our
civilization. Every new strike plainly demonstrated a growing tension in society. Yet "we continue to assume with easy-going confidence that in each new case, somehow or other, the parties to the
dispute will find some solution . . . we leave the situation such that
industrial disputes lead inevitably to a state of industrial war."
We must learn, Taft asserted, how to prevent catastrophes. "Not
during the rainstorm but in fair weather should the leaking roof
be examined and repaired." [19]

Present-day machinery for mediation, the President admitted,
could not bear the strain of modern conflicts. He called for a new
instrument of great responsibility and power. This commission
would re-examine all state and federal laws, assemble and digest
all relevant industrial information, study arbitration and mediation
methods, and investigate the general condition of labor in all principle industries. Previous surveys, the Chief Executive maintained,
whether public or private, had proved fragmentary and incomplete.
Now the times demanded "a searching inquiry. . . official, authoritative, balanced." [20]

Most of the nation's press greeted Taft's idea with approval.
In Chicago, the *Tribune* thought the commission proposal the most
significant part of the President's message. "It is a step of great
importance," asserted reformist *Nation*, "but one for which the
time is evidently ripe." President Taft alone among America's
statesmen, declared the Brooklyn *Tribune*, "has observed with
anxiety the dangers to society that follow discord in the relations
between capital and labor, discord bringing in its train all of the
evils of the general strike." The *Independent*, in agreement with

* Taft's message contained another item that indicated his responsiveness to
the appeals of the learned professions. He recommended a National Archives
Building, the result of a request by J. Franklin Jameson of the Carnegie
Institution of Washington, on behalf of the American Historical Association.

the Boston *Record,* the New York *Evening Post,* and the Chicago *Record-Herald,* termed the scheme "wise and timely." It pointed out that Canada, New Zealand, Germany, and England had all enacted labor laws in advance of our own. Industrial relations, the publication said, is a matter of nationwide concern; its proper sphere is in the federal government. "A spirit of bitter war," *Outlook* wrote, exists between many employers and workers. "Public knowledge of these conditions ought not to depend upon newspaper gossip or upon the reports of occasional and sporadic cases in court. . . . The whole Nation ought to know what is going on." [21]

4

Up to this point intellectuals had run the show. Successful in persuading the President to sponsor their legislation, they hastened to consolidate their victory. But this investigation during a time of ferment bore upon almost every segment of society. Other interested parties now moved onto the scene. Union labor, as represented by the AFL and Samuel Gompers, with the Railroad Brotherhoods following their lead, emerged as among those most concerned. Still near its zenith as a labor-management arbiter, the National Civic Federation (NCF) started to exert its authority. Finally, the wealthy and powerful NAM mobilized for battle. All four converged as the commission bill reached Congress.

Pleased with their initial triumph, the reformers organized a Committee on Industrial Relations designed to bring pressure on the legislative branch. Under the leadership of Edward T. Devine, their lobby embraced fifty-three eminent lawyers, professors, journalists, and social workers. Committee members worked directly with Taft to draft a bill for presentation to Congress. At the outset, wealthy Adolph Lewisohn contributed $5,000 to the cause, and later merchant Julius Rosenwald joined soap manufacturer and single-tax advocate Joseph Fels to augment its treasury.[22]

These funds enabled the Committee not only to operate in Washington but also to publish a series of pamphlets and broadsides to arouse popular opinion. In *Work Relationships and the Democracy,* for example, Paul Kellogg denounced American "Simple Simonism" in industrial relations. We have paid a high price for our neglect, he asserted. "We pay it in bitterness and in disenchantment, in disrupted industry, in vast money loss, in bloodshed and in mute and obscure suffering." Even Taft's rival, Theodore Roosevelt, furnished an article in support of the President's Commission. "It is earnestly to be hoped," wrote the Colonel, "that Republicans and Democrats, wise Progressives and wise Conservatives will all alike back up his [Taft's] decision." "For half a century," asserted reformer-economist Walter Weyl, "we have blundered through a succession of fatuous errors because we did not know. It is time to know." [23]

Samuel Gompers watched this agitation with great anxiety, for he desperately needed a sign of salvation. A bitter employers' counterattack against unionism, climaxed by the McNamara case, had all but floored organized labor. Even Gompers, who with the exception of one year had ruled the AFL for a quarter of a century, discovered his position jeopardized. Many suspected the labor chief of deeper involvement in the dynamite conspiracy than he had admitted. Indeed, Gompers swore that Burns was still waging a relentless campaign to put him behind bars. "He was determined," later wrote the AFL President, "to besmirch and if possible to destroy my work and the cause of labor." Where Burns failed, the judiciary threatened to succeed; Gompers found himself in the midst of an appeal of a one-year jail sentence for contempt of court. All previous difficulties, lamented the Federation leader, "were as nothing to the trial by fire that came with the McNamara case." [24]

His back to the wall, Gompers, like the rest of organized labor, searched for a way out. Now he thought he saw his chance. Since 1878, the union chief boasted, he had always contributed to every government commission concerned with industrial problems. But every time he had failed to achieve his major objective—official labor representation on such a body. In this new project before Congress, the AFL executive believed that he could attain his lifelong ambition and also reinvigorate a badly shaken labor movement. [25]

When Devine and Kellogg first approached him with a tentative draft of the bill, Gompers balked. "It was rather a hard time I had with these gentlemen," he later recalled, "in convincing them of the necessity of labor being represented on the commission." He further insisted that labor should at all times enjoy exact and intimate information not only at public hearings but also during the private executive sessions. In order to insure AFL support, the Committee added a provision that not less than two commissioners should come from labor's ranks. For the sake of balance, they added an identical section with respect to employers. The AFL executive council approved and went to work on Congress.[26]

Soon the National Civic Federation enlisted in the cause. Formed in 1900 by notables from business, labor, and government, NCF had rapidly developed into a major agency for the arbitration of industrial disputes. Its sponsors included such important figures as Mark Hanna, Grover Cleveland, Oscar Straus, Charles M. Schwab, Samuel Gompers, John Mitchell, and Seth Low. Although a private institution, it cooperated with federal and state agencies and usually volunteered its services during any important labor-management altercation. At the peak of the NCF, its members participated in the settlement of some of America's greatest strikes. Hanna had envisioned the Civic Federation as a league to unify capital and labor against socialism.[27]

Ralph Easley, full-time Chairman of the NCF executive committee, disliked the federal commission. He scored its creators as "radical preachers and charity workers" bent on promoting "a political Socialistic inquiry." Easley had already devised his own program for an investigation of industrial relations free from such dangers. In his study he determined to prove that, contrary to socialist doctrine, capitalism had provided the American worker with ever-expanding prosperity. Easley initiated an elaborate research project which by 1914 boasted twenty-five subdivisions and employed over 400 people, all of whom diligently toiled to verify a preconceived conclusion.* As ruler of such an empire, the NCF chair-

---

* Easley's grand enterprise marched onward through 1915 with plans, projections, and revisions. Then it hit a number of snags which included opposition from the labor men. Warren Stone, chief of the Locomotive Engineers, for example, called it "an absurd piece of work." In addition, the Commission's report ran counter to Easley's conclusions. When World War I broke out, NCF suppressed the report because it believed it wise not

man, with lofty disdain, dismissed the proposed federal commission as "just another . . . muckraking scheme." But Easley did not dare to oppose the legislation openly, for both Taft and Gompers sat on NCF's executive council. He stood by helplessly as his own institution at its annual meeting unanimously endorsed the President's proposal.[28]

A fourth group, the National Association of Manufacturers, approached the controversy more covertly. Rich and militant, NAM represented about 4,000 employers. Under the banner of the open shop, it battled all efforts to limit working hours, insisted that the Sherman Anti-Trust Act apply to unions, and backed the right of the courts to issue antistrike injunctions. NAM not only objected violently to AFL and the closed shop, but also resisted such political reforms as initiative, referendum, and recall and the direct election of senators. Association President John Kirby, Jr., so distrusted progressive elements among both Republicans and Democrats that he asked his membership to consider formation of a third party. At this time, NAM probably sustained the mightiest legislative lobby in the United States.[29]

In the last few years the Association had led the assault against labor which had slowed the growth of the AFL to a dead stop.* Now with the McNamara case, NAM closed in for the kill. It unleashed, especially in its official organ, *American Industries,* an unparalleled campaign of vituperation obviously designed to stamp out trade unionism in America. At the Association's 1912 convention, President Kirby sounded the keynote. He held Gompers and the AFL morally and possibly legally culpable for the Los Angeles out-

---

to promulgate such an optimistic analysis of American institutions at that time. Not until the mid-1920s did NCF deem conditions safe enough to issue Easley's "proof" of the beneficent nature of American capitalism. (Green, pp. 188-89; Stone to Easley, Nov. 11, 1915; Gompers Papers as cited in Green, pp. 187-88; Easley to Mitchell, Mitchell Papers.)

Nor did Easley's denigration of the Commission prevent him from selecting for his own advisory committee such Commission sponsors as Lewisohn, Lindsay, and Seligman. He later added four of the eventual nine commissioners to his staff as well as the Commission's first director of research. ("A National Stocktaking of Social Assets and Liabilities," *National Civic Federation Review,* III [Dec. 1, 1913], pp. 2-3.)

* Between 1905 and 1910 AFL membership remained at a standstill. (Taft, *The A.F. of L.,* p. 233.)

rage. "These assassins," he charged, "acted in a representative capacity." But the American Federation's depravity neither began nor ended with this isolated atrocity, for Kirby blasted it as a lawless syndicate guilty of "constantly recurring crimes." "No country can exist," he thundered, "half free and half throttled by criminal unionism." [30]

Since the National Civic Federation reckoned such labor stalwarts as Gompers and Mitchell among its most active members, it earned the fury of NAM. Kirby censured it as a "a huge joke" that condoned "an un-American and un-Christian institution." In a somewhat lighter vein, an anonymous NAM writer tried to imitate humorist Finley Peter Dunne's Irish brogue and pictured the NCF as a haven for social climbers, "gallant ladies an' gentlemin wid slathers iv money . . . an' a big warrum spot in their hearts for th' toilin' masses." More characteristically, *American Industries* flogged the group as "disloyal," "unpatriotic," and "a menace to free American industrialism." [31]

5

As these organizations assembled their forces, the Commission bill was launched on its legislative career. Taft's project found able champions. In the lower chamber, Representative William Hughes, a Democrat of New Jersey, soon to rise to the Senate, introduced the measure on February 29, 1912. On that same day Republican Senator William E. Borah of Idaho placed it on the Senate calendar. Organized labor entertained high hopes because the Democrats, with whom the AFL had an informal alliance, now controlled the House. Labor's bloc in Congress had recently increased its number to fifteen. In addition, at the AFL's request, William B. Wilson, a Democrat from Pennsylvania, destined to become the first Secretary of Labor in American history, chaired the House Labor Committee.[32]

When this committee opened its public hearings, the social reformers descended en masse. Every witness spoke in favor of the proposition. Throughout much of the testimony ran a theme of urgency and of fear of impending disaster. Washington Gladden, reformist minister of Cleveland and a leader of the "social gospel" movement, warned against the acceleration of industrial warfare. Congress must create the Commission, he pleaded, because "the interests concerned are more vital and more fundamental than any other interests into which Congress has made special inquiry. . . . More people are affected by them," he declared, "the whole economic and political scheme rests upon them." This proposal, Louis Brandeis believed, was "the most far reaching step we have yet undertaken to meet the crisis upon us." Another witness best expressed the sense of alarm felt by so many: "There is unrest everywhere. Never before have conditions been so miserably bad. Capital and labor are not satisfied, and we are having clash after clash. The situation looks worse and the future gloomy. It has been said that we are now experiencing such times as preceded the French Revolution." Perhaps impressed, the Labor Committee accepted Devine's counsel and called for an appropriation of half a million dollars to finance a commission on industrial relations.[33]

Gompers and indirectly NCF now exercised a formative influence on the legislation. The AFL President persuaded W. B. Wilson's committee to expand the number of labor commissioners from two to three, with a corresponding increase in employer and public repesentation. Gompers had also long worried about the influx of Orientals into the United States because he believed their acceptance of low wages undermined American standards. When NCF's Ralph Easley submitted evidence to him with respect to the illegal entry of Asians, the union chief drew up an amendment that empowered the Commission to investigate this subject.* At his request Senator Borah worked this somewhat extraneous matter into the Commission bill.[34]

NAM operated in a more subtle fashion. No one from the Association overtly lobbied to quash the proposal, but some Con-

* Later the Commission hired an Easley-recommended investigator under special arrangement. Complications growing out of this led the Commission Chairman to suggest to the Department of Justice that Easley had violated certain statutes and had misused the mails. As a result of the charge, the Justice Department almost investigated three members of the Commission on suspicion that they had violated the criminal law of the United States. (Justice Department File 177373.)

gressmen inserted an amendment which forbade the proposed Commission to pay anyone more than $3,000 per year. Its advocates wanted the Commission to employ distinguished social scientists and claimed that such a salary limitation threatened to cripple the whole investigation. A Senate-House compromise raised compensation for experts to $5,000 but retained a ceiling of $3,000 for all others except those hired temporarily as stenographers. "These final touches," Representative Hughes later remarked, "were given to the act by the National Association of Manufacturers. In the closing days of that session of Congress I rescued the bill from the hands of a gentleman who afterwards, in the lobby investigation, turned out to have been in very close touch with these people." [35]

A crackling debate erupted when the bill reached the House floor. Opponents first ripped into the cost of the Commission. "It is proposed," J. H. Moore, a Republican of Pennsylvania, complained, "to take $500,000 of labor's money and spend it to obtain information that the country already possesses." Congressman Wilson retorted that the very nature of the study demanded this sum "because the subject matter is one of the greatest that has ever been investigated by any commission." Indeed, argued Wilson, the government had already expended over $700,000 to examine the more limited topic of immigration. "Yes; over $700,000," snapped Democrat John J. Fitzgerald of New York, "and not a thing of value resulted. . . . So far nothing of value has resulted from the Monetary Commission. I hazard the prediction that if you spend $500,000 on this Commission the greater part of it will be wasted." [36]

Its critics also blasted the Commission as unnecessary. We did not need a scientific investigation, Moore contended, "everyone of us has a sort of instinct that we understand what are the causes of unrest." "Instinct" seemed unreliable to one progressive Republican, Henry A. Cooper of Wisconsin. "There is unrest everywhere in the industrial world," he cautioned. "We have been merely skimming the surface in our attempts to find a remedy." But Moore remained unsatisfied: "The country has had enough investigations. . . . The Democratic Party has deemed it wise to use the money of the people of the United States in a series of investigations into all sorts of questions. . . . Inquisitors are again to go into the industrial

establishments of the country and possibly widen the breach between capital and labor. [Applause]" [37]

Other congressmen rose to defend the legislation. Frank M. Nye
of Minnesota and James R. Mann of Illinois, both Republicans,
ranked among its staunchest supporters. This Commission could
travel around the world with his blessing, Mann declared, if only it
could discover a means of settling disputes without "riot and bloodshed." It remained for representative William Wilson, however, to
deliver the final benediction:

> I have no idea that it will solve all the problems existing between
> employer and employee. Those I scarcely hope to see solved in my
> time; but I do believe that it will have a tendency toward the solution
> of those problems . . . this bill, if enacted into law, will tend to show
> the employer and the employee alike the necessity of getting together
> and thrashing out their differences over the table instead of in the
> industrial battlefield of strikes. [Applause] [38]

In order to guarantee passage of the bill, Wilson partially yielded
to the economy-minded. Instead of an immediate grant of $500,000
to cover the total cost of the Commission, the legislators appropriated
only $100,000 as a first installment. Wilson fully expected that his
project would need the rest of the money, but this new arrangement
gave the House Appropriations Committee the right to review the
Commission's work. Congress insisted on retaining the $5,000
remuneration limit for experts and provided the commissioners
themselves with an honorarium of $10 a day and expenses. These
financial restrictions, Representative Hughes reported, "were obnoxious to me and objectionable to the supporters of the measure,"
but they preferred "to take half a loaf rather than no bread." [39]

On August 22, 1912, both houses dispatched the bill to the
White House. It called for nine commissioners, three each from
labor, management, and the general public. Congress required a
preliminary statement within one year and a final report within
three. Considerable power would accrue to these nine men. They
were granted the right to "hold sittings and public hearings anywhere
in the United States, to send for persons and papers, to administer
oaths, to summon and compel the attendance of witnesses and to
compel testimony." Congress further authorized the Commission

to investigate a breathtaking array of topics that embraced almost every phase of modern industrial life. This Commission, Congress finally enjoined, "shall seek to discover the underlying causes of dissatisfaction in the industrial situation and report its conclusions thereon." On August 23, 1912, with William Howard Taft's signature, "An Act to Create a Commission on Industrial Relations" became law of the land.[40]

6

"I regard the personnel of the Industrial Commission . . . as of the highest importance," President Taft declared soon after he signed the bill; most of the press concurred, "In the hands of a discreet and intelligent commission," declared the New York *Tribune*, "it might contribute to industrial peace," but, cautioned New York's *Evening Mail*, "big men would be needed." A dangerous weak spot in the entire project, admonished the New York *Commercial*, lay in "the difficulty of selecting a Commission that will command public confidence." "Everything," stated the *Nation*, "depends on the character and ability of the investigating Commission and on the spirit in which its work is undertaken."[41]

Those who had most directly molded the form of the Commission now tried to determine its membership.* Gompers wasted no time. Twenty-four hours after Taft had signed the bill, the AFL chief sent his Washington emissary, Frank Morrison, to the White House with a list of nominees to "see to it that the rights and interests of organized labor would not be frittered away." Gompers insisted that, in both tentative and final drafts of the legislation, it had been clearly understood that the three labor delegates should be "members of the organizations affiliated to the American Federation of Labor and the railroad brotherhoods." He warned Taft that unless his appointees received presidential confirmation, organized

* Lindsay, Wise, and Devine conferred with President Taft regarding the membership of the Commission at Taft's home in Beverley, Mass. (Wise to Lillian Wald, August 24, 1912, Wald Papers; Lindsay to Committee on Industrial Relations, Sept. 3, 1912, Devine to Jane Addams, Sept. 11, 1912, Addams Papers; Wise to Jane Addams, Sept. 3, 1912, Breckinridge Papers.)

labor would not cooperate with the Commission except as compelled by law.[42]

Even before Congress enacted the measure, the AFL had selected two favorite sons, James O'Connell, third vice-president of the AFL, and John B. Lennon, its national treasurer, as candidates for the Commission. Soon afterward, Austin B. Garretson, president of the Order of Railway Conductors, was named by the Railroad Brotherhoods. Morrison, at Gompers' direction, then sped to New York to keep the social reformers in line. A large part of their committee regarded Lennon and O'Connell as mediocrities, but they agreed to the Federation president's demands and submitted both names to Taft along with others.[43]

NAM, which had lurked in the shadows during the legislative phase of the bill, now emerged into the light. "This Commission has tremendous power," wrote NAM counsel James A. Emery, "and will be, in fact, a universal smelling committee with the authority to stick its nose into everybody's business." Emery feared that the "socialistically inclined will press this matter and endeavor to see that it is constituted of men with exceedingly long noses, with highly developed powers for detecting strange odors." NAM, he predicted, would have to appear before the Commission at great length. "It can cause a vast deal of trouble, and the opinion which it will express will have a great deal of effect on the public." We need men, he asserted, who are "good mixers, but firm as rock in their principles" [presumably with weak noses].[44]

Leaders of this lobby soon reached Taft. They beseeched him to protect the Commission "from weedy-headed individuals or others who intended to make it a vehicle for the propagation of theories or grouches." In letters and conferences with the President and with Secretary of Commerce and Labor Charles Nagel, Association executives darkly prophesied that "we have more to fear from erratic college professors than any other source." So many scholars, they complained, "hang on the ragged edge of socialism and lack experience, poise, and practical contact with industrial affairs." If university representation became an unavoidable evil, NAM held Nicholas Murray Butler of Columbia and Professor Laurence

Laughlin of Chicago closest to its heart. Not really in need of persuasion, Taft assured the NAM that he would name "the right kind of people." [45]

Atop the Association's roster stood St. Louis engineer and executive Ferdinand C. Schwedtman.* An NAM vice-president, Schwedtman had published a book on the operations of social insurance in Europe; both French and German critics had highly praised his recommendations on accident prevention and workmen's compensation. His deepest convictions, however, landed him squarely in NAM's camp. "The signs of the times," he told President Kirby, "indicate that before we die of old age we will have to be ready for many a strenuous campaign." When he witnessed a band of IWW zealots march up Fifth Avenue, Schwedtman "could not help but feel that we may have to defend personal liberty and Constitutional freedom with guns as well as words before many years older." [46]

Ralph Easley of NCF, who distrusted the whole idea of a federal commission, now zealously schemed to see that Taft chose his kind of "right people." He pressed his case through Secretary of the Treasury Franklin MacVeagh, Commissioner of Labor Charles P. Neill, and mining engineer John Hays Hammond, all NCF members and all men who carried weight with the administration. Like NAM, Easley most dreaded those "sentimental and theoretical" social reformers. "The labor question," he protested, "is a big, practical problem and can't be dealt with in terms, as they put it, of 'vision, imagination and enthusiasm.'" A visit to the White House by the intellectuals so alarmed the NCF official that in order to blunt their effectiveness he solicited a parley of all four parties to endorse

---

* Schwedtman, a businessman who had expressed interest in mild forms of worker amelioration, impressed NCF and the social reformers as well. Both mentioned him among their choices for an employer representative. (Easley to William B. Wilson, Dec. 24, 1913, Labor Department File 16/184, Easley to Taft, Sept. 28, 1912, Taft Papers.)

Fear that certain conservative midwestern manufacturing interests might influence Taft led to an energetic counter offensive by social work leaders Graham R. Taylor and his son, Graham Taylor. (Telegrams, Graham R. Taylor to Jane Addams and to Mrs. Emmons Blaine [n.d.]; Graham Taylor to Ethelbert Stewart, Sept. 7, 1912, to Walter L. Fisher, Sept. 9, 1912, to Charles Nagel, Sept. 12, 1912, Taylor Papers).

a common slate of nominees. But NAM, enraged over the Civic Federation's choice of John Mitchell as a labor commissioner, quickly scotched Easley's dream of a summit conference.[47]

7

Taft purposely delayed public announcement of his Commission until after the 1912 presidential election. With so many interests involved, an announcement, no matter who his appointees were, would only have furnished more ammunition to his enemies. Taft had enemies enough. When Woodrow Wilson was elected in November, the Chief Executive hesitated no longer. He preferred designating his own Commission to bequeathing that authority to his Democratic successor.[48]

On December 17, 1912, Taft published the long-awaited list. It plainly demonstrated the effect of those who had brought pressure to bear on the White House. In naming the labor delegation, Taft acceded completely to the AFL. For a time the President had considered two other candidates, but Gompers' threat apparently drove away any thought of independent action. Since the social reformers had endorsed these same three men, Taft undoubtedly believed that he had satisfied both groups. John B. Lennon and James O'Connell of AFL and Austin B. Garretson, choice of the Railroad Brotherhoods, all earned the Presidential nod.[49]

For his business appointees, the Chief Executive clearly followed the lead of NAM. Schwedtman, first choice of the Association and a name high on the list of both NCF and the reformers, appeared as an obvious "shoo in" for the Commission. Taft then picked Adolph Lewisohn, wealthy New York copper magnate, financial angel of the reformers' Committee, and, according to Taft's secretary, Charles Hilles, "the most important Jew in New York." Lewisohn represented closed-shop employers, while Schwedtman spoke for open-shop management. Frederic A. Delano, president of the Wabash Railroad and an uncle of Franklin D. Roosevelt, completed this trio. A man who had worked his way up from the lowest shop levels, Delano possessed first-hand experience in railway labor matters. In addition, he had contributed his services to the War Department as a consulting engineer. Taft had studied the dossiers of several railroad presidents and may have selected Delano on the advice of Secretary Nagel, who counseled that, of those under scrutiny, "Mr. Delano is more safe." [50]

Crucial to the entire Commission were those who acted for the public. In all likelihood they would command the balance of power. For the most important post of Chairman, the Chief Executive named Republican Senator George B. Sutherland of Utah (later a justice of the Supreme Court). A conservative, a Westerner, and highly esteemed by NAM, Sutherland also came from the body that would have to confirm all of the nominees. [51]

President Taft also appointed Charles S. Barrett, Georgia Democrat and president of the Farmer's National Union. Both Easley and William B. Wilson had endorsed Barrett as a spokesman for Southern farmers. In addition, he enjoyed a close friendship with Senator Hoke Smith of Georgia, who as chairman of the Labor and Education Committee would wield great authority during the Senate's examination of the commissioners. [52]

Taft produced one "sleeper"—George B. Chandler of Connecticut. An agent of the American Book Company, Chandler had also served as a Republican member of the state legislature and chaired its Committee on Labor. Since Connecticut was an industrial state, the President had requested Republican Senator George P. McLean to suggest a candidate. McLean took Taft too literally and directly offered the position to Chandler. Taft then felt that he could not embarrass McLean and appointed the Connecticut legislator. [53]

The National Civic Federation joyously hailed Taft's industrial relations team. "It is bully," exulted Ralph Easley. Sutherland's appointment as Chairman especially gratified the Federation executive, for the Senator had promoted their workmen's compensation bill in Congress. Easley asked the Utah Republican for a "heart to heart talk." He promised to give the Senator the inside story of the Commission, so that the lawmaker would understand why he had to avoid installing Socialists or socialistically inclined thinkers on his staff. Taft's labor men, "anti-socialist to the core," equally delighted the Civic Federation official. [54]

Nor did NAM voice any public complaint. As compared with its previous frenetic outbursts, *American Industries* accepted the Commission with cool dispassion. Only O'Connell, "who is frankly recognized as a radical," disturbed the magazine at all. Privately, however, Emery nourished a few misgivings. While he distrusted Lewisohn as "not really an employer but a banker," he commended Delano as a "strong man." Emery further suspected that Barrett really belonged with the labor commissioners and expected him to side with AFL. Chandler bothered the NAM counsel because he appeared "weak and yielding" with a "tendency to coddle the labor element." Sutherland as chairman, however, signified "the best stroke of all." "It will give the Commission," Emery asserted, "a sound, well balanced, remarkably able and conservative lawyer as presiding officer. He will be a guiding hand throughout its deliberations." Gleefully Emery noted, the "college element is utterly without recognition." [55]

No one needed to tell the "college element" that Taft had dumped them. In New York the original sponsors condemned the presidential roster as "a great disappointment." "There is no well known economist or social worker," they lamented, "to speak for the increasingly effective work that is being done by our universities and colleges." Taft's Commission also failed to include a woman, although millions of women now toiled in industry. Finally, the reformers damned the slate because it lacked men of sufficient prominence to represent enlightened public interest. Perhaps an exasperated telegram from *Survey* best illustrated this last point: "Who is George B. Chandler?" [56]

A cry of indignation rang out from intellectuals across the nation. In Boston, during a convention, over 100 social scientists whipped off a petition to the Senate demanding the rejection of Taft's nominees. "Disappointed and disgusted," a leading Midwest economist exclaimed, "I will not be a party to another capitalistic humbug." A prominent labor expert protested that "the Commission lacks weight; will fail to carry conviction; money wasted, better none." Another tore into the business delegates because not one "stood head and shoulders above his fellow employers in insisting on the preservation of the spirit of democracy in industry." They also ostra-

cized Lennon and O'Connell as unprogressive labor leaders and upbraided the President for his failure to appoint at least one member
of the reformers' original committee. As one social worker summed
it up, "The President faced the great constructive opportunity of
his term, and he hands us, pardon me, a lemon." [57]

This vituperative assault stung the AFL leadership, which found
itself quite content with Taft's Commission. Timothy Healy, president of the Brotherhood of Stationary Firemen, expressed shock
at public statements that had denounced the AFL nominees as
"typically reactionary" and "what in politics we should term the
'Old Guard.'" He pointed out that the reformers' committee had
placed these very men at the top of its own list for President
Taft along with the names of Lewisohn and Schwedtman. "Why
this change?" he asked. Lennon and O'Connell did not represent
reaction. "The only opposition to these people," Healy maintained,
"comes from revolutionary Socialists and the Industrial Workers of
the World. Are these latter the people you and your committee of
social workers and economists think President Taft should name
on such a commission?" [58]

Healy had intended this last question only as rhetoric, but to his
astonishment the replies shot back in the affirmative.* "We, as
students, see within the labor movement and the labor world this
great radical fact looming up," answered Paul Kennaday, "and to
ignore this radical element and dismiss lightly the Socialists or the
Industrial Workers of the World is impossible." We believe,
Kennaday continued, that "to leave this new and tremendous
radical wing represented by those and those only who are in open
and bitter hostility . . . is highly improper and unwise." [59]

Similarly, John A. Kingsbury of the New York Association for
Improving Conditions of the Poor and Lillian Wald of the Nurses'

---

* In a somewhat befuddled reply, Samuel McCune Lindsay, chairman of
the Committee, told Healy that originally his group believed the AFL entitled
to one but not two of the Commission seats. "We did endorse the nomination
of Mr. John B. Lennon," Lindsay explained, "without suggesting any
alternative name, and also submitted Mr. James O'Connell's name to the
President with two alternative suggestions." Perhaps Taft could be pardoned
for not quite understanding when an endorsement was not an endorsement.
(Lindsay to Healy, Jan 2, 1913 [copy], NCF Papers, contains quotations;
Nagel to Borah, Jan. 8, 1913, Commerce and Labor File 68117/15.)

Settlement both pleaded for the inclusion of at least one radical commissioner. The Reverend John Haynes Holmes of New York pulled no punches: "I believe they are quite right in describing the representatives of labor as men who are wholly reactionary. Indeed, if I were speaking for myself, I should extend these criticisms not merely to these appointees, but to the Federation of Labor itself." "Wake up, A. F. of L.," he cried, "you are today a hopeless drag upon the labor world." [60]

A furious Samuel Gompers now lashed back at these reformers, whom a few months before he had termed "a group of high-minded citizens." [61] "The workers are not bugs to be examined under the lenses of a microscope by the 'intellectuals' on a sociological slumming tour. . . . By their very intolerance and arrogance they manifest their personal unfitness to consider Labor's problems. . . . Wisdom and understanding do not always accompany diplomas, degrees, or attach themselves to endowed chairs." [62] In a public letter the aroused labor chief spanked the Committee: "You should all be thoroughly ashamed of yourselves, and you will have cause to be for this piece of stupidity and arrogance." [63]

In order to drive Taft's candidates through the Senate, NAM, NCF, and AFL banded together in a bizarre alliance. Ralph Easley predicted that their collective power plus administrative pressure and the caliber of the nominees would win them an easy triumph. But political events militated against his prophecy. A hungry Democratic Party, out of office for sixteen years, felt in no mood to carry out the wishes of a defeated lame-duck President. Even Senator Hoke Smith, whom Taft may have tried to pacify through his nomination of Barrett, turned a deaf ear. He declared that the Republicans had been repudiated and advised the Senate to ignore any further Taft appointments.[64]

In a last-ditch struggle to win endorsement, Republicans, joined by some Progressives, forced the upper chamber to remain in executive session. As a countermove, the Democrats, although a minority, filibustered until they successfully prevented a vote. Emery of NAM remarked sadly, "The Democratic Senators discussed everything on earth but the nominations and showed every evidence of their ability to keep it up indefinitely, with the result that the effort has now been abandoned. . . . There is no possibility of confirming the present Industrial Commission." Emery was right. The Senate never approved Taft's commissioners.[65]

As Inauguration Day approached, the Chief Executive may have nurtured gloomy forebodings. At his request Congress had entrusted the Commission with vast power. His own appointees would have used this authority discreetly and produced a sober, limited report without a hint of sensation or a disturbing idea. But political change doomed the President's plan. For all his care, Taft had placed this potentially dangerous weapon directly into the hands of his enemies. They now entered Washington with a promise of sweeping reforms under the banner of the New Freedom.

III

MR. WILSON MAKES HIS CHOICE

1

"THE NINE MEMBERS of the Industrial Relations Commission," Walter Lippmann declared, "have before them the task of explaining why America, supposed to become the land of promise, has become the land of disappointment and deep-seated discontent." On the shoulders of a new President rested the responsibility of choosing the men to carry out this awesome duty. Once again, powerful interests pressured the White House. Woodrow Wilson chose carefully. He consulted cabinet officers and his closest advisers. His new Commission differed markedly from Taft's and in many ways demonstrated the direction of the New Freedom.

In so varied a nation as America, no small group of individuals could ever be a true cross section, but the U.S. Commission on Industrial Relations came close. Geographically, its membership spanned the continent. Catholic, Protestant, and Jew all joined in the inquiries. A millionairess sat next to a former tailor; an internationally famous scholar rubbed shoulders with an ex-railroad mechanic. All possessed experience in industrial relations, and all came to the Commission with enthusiasm. "If they do their work with imagination and courage" Lippmann predicted, "they will do more than any other group of people in this country to shape our history." [1]

2

All those who had pressed Taft with respect to the Commission now descended on President Wilson. The social reformers wasted no time. Bitterly disappointed by Taft, they sped to Wilson at a secretly arranged meeting. Samuel McCune Lindsay of the Committee blasted the existing slate of nominees. He expressed hope that the Senate would not confirm these candidates and would grant the new adminstration a free hand in selecting its own people. Wilson welcomed the reformers cordially: "You are all to regard yourselves as forces playing upon the Government, and I hope that during the next four years you will find a sensitive part of the Government at the top." [2]

In further letters, telegrams, and interviews with the President, the intellectuals pushed their case. They dropped their opposition to Taft's AFL candidates and called for reappointment of Lewisohn, Delano, and Schwedtman on the employers' panel. "Most important of all," Lindsay said, "we hope they will designate a Chairman of this Commission who will be recognized throughout the country as a strong and forceful leader." Labor authorities Louis Brandeis and Father John A. Ryan ranked high on their list.[3]

Special requests for appointment of a woman flooded Wilson's desk. Petitions and resolutions from the National Women's Trade Union League demanded nomination of at least one member of their sex. At their national convention, WTUL members specifically endorsed Agnes Nestor, president of their Chicago branch. The social reformers joined this chorus and urged that the prospective woman commissioner also be one who could speak for the "more radical elements." They picked humanitarian Jane Addams as one of their special favorites.[4]

Samuel Gompers of the AFL still regarded the Commission as of paramount importance; he even beat out the reformers in their race to Wilson. As early as August, 1912, before the election, a worried Gompers and AFL Secretary Morrison went to Trenton to see the Democratic standard-bearer. Of all issues he wanted to discuss, Gompers placed the matter of the Commission first. "I left Trenton," he admitted, "feeling very much relieved." Even though Wilson had reassured him, even though intellectuals no longer crossed him, Samuel Gompers still fretted. He wrote William B. Wilson to make sure that the new Secretary of Labor definitely recognized that in both tentative and final drafts of the bill, "it was clearly understood and provided for that there should be on the Commission three representatives of organized labor." [5]

As usual, Ralph Easley of the National Civic Federation fumed about the intellectuals. He had grown disillusioned, he told Presidential secretary Joseph P. Tumulty, over a report that "a group of radical social reformers, Socialists and Anarchists," had tried to foist an IWW on the Commission. A shocked Easley also informed William B. Wilson that John Fitch of *Survey* actually favored designation of Wobbly chief Big Bill Haywood. Those who promoted appointment of a woman radical equally distressed Easley. These reformers have a right to make recommendations, he granted, "but when they put themselves on record in favor of a Red Flag revolutionary socialist to represent the women of this country," they went too far.[6]

In order to deflect the reformers' influence, Easley lobbied for two safer candidates. First he advanced the name of wealthy Mrs. J. Borden Harriman. An NCF member, Mrs. Harriman possessed experience in the labor field and in Easley's eyes fulfilled the requirements of intellectuals for a woman commissioner. He also chose Professor John R. Commons, a well-known labor historian from Wisconsin University: "Mr. Commons would meet the expectations of the saner elements among what are termed the radicals and at the same time would be very pleasing to Senator LaFollette and all his friends." [7]

Once more the National Association of Manufacturers and other conservative businessmen trained their guns on the White House. NAM especially strove for retention of its favorite son and vice-president, Ferdinand Schwedtman. Perhaps as a selling point to the progressive President, they stressed the favorable response given to Schwedtman's studies of accident prevention and workmen's compensation. F. D. Underwood, head of Erie Railroad, warned Secretary Wilson against renomination of AFL executive James O'Connell. The Erie's chief considered O'Connell "extremely radical": "There are very potent reasons why Mr. O'Connell should not be appointed. If you will send your representative to me I will be glad to explain." [8]

3

Each of the outside groups that played upon the White House represented an important force in American life. Woodrow Wilson therefore turned to his cabinet and his official family for advice. At the President's request, Secretary of Labor William B. Wilson canvassed trade associations, railroad corporations, manufacturers, labor unions, and public service institutions. He asked what changes, if any, they desired in Taft's original slate of commissioners. After he had analyzed the responses, the cabinet official submitted a revised schedule to his chief.[9]

Secretary Wilson modified Taft's Commission only slightly. He retained all three labor men as well as Delano, Barrett, and Schwedtman. Only Sutherland and Chandler felt the axe. As alternatives the Secretary placed Louis Brandeis and Edward T. Devine at the top of his list. He also recommended appointments from a roster that included Seth Low, President of Columbia University, millionaire banker August Belmont, and social workers Florence Kelley and Jane Addams. William Wilson had preserved the generally conservative tone of the first Commission but nodded faintly in the social reformers' direction.[10]

A far more potent influence on the President, however, was from Colonel Edward M. House. A Texas newspaper publisher, the Colonel had quietly but swiftly emerged as Woodrow Wilson's closest adviser. House too had drawn up a roll that he deemed "excellent" for the Commission. First he showed his selections, fourteen in all, to William G. McAdoo, Secretary of the Treasury, with the request that he forward them to the Chief Executive. This memorandum stands as a testimony to House's authority—eight of the nine commissioners finally installed appeared on the Colonel's list.[11]

In choosing his men, House employed three basic criteria: each candidate's ability, the special groups most interested in the Commission, and congressional politics. All these elements, for example, operated in his selection of commissioners to represent the public. House chose Brandeis to chair the Commission. In the Colonel's estimation, this attorney's legal, economic, and practical experience especially qualified him. Brandeis already enjoyed cheerful approval from both labor and social reformers, the Colonel noted, and his appointment would please Senator LaFollette and other progressive Republicans. Like Taft, House suggested Charles S. Barrett. A Southerner and president of the Farmers' Cooperative Union, Barrett spoke for some 2 million rural voters. In addition, he ranked as the favorite of Hoke Smith, powerful chairman of the Senate Education and Labor Committee. Finally, the Colonel endorsed Professor John R. Commons of the University of Wisconsin as a "very able man and also a protegé of La Follette's." [12]

House emphatically promoted enlistment of Mrs. J. Borden Harriman. She stood out in his mind as "the most logical, the most representative and the best woman appointee." All her sympathies, the Colonel maintained, resided with wage-earners; labor men in New York warmly supported her. "They know how, among other things, she went down into the basements to study conditions under which the stationary firemen work and how she helped to get the employers to improve those conditions. . . . I am told that Mr. Gompers, Mr. Mitchell and other labor leaders are heartily in favor of Mrs. Harriman's appointment." [13]

With respect to labor and business, House accepted some Taft nominees but added a few of his own. He ratified all three original employee panelists and sanctioned Delano as the finest possible recruit from railroad management. Then the Colonel advised two new and rarely mentioned candidates: S. Thruston Ballard and Harris Weinstock. Kentucky mill-owner Ballard had distinguished himself as a paternalistic and highly progressive employer. Weinstock qualified on a number of counts: he hailed from the West Coast, operated a closed shop, understood immigration, and had traveled around the world as a student of labor. "He is a Bull Mooser," the Colonel added. President Wilson's anti-monopoly policies decidedly influenced House's thinking. "In making up a list of employers," he remarked wryly, "it is well to remember that there are no employers of national reputation excepting those in the large trusts, most of whom are either under indictment or ready to be indicted." [14]

4

On June 26, 1913, President Wilson announced his U.S. Commission on Industrial Relations. With only one exception, the Chief Executive completely accepted House's counsel. Labor delegates Garretson, Lennon, and O'Connell sailed in without contravention.

For a time the President seriously considered nomination of an IWW. He asked Brandeis to recommend a candidate and informed the attorney that he awaited his reply "with greatest interest." Brandeis, along with journalists Lincoln Steffens and Walter Lippmann, sponsored Frank Bohn, a former Wobbly and editor of the *International Socialist Review*. But the President, perhaps mindful of Gompers and the NCF, dropped the idea. He scrupulously avoided any direct representation from radical labor.[15]

Wilson expelled Schwedtman and Lewisohn from the business panel; Frederic Delano survived. As replacements the Chief Executive named both House's favorites, Harris Weinstock and Thruston Ballard. A former California state official, Weinstock had performed some government service; Ballard had stayed out of public view almost entirely. Indeed, no one registered greater amazement than the mill-owner himself: "I had received no intimation that it [the appointment] was to come. . . . I was really deeply touched that my work here at the mills should have had this recognition." The Louisville *Courier-Journal* reported that President Wilson, "in going over a great mass of papers" those which gave details of Ballard's achievements "had struck him so forcibly he decided to appoint the Louisville man." A check with Kentucky senators assured Wilson that Ballard ranked among the most respected and prominent citizens in the city.[16]

For the all-important segment to represent the public, Wilson discarded all Taft nominees. Obviously neither arch conservative Sutherland nor obscure, accidentally designated Chandler qualified. Despite House's admonition, Wilson also dislodged Charles Barrett. Not even Hoke Smith's personal letter, which blessed this agrarian leader with the Senator's "cordial recommendation," swayed the President. In order to meet demands of reformers for a trained economist, the Chief Executive first tendered a place on the Commission to Edward T. Devine, but the latter declined. Wilson then granted this spot to House's candidate, Professor John R. Commons of Wisconsin.[17]

Strong reasons dictated the President's installation of Mrs. J. Borden Harriman. At the Democratic convention Mrs. Harriman had helped swing William Jennings Bryan from his support of Speaker Champ Clark of Missouri to Woodrow Wilson. In the pre-election months she captained the women's division of the Democratic campaign. Through her work with NCF, she had already won the gratitude of many labor chiefs. Mrs. Harriman, Colonel House attested, "is more interested in this [the Commission] than anything else and I hope she may have her desires gratified." By her nomination Wilson answered the reformers' request for a woman commissioner, delighted AFL and NCF, and paid off a political debt as well.[18]

Woodrow Wilson regarded the Commission as important enough to offer its chairmanship to Louis Brandeis, a man whose judgment he prized most highly. Originally the President had wanted this legal expert to join his administration either as Attorney-General or as Secretary of Commerce, but political pressures blocked these plans. Now Wilson appealed to his friend to lead the industrial probe. "There is no one in the United States who could preside over and direct such an inquiry so well as you could," the President assured him. "It would gratify me very deeply if you could." [19]

Brandeis refused the office, however, and the Chief Executive had to continue his search. But the jurist did advise Wilson to sound out Charles R. Van Hise, president of Wisconsin University. In reply President Wilson declared, "I have recently been thinking of Frank P. Walsh of Kansas City. What would you think of him as Chairman?" This question marked the first mention of the man who eventually dominated and, in the public mind, personified the entire federal study. Brandeis responded that he knew little of Walsh except that social workers in New York held the Missourian in great esteem. He doubted Walsh's suitability only on grounds that the Midwestern lawyer lacked a national reputation.[20]

Actually Woodrow Wilson had first met Walsh through Mrs. Harriman during the 1912 campaign. A newspaperman had told her about an influential, progressive, pro-labor Missouri attorney who could not decide between Wilson and Roosevelt. If Frank Walsh could be induced to champion the New Jersey Governor, this writer claimed, he could deliver a big bloc of this border state's vote into the Democratic column. Mrs. Harriman quickly arranged for Walsh to visit Wilson at his headquarters in Sea Girt, New Jersey. After lunch she and Wilson's daughter Eleanor left the two men alone. "When we came back to the cottage," she remembered, "there was Mr.

Walsh, convinced that Mr. Wilson's progressiveness was more progressive than the Colonel's; and within a week Democratic headquarters hummed with the news that a bureau for social workers was to be established as a part of the Democratic campaign and that Frank P. Walsh of Kansas City was to be in charge of it." [21]

President Wilson also consulted Treasury Secretary McAdoo about Walsh and Van Hise. McAdoo lauded the Wisconsin educator but shoved in an especially strong oar for the Kansas City lawyer: "I think it would be worth your while to consider Mr. Walsh. . . . I understand he is acceptable to Labor. . . . I know from my own association with him at the Democratic headquarters last year that he is a man of vigor and capacity, animated by an earnest desire to serve unselfishly the cause you represent." Three weeks later Woodrow Wilson formally signified his designation of Frank Walsh as Chairman of the U.S. Commission on Industrial Relations.[22]

5

President Wilson's new Commission revealed, in part, the early course of the New Freedom. Some Taft men survived, but the President had distinctly altered the character of the investigative body. This new slate indicated which groups, among competitors, the new administration favored and which it tended to ignore. Certainly the reaction of the interested parties plainly underscored their own awareness of the meaning of Wilson's Commission.

The fortunes of the NAM had declined most disastrously. As Taft had slighted social workers, Wilson obliterated the businessman's lobby. From the NAM point of view every change was noxious. Despite all pleas, the new President had completely ignored their idol, Schwedtman, and had substituted progressive Thruston Ballard. Even worse for NAM, Wilson had dethroned conservative Senator Sutherland and crowned in his stead outspokenly pro-labor Frank Walsh. Hopefully perhaps, *Nation's Business* consoled its readers with the thought that a former industrial commission, authorized by McKinley, had unloaded a nineteen-volume report which now stood "almost forgotten." [23]

AFL and NCF rejoiced. Gompers could ask no more. His labor slate had triumphed, and the new commissioners augured a turn for the better. "Speaking of the Industrial Relations Commission, how about that now?" exulted Ralph Easley. "I do not see many of the I.W.W. or in fact Socialist promoters of the movement on the line." Even though he had exercised only an indirect influence on the President, Easley proudly declared that eight out of nine commissioners belonged to NCF. The *National Civic Federation Review* acclaimed the Commission's personnel "as the best possible guarantee of its fairness, independence and capacity for usefulness." [24]

Even Frank Walsh as Chairman did not distress NCF's chief. Originally, Easley had preferred Brandeis but had grown disenchanted when the Bostonian promoted an IWW for the Commission. True, the Civic Federation executive suspected Walsh of Socialist views. He interpreted this, however, just as evidence that the Missourian had "a great big heart." Walsh, explained Easley, was "a new man in this work and it is not surprising that he should be largely impressed by the promoters of the bill creating the Commission." [25]

"There was great disappointment in progressive circles," reported the New York *Times*, "and at first this disappointment threatened to take the form of open opposition. At one time there was talk that President Wilson would withdraw several names and submit new ones." Wilson had moved closer to their ideals but not far enough. They still disliked a labor panel completely dominated by conservative unionists. Furthermore, the President had ousted Schwedtman and Lewisohn, two men they greatly esteemed. Although the new Chief Executive had nominated a woman, these intellectuals still yearned for a more widely known feminist such as Jane Addams. Only Professor Commons satisfied them. He is, *Survey* concluded, "the one man in America who as economist and investigator has thought out industrial reforms." Nevertheless, the social reformers acquiesced; their committee disbanded.[26]

Woodrow Wilson submitted his candidates to the Senate, and that chamber promptly consigned them to its Education and Labor Committee. In addition, the Chief Executive took pains to stress the importance of this federal investigation. Instead of a routine request for funds, the President wrote a personal letter to the chairman of the House Appropriations Committee. "So much is expected of this commission and so many people are looking forward to its labors with confidence and hope that we may find valuable guidance in its final report," Wilson pleaded, "that I feel justified in calling your attention in this special and separate way to the necessity for this appropriation." [27]

In spite of Wilson's efforts, the Senate locked his nominations in committee all summer long. Soon rumors spread that the "interests" and their political henchmen were plotting to knife the Commission. Beware of Walsh's old rival, Senator James A. Reed, journalist Boyd Fisher admonished the President. Reed, as "head of machine democracy in Missouri," might spearhead a drive against the federal team. Walsh himself fidgeted. "If the Senate of the United States does not act pretty soon," he swore, "I will have nervous prostration as this is the first office that ever seemed to be within my grasp." [28]

Walsh could bear the suspense no longer. Through Missouri Senator William J. Stone, he unraveled the mystery. "Nothing the matter," Stone wired, "except Smith he was miffed." As chairman of the Education and Labor Committee, Hoke Smith had deliberately stalled the nominations in order to spite the White House. President Wilson, perhaps always a bit careless about senatorial sensibilities, had failed, of course, to appoint the Georgia solon's protegé, Charles Barrett. When Stone divulged the truth to Wilson, an angry Chief Executive immediately lit a fire under the Southern statesman. Soon afterward, the entire Senate, with little debate, ratified the new Commission.[29]

6

Those individuals whom the Senate confirmed represented a rough cross section of American life. Congress had empowered them to study the most inflammable issues of their time. Six commissioners were delegates from the two chief contending interests—capital and labor. Their backgrounds, personalities, and philosophies would deeply affect the character of the Commission's work.

On labor's side, Austin Bruce Garretson spoke for railroad unionism. His father, an Iowa Quaker, believed that every boy should
learn a trade, and young Austin apprenticed himself to a wheel-
wright soon after completion of his public school education. But
railroading fascinated him. Soon he discarded his original vocation
and began to work as a brakeman. From his travels as an employee
of a number of lines, Garretson learned about America's changing
industrial life. With others he fought and won the battle to trans-
form the Order of Railway Conductors from a purely fraternal
organization into an effective bargaining agent for economic betterment. Soon after the turn of the century he assumed its leadership.[30]

As a unionist, Garretson pursued a policy of enlightened aggres-
siveness. He resisted every attempt to limit the right to strike but
employed that weapon sparingly. Though opposed to violence, Garretson advocated more fundamental economic reforms than did
many contemporary labor officials. As a force behind the Newlands
Act, which strengthened railroad regulation, he later championed
government ownership of the railroads. Even though Garretson favored high salaries for union executives, he had declined an increase
in pay voted to him by his own brotherhood.[31]

Tall, angular, deeply sincere, genial Austin Garretson reminded
some of Abraham Lincoln. A constant reader, this union official
grew well versed in ancient and modern history; he quoted Plato or
the Bible with equal facility. Railroad management respected Garretson, as did the social reformers, who deemed him the strongest
and most independent of the labor commissioners. At age fifty-seven,
Austin Garretson joined the federal board as the able chief of one
of the most capable craft unions in the country.[32]

James O'Connell, Gompers proclaimed, "was the man who made
the International Association of Machinists." A Pennsylvanian by
birth, O'Connell had injected new energy into his union and had
served as its president for almost two decades. But pragmatic craft-
unionist O'Connell had felt the wrath of a Socialist revolt within
his own bailiwick. In 1910 the Socialists, according to Gompers,
launched a "sniping campaign" against those officers whom they
considered "most obnoxious." Their insurgency drove O'Connell

from power. Nevertheless, he continued to function as an AFL vice-president and also directed its increasingly important Metal Trades Department.[33]

Controversy had always raged about O'Connell's head. When he joined the Commission, the *New Review*, a Socialist publication, disparaged him as an "old hack" who possessed a limited "business mind." Progressive reformers scorned him as a reactionary, NCF hailed him as a "level-headed conservative," and NAM castigated him as a radical. A Catholic, a Democrat, slightly gray, and a fault-less dresser, this commissioner did not approve of women in public life. Mrs. Harriman complained that at first O'Connell "made me feel like a specimen from the zoo, but after a few months his voice lost some of the growl and I liked him." [34]

Of all those on the Commission, AFL treasurer John B. Lennon had most eagerly sought the post. Once his union sponsored him, Lennon strove tirelessly to obtain confirmation. During Taft's administration, he induced John Mitchell to operate as a one-man lobby on his behalf. "My interviews with the President and Sectry. Nagel convinced me," Lennon later informed the UMW chief, "that you were my most effective friend in this matter." When Wilson considered a new slate, Lennon aspired to the chairmanship. These commissioners, Lennon asserted, "should devote all their time to their work, and do the best work possible, that is what I should expect if I am named." [35]

An unusual combination of Socialism and liquor, John Lennon believed, had marred his career. He rose from a small shop in Denver to the presidency of the national Journeyman Tailors' Union and for over two decades acted as its general secretary. But the same Socialist rebellion that toppled O'Connell also swept Lennon out of office. Nevertheless, he attributed this defeat primarily to liquor interests. At a time when the *American Federationist* reeked of ads for Good Old Guckenheimer, Hunter's Baltimore Rye, I. W. Harper, Old Taylor, and Evans' Ale, teetotaler John Lennon had launched a fervent Prohibitionist crusade. Once he embarked on a two-and-a-half-week tour for the Anti-Saloon League, orated three times a day, took constant abuse from hecklers, and reported, "My throat is like a wood file. . . . I know I am somewhat of a fanatic on the subject, but I know in the main I am right." [36]

On the Commission, despite brickbats from the left, Lennon won the approbation of his colleagues. The Socialist *New Review* denigrated him as "not even ordinarily bright," and insinuated that he functioned only as O'Connell's puppet. It provided no substantiation for this charge. Mrs. Harriman thought Lennon "one of the most sympathetic men I ever knew. . . . Distressing testimony would make the tears run down his cheeks and yet he was always tolerant of the employers' side." To Frank Walsh, Lennon appeared "an intensely practical man" yet gifted with "a philosophic turn of mind. . . . He is the only man who seems to have the confidence and affectionate regard of workers everywhere." [37]

On the employers' side, Frederic A. Delano represented railroad management. Although born in Hong Kong, son of a wealthy merchant, he spent most of his boyhood in Newburgh, New York. A Harvard degree notwithstanding, the young man determined to learn railroading from the ground up; he started as an apprentice machinist on the Chicago, Burlington, and Quincy. Fifteen years after his college graduation, however, Frederic Delano had achieved the post of general manager. A short time later he became president of three other railway systems. In addition, Delano had seen government service as a consulting engineer for the War Department in the Philippines. Most rail executives recognized him as without peer in his intellectual grasp of the industry's labor problems.[38]

While a commissioner, Delano ranked in influence second only to the Chairman. Indeed, Frank Walsh praised him as "my bulwark of strength," a man of "splendid judgment and tact." Equally, Mrs. Harriman found the engineer "a delightful and cultivated gentleman, greatly in the confidence of both railway owners and railway employees." While Delano investigated labor, his young nephew, Franklin D. Roosevelt, had just started his own career as Woodrow Wilson's Assistant Secretary of the Navy. Shortly before the completion of his first year as a commissioner, Delano resigned in order to join the Federal Reserve Board as vice-chairman. [39]

When Delano departed, Richard H. Aishton filled the vacancy. A self-made man, Aishton as a teen-ager had swung an axe on the right-of-way of the Chicago & North Western. When he reached the age of forty, however, he ran the line as its general superintendent. Later he assumed its presidency as well as that of the American Railway Association. Aishton had gained great experience in dealing with the Railroad Brotherhoods, a fact that probably influenced the decision to appoint him. His service on the Commission, however, lasted only a few short months near the close of its hearings.[40]

Harris Weinstock, one newsman declared, was a "live wire." Indeed, the Commission's employer delegate from the West Coast had pursued an energetic and varied career. Offspring of English-Jewish immigrants, young Harris ended his formal schooling at age thirteen, but educated himself well enough to publish a number of articles and books. His works ranged from labor relations tracts to a religious study, *Jesus the Jew*, which boasted an introduction by David Starr Jordan, President of Stanford University. In Sacramento Harris and his half-brother founded the Weinstock-Lubin Department Store, developed it into a leading emporium, and branched out into far-flung real-estate ventures. As a National Guardsman, Weinstock worked his way up from Private to Lieutenant Colonel and thereby acquired a lifelong title.[41]

With equal gusto the Colonel plunged into public affairs. Active in the National Civic Federation, he also presided as the first president of San Francisco's Commonwealth Club. In 1906, unlike most of his fellow businessmen, Weinstock vigorously supported the graft prosecutions which implicated some of San Francisco's wealthiest citizens. As a Bull Mooser, he championed the cause of his close friend, reformer Hiram Johnson, in Johnson's successful gubernatorial fight. A many-faceted man of action, Weinstock resembled that other apostle of the strenuous life, Theodore Roosevelt, whom, indeed, along with Hiram Johnson, he worshipped as a personal hero.[42]

This new commissioner had already acquired considerable experience in industrial relations. As a state commissioner in 1908, he traveled over several continents in order to study labor laws. Germany's special courts of arbitration particularly interested him. Four years later, Weinstock earned more than local fame for his thorough and penetrating analysis of IWW free-speech riots in San Diego.

"Organized labor has come to stay," closed-shop employer Weinstock announced. "Unionism is destined to be a permanent and growing institution of modern industrialism." [43]

Abounding in energy and buoyant in spirit, Samuel Thruston Ballard arrived on the Commission as its only Southerner. In the 1880's this Kentuckian and his brother reorganized and rebuilt a bankrupt flour mill in Louisville until it flourished as the largest winter wheat refinery in the world. Ballard's Obelisk Brand became a household word. The firm also enjoyed renown for its progressive labor policies. Thruston Ballard's company ranked among the very first to introduce profit-sharing; as early as 1899, one-third of all annual profits accrued to employees. A few years later the Ballard mills initiated the first eight-hour day in the industry. Management also provided its workers with rest rooms, recreational halls, a dining room, and other facilities.[44]

Although Ballard was well known as a businessman, his politics at the time appeared vague. Secretary of Labor Wilson considered the mill-owner a Democrat, but another White House adviser pegged him as a Republican. During the 1914 congressional election Ballard had invited Woodrow Wilson to visit him if the President campaigned in Kentucky. Fortunately for the executive, the President did not accept, for subsequently in his career Ballard ran for office on the opposing party ticket. In 1919 Republican voters elevated him to the position of Lieutenant Governor. Republicanism persisted in his family, for Ballard's grandson, Senator Thruston Morton of Kentucky, officiated as GOP National Chairman during the 1960 presidential election campaign.[45]

Forthright Thruston Ballard, Mrs. Harriman later wrote, "was one of the most amusing and original men I have ever met." Only Frank Walsh could match the Kentuckian's zeal, yet in background these two men differed markedly. A Cornell graduate, of old American stock, Ballard belonged to the Sons of the American Revolution, the Society of Colonial Wars, and the Society of the Cincinnati. Walsh, on the other hand, came from an Irish immigrant family, had worked as a boy, and identified with the laboring classes. Yet Ballard and Walsh became inseparable friends. Despite their dissimilarities, they resembled each other in exuberant individuality, good humor, and personal warmth. To Thruston Ballard, Walsh was always "the Chief." [46]

7

Those who represented business and labor on the Commission had pursued generally orthodox careers. On the public panel, however, sat three individuals each with a decidedly nonconformist history. Irreverent *Masses* stereotyped Mrs. Harriman, Commons, and Walsh as "My Lady Bountiful," "Professor of Academic Truth," and "Militant Altruist," but actually each possessed a highly complex personality. They, more than the others, could shape the investigation. In their hands lay the balance of power. [47]

Florence Jaffray Hurst Harriman, nicknamed "Daisy" and known to the world as Mrs. J. Borden Harriman, emerged from a life of opulence. In every sense of the word at that time Florence Harriman was "society." As a child she resided in a fashionable townhouse on Fifth Avenue in the winter. Summers the family spent at their country estate overlooking the Hudson, and adjoining Washington Irving's former home. As a little girl Daisy would peep over the upstairs railing and stare at the tops of the heads of Chester Arthur, William Evarts, Henry Patterson, John Hay, and Henry George. One day, she later recalled, "Grandpapa had gone off in his steam yacht to meet President Garfield and bring him up to Mr. Cyrus Fields'. He came back alone. The President had been shot at the station in Washington." [48]

During her girlhood, Florence Hurst enjoyed every privilege of America's elite. She attended private classes at J. P. Morgan's home with the banker's daughter and ice-skated with young "Jack" Morgan in Central Park. As a debutante, she swirled through a world of constant gaiety. From New York to Bermuda, from England to Egypt, pretty Daisy watched thrilling regattas and danced at brilliant balls. She moved as an equal among Vanderbilts, Belmonts, Roosevelts, and Astors. At nineteen she married J. Borden Harriman, a Wall Street broker and a cousin of the railroad tycoon. [49]

Yet the trivial nature of her life troubled Daisy Harriman. "Sometimes," she mused, "Society has seemed to me like pink frosting on a cake—cake in a world that hungered for bread. Parties seemed feathers and fuss, nothing more." Tentatively, hesitatingly, she started to pierce her insulated environment. Along with some other women she founded the Colony Club and became its president. There the women listened to discourses on social problems from such lecturers as Terrence Powderly of the Knights of Labor. With a firmer step the young matron joined the National Civic Federation, where she met John Mitchell of the UMW and Timothy Healy, head of the Stationary Firemen. On one occasion Healy and 150 sturdy members of the brotherhood dined and spent the evening at Mrs. Harriman's sumptuous home. They granted her honorary membership.[50]

Florence Harriman's Civic Federation work deepened her knowledge. She rose to chair its women's welfare department and embarked on a series of labor studies. In New York she helped to reform conditions among Healy's firemen and personally investigated the textile strike at Lawrence. On behalf of NCF, Mrs. Harriman trekked all through the Carolinas and Georgia to analyze the effects and causes of child labor. National magazines purchased her articles based on these explorations. "It was the first money I had ever earned," she recalled, "and I was very proud." [51]

Soon Daisy Harriman jumped into politics; she did not lack confidence. At the Democratic convention of 1912, William Jennings Bryan, by his support of Speaker Champ Clark of Missouri, obstructed nomination of her candidate, Woodrow Wilson. Mrs. Harriman charged into the Commoner's suite, shoved through the crowd, and bagged her quarry. Without authorization she assured the orator that a Wilson victory would guarantee his nomination as Secretary of State. Many other considerations undoubtedly influenced Bryan, but at the conclusion of his long dialogue with Mrs. Harriman he truthfully announced, "I will never cast another vote for Clark." [52]

In practical politics Florence Harriman caught on fast. At her suggestion, Wilson created a Democratic women's division, and Mrs. Harriman seized the helm. Then she hit the hustings. In poor immigrant districts, crowds hooted her because of her wealth. She won cheers, however, when she proclaimed herself the daughter of an immigrant and promised that their children might someday be as rich as she. Vote for Wilson, she shouted, for "everything is so high now that if you wanted to throw a bad egg at me they're so expensive that you couldn't afford to do it." [53]

Florence Harriman had traveled a long way since her frivolous girlhood. "The best thing in the world is creative work," she said, "but I did not know that then." She took her new duties seriously: "I was on my honor as a woman . . . to make as few mistakes as possible. There were too many critics of women in public life." At age forty-two, Mrs. J. Borden Harriman, now "a handsome woman with white hair and fine gray eyes," became the first of her sex ever to serve on a federal commission [54]

Professor John R. Commons arrived on the Commission its unchallenged intellectual leader, yet his early career had shown him to be almost a complete failure. His father, a ne'er-do-well Indiana editor, passionately admired Herbert Spencer. His mother, during Commons' boyhood, had to rescue the family from financial disaster by running a boarding house. "I was brought up," the Professor asserted, "on Hoosierism, Republicanism, Presbyterianism, and Spencerianism." Frail physically, even as a college undergraduate, the young man suffered from what he described as a "nervous breakdown." With his bad academic record, Commons graduated from Oberlin only by special dispensation. For a while he worked as a printer and then vaulted into the Anti-Saloon crusade. Commons swore off smoking and drinking and cast his first ballot, in 1884, for the Prohibitionist ticket. "Here I began," he later wrote, "my fifty-year record of voting for third parties." [55]

Even when Commons embarked upon higher education, defeat plagued him. Although he studied at Johns Hopkins for two years, the young Indianian completely failed his history examination and never secured his doctorate. At Wesleyan, in Connecticut, where he first taught political economy, the University quickly sacked him as incompetent. For the next few years he meandered from campus to campus—Oberlin, Indiana, and, finally, in 1895, Syracuse. As soon as he set foot on this new soil, Commons blatantly proclaimed that he was a Socialist, a Single Taxer, a Greenbacker, a Free Silverite, and a Municipal Ownerist. Nevertheless, they hired him.[56]

Even at Syracuse, Commons stirred up a storm. Somewhat novel in his teaching methods, he once dragged a half-crazed tramp into his sociology class to be interviewed. The experiment succeeded, but for the next two weeks the derelict insisted on breaking into other professors' classes demanding the right to lecture. On another occasion, Commons arranged for his pupils to inspect a local penitentiary but discovered to his astonishment that half the student body had followed him. Correction officials accused these undergraduates, said Commons, of "frisking with prisoners, men and women." Some clergymen protested that this educator preached irreligious ideas, but the chancellor of the University stoutly defended his faculty's right to academic freedom. Later, however, when potential benefactors refused to contribute money to Syracuse because of Commons, this same administrator suddenly discontinued all Commons' courses. "I was not dismissed," the scholar later quipped, "my chair was pulled out from under me." [57]

Commons now turned his back on ivy-covered walls. With financial aid from George H. Shibley, a wealthy Free Silverite Democrat, the scholar organized a Bureau of Economic Research which issued a weekly index of wholesale prices. But his patron, who had poured some $3,000 into the venture, lost interest. "I had been fired twice within eighteen months," the Professor ruminated, "once by the conservatives and once by the radicals." In 1901 the U.S. Industrial Commission afforded him a temporary berth as its immigration expert. Commons impressed Ralph Easley, who then engaged the economist as his assistant on NCF. In his new capacity Commons participated in the settlement of some of the country's most important labor-management feuds, including the 1902 anthracite coal strike.[58]

Economist Richard T. Ely slipped the controversial scholar back into academic life. At exciting and reformist Wisconsin University, "I was born again," Commons declared. Here the scholar initiated his highly important studies of American labor and economic life, to which he devoted the next thirty years. Commons also examined municipal gas and utility companies in Europe, guided an investigation of Milwaukee city government, and assisted Edward T. Devine with his notable survey of Pittsburgh. Between teaching chores he plunged into LaFollette's Progressive movement. Commons drafted and promoted the bill which created Wisconsin's industrial commission and served on it as an active member.[59]

"A pigmy physically, but a giant when it comes to intellect," John Commons enjoyed universal respect from the educated world. "He is a thoroughly good fellow," said Theodore Roosevelt, "more of a radical even than I am, but a sane radical." Frank Walsh heralded the Wisconsin educator as "the most accomplished political economist of this time." An expert among experts, the professor was bound to become a power on the Commission.[60]

"A great lawyer, a persuasive speaker, and the most authentic liberal I have known"—so journalist George Creel described Frank P. Walsh, who now rose to command the industrial probe. One of a large Irish Catholic family, the Chairman grew up in the raw frontier atmosphere of early Kansas City. In his youth Walsh had known poverty, fought it, hated it, and never forgot it. Of thirty boys he remembered in his neighborhood, only three had survived to normal manhood. His formal education ended at an early age. To help his widowed mother, he hawked newspapers, delivered Western Union messages, and roamed all over the West as a railroad worker. Embued with confidence from this last adventure, Walsh returned to read law in a local office and in 1889 won admission to the bar.[61]

"If you asked a lawyer who was the greatest advocate in Missouri," a reporter wrote, "it's dollars to jitneys he will mention Mr. Walsh first." Immense vigor, oratory, shrewdness, and human warmth rapidly propelled him. At this time law was one of the few occupations in which a man could obtain a substantial income without aligning himself with big business. Walsh's early privation and his sympathy with the underprivileged drove him to abandon all corporate practice by 1900, but he still earned up to $50,000 a year in legal fees. Dramatic courtroom duels against James A. Reed, later a Democratic U.S. Senator, greatly enhanced his reputation. In almost every major case, if one party engaged Reed, the other hired Walsh. "I'm raising eight children," Walsh quipped, "by practicing law against Jim Reed." [62]

A trial that involved Jesse James, Jr., helped catapult both attorneys to prominence. Son of the immortal bandit, young Jesse stood accused of carrying on a family tradition by holding up a Missouri Pacific train near Kansas City. Without warrant, detectives had arrested and questioned James on suspicion before they jailed him. Many persons in the community who had liked this hitherto exemplary young man bridled at the dubious circumstances of his apprehension. Hundreds jammed the courtroom; grimly serious, they followed every motion intently.

Frank Walsh delivered an impassioned defense. In a paraphrase of a famous editorial on the death of Jesse James, Sr., the attorney damned police malpractice. "What a spectacle!" he shouted. "Is it possible that this great commonweath had to ally itself with hired detectives, with paid bloodhounds of the law, that the majesty of the law might be vindicated?" If so, Walsh cried, then the two symbolic bears in Missouri's flag should be ripped out and replaced with "the leering face of a detective and the crawling, snake-like shape of an informer!" Out for only a short time, the jury shot back a verdict of not guilty, and the courtroom rocked with cheers. Prosecutor Reed knew when he was beaten. Then and there he dropped all other indictments in the case. This drama so enthralled young James that he determined to study law. Later, as an attorney, he trod in Frank Walsh's footsteps and battled the Pendergast machine as a clean-government insurgent.[63]

Another colorful case, that of Colonel William Rockhill Nelson, publisher of the Kansas City *Star*, further broadcast Walsh's fame. Flamboyant and anti-Pendergast, "Baron Bill" Nelson had expanded his newspaper from a four-page daily into a major enterprise. For years he had attacked judges and lawyers for corruption and fee-splitting. *Star* headlines frequently proclaimed, "COURTS PROMOTE ANARCHY" or "BILL HITS SNITCH LAWYERS." One Pendergast judge waxed so indignant over what he considered an abusive slur that he charged the Colonel with contempt of court, refused to accept a fine, and demanded that the publisher go to jail. Newspapers all over the nation howled over this alleged challenge to freedom of the press. Colonel Henry Watterson of the Louisville *Courier-Journal* threatened to lead 100,000 Kentucky riflemen into Missouri to rescue embattled Nelson.

Even Walsh's skill could not save Baron Bill. Pendergast henchmen piled into court to gloat over this humiliation of their ancient foe. At the conclusion of the trial, without any adjournment, the judge immediately pronounced an opinion in unusually precise and fluent language. A Walsh aide peeped over the rostrum and noted that the judge read from a carefully prepared statement. Under Walsh's interrogation the judge confessed defiantly that he had written this verdict before the close of the testimony.

The judge then insisted that police immediately escort Colonel Nelson to prison instead of allowing his lawyers time to secure a writ to keep their client out of jail pending appeal. By sheer physical force, the husky Walsh and his aides blocked deputies from seizing the publisher until other members of the defense staff procured the necessary documents. Walsh not only saved Baron Bill from incarceration but also discovered an improper trial procedure that armed him with a needed point of law. On appeal, a higher court rescinded the Colonel's sentence.[64]

"An idealistic and optimistic Irishman," one observer noted, Walsh, "combined radical agitation and practical politics in a most uncommon fashion." In Kansas City's rough-and-tumble public life, Walsh allied himself with Pendergast's archrival, Joseph B. Shannon. Although Shannon's "Rabbits" and Pendergast's "Goats" clashed mainly over spoils, Walsh used his connection as a lever for social reform. On the Tenement Commission he helped expose the rat-ridden, unsanitary squalor which contaminated large areas of the city. Walsh personally drafted plans to erect a housing project to replace these slums. As president of the local Civil Service Board, he devoted himself in addition to the Board of Public Welfare, which established and enforced better conditions for industrial workers.[65]

In 1902 this attorney burst forth as a maverick in state politics. At Missouri's Democratic state convention, he sponsored a platform plank that denounced corporation contributions to campaign funds.

With blandishments and threats, financially pressed party regulars begged him to pocket his resolution or aim it solely at Republicans. Instead, Frank Walsh rented a separate hall and in a roaring speech tore into the bosses and their moneyed masters. Before the convention ended, the machine Democrats reversed themselves and Walsh's amendment triumphed. Two years later, he and Shannon carried important Jackson County for reform gubernatorial candidate Joseph W. Folk, and Progressivism swept into Missouri's statehouse. Despite his reformist convictions, the attorney refused to run for elective office: "What we need more than lawmakers and law governors is agitators. An agitator is a man who won't stand for lies [just] because they are old." [66]

"Broad-shouldered, deep-chested, wide of brow, and granite-chinned," Walsh exuded vitality. A boxer, crack handball player, swimmer, and dancer, he lost patience with people who didn't "stretch their muscles." Given to long walking tours, Walsh usually hiked with one or more of his numerous brood, who puffed and slipped as they tried to match their father's giant strides. Sanguine in temperament, the Chairman sometimes moved impulsively. He loved a good fight. Frank Walsh, declared Paul Kellogg, "would give dynamic force to any commission" even if it sat on weather reports.[67]

8

Woodrow Wilson had named some highly distinctive individuals to his Commission. Before them lay an immense task. They would have to traverse the continent many times. Their job would entail the examination of almost every phase of the nation's life. Success demanded that they plan carefully. They needed to formulate a basic philosophy and a plan of attack.

Even before Wilson announced his Commission, two of its most important members had already conferred. On June 20, the Chief Executive telegraphed Walsh requesting him to act as Chairman. That very day John R. Commons happened to pass through Kansas City and heard rumors of Walsh's appointment. Wilson, through Senator LaFollette, had offered the scholar a seat on the federal board, but Commons had not yet committed himself.* Now he hurried to Walsh's office. There the attorney persuaded him to join the Commission: "I shall lean heavily on such experts as you," Walsh assured him, "and I promise you that I will work." Simultaneously both men dispatched their acceptances.[68]

Walsh consulted not only Commons but all groups directly concerned with the Commission. In their Kansas City talks and later at Madison, the two men had already sketched their basic design. They divided the Commission's work into two major sections: Walsh would conduct public hearings and Commons would supervise research. Then the Chairman traveled east, conferred with the social reformers, and visited AFL's executive council in Washington. Ralph Easley of NCF, who had caught wind of Walsh's previous parleys, immediately sped to the capital to bestow the benefits of his advice upon the Chairman.[69]

In the fall of 1913 the entire Commission met for the first time. Collectively they confirmed the hearings-research division of the federal investigation. In addition, they elected Mrs. Harriman resident commissioner in the District of Columbia. Their function, the commissioners agreed, was neither administrative nor arbitrational. Nor did they intend simply to present Congress with unevaluated statistical evidence. Their work, they declared, "is meant to be interpretive and remedial. . . . The Commission's duty is to get behind the facts." "It's *causes* that we are after," Walsh insisted, "not *symptoms*." [70]

Generally the investigation enjoyed a good press, but two particular comments flashed out like danger signals. Big Bill Haywood of IWW blasted the Commission as a "tragic joke" perpetrated by legislative jugglers. He foresaw no improvement in the social order until the distinction between capitalist and worker was destroyed. "We say that this struggle will go on," Big Bill later avowed, "in spite of anything that this commission can do or anything that you

---

* In his autobiography Commons states that Wilson offered the chairmanship to him. No evidence in either the Wilson or the LaFollette papers supports this claim. Commons wrote *Myself* when past seventy without any records and may have confused the offer with some other federal chairmanship tendered him by the President. Commons did not retain his own papers for this period. (See *Myself*, p. 166.)

may recommend to Congress." Detective William J. Burns, on the other hand, urged the Commission to look into alleged connections between organized labor and the McNamara dynamite conspiracy. Walsh replied, "There you have a warning of a malign division . . . on one side your Haywoods, sullen and distrustful, and on the other your Burnses, eager for persecutions and prosecutions. . . . It is an alignment that must be prevented, for I can conceive of nothing that will so hamper the work of the commission as being compelled to run the class gauntlet." [71]

The Commission, for almost two years an arena of contention among some of America's major interests, stood on the threshold of its mission. Most of the commissioners embraced progressive views. None approached the conservatism of some of Taft's appointees. Sectionally, they hailed chiefly from midwestern or border states with some also from the Far West and the East. Most were self-educated; only three boasted college degrees. All had acquired experience in tripartisan (labor-capital-public) activities mainly through the National Civic Federation. Conservative labor and small business triumphed; at this time Wilson's New Freedom excluded both big industry and radical unionism. Members of the public panel, with their extremely varied backgrounds, gave promise of acting as the creative force within the Commission. These nine investigators now embarked on their journey through a troubled America. Establishment of this Commission clearly showed how important the social implications of industrial violence loomed in the minds of many progressives.

IV

WAR IN PATERSON

1

"THERE'S WAR IN PATERSON!" cried journalist and strike sympathizer John Reed. "But it's a curious kind of war. All the violence is the work of one side—the Mill Owners." "I say *they* declared war the first morning," asserted Paterson's Police Chief John Bimson in reference to the IWW. "I have been 28½ years in the police business in this city, and I have never seen any such tactics used in any strike."[1]

In 1913, Paterson, New Jersey, indeed exhibited many of the characteristics of open warfare. Two armies faced one another, each determined to achieve victory. Police arrested hundreds, many men were wounded, and some died. Parades, slogans, banners, and impassioned oratory kept combatant morale high. Explosions destroyed property; both sides battled openly with clubs and guns. Peace signified only a temporary truce.

"The struggle at Paterson is but one phase of the industrial problem that is characteristic of our times," declared *Outlook*. "It is for the study of that problem that this Commission was created." What caused this war? Why did it last so long? What prevented a solution? Paterson's ordeal revealed something important about America.[2]

2

In 1912 New Jersey's silk mills and allied industries employed about 30,000 operatives, of whom 90 percent, chiefly adults of both sexes, worked in the Paterson area. They wove and dyed the raw material brought from the Orient; their labor elevated the state to a top position in the silk industry.

At the turn of the century, however, Pennsylvania rose to challenge New Jersey's supremacy. A plentiful supply of female and child labor existed in the mining communities of the Keystone State. These employees toiled three to five hours per week longer and received about half as much pay as the New Jersey silk workers. In addition to this cheap labor, Quaker State silk manufacturers obtained exemption from local taxation, free land for their mills, and inexpensive coal.[3]

Technology, however, really changed the character of this industry. Paterson mills manufactured high-grade broad and ribbon silk woven on jacquard or German looms. A weaver had to watch one of these machines constantly in order to stop it if a thread broke. Pennsylvania mills made a lower grade of silk on new looms that ceased automatically when a break occurred. One worker could tend as many as six of these newer machines at once. Pennsylvania thus produced great quantities of cheap silk at low labor costs.[4]

At first the two states did not compete, since each fashioned a different grade of fabric. But in the six-year period preceding 1912, Pennsylvania factories increased their output by 97 percent, while those in Paterson advanced theirs by only 22 percent. Impressed by the profits in cheap silk, New Jersey manufacturers began to convert to the multiple-loom system. Paterson weavers feared that this change meant increased unemployment, lower wage rates, and additional hardships for themselves. Manufacturers viewed the transition as a natural economic development; they were surprised when, in November, 1911, the workers went on strike.[5]

The walkout lasted until the following May and resulted mainly in a rise in the minimum wage rate to $14 a week for some broad-silk weavers. Rudolph Katz, local IWW (Detroit faction) chief,*

* In 1908 the Industrial Workers of the World divided into two factions. Daniel De Leon's Socialist Labor Party dominated the Detroit organization. It endorsed the use of parliamentary political action and the economic weapon of the strike. De Leon's group, however, deplored the use of "direct action," i.e., force or violence.

The Chicago branch, headed by Haywood and Vincent St. John, scorned political methods and accepted the utilization of sabotage and violence when necessary. Both they and the Detroit organization favored a form of syndicalism.

led this successful campaign. He failed, however, to consolidate his organization, and it soon disintegrated. Within six months Paterson's toilers prepared to march out again, this time under more militant leadership.[6]

3

On January 27, 1913, all 800 employees of the Henry Doherty Silk Company in Paterson struck. They did so because management fired a workers' committee which protested against the multiple-loom system. During the following weeks, the rest of the broad-silk weavers, the ribbon weavers, and the dyehouse laborers joined the strike. By the end of the first week in March, some 10,000 silk operatives had quit their jobs. Apparently these workers left spontaneously. They did not receive the support of the local AFL, and the local IWW (Chicago branch) possessed only 100 scattered members.* Not more than 5 percent of those striking belonged to an organization.[7]

But now IWW's small local expanded enormously. Paterson's overworked, underpaid, and mainly unskilled immigrant laborers quickly swelled its ranks. Union leaders rapidly organized picket brigades, established a strike committee, and formed a large number of departments, such as publicity, information, and relief. "Show your disapproval by striking altogether," IWW cried. "The bosses are after our lives. . . . It is better to starve fighting than to starve working." The local leaders soon declared a general strike for the entire industry.[8]

Although the multiple-loom system was the basic issue of the strike, it was not the only cause of dissatisfaction. An assortment of indignities, injustices, and petty tyrannies helped touch off the conflict. Men complained that employers, by the use of subtle devices, constantly cheated the workers out of their just wages. Employees

---

* At one time nearly all Paterson's workers were enrolled in the United Textile Workers Union (AFL). A series of unsuccessful strikes, however, led to the collapse of that organization. (*Statistics*, p. 181; Paterson *Press*, Paterson *Guardian*, January–March, 1927.)

protested that managers would give some favored worker an easy material to loom and then use him as a pacemaker for the rest of the weavers. One mill-owner lectured his workers on how to cook soup and leftover foods in order to demonstrate to them how they might reduce their cost of living. If they followed his advice, he assured them, they would not need a wage hike.[9]

Some mills employed little girls as apprentices. A child worker would contract to allow the employer to withhold half her wages until the end of a full year. Many bosses would fire these trainees just before the twelve-month period expired, thereby releasing themselves from the obligation to pay the remaining wages due. One of these companies fined its operatives 50 cents for talking, 50 cents for laughing, 50 cents for opening a window, and 50 cents for a torn apron. "Maybe you could not believe it," one little girl reported, "but they steal our hooks and scissors from us and then we have to buy them back again for thirty-five cents." [10]

If laborers protested against these and similar practices, a silk worker told the Commission, "they would be singled out and systematically discharged." "It was this continual nagging at the employees," he explained, "demanding more work, always taking advantage of an opportunity that presented itself to reduce the wages that filled the workers with so much indignation and hard feeling against employers." [11]

Originally the strikers asked only for the elimination of the new looms, a forty-four-hour week for the entire industry, an increase of 25 percent in piece prices, and a minimum of $12 a week for dyehouse helpers. Later the dye workers added new requests, chief of which included an eight-hour day and time and a half for overtime. On no occasion did IWW demand formal recognition.[12]

Paterson mill-owners flatly refused to negotiate with the union. They asserted that it would be futile to deal with an organization admittedly aimed at the overthrow of private property. If they granted the strikers' demands, the silk entrepreneurs further declared, their industries could not meet the Pennsylvania competition. Each manufacturer expressed a willingness to discuss problems with his own employees, but only after they had returned to work and quit IWW. "No legitimate business can stand the method of attack of the I.W.W.," said Samuel McCollom, president of the Manufacturers' Association, "but we'd rather go to the wall at once than yield everything we own to them by degrees." [13]

4

Since management had completely declined even to discuss the issues, the workers prepared for battle; the local IWW had already laid the groundwork. Now onto the scene came its dramatic national leaders—Big Bill Haywood, Elizabeth Gurley Flynn, and Carlo Tresca. With the arrival of these three and their lieutenants, Patrick Quinlan and Joseph Ettor, Paterson's struggle took on new dimensions. It ceased to be a purely local affair and grew into an event of national importance.

Big Bill Haywood led the radicals. "Huge, burly, six-feet-two, with a great blunt face, all pocked and seamed," Haywood was a powerful orator. He already bore scars from some of the most violent labor wars in America—including Cripple Creek and Lawrence among the most prominent. Born in Salt Lake City, Big Bill had worked as a miner since the age of sixteen and when still a boy had lost an eye. "His gigantic frame and one eye gave him the appearance of a sinister Cyclops," Elizabeth Flynn wrote, "but his face lit up with kindness in talks to workers." In the labor movement Haywood rose to the position of secretary-treasurer of the Western Federation of Miners (WFM) and in 1905 was among those who founded IWW. But Haywood's advocacy of direct action syndicalism had led to his expulsion both from the WFM and from the Socialist Party. He represented IWW's most radical faction. [14]

Bill Haywood completely accepted the inevitability of class conflict; he envisioned no alternative to constant warfare and the eventual triumph of the proletariat. "I have had a dream that I have in the morning and at night and during the day," he proclaimed, "and that is that there will be a new society sometime in which there will be no battle between capitalist and wage earner." To achieve that utopia, Big Bill looked forward to a great general strike, during which the workers would confiscate every factory and elect their own representatives to a new industrial congress. Haywood scorned politics, scoffed at contracts, and favored sabotage. "I would hold that the property does not belong to you," he warned his enemies. "What you as a capitalist class have piled up as property is merely unpaid labor . . . you have no vested right in that property." Although a third-generation Midwesterner, Haywood loomed as one of the most revolutionary figures in American history.[15]

Elizabeth Gurley Flynn was only twenty-two, but Haywood called her "the greatest woman agitator that the cause of those who toil with their hands has produced in a generation." New England born and bred, she had absorbed the socialism of her parents. At the age of sixteen, she delivered her first speech at the Harlem Socialist Club. It quickly won her invitations from groups which stretched from Philadelphia to Boston. Soon she plunged into IWW agitation. Author Theodore Dreiser described this girl as "a typical Irish beauty, with blue eyes, filmy black hair and delicate pink complexion." But, cautioned the novelist, "she has the mature mentality, the habit of thought and finished expression of a woman twenty-five." Struck by Miss Flynn's comeliness and forensic power, David Belasco, the famous theatrical producer, once tendered her a part in one of his plays. But Miss Flynn spurned the idea of reciting other people's lines. "I don't want to be an actress!" she cried. "I'm in the labor movement and I speak my own piece." [16]

Wobbly captain Carlo Tresca had escaped from his native Italy in order to avoid a politically inspired jail sentence. Scion of a wealthy landed family, he was called "Don Carlo" by Italian peasants even as he led them in socialist agitation. Tresca's rosy cheeks, sensitive mouth, kindly smile, and beard, Max Eastman noted, gave him the gait and bearing of a "mildly liberal gentleman of the old school." Once during a bloody riot, Tresca stooped to aid a wounded picket. A policeman respectfully tapped the labor chief on the shoulder. "Please step aside, Doctor," the officer requested. "We're arresting these men." As a person of culture and an impressive orator, Carlo Tresca enjoyed vast authority among Italian immigrants, but he never learned to speak English properly. If

Tresca had mastered this new tongue, Eastman speculated, he could have become one of the greatest labor leaders in American history.[17]

These IWW champions and their associates, who now entered Paterson, appealed to more than the simple economic needs of their followers. Rhetorical, emotional, excitable, fascinated by the concept of violence, they lent an air of romanticism to the movement. Irish-born orator Patrick Quinlan, for example, joined their ranks. During times of discouragement, Quinlan had found consolation in poetic tributes from Rose Pastor Stokes. Canadian authorities had recently ransacked the possessions of Wobbly agitator Joseph Ettor in search of subversive pamphlets. They discovered only a volume of Shelley's poetry. Critics had already acclaimed the powerful poems from prison by another IWW leader—Arturo Giovanitti.

Elizabeth Flynn and Carlo Tresca were lovers. "We lived and worked together for the next thirteen years," she later wrote. "This was according to our code . . . to honestly and openly avow a real attachment." On one occasion, during a riot, Tresca lost half of his vest. Those who found the garment noticed that it held a tiny copy of Elizabeth Barrett Browning's love poems. Miss Flynn had underlined the most tender passages and inscribed them to Tresca.[18]

5

As soon as these lords of the IWW set foot in Paterson, city officials cracked down. On the very day that the union declared a general strike, police charged into their principal assembly hall and smashed the meeting. Then Police Chief Bimson immediately arrested Tresca, Miss Flynn, and Quinlan. Although he admitted that this gathering was peaceful, the chief defined this move as "preventative [sic] medicine." Officers then apprehended twenty-five more union leaders who were trying to stage a parade. These strikers had conducted themselves in good order, but Bimson claimed that his action would avert a riot. Finally, the city fathers closed all assembly halls to strikers. Auditorium owners were directed to lock their establishments securely to bar laborers from breaking in to hold meetings.

On behalf of the strikers, a citizens' committee appealed to Mayor Andrew F. McBride to restore the rights of free speech and assembly. Paterson's executive retorted that such rights extended only to residents of the city: "I cannot stand for seeing Paterson flooded with persons who have no interest in Paterson, who can only give us a bad name," he snapped. "I propose to continue my policy of locking up these outside agitators on sight." [19]

On that same day, police raided a meeting of non-IWW Socialists who were quietly listening to an address by Wilson R. Killingbeck, state secretary of the Socialist Party. When detectives and uniformed officers raced to the platform and seized Killingbeck, the entire audience jumped to its feet and shouted protests. A forward section of the crowd closed in on the police, who blocked this move with a quick call for reserves. One officer then read aloud to the astonished group the entire ancient Riot Act including its final phrase, "God save the King!" An angry mob followed police as they escorted their prisoners to headquarters. Chief Bimson demanded to see a copy of what the Socialist leader had previously been reading to his audience. To that official's embarrassment, Killingbeck showed him that it was a section of the New Jersey constitution.[20]

In his paper, the *Weekly Issue*, Socialist Alexander Scott blasted these violations of civil liberties. Police, without a search warrant or any written authorization, then swooped down on Socialist Party headquarters and confiscated from 5,000 to 10,000 copies of the offending journal. They also arrested Scott on a charge of inciting "hostility to government." Bimson held the editor until payment of a $2,000 bail bond.[21]

Haywood soon got his first taste of Paterson justice. Barred from indoor halls, the strikers congregated in an open field within city limits to listen to Big Bill. On orders from Chief Bimson, police forbade the rally. Someone suggested that the workers march to the neighboring town of Haledon, where the Socialist mayor had granted them complete freedom of assembly. With Haywood in the lead, the laborers walked toward this community until they arrived within a few hundred feet of the county line. At this point, Paterson police stopped them and arrested Haywood and local IWW leader Adolph Lessig.[22]

Authorities kept both men overnight in the county jail. On the next day, without a trial, recorder James F. Carroll sentenced each to a $5,000 fine and six months of servitude on a charge of disorderly conduct. Carroll also held them for unlawful assembly pending an investigation by a grand jury. Justice Minturn dismissed the first charge of unlawful assembly when Haywood appealed to the state Supreme Court. At the same hearing, however, Paterson's prosecutor claimed that, since a large crowd followed the Wobbly boss to Haledon, Haywood was guilty of leading a parade without a permit. Judge Minturn responded, "Crowds follow a circus. Do you arrest the circus? The case is dismissed." Later the state Supreme Court also released both men from the charge of disorderly conduct.[23]

Perhaps because of public clamor, Paterson authorities temporarily relaxed their restrictions and allowed the assembly halls to reopen. But the city prosecutor, ever alert for sedition, insisted on sending a stenographer, guarded by detectives, to every important meeting. On May 19, when a speaker at a strike rally, noting the police stenographer, growled, "The spy is in the rear of the hall," 3,000 workers, according to Captain Bimson, "turned like tigers" and threatened this unwanted guest. Revolvers drawn, detectives steeled themselves to stand against the crowd, but their fears had no justification. According to the police chief himself, no one in the audience made any further advances; the gathering proceeded to a peaceful conclusion. Some of the strikers jeered at the detectives afterward, but no violence erupted.[24]

After this incident, Paterson shut down all public halls permanently. When questioned as to what law justified this restriction on liberty of assembly, the police chief responded, "No law. We could close them if there had been a complaint that they are disorderly places, and there hasn't been any complaint, yet. But we could have a complaint quick enough if we needed it." [25]

Only a few publications bothered to notice these violations of basic constitutional rights. The New York *World* excoriated

Paterson's police for "demonstrating its stupidity in the presence of a strike." It noted that the authorities handled the nonviolent Socialists just as they did the IWW. The Socialist New York *Call* pointed out that "it was the possessors of the law that violated, prostituted and degraded it." William Z. Foster's *Syndicalist* saw Paterson's activities as proof that "the real strength of capitalism lies in the fact that the capitalists have no regard for their own laws when those laws stand between them and victory." Haywood, however, reacted differently. "This action on the part of the police," he asserted, "so thoroughly aroused the working class of Paterson . . . that it resulted in bringing about an amalgamation that would otherwise have required much hard work and a longer period to accomplish." [26]

6

These infringements by police in the early stages of the strike continued throughout the struggle. Paterson officials also turned to the courts as an additional weapon. Judicial aggression, particularly in respect to freedom of speech, reached its peak at the trials of Tresca, Flynn, Quinlan,* and Scott.[27]

On the opening day of the trials, 5,000 spectators swarmed around the courthouse. Every time policemen forced back those who tried to push into the building, the crowd retaliated with boos and hisses. Some in the gathering stood at the doors and windows of stores, others on the tops of houses. "There they come: hurrah for Big Bill Haywood!" someone shouted. "The response was deafening," a newsman recorded. "It seemed as if every person in the great throng was leather-lunged." Miss Flynn, resplendent in a claret-colored dress, walked with Carlo Tresca. In his Vandyke beard and glasses, the Italian resembled a poet. "Haywood accepted the plaudits with the bearing of a King acknowledging the tributes of his subjects," said one observer. "He bowed and smiled at inter-

---

* Specific indictments were: Tresca: inciting to assault police; Quinlan: advocating the burning and destruction of property, inciting to assault, inciting to personal injury; Flynn: inciting to assault. (New York *Times*, May 1, 1913.)

vals, not, however, displacing the large black sombrero hat which he wore, nor the cigar."[28]

Black-haired, good-natured Patrick Quinlan first stood trial. According to the prosecution, Quinlan, during a strike rally, urged the use of physical violence against strikebreakers. Police officers served as the major witnesses against him. In his defense Quinlan produced more than thirty persons who swore that he did not even address the assembly in question. A Paterson newspaper reporter who had taken notes throughout the entire rally corroborated their testimony. Although the first trial resulted in a hung jury, a second led to Quinlan's conviction.[29]

According to an agreed procedure, none of the guilty were to receive sentence until completion of all the cases. During a recess in Miss Flynn's trial, however, the fun-loving Quinlan and a journalist passed the time by burlesquing a courtroom scene. In this mock drama the reporter, acting as both prosecutor and judge, accused "defendant" Quinlan of "failing to get a haircut and shave" and sentenced him to fifteen years in a brewery. This, remarked the labor leader, was the most pleasant punishment he had ever received in America or Ireland. Suddenly a deputy sheriff burst into the room and exclaimed that they were making a show of Passaic County justice. This officer immediately escorted Quinlan into the presence of a judge. Within moments the judge slapped the IWW chief with a $500 fine and a prison term of up to seven years.[30]

Quinlan's conviction hit Paterson like a bombshell. It signified that all the IWW leaders might suffer imprisonment. A little girl, Carrie Torello, ran out of the courthouse and first gave out the news to the crowd of incredulous strikers who surrounded her. "Guilty as charged," she cried. "It's true, I tell you! I heard them say it." Hordes of workers then descended on Helvetia Hall, where the other Wobbly leaders awaited the news. "The verdict is a class verdict," thundered Elizabeth Flynn. "It is an outrage." Carlo Tresca grew so overwrought that he could hardly express himself even in his native tongue. "They shout for law and property," he yelled, "but for human life they say nothing." A reporter quoted members of the audience as muttering, "We will put dynamite under the court. . . . Yes, they will get what's coming to them now."

At a mass meeting the following day, 15,000 strikers stood for hours and hurled invectives at Paterson authorities. "You want to tie up every garage, every streetcar line and then see to it that the lights are put out for a couple of nights," local IWW chief Lessig told his cheering audience. "Do that and see how the bosses will like it." As sweat rolled down his face, Big Bill Haywood roared denunciations of Paterson's jury, while Joseph Ettor rapped the police as "hired assassins of the capitalists." Jumping up and down, his eyes ablaze, Carlo Tresca spat out his own tirade in broken English: "Police, thieves, liars, loafers, cowards!" he screamed.[31]

This sentence whipped up a storm of protest from many different quarters. The DeLeonite *Weekly People* blasted the jury as a "worse bunch of Anarchists than Quinlan." A man would have to spend as long as seven years in jail, exclaimed the New York *Call*, because "a rag, or a phrase, or a tattered sentence was taken from many hours of talk." In the Midwest, Socialist *Appeal to Reason* donated its entire reserve fund ($5,000) to pay for the union leader's bail and appeal: "Quinlan's release will give all our comrades in the state of Woodrow Wilson and his 'New Freedom' the right to carry on their agitation." Progressive Amos Pinchot also sent a check. Although he disagreed with many of the principles of the IWW, Pinchot swore, he did believe in justice. All in vain. Both the New Jersey Supreme Court, and the Court of Errors and Appeals upheld the conviction. The union leader served nine months in jail.[32]

As a result of the Quinlan case, IWW attorneys petitioned Justice Minturn to allow the other defendants to be tried before a "foreign" jury, that is, one chosen from outside Paterson. Defense lawyers asserted that the press and public were so hostile in Paterson that they would prevent a fair hearing. Despite objections from the prosecution, who claimed that such a move would cast a stigma on the town, the judge granted this request, Paterson's first such ruling in thirty years.[33]

Under these new conditions, the prosecution then called for the trial of Elizabeth Gurley Flynn. The prosecutor tore into his witness relentlessly, but she withstood every onslaught. Even the anti-IWW New York *Times* admiringly reported, "for once the hard fighting prosecutor met his match in this pale-faced young woman from upper Manhattan." Toward the end, the exasperated attorney found himself shouting at her, a technique at once denounced by the defense as bullying. Miss Flynn faced a charge almost identical with that brought against Quinlan. Her trial followed the same pattern. At its conclusion, the jury disagreed and did not render a verdict.[34]

Paterson officialdom delayed a long time before retrying the redoubtable girl orator. It was not until 1915, when she returned to the city during a new labor war, that they suddenly reactivated her case. This apparent persecution of an individual on a charge now two and one-half years old aroused the anger of a group of prominent women, who organized a fund-raising committee for Miss Flynn's defense. Within an hour the jury delivered a verdict of not guilty. As the Paterson *News* commented, "the police witnesses displayed that superhuman perfection of memory which is always suspicious and the jury did not believe them." Even the New York *Times* admitted that the case cast some doubt on the veracity of police officers and found the evidence disquieting.[35]

Carlo Tresca's first trial also terminated with a hung jury. During the Commission's hearings, the defense attorney chided the prosecutor for his tardiness in retrying this IWW case. Soon afterward the Italian again stood before the bar of justice. In only twenty minutes the jury judged him not guilty. Police had originally arrested Tresca for uttering the words, "This strike is the start of a great revolution." Snapped famed editor Arthur Brisbane: "It is just as well for our judges and district attorneys to remember that this country BEGAN WITH A REVOLUTION." [36]

Although not a member of IWW, Alexander Scott, editor of the Socialist Passaic *Weekly Issue*, had roasted Paterson's police with irritating regularity. "Hot-headed brass-buttoned anarchists" and "a bunch of drunken Cossacks" ranked among Scott's choice epithets for the local constabulary. Paterson dignitaries could stand it no longer and accused the journalist of inciting "hostility to government." This charge referred to a rather dusty piece of legislation passed after the assassination of President McKinley. The statute sought to prevent anarchists from instigating violence against public officials. Scott's attorneys believed the accusation so ridiculous that they did not trouble to prepare a defense. A jury of Paterson businessmen and manufacturers, however, brought in a verdict of guilty. A local judge fined editor Scott $250 and condemned him to a prison term of up to fifteen years.[37]

Publications throughout the United States, regardless of political ideology, cried out with indignation. "If New York had such a law and it was interpreted as the New Jersey law has been interpreted," argued Pulitzer's *World*, "most of the inhabitants in this city would be in jail. Indeed . . . the town would be practically depopulated." Every interest fears publicity and is always ready to say, "Send the editor to jail; teach him a lesson so he won't interfere with our game," declared the Kansas City *Star*. The Boston *Transcript* blasted the legislation as a gag law. "Scott's conviction," *International Socialist Review* flatly announced, "makes the constitutional guarantee of a free press a dead letter." [38]

As if in accord with these sentiments, the New Jersey Supreme Court set aside Scott's conviction. The higher bench ruled that the original trial judge should have quashed the indictment or directed the jury to render a not-guilty verdict. In Scott's case, as in the other important IWW trials, Paterson authorities had employed the judiciary to violate basic constitutional rights. Juries outside Paterson did not convict a single Wobbly leader. With the exception of Quinlan, all appeals to higher courts ended in favor of the defendants.

7

This harsh treatment accorded their leaders angered rank-and-file strikers. Violence broke out with mounting intensity. Weidmann Silk and Dyeing Company ranked among the worst trouble spots. Many mechanics, electricians, and engineers who lived near the plant took advantage of the strike to repair their idle machinery. Those on picket lines, however, regarded these men as strike-breakers. During the first part of April, a number of bombs exploded in the residential area close to the mill. These incidents provoked the company to hire detectives to escort their employees as they entered and left the factory. [39]

On April 17 jeering pickets surrounded a group of Weidmann workers and their guards. Suddenly a battle erupted. Stones flew in all directions, killing one man and injuring others. About twenty gunshots barked out, and a bystander, Modestino Valentino,[*] fell mortally wounded. Hundreds of pickets encircled two detectives, who held their assailants at bay with pistols until police reinforcements came to their rescue. Patrol wagons hauled away twenty-three rioters. [40]

Two detectives stood accused of the murder of Valentino; three persons, according to an IWW attorney, positively identified them as the killers. At each of the first two hearings the presiding judge stressed that a perfect prima facie case existed against at least one of the accused. Each time the magistrate directed the jurors to bring in an indictment for murder. Each time they refused. Upon completion of the third investigation, Justice Minturn spoke with considerable feeling: "What invisible hand is there in this community that is strong enough to prevent the indictment of this man? Are you willing to say that our laws are respecters of persons? What power is there in this community that is greater than the power of the law?" Nevertheless, the jury again failed to indict; neither of the detectives ever had to face trial.[41]

Arrests of laborers proceeded with monotonous regularity. In one instance, authorities jailed 200 strikers at the same time; most of them were seized while picketing and charged with disorderly conduct, unlawful assembly, or both. Testimony leading to their conviction derived almost exclusively from police officers. Recorder Carroll, perhaps the most hated man in Paterson, simply meted out sentences and fines. Few were even granted trial by jury. [42]

Paterson police once hailed journalist John Reed into their prison. In "Sheriff Radcliff's Hotel," as Reed dubbed the jail, he choked in foul air and was revolted by the vermin which swarmed over

[*] The New York *Times* referred to this man as Vareche and Varecho. Sometimes he was also called Valentino Modestino. In the *Testimony*, however, most witnesses used the name Modestino Valentino. (*Statistics*, p. 209; *Pageant of the Paterson Strike*, pp. 16–18.)

the walls. Prisoners ate rancid meat, rotting vegetables crawling with insects, and soup full of dead rats. But the high spirits of the strikers really impressed the young writer:

> In about an hour the outside door clanged open, and in came about forty pickets in charge of the police, joking and laughing among themselves. They were hustled into cells, two each. Then pandemonium broke loose! With one accord the heavy iron beds were lifted and slammed thunderingly against the metal walls. It was like a cannon battery in action.
> "Hooray for I.W.W.!" screamed a voice. And unanimously answered all the voices as one, "Hooray!"
> "Hooray for Chief Bums!" [Chief of Police Bimson]. . .
> "Boo-oo-o!" It was an awful voice in that reverberant iron room, full of menace.
> "Hooray for Haywood! One bigga da Union! Hooray for da strike! To hell wit' da police!" [43]

Paterson had a formative influence on Reed's character. He had joined the strike as a lark, but the suffering of the workers aroused his deepest feelings:

> When it came time for me to go out I said goodbye to all those gentle, alert, brave men, ennobled by something greater than themselves. *They* were the strike—not Bill Haywood, not Elizabeth Gurley Flynn, not any other individual. . . . Think of it! Twelve years they have been losing strikes—twelve solid years of disappointments and incalculable suffering. They must not lose again! They cannot lose! [44]

Acts of violence rocked the city all through the long struggle. Vandals stoned more than forty houses and exploded fourteen bombs. Three attempts to wreck railroad trains occurred, one of which damaged and almost derailed a Chicago express. Twenty policemen suffered injuries, and combatants assaulted at least fifty persons with lead pipes, bludgeons, and clubs. The strike accounted for at least five deaths. Before the end, police had arrested 1,800 people.[45]

Each side blamed the other for this turbulence. Strikers placed the responsibility on private detectives and police brutality. New York's Socialist *Call* suggested that Chief Bimson and Mayor McBride deliver a series of lectures on the theory and practice of direct action and physical violence, which they, as experts, had applied to workers. City authorities insisted that the IWW leaders had deliberately lashed their followers into riotous outbursts. McBride complimented his law officials on their "patient forbearance." IWW, he charged, "threatened to make Paterson a howling wilderness, an industrial graveyard, and to wipe it off the face of the map. . . . the fight which Paterson is making is the fight for the nation." [46]

8

Despite these mutual recriminations, certain groups in Paterson tried to settle the dispute in a more civilized manner. In March the silk workers' press committee made the first overture. They indicated their willingness to meet at any time with the Silk Manufacturers' Association. Those on strike, this committee affirmed, asked only for the right to bargain through an agency of their own choosing. In reply members of the Association reiterated their previous position. Each manufacturer would deal solely with his own employees and only after they had returned to the mills. [47]

A day later the Paterson *Press* telegraphed Governor James F. Fielder and requested that he appoint a Senate committee to investigate the strike. Each party was to agree in advance to accept the senators' recommendations. Governor Fielder, although willing to comply, refused to act unless both sides solicited his intervention. While the mill workers endorsed this plan, the manufacturers spurned it. [48]

Paterson's hopes for peace temporarily brightened when a joint committee representing both sides petitioned the state legislature to investigate the conflict. Their supplication failed, however, and the employers stubbornly declined to participate in any further discussions. "These people," an industry spokesman said of the IWW, "will not be bound by any agreement and will continue to strike again and again until they own the mills. It would be foolhardy to treat with an organization of that kind." [49]

Now Paterson's AFL launched a membership campaign in

order to capitalize on management's hatred of IWW. Although conservative newspapers prayed for its success, the Gompers union met with a cool reception. In a last-ditch effort to split the Wobbly ranks, AFL obtained permission to hold an open meeting in an armory, where 15,000 workers filled the auditorium. For almost an hour this multitude kept up such a steady roar of hooting that the Federation leaders could not speak. When Haywood, Tresca, and Miss Flynn burst into view, the crowd responded with frenzied cheers. These IWW heroes challenged the AFL to a debate, but the latter declined. Denied the opportunity of hearing their Wobbly chiefs, a great majority of the audience stamped out. Soon after, the Federation abandoned its recruiting drive.[50]

One cluster of workers, disillusioned with both unions, sued for a separate peace based on a wage scale already in effect at one of the higher paying mills. These operatives planned to form a permanent association of employees in the broad-silk industry entirely free of any existing organizations. This move by the independents might have broken the strike, but the mill owners rebuffed it. Acceptance of this scheme, manufacturers declared, meant abandonment of their basic principle: grievances must be settled only between each proprietor and his own laborers. "It is not alone against the I.W.W. that the employers have set their faces," observed John Fitch. "Union organization, under whatever name, is opposed whether its terms be 'reasonable' or 'revolutionary' because it interferes with business." [51]

On June 6, IWW tendered its final appeal. The Union Strike Committee again proposed a joint conference. It maintained that

> To ask the workers to return without even talking about their grievances is nothing else than asking a complete and unconditional surrender, a proposition which in our judgment will not be accepted. To starve the workers back into the mills does not appear to be a policy that should commend itself to intelligent men. The handling of immense quantities of costly material by men having nothing but black hate in their hearts and a desire for revenge in their souls, seems to be a rather dangerous proposition.

Officials of the Manufacturers' Association ignored the proposal. Informally, they characterized it as "mere bluster" and remained inflexible. Their refusal signified the end of the last important attempt to terminate the strike by negotiation. [52]

9

All peace proposals, regardless of origin, smashed on the rocks of employer obduracy. Paterson Rabbi Leo Mannheimer * concluded that the strategy of management was evidently "to starve the workers into submission, so that they will return to the mills disheartened and broken." Avoiding starvation became a chief concern of the IWW. [53]

Wobbly leaders recognized the urgency for large-scale aid and created a Strike Relief Fund, which procured money from other IWW locals, Socialist groups, and Italian societies. In addition, benefit performances, cake sales, dances, and contributions from local merchants swelled their treasury. Later the union opened its own grocery store. In order to relieve married workers of some of their financial distress, Miss Flynn arranged to send the children of strikers' families out of Paterson. Foster parents in New York, Pennsylvania, and New Jersey communities cared for about 400 of these youngsters free of charge. [54]

This need for funds led to the most startling episode of the entire strike—the Paterson Pageant. During a gathering at the home of intellectual salon hostess Mabel Dodge Luhan, Big Bill Haywood complained bitterly that New York laborers had not learned about the Paterson struggle because metropolitan dailies ignored the story. "Why don't you bring the strike to New York and *show* it to the workers?" Mrs. Luhan ventured. "Well, by God! There's an idea!" Haywood exclaimed. "But how? What hall?" According to Mrs. Luhan, a young man among the guests jumped forward. "I'll *do* it!" he shouted. "My name is Reed. . . . We'll make a Pageant of the Strike! The first in the World." [55]

Over the next few weeks, energetic John Reed, a recent Harvard

* Rabbi Mannheimer also suffered at the hands of the employer sympathizers. Influential members of his congregation expelled him from his post because of his efforts to settle the strike. (New York *Times,* April 19, 1913.)

graduate and drama critic for *American* magazine, toiled feverishly on this prodigious undertaking. He drilled Paterson workmen of varied nationalities into a theatrical company and led masses of them in song. Laborers grew fond of this vital young man: "You make us be happy," a smiling immigrant told him. "One of the gayest touches," Mrs. Luhan later recalled, "was teaching them to sing one of their lawless songs to the tune of 'Harvard, Old Harvard.' " [56]

When the great day arrived, thousands of cheering strikers marched forth from Paterson, crossed the Hudson, and paraded down Manhattan's waterfront. Overhead, on the four sides of the Madison Square Tower, a huge ten-foot sign of blazing red lights spelled out the letters IWW. This final touch had remained a secret until the last minute. "Then it was too late," Mrs. Luhan reported, "to get the heavy municipal machinery in motion to have the Seditious Blaze turned off. By the time the red tape unwound, the show was over." [57]

"It is doubtful," noted the New York *Times,* "if Madison Square Garden, even at the close of the bitterest of political campaigns, ever held a larger audience." Thousands of people of almost every nationality crammed themselves into the amphitheater. Robert Edmond Jones, Reed's college friend and later a noted Broadway scenic designer, had decorated the whole interior in flaming red. A gigantic poster drawn by Reed depicted the heroic figure of a worker rising from the factories and smokestacks. "Every man, woman and child" in that audience, the *Times* observed, "seemed to be enthusiastic for the Haywood organization and all that it stands for." [58]

Inside the hall the audience sang Wobbly songs and lustily chanted union slogans. Sheriff Harburger of New York sat in a box seat. "Just let anybody say one word of disrespect to the flag," he swore, "and I will stop the show so quickly it will take their breath away." He could not prevent the singing of the *Marseillaise,* however, though he had checked on the matter. "The courts," he murmured glumly, "have decided that the *Marseillaise* is legal." [59]

On a huge platform in the center of the arena, striker-thespians re-enacted the major incidents of their Paterson ordeal. Once again, as whistles blew and workers shouted, police persecuted the press, broke up rallies, and clubbed innocent victims. Once again Paterson's children, hundreds of them now on stage, trekked out of town to foster homes. Similarly, these actors dramatized the murder and funeral of Modestino Valentino. As a climax, Haywood, Miss Flynn, Tresca, and Quinlan all addressed the excited multitude. Then the band struck up, and thousands of voices rang out with the *Marseillaise* and the *International*.[60]

Although the New York *Times* blasted this pageant as a display of "mad passion against law and order," anarchists in *Mother Earth* found it "lacking in revolutionary spirit." Most publications, however, regardless of ideology, praised the spectacle. "Probably few witnessed the exhibit without sympathy," said the New York *World*. "It would have pleased any dramatic critic because of the sincerity with which the simple plot was carried out." New York's *Tribune* considered it a "very effective appeal" which stamped IWW leaders as "agitators of large resources and original talent." Not even the Elizabethans, proclaimed *Independent,* had ever presented a play "with more effect than this performance where actors and audience were of one class and one hope." *Survey* also remarked on the surprising exhibit of unity among so many conflicting nationalities. "We're all brothers and sisters," one worker had assured them. As a demonstration of "the solidarity of the working class," declared the Socialist New York *Call*, the Paterson Pageant was "a stroke of genius." [61]

Paterson, and especially this rally in the Garden, profoundly affected a number of intellectuals. The strike, it seemed to them, fulfilled all their visions of a perfect proletarian revolt—working-class unity that cut across the barriers of nationality and language; gaiety in the face of oppression; speeches, songs, poetry, banners, and drama. "I just simply could not stand it any longer and I let my books go and came down here to congratulate you," writer Upton Sinclair told Paterson's workers. "Yours is the finest exhibition of solidarity ever seen in the Eastern states." Novelist Ernest Poole, along with Lincoln Steffens and Margaret Sanger, joined the battle. In his novel *The Harbor*, Poole created the character of Joe Kramer who assisted Haywood in the 1919 New York dock strike. Intellectual playboy John Reed had gained his first taste of active labor warfare. "Paterson shook Reed," one writer commented. "He learned for himself the things books and talk could not teach." [62] This experience started the young man on his serious journey leftward, which he climaxed by participation in the Russian Revolution.*

A dramatic success, Paterson's extravaganza threatened to erupt into a major financial scandal. On the night of the play, its managers proudly announced a $10,000 profit. Then days passed, and not a penny entered the strikers' relief fund. Finally Bill Haywood sorrowfully declared that contrary to the original estimate, the venture had netted only a paltry $348 above expenses. Workers wanted to know why one of the biggest shows ever staged in Madison Square Garden had yielded so microscopic a return. Gleefully, some newspapers noted that Haywood had hastily departed for Europe and that John Reed had just recently booked passage on the Hamburg Line. What happened to all that money? demanded *Miners' Magazine.* "Thousands have been duped by the . . . professional flim-flammers of the I.W.W." [63]

In order to avert further accusations, the Pageant's executive committee quickly published a full, authoritative statement of its finances. These members disclosed that the big spectacular had actually sustained a loss of over $1,000. They had overestimated their receipts; they had admitted too many free of charge. Only last-minute pleas to sympathetic donors erased this deficit. "Alas!" sighed Gompers ironically, "dazzled by the glamor of the footlights I.W.W. expected to bring back barrels of gold." Anyone on Broadway could have told Haywood that he was sure to "'come out a

---

* The Russian Revolution deeply affected the careers of three major leaders of the Paterson strike. John Reed helped to write the Soviet Constitution. In 1920 he died in Moscow, and for several years his grave at the foot of the Kremlin's walls served as a mecca for American tourists. While awaiting trial for sedition in 1921, Bill Haywood forfeited bail and departed for Russia. He remained there until his death in 1928 and a portion of his ashes were placed next to the grave of Reed. Elizabeth Gurley Flynn joined the American Communist Party and became its chairman in 1961. Three years later she died while visiting the Soviet Union.

loser,' " cracked the New York *Times*. IWW, it asserted, had a talent for "arson, murder, pillage" but not for show business.[64]

10

After the failure of their Pageant and the attrition of other sources of income, the workers gradually drifted back to the mills. As a preventive measure the IWW tried to revive aggressive picketing. Police smashed their lines so effectively, however, that all such activity ceased by mid-June. In July even Elizabeth Gurley Flynn advised the laborers to return "with a spirit of hatred in your hearts not for the starving brothers and sisters who have fought this battle with you, but for the capitalists of Paterson, who have had no mercy on the downtrodden working class." [65]

Starvation, not benefits, drove the laborers back into the mills. A few dyehouse workers secured a 5 to 10 percent increase in piecework rates, but they had to accept the retention of the fifty-five-hour week. Most returned unconditionally and acquiesced to whatever terms their employers offered. Some manufacturers refused to dismiss striker replacements, which made rehiring old hands difficult and gave rise to persistent rumors of the presence of a blacklist. Defeat shattered the IWW and left the operatives without any permanent labor organization. Paterson's workers lost $4,160,000 in wages during the conflict.

At best, however, the owners won a Pyrrhic victory. Their adamant refusal even to discuss a settlement had prolonged the strike until it cost them $5,225,000. Neither they nor anyone else had devised any satisfactory method for adjudicating future disputes. Within four months the mill-owners faced the possibility of a new walkout; serious labor troubles plagued Paterson far into the next decade.[66]

Conservative newspapers breathed a sigh of relief with the termination of the strike. The whole country, admonished the New York *Times*, should be grateful to the Paterson officials who had stood so firm against the Wobblies. No one profited from the conflict, observed Philadelphia's *Inquirer*, except the "blatherskite and blood-sucking [union] leaders." Both the New York *Herald* and the *Journal of Commerce* hoped that Paterson meant death for IWW.[67]

Even most of the noncapitalist press drove nails into the Wobbly coffin. Socialist *Call* and the DeLeonite *Weekly People* interpreted Paterson as proof of the failure of direct action. Now, swore *Miners' Magazine* in its usual gentle tones, IWW's "dead-beats and bilks shall be given to understand that no more money shall come from the sweat of labor to put on *Easy Street* the flim-flamming gang whose dirty vocabulary would pollute a garbage barrel and befoul a sewer." In less colorful language, Samuel Gompers pronounced a similar judgment: "They mislead the toilers into striking for impossible ideals and leave them betrayed and helpless and at the mercy of vengeful employers." Perhaps Rose Pastor Stokes best expressed the tragedy of the strike for the workers:

> . . . Our fingers do not cease!
> We've starved—and lost, but we are weavers still;
> And Hunger's in the Mill! [68]

11

When the Commission went to Paterson, its hearings revealed that behind the strike's violence lay a deep ideological conflict. An uncompromising commitment to the class-struggle doctrine certainly characterized IWW leadership. "The struggle between the working class and the capitalistic class is an inevitable battle." Big Bill Haywood told the Commission. "It is a fight for what the capitalistic class has control of—the means of life, the tools and machinery of production." Once again, Haywood advocated refusal to make contracts, deliberate halting of production lines, defiance of judicial decisions, a general strike, and seizure of factories. "The Industrial Workers of the World," he declared, "do not recognize that the bosses have any rights at all." [69]

Adolph Lessig informed the Commission that his local did not counsel violence during the Paterson strike. But this peaceful policy was just a strategic maneuver. If a strike could be won by blowing up a mill, Lessig predicted, "we probably would not hesitate to pursue that course." When commissioners asked Vincent St. John, national IWW secretary-treasurer, if this philosophy of violence applied to persons as well as to property, he responded with one word, "Certainly." [70]

Many of those on the manufacturers' side also advanced extremist ideas. During the hearings, John A. Ferguson, an engineer and building contractor, asserted that any means, legal or illegal, were justifiable to rid the city of Wobblies. Frank Walsh elicited Ferguson's formula for dealing with this "outside element":

CHAIRMAN WALSH: In other words, did you think that they would be justified, if a man was a known agitator and had caused trouble, as you understood it, at other places, to arrest him as he got off a train and not give him a chance to be heard?

MR. FERGUSON: Not give him a chance; simply say, "When the next train goes out you go out on it."

These remarks created the first interruption in the Commission's proceedings. Spectators broke out in hisses and boos that spread throughout the room. Chairman Walsh rapped for order and finally regained control. [71]

James W. Cooke, former president of the Charity Organization Society of Paterson, defended the suppression of free speech and assembly as necessary in order to preclude "a stoppage of work." Those public officials who by their actions broke their oaths to uphold the Constitution were only technically, not morally, guilty of a crime. [72]

Finally, the commissioners read a series of editorials which the Paterson *Press* had published during the strike. These articles described various illegal and violent tactics employed against IWW in other cities. The *Press* then asked its readers to consider using such measures against Paterson's labor agitators. One such editorial asserted, "Akron could not find a law to banish this dangerous revolutionist and his cohorts, but a citizens' committee of 1,000 men did the trick in short order. Can Akron accomplish something that Paterson, N.J., can not duplicate?" [73]

The Commission's probe of Paterson's strike scored a triumph with most of the press. Paterson's *News* hailed the federal body as an agency which would dig down to the roots of industrial strife. Two other papers praised Chairman Walsh for his absolute impartiality. Undoubtedly, the Paterson *Call* predicted, this hearing will play a pronounced role in the legislation of proper labor laws. The Paterson *Press* concluded that the work of this Walsh group "should be far reaching in preventing other great labor wars and in handling them effectively where they do break out." In New York, the *Journal of Commerce* sounded one of the few sour notes. This "meddling commission," it snapped, "is not calculated to promote a rational settlement of the conflict between capital and labor. . . . It has no right to go into a local community and rake up its past troubles." [74]

One major fact struck many observers: the Commission had exposed the extent to which social irresponsibility and violence had dominated the entire Paterson episode. Defiant lawlessness has never before been so boldly expressed," asserted the New York *World*. IWW leaders, it protested, should have appeared not before the Commission but before a grand jury. "Crime is crime, and those who preach and practice it should be addressed not by professors of economics but by the policeman, the jury, and the judge." Horrified by the ferocity of this labor war, New York's *Sun* stated that "the sole virtue in the I.W.W.'s case appears to be its candor." Paterson's businessmen and civil officials, John Fitch of *Survey* noted, had favored illegal methods just as much as the IWW. In analyzing Paterson, Fitch caught the dominant theme of Commission strike hearings all over America: "Here were men on both sides who advocated breaking the law—each for his own reasons; each with his own sanctions . . . for employing force, if necessary, to accomplish their ends." [75]

V

REVOLT IN NEW YORK

1

"THIS IS MORE THAN A STRIKE!" cried Samuel Gompers to a tumultuous rally in Madison Square Garden "It is an industrial revolution." The AFL president prophesied correctly. His words signaled the start of the 1910 New York garment workers' strike. This struggle soon engulfed 60,000 to 70,000 employees and prostrated an entire industry.[1]

When the battle ended, after weeks of dramatic violence, both sides agreed to a unique form of industrial government generally known as the "Protocol of Peace." Under the Protocol's system of grievance machinery, quiet discussion and judicious reasoning replaced strikes and lockouts. Employers enjoyed uninterrupted production and profits. Wages, hours, and conditions substantially improved. Men of good will praised this bold new venture and hailed it as a bright omen for the future. Yet despite all the benefits the whole governmental structure seemed about to crash only two years after its construction. Friends of the Protocol called to the Commission for rescue. How had capital and labor fashioned so fine a work? Why now did it appear doomed? Could it be saved? The Commissioners sped to New York to find out.

2

From 1880 to 1910 the women's clothing industry in the United States expanded at a prodigious rate; the value of its factory product leaped from $32 million to $384 million. New York City alone accounted for 70 percent of this total, although centers also developed in Boston, Chicago, and Philadelphia. New York employed 98,000 workers, more than 60 percent of the entire labor force in the trade. Most of these toilers had recently emigrated from Jewish communities in Russia or in eastern and central Europe, although by 1900 Italians comprised over 15 percent of the wage-earning population.[2]

Three groups exercised a formative influence on this preminently Jewish society—workers, businessmen, and intellectuals. European persecution had induced the first two classes to live in isolated communities dominated by ancient Jewish religious beliefs and customs. Workingmen within this self-contained world traditionally looked forward to the time when they could leave the laboring class and gain entrepreneurial status. Jewish intellectuals, however, possessed a more sophisticated point of view. European ideas of agnosticism, positivism, anarchism, and socialism deeply affected their thought. As recent immigrants, these educated Jews found few career opportunities outside the garment trade. They exerted a strong influence over the other Jewish workers, however, and a close association evolved between the unions and socialist leadership.[3]

Conditions within the industry, these intellectuals discovered, cried out for alert and imaginative unionism. Fierce competition among many firms, all of whom operated on a tiny margin of profit, drove down wages, lengthened hours, and produced foul environments. A state investigator in the mid-1880s visited tenement factories where "the air was stifling," and the temperature "well up in the nineties and odiferous with sewer gases. . . . The women were scantily clad, their hair unkempt, their pale abject countenances, as they bent over their work, formed a picture of physical suffering and want that I certainly had never seen before." These workers earned 50 cents for sixteen hours of labor.[4]

Ten years later the same situation prevailed. Studies showed that a garment employee still toiled an average of fourteen hours per day with no time limit at all during the busy season. In 1895 a researcher blasted these practices as "a system of making clothes under filthy and inhuman conditions . . . a process of grinding the faces of the poor." [5]

These brutal circumstances impelled workers during the 1890s to form local labor societies. In 1900 a convention of leaders created the International Ladies' Garment Workers' Union (ILGWU) to unite all clothing employees in the United States and Canada; shortly afterward they joined AFL. Antagonistic bosses and fluctuations in the business cycle buffeted the young International from the outside. Disputes between eastern and western locals, invasions by IWW, and warfare among Socialist factions ripped it internally. In 1907 successful strikes by Boston cloakmakers and New York reefermakers (children's coats) boosted its membership to a new high. A depression one year later devastated it. A union of many nationalities, languages, and ideologies, a union which functioned in a highly unstable industry, the ILGWU in its first decade offered little promise of salvation to the crushed garment worker.[6]

3

An unexpected event in 1910 touched off a revolutionary transformation in the International. Impetus for this change sprang not from experienced trade unionists but rather from young girls who worked at the shirtwaist trade. Their dramatic uprising captured the attention not only of the labor world but of almost every section of society in New York and the nation. For a time it unified divergent reform groups behind a single purpose. It lifted the garment girl from obscurity and made her a *cause célèbre*.[7]

Shirtwaist-making as a business did not develop until the decade after 1890, but by 1909 it encompassed about 450 factories in New York and employed 40,000 operatives. Unmarried women between the ages of eighteen and twenty-five accounted for 80 percent of the trade's wage earners. Most of the shops, of medium size, utilized the services of 20 to 30 employees, but a few larger firms that hired 100 to 300 girls ruled the industry. Working hours ranged from fifty-six to fifty-nine per week, but they climbed as high as seventy during a busy season. Since most concerns ran on a piecework basis, frequent style changes forced constant readjustment of the pay scales. Incomplete statistical studies of the time suggest that over 50 percent of the employees earned from $7 to $10 weekly, but these figures do not reflect the fact that periods of idleness, sometimes as long as three months, reduced annual incomes far below that average. In addition, many labored together in groups known as "sets." A company's payroll displayed only the name of the head of a set; he divided among the members of his team what appeared on the record as a good individual wage. Some 15 to 30 percent of the workers, when employed, averaged only $4 a week under this system.[8]

An accumulation of petty tyrannies, however, really precipitated the strike. Management, contrary to its obligation, charged employees for the use of electric power and for needles and thread. If an operator arrived only five minutes late, the girls complained, the owner would dock her half a day's pay. Some manufacturers cheated workers out of a portion of their lunch hour by placing a piece of cloth over the clock. If an employee left the room, a forewoman would follow and hurry her back to the bench. If a girl felt ill, few owners would allow her to leave the factory. When some women objected to overtime work, the employers locked them in the shop and compelled the girls to "eat the suppers furnished to them with one hand, while running the machines with the other." Management "simply refused to recognize the girls as human beings." These constant nagging indignities mounted until they grew unbearable; then the girls reacted—quite humanly.[9]

Few major strikes ever broke out so unexpectedly. In the summer of 1909, two large manufacturers, Triangle Waist Company and Leiserson's, fired some employees whom they suspected of union agitation. All other workers in these two shops then walked out and declared a strike for union recognition. Ordinarily such minor labor disputes attracted scant notice, but the brutal tactics directed against these young girls aroused the ire of social reformers and newspapers. At first, owners tried to play off Italian against Jewish workers, but this met with small success. Leiserson then hired professional thugs as "special police" to guard the factory. A list of these men and their criminal records appeared in the *Jewish Daily Forward*. Next to it the *Forward* printed dramatic photographs of some battered and bloody girl strikers whom these toughs had assaulted. Five ruffians beat one striker, Clara Lemlich, so badly that she was hospitalized for several days. Public protest forced Triangle to adopt a new strategy—girls against girls; it stationed prostitutes outside company gates. These unique guardians of private property not only fought off pickets but also tried to persuade some of the young strikers to join their own profession.[10]

Police exhibited an obvious bias in favor of capital. New York state law sanctioned the right to picket, but authorities nevertheless arrested and convicted the girls on this alleged offense. While magistrates acquitted men who assailed young women, they penalized strikers on the slightest excuse. Class distinctions clearly influenced law enforcement. Once an officer apprehended, along with a group of other pickets, Miss Mary Dreier, socially prominent president of the Women's Trade Union League (WTUL). When he learned her identity, the policeman refused to bring Miss Dreier before the magistrate along with the rest of the culprits. "Why didn't you tell me you was a rich lady?" he exclaimed. "I'd never have arrested you in the world." [11]

This situation provoked union leaders to hold a mass meeting to discuss the possibility of a general strike. On November 22, 1909, 3,000 shirtwaist-makers jammed into the auditorium of Cooper Union. Orator after orator denounced the bosses and deplored conditions; all stopped short of an appeal to strike. Samuel Gompers warned against hasty action; he advised a walkout only if all other means failed. Then from the back of the auditorium a small, dark, quick-eyed girl, only twenty years old, requested permission to speak. Many in the audience recognized her as Clara Lemlich, who had just returned from the hospital after the savage assault she incurred on the picket line. Miss Lemlich's name did not appear on the program, and the chair granted her the floor grudgingly. She unleashed a fiery tirade and concluded, "I have listened to all the speakers. I have no more patience for talk, I am one of those who feel and suffer from the things described. I move that we go on a general strike." From every corner of the hall surged a roar of approval. Excitedly the chairman called for a vote. Three thousand voices shouted their unanimous consent.[12]

"Do you mean faith?" cried the chairman. "Will you take the old Jewish oath?" [13]

Thousands of right hands shot up as the throng swore in Yiddish, "If I turn traitor to the cause I now pledge, may this hand wither and drop off at the wrist from the arm I now raise." [14]

In a spirit of joyous bedlam the strike began. At 9:00 A.M. the shirtwaist girls quit their factories. As they crowded into the streets and marched toward union headquarters they cheered and sang in English, Yiddish, and Italian; traffic stopped all over the lower East Side. Union chiefs found themselves as unprepared for the strike as the employers. Armies of women invaded the International's offices. All wanted to sign up, pay dues, and start picketing at once; it took three days to restore order. Finally, strike leaders obtained twenty assembly rooms for periodic local meetings. Additional aid came from the WTUL and the United Hebrew Trades.[15]

Many of the smaller shops quickly signed, and by early December 160 of these concerns had reopened. But the more important larger firms refused to capitulate so easily. They formed the Associated Waist and Dress Manufacturers and on November 27 declared war against the union. A member of this organization sounded its keynote when he characterized local International leaders as "a lot of irresponsible blackguards." This association advised manufacturers who had made contracts to repudiate them; it denied admission to its ranks to any company that did not oppose unionism. "We insist upon open shops," its president asserted, "and from that stand we will not budge." [16]

Immediately after the vote for a general strike, violence was magnified. Almost every day newspapers carried stories of disturbances, arrests, and assaults. Gangs of men used their fists against girl strikers. Two strikebreakers hurled a picket to the ground and then stamped on her. A group of thugs pounced on a strike committee chairman while he was collecting funds and injured him so badly that he had to remain in bed for three weeks. Another assailant jumped upon a nineteen-year-old girl, smashed her side, and broke one of her ribs. He disabled her for life.[17]

Suspicious of the manufacturers' augmented staff of special police, the WTUL engaged private detectives to make an investigation. A report issued by the League based on this research disclosed that certain employment agencies deliberately furnished professional rowdies to factory owners. Bosses, the WTUL concluded, apparently held the theory that rough treatment and several arrests would drive a girl striker out of the union. A spokesman for the manufacturers retorted, "I shouldn't blame the employers if they did use toughs." He claimed that pickets constantly intimidated non-striking workers.[18]

New York courts offered no redress to the girls; instead, they acted as an ally of the manufacturers. When a young woman striker demanded a warrant for the arrest of a man who had attacked her, the judge rejected her plea. "You had no right to be picketing," he asserted. "You only got what was coming to you." [19]

At another time a picket was trying to talk peaceably to some strikebreakers when a company guard punched her breast and knocked her to the ground. The young lady appeared in court accompanied by a number of witnesses on her behalf, but the magistrate released the ruffian and passed sentence on all the girls. One judge admitted in court that he had no desire even "to bother with witnesses for these strikers." [20]

In a carefully prepared study, the WTUL presented documentary evidence of case after case in which authorities ordered bruised and bleeding girls to prison while exonerating their assailants. "You are on strike against God and nature, whose prime law is that man shall earn his bread in the sweat of his brow," one magistrate ruled. "You are on strike against God." When he learned of this remark, George Bernard Shaw quipped, "Delightful, medieval America always in the most intimate personal confidence of the Almighty." [21]

When fines and jail terms based on denial of the right to picket failed to break the strike, magistrates tried a different maneuver. They convicted girls on the vague charge of disorderly conduct and committed them to the workhouse on Blackwell's Island. Previously, the courts had reserved this punishment for far more serious violations. Blackwell's Island threw adolescent girls into association with prostitutes, degenerates, and criminals, a fact that brought expressions of dismay even from some of the veteran inmates. But the strikers persevered as a bleak and frigid winter descended. "There never was anything like it," an experienced union official declared. "An equal number of men never would hold together under what these girls are enduring." [22]

This cruel treatment stirred up a storm of protest from leaders in the upper and middle classes. Almost every reform organization in the city and many of the wealthiest women in the United States arose to defend the strikers. Feminist agitation joined the cause of labor. "Social compunction" motivated these ladies. One periodical defined this emotion as "intense feeling of the more fortunate classes that they owed much to the others." These new allies of the workers transformed the conflict into a fervent moral crusade. [23]

Intellectuals like Professor E. R. A. Seligman of Columbia, the noted journalist Ida Tarbell, and social worker Lillian Wald promulgated a blistering indictment of law-enforcement brutality and judicial favoritism. These writers perceived the crisis as part of a larger question "concerning the place of the police in our modern industrial and social life." When the New York *Times* challenged the factual basis of their statements, victimized shirtwaist girls submitted affidavits in support of the accusations. Shortly afterward, thousands of angry, silent dissenters, suffragettes and Socialists in the lead, marched on City Hall. A committee of five presented the mayor with a protest against police and court depredations. An eighteen-year-old girl told of the time two patrolmen had seized her, torn her dress, insulted her, and made improper proposals while superior officers looked on without objection. His Honòr expressed a special interest in this incident, which the young lady depicted as typical. [24]

The next day, Mrs. O. P. H. Belmont, mother of the Duchess of Marlborough, engaged the Hippodrome theater for a strike rally; she packed it to the roof. Most factory girls walked to and from the auditorium in order to save carfare, but of the $300 collected during the meeting, $70 came in the form of pennies. Close by Mrs. Belmont and other society women sat an Episcopal bishop, a deputy from the Catholic archbishop, and the New York health commissioner. An "equal rights feast," scoffed the New York *World*. These representatives of the established order listened with rapt attention as Socialist Rose Pastor Strokes declaimed, "Friends and sisters, I bring to you the message of 40,000,000 men and women, working men and working women the world over, and the message is: 'Workers Unite! You have nothing to lose but your chains, and you have the world to gain!' " [25]

Society and feminist leaders contributed to the strike in a variety of ways. A secretary to one of the matrons joined a picket squad; she had her clothes ripped off and her skull nearly fractured when a policeman hurled her against a fire hydrant. At the highly exclusive Colony Club, Mrs. Belmont and the suffragette Political Equality Association invited a number of shirtwaist girls, who had previously suffered beatings or jailings, to relate their experiences. "I could tell you ladies, how I spend my life and live on fifteen dollars," Clara Lemlich, one of the better paid workers, attested, "but I have no right to speak when there are others who make three dollars a week." Impressed, the women donated $1,300 within a few minutes. [26]

Anne Morgan, daughter of banker J. P., proposed to build a shirtwaist factory complete with every modern sanitary and architectural detail; it would observe strict union conditions. Her first order arrived from Wellesley College students, who asked for 1,000 waists cut to a special Wellesley pattern. Benefit ticket sales and special performances staged by producers such as the Shuberts and Klaw and Erlanger raised thousands of dollars for the strike fund. Finally, Mrs. Belmont called for a sympathetic strike by all women in the city. [27]

Student delegations from a number of women's colleges reinforced the cause. They delivered speeches, helped inexperienced strikers stay within the law, and talked back to bosses from picket lines. A squad from Barnard scrutinized the circumstances under which police arrested pickets and served as witnesses if the officer committed an illegal act. Vassar girls sold special copies of the Socialist *Call* on the sidewalks of Wall Street. [28]

Helen Taft, daughter of the President and a charter member of the Bryn Mawr Suffrage Club, drew detailed front-page coverage when she visited the strike area. "I never knew they were so down-trodden!" she exclaimed. "Really, I'll never put on a shirtwaist again without a shudder." Miss Taft stated that she might go on the picket line and run the risk of arrest. "I shall certainly speak to papa about the terrible conditions. . . . Why, it's just like reading Neitzsche, isn't it?" And with that Miss Taft and her party took off to the opera.[29]

A mammoth demonstration at Carnegie Hall climaxed the drive. Socialists, radicals, and Single Taxers stood shoulder to shoulder with Anne Morgan, Mrs. Belmont, the WTUL, and the Liberal Club. On stage, factory girls, arrayed in sashes which bore the word "arrested" in huge black letters, promenaded in a colorful pageant of slogans and banners. A sixteen-year-old girl told how a judge condemned her to the workhouse simply because she protested to a police captain about the bullying of a fellow striker. Lawyers Samuel Untermyer and Morris Hillquit excoriated the city's magistrates for their refusal to enforce the state law that secured the right to picket. Nor could the judiciary, they maintained, legally sentence anyone to the workhouse on the charge of disorderly conduct. Resolutions damned these court actions as examples of "a prejudiced and vindictive mind." "The office of Magistrate," they announced, "has thus been perverted into an instrument of persecution and oppression." [30]

In December, 1909, the first serious attempt to end the strike came when two members of the National Civic Federation suggested that a board of arbitrators decide the issues. Employers accepted the invitation to a conference, but the union hesitated because it wanted recognition first. Then the Associated Manufacturers announced that its members, "would under no circumstances . . . enter into union agreements," and negotiations collapsed. Later in the month, however, Philadelphia shirtwaist-makers also declared a general strike. Their action cut off production so completely that New York's manufacturers exercised a more conciliatory attitude. Hectic days of discussion produced a compromise which granted some concessions to labor with respect to hours and conditions but ignored demands for a closed shop. Workers voted to reject this proposal.

Later efforts by the State Board of Arbitration proved equally fruitless.[31]

By mid-January the strike started to decline, chiefly because workers could not shut down the big shops entirely. In addition, the union treasury was empty; needy strikers had drained it of $2,500 per week. On January 11, 1910, labor leaders offered to submit all questions to arbitration, but the manufacturers turned them down. Settlements between individual shops and the union then began, until by the end of the first week in February even the larger establishments had reached accord with their employees. Most companies ratified pacts that provided a fifty-two-hour week, time and a half for overtime, a fixed wage scale, elimination of subcontracting, and hygienic working conditions. These labor gains represented only partial victory. Nothing guaranteed that the large firms, which set the pattern of the trade, would not as before violate their agreements during slack season. The Associated Manufacturers itself still refused to recognize the union at all.[32]

As a result of the strike, the shirtwaist-makers' local had grown to major proportions. When the fray commenced, the organization elicited loyalty from only 800 workers, but at its termination union rolls boasted of 20,000 members in good standing. Shirtwaist girls had demonstrated their capacity for cohesive action; they had created an important instrument for their future. Most significant of all, their battle captured the interest and support of a multitude of articulate people outside the labor movement. It publicized the plight of the garment worker and acted as an advance agent for reform.[33]

4

The girls emboldened the boys. Men in the cloak-and-suit division of the garment industry took heart when they witnessed the publicity and aid which the shirtwaist workers acquired. While the women's strike had erupted suddenly in a burst of spontaneous emotion, the male laborers planned their own revolt with detailed precision. Exploited young girls could awaken social compunction among sympathetic outsiders; men might have to storm the battlements alone.

Laissez-faire individualism reigned supreme in the cloak-and-suit business. In 1890 a few large manufacturers, usually known as the "giants of Broadway," exercised royal sway. But down on the lower East Side, centered on Division Street, immigrants penetrated the industry as small entrepreneurs. These "moths of Division Street" challenged the "giants." Unlike his wealthier rival, the small manufacturer dispatched no designers to Paris, maintained no showrooms, and employed no models. He operated in a loft at the lowest possible rent and hired the cheapest possible labor. Soon after the turn of the century, the omniverous "moths" destroyed the "giants." In a triumph for the lower East Side, the "Jewish needle made America the best dressed nation in the world." But the most successful developed a taste for the carriage trade. They moved to Broadway, opened showrooms, and followed all the expensive practices of their former competitors. By 1910, however, a new generation of "moths" hatched and started to gnaw away at these *arriviste* "giants." [34]

Whether he toiled for a "giant" or for a "moth," the worker fared badly. A board of inquiry concluded that "all of the shops, from the 'poorest' in the attic or cellar of some old, converted tenement to the 'richest and biggest' in loft buildings of the most modern type," suffered "from various sanitary defects." These included dirty floors, defective plumbing, bad ventilation, inadequate toilets, and poor fire prevention facilities. Most bosses expected their employees to furnish their own machines. Every time a laborer changed jobs, he had to hire a helper to carry his equipment. All the men paid for their needles, thread, oil, and electricity. [35]

By 1910 subcontracting had evolved as the greatest evil in the trade. Under this system, a manufacturer remunerated only two or three workers directly. These cloakmakers then hired a number of assistants, who in turn engaged sublaborers. This method forged a chain of smaller employers, all interested in holding down wages. In the decade during which subcontracting soared, most wages remained stationary or declined; hours averaged from fourteen to sixteen per day. Many employees, contrary to law, carted additional bundles of work home. [36]

After twenty years of stagnation, cloakmakers realized that only drastic measures promised redemption. Various local and International leaders had been arguing about the need for a general strike since 1908. Now they moved into action. Union chiefs appointed a forty-five-man general strike committee and nine special subcommittees. They mapped schemes to cover every possibility—picketing, meeting halls, speeches, press relations, finances, law, printing, and relief. Finally John B. Lennon, treasurer of the AFL and later a member of the U.S. Industrial Relations Commission came from Washington to represent the national union during the strike.[37]

At the end of June, 1910, ILGWU leaders took a chance—they rented Madison Square Garden for a pre-strike assembly. Many warned that the number who would attend would not fill the huge auditorium, but to their astonishment the demonstration broke records. Arrangements called for proceedings to start at 6:00 P.M., but at 5:30 police had to send out for reserves to handle the swollen crowd; at 7:00 they closed the doors. A police inspector estimated the crowd to be the largest he had ever seen. Some 15,000 to 20,000 poured into the Garden, while 25,000 more clamored to gain entrance. Time and time again, a band struck up the *Marseillaise*. Time and time again, ovations greeted every speaker. Union leaders knew that the time had come.[38]

But this mass meeting did not officially proclaim a strike. Officials insisted on a secret poll of their membership. Almost 20,000 cast ballots, and only a few hundred voted in the negative. On the morning of July 7 the strike committee convened at 6:00 A.M. and took the big step. Within an hour, circulars printed on red paper appeared in all the shops. In Yiddish, English, and Italian, they proclaimed the start of the strike at 2:00 P.M. that day. In addition, the notice divided the garment area into seven districts and presented detailed instructions on how to travel to each of the 145 separate smaller meeting halls obtained for the occasion. Union leaders waited tensely. Would workers respond to the first call for a general strike of cloakmakers in sixteen years?[39]

At two o'clock, women workers, about 10 percent of the labor force, marched out of their factories two by two in a gay holiday mood. Then endless streams of men poured from every door, surged up every side street, and converged on Fifth Avenue. More than

60,000 workers walked out of their jobs and paralyzed the industry. "Many of our most devoted members cried for joy, at the idea that their lifelong labors had been crowned with success," recalled Abraham Rosenberg, ILGWU president. "In my mind I could only picture to myself such a scene taking place when the Jews were led out of Egypt." [40]

On July 5 the strike committee dispatched a list of demands to each manufacturer. Their requests included a forty-eight-hour week, a limit to overtime, the elimination of subcontracting, the arbitration of disputes, worker-management piece-price committees, and the restriction of employment to unionists. In reply, owners formed a Manufacturers' Protective Association. They scorned the union proposal. Members of the MPA vowed never to sign any agreement that would involve "surrender of the control and management of factories to any set or group of men, whether calling themselves a 'union' or anything else." [41]

From the outset, both adversaries employed belligerent methods. MPA recruited over ninety special policemen and imported workers from Cleveland and Chicago. When some of these out-of-town auxiliaries, protected on either side by two rows of company guards, advanced toward the shops, 500 pickets jeered, hooted, and blocked their passage. Police then swung their clubs, and union sympathizers hurled stones, sticks, and brickbats. On that same day fistfights, beatings, and riots erupted all over the garment area.[42]

A resumption of work by some former strikers drove loyal union members into a frenzy. At one reopened shop, 300 strikers rammed through a police line and stormed into the factory. First the invaders bowled over strikebreakers at work and pummeled them. Then they tossed tools on the floor, overturned machines, heaved cloth out of the shattered windows, and smashed chairs over tables. Police rushed in to stop the costly demolition but caught only three culprits. This time manufacturers accused the union of hiring thugs—a charge vehemently denied by labor.[43]

All during the next weeks garment industry reports followed the same turbulent pattern. Clashes among police, pickets, and strikebreakers added to an ever-mounting toll of arrested and wounded. In one instance, mobs were trying to impede guarded strikebreakers with shouts of "scab" and "dirty kike," when sharp screams from another melee distracted them. Spectators discovered a number of toughs with sticks thrashing two girls whom they had just kicked to the ground. On August 17, 1,000 unionists surrounded a factory, flung bricks and other missiles through windows, wrecked a good deal of property, and injured several people. That same night an army of strikers raided another concern, laid waste equipment, and battered workers. While men charged with assault and property damage deluged night courts, several owners resolved to close completely rather than risk further vandalism.[44]

This recurrent breakdown of law and order alarmed Acting Mayor John Purroy Mitchel, who had just assumed the duties of ailing Mayor Gaynor. As his first official act of importance, Mitchel ordered an investigation of strike turbulence. Its findings convinced him that "both sides have been violent and disorderly, if not worse." In an open letter to his police chief, New York's executive insisted that patrolmen apply absolute impartiality toward strikers and strikebreakers. Mitchel strongly rebuked the courts for anti-union bias; some judges, he asserted, "have forgotten that they are the servants of the people." He pleaded for judicial tolerance and patience, especially toward those who spoke little English. Strikers cheered the mayor, but manufacturer Paul Bonwit of Bonwit Teller grumbled that Mitchel's decree reduced law enforcement to an "unmitigated farce." Further complaints from both parties finally prompted the mayor to summon a grand jury inquest of the whole controversy with particular attention to the role of the police.[45]

Union elation over City Hall's policies soon collapsed. On August 25 a judge dealt workers the hardest blow of the conflict. In response to an appeal by the MPA, Supreme Court Justice John W. Goff issued a sweeping injunction against the toilers. Goff contended that the strike aspired to an illegal goal—the closed shop. Such action, he held, constituted a "common law and civil conspiracy." Any employer who accepted these terms violated the statutes. The Justice stigmatized the union for condoning "a systematic course of aggression by criminal acts." He cited forced entry of shops, destruction of property, "assaults and batteries of a serious nature," and threats to "beat or kill" members of strikebreaker's families. For the first time in the history of labor disputes in the state, an injunction not only permanently restrained men from peaceful picketing but also forbade them to interfere in any way at all with those who wished to work. Previously most people had regarded these activities as lawful.[46]

This all-inclusive mandate even impressed Julius Henry Cohen, attorney for the manufacturers. He termed it "the strongest one ever handed down by an American court against trades unionism." Garment-worker leaders, manufacturer Eugene L. Sealinsky asserted, "have used methods by which they have created a Frankenstein, which is ready to devour them." A higher court, swore strike chairman Alexander Bloch, would overrule this "blow at freedom." Samuel Gompers decried Goff's pronouncement as another example of the "tyranny of the autocratic methods of concentrated capital and greed." Mayor Mitchel threw up his hands. Under this ruling, he announced, he had no choice but to revoke his previous directive with reference to the rights of pickets. Strikers tested the mayor's words, and police arrested seventy-four men in one day.[47]

Meanwhile, the strike worked its baneful effect on both capital and labor. A number of smaller companies acceded to union contracts, and the larger shops felt the pinch. One harassed owner stressed that unionists "ought to understand that things have reached a crisis and that we are manufacturing nothing. They may understand then that their action is destroying the trade by which they live." As business in the garment industry ground to a standstill, suffering intensified. Some restaurants provided free meals, and a few banks lent money to strikers. On August 20 those in settled shops voted to contribute 15 percent of their pay to those still on strike. Requests for aid swamped the offices of the United Hebrew Trades, and pawnshops bulged with possessions of striker households. All over the East Side, the number of evictions increased catastrophically. On a single day, 1,100 cases appeared on the court docket; corridors and waiting rooms echoed with the weeping of women and children.[48]

Seriously hurt, both opponents turned a more favorable ear toward compromise. Earlier, in July, Boston merchant and reformer A. Lincoln Filene had persuaded Louis D. Brandeis, who recently had resolved the Boston cloakmakers' strike, to act as peacemaker in New York. Brandeis brought the adversaries together, and at first their conference progressed smoothly. They concurred on most minor questions and agreed to submit the more complicated problem of wages and hours to arbitration. But the parley foundered on the closed-shop issue. Labor negotiators believed other concessions meaningless unless employers consented to hire only union men. Manufacturers staunchly resisted this proposal on the grounds that it denoted surrender of management control to the International.[49]

At this juncture Brandeis volunteered his own favorite idea. Instead of the closed shop or the open shop, he suggested the "preferential shop." Employers would adhere to union conditions, wages, and hours and would employ a majority of union men. When a job fell open, owners would hire an ILGWU member over a nonunion man if both applicants possessed equal ability. With misgivings the manufacturers acceded to the proposal, but worker representatives firmly rejected it. Labor spurned any scheme which afforded bosses an opportunity to employ unorganized workers.[50]

"The open shop with honey," so the *Jewish Daily Forward*, the largest Yiddish newspaper of its time, derided this tentative pact. Most New York newspapers, however, with the exception of the Socialist *Call*, upbraided the union for its refusal to compromise. This almost universal castigation by the press only hardened worker determination. When the *Forward's* editors inaugurated a new fund-raising drive, the response overwhelmed them. They amassed $50,000 almost overnight. Young boys and bearded grandfathers swarmed into the publication's offices; some offered to contribute 50 percent of their wages to the cause. "These were men and women accustomed to enduring hardships for a principle," noted one commentator. "Men and women who had fought in Russia, who were revolutionists, willing to make sacrifices, eager to make sacrifices. Their blind faith was the backbone of the strike." [51]

Pained by the distress he beheld among his own people, Jacob Schiff, a prominent Jewish philanthropist, convinced both sides to resume negotiations. Their new stipulation bestowed further awards to labor but still contained a clause in favor of the preferential shop. Rank-and-file members reacted decisively. At meetings all over the garment district, when union chiefs read the new proposal aloud, workers jumped off chairs, dragged officials from platforms, and threw them out of halls. Even John Lennon, national treasurer of AFL, had to flee from an auditorium just before irate strikers laid violent hands on him. "We'll stay out and starve until the union is recognized," laborers shouted. A rhythmic chant of "closed shop, closed shop, closed shop" rang out through the night. Some believed that the Jewish periodical *Wahrheit* had endorsed this second agreement. Several thousand infuriated workers besieged its headquarters, smashed its windows, and wounded a number of employees. Without permission from the city, 5,000 strikers paraded up Fifth Avenue to protest any settlement except that of the closed shop.[52]

High spirits braced workers in the teeth of evictions, beatings, arrests, and starvation. Justice Goff's decision, however, robbed them of their only effective weapon. The leaders, therefore, consented to a third round of discussions. On September 2, 1910, these representatives of capital and labor drafted a compact which, among many articles, barred subcontracting and conferred a 25–30 percent wage increase, a fifty-hour week, and extra pay for overtime. Management also promised to supply work materials and to formulate piece prices in consultation with individual shop committees. This new document still called for a preferential shop, but company officials avowed their "belief in the union and that all who desire its benefits should share in its burdens." [53]

In order to avoid the riotous behavior that had followed the previous vote, ILGWU officials this time issued no public announcement and held no public assemblies. Instead, the strike foreman in each shop explained the proposed contract to his people and solicited suggestions for any desired alterations. These chairmen then convened, debated last-minute modifications, and officially ratified the bargain which terminated the strike. Jubilation heralded the advent of peace. Laborers marched through the streets to the music of brass bands and the pageantry of flags, floats, and streaming banners. For the first time, garment workers had won a favorable collective agreement with a majority of their employers.[54]

5

Manufacturers and workers had agreed to many covenants before, only to see them abrogated. This constant instability had racked the garment trade for generations. Workers had battled for the closed shop because they saw it as the only way they could solidify their gains. Yet they settled for the preferential shop, which approached but did not achieve this end. Could labor retain its benefits? Could manufacturers avoid costly strikes and incessant interruptions of production? Could civilization so quickly dispel barbarism?

Those who framed the new pact answered "Yes" to these questions. They introduced the most original idea in American industrial relations of their generation. Chiefly a product of the mind of Louis Brandeis, the Protocol, its official designation, provided a system for the settlement of labor disputes without strikes or lock-outs. This plan created a Board of Arbitration on which served one representative from capital, one from labor, and one neutral member. Below this high court sat a Board of Grievances composed of an equal number of delegates from each side. Both groups on this grievance panel had a chief clerk, who in turn directed a number of deputy clerks. If discord arose in a shop which those on the premises could not rectify, two deputies intervened. If they failed to achieve an accommodation, the matter then reached the chief clerks. If the problem could still not be settled, it came before the entire Board of Grievances. Only a deadlock of this body would send the issue to the Board of Arbitration for final judgment. Concurrent with this machinery, the Protocol established a Joint Board of Sanitary Control, in which owners and unionists cooperated to examine, correct, and improve health and safety conditions throughout the industry.[55]

Many of the Protocol's fathers truly believed that they had embarked on a great new departure in industrial government—an experiment that would influence events in the whole nation. A moment in history had arrived, Brandeis thought, when enlightened businessmen realized that they must accept and cooperate with organized labor. In return, workers had to renounce violence and their desire for the closed shop. An open shop meant the "disintegration of the union," but the closed shop denoted the "exchange of the tyranny of the employer for the tyranny of the employee." Julius Henry Cohen, counsel for the manufacturers and coauthor of the Protocol, asserted that responsible employees had resented the indiscriminate abuse heaped on all entrepreneurs because of the rapacity of an antisocial minority. Protocolism promised these men relief from strikes, standardization of labor costs, and elimination of unfair competition by unscrupulous sweatshop operators. It placed industry on a "higher plane," where "law and order should take the place of anarchy." [56]

Visions of a "higher plane" played little part in the thinking of most laboring people. Some still bore scars from combatting autocratic Czarist ukases; European socialistic ideologies of class struggle governed their outlook toward businessmen. "It is hard for our people to be reconciled with the idea that the union should go and make a compact with the employers," John Dyche, secretary of the ILGWU, told the Commission. His people, Dyche explained, "have been engaged for years in a life-and-death struggle with the manufacturers." Few indeed grasped the significance of the preferential shop. Dyche, himself, admitted that he possessed no "clearer idea of what it meant than the rest of my colleagues." After decades of struggle, however, union men wanted to consolidate their benefits. True, they had relinquished the right to strike, but most of the older men felt no great loss—twenty years of fruitless battle had persuaded them to try a different path.[57]

In its first two years (April 15, 1911, to October 31, 1913) the Protocol produced salutary results. Records show that of some 7,656 complaints filed, the chief clerks or their deputies adjusted 7,477, or 97 percent. Only 179 disputes reached the Board of Grievances, and that body resolved 159 of them. Only a tiny remainder of twenty cases ever developed into quarrels important enough to command the attention of the Board of Arbitration. In addition, the Board of Sanitary Control functioned remarkably well. Hundreds of employers cleaned up their shops, introduced electric power, and enforced stricter safety regulations. Subcontracting diminished, wage rates rose, and some 70,000 workers augmented the ranks of the New York International. In practice, the preferential shop evolved into the closed shop. At the same time company earnings swelled, and by the start of 1913 the Manufacturers' Protective Association boasted a membership of over 1,200 shops.[58]

Individuals and publications throughout the nation heaped praise upon the Protocol. Such varied publications as the *New Republic,* the New York *Times, LaFollette's, Outlook,* and *Everybody's* rejoiced in New York's triumphs. Brandeis, his dream now a reality, extolled the people of the garment industry for "the most creditable and hopeful effort yet made in America to solve the proper relationship of employer and employee." "It is creating a whole new economic order," asserted a writer in *Munsey's,* "and is helping perhaps more than any other agency to realize the long cherished dream of an industrial democracy." A management publication, the *Cloak and Suit Review,* and the ILGWU *Ladies' Garment Worker* both pronounced the experiment a decided success. The *Independent's* editor, Hamilton Holt, predicted that Protocolism indicated that "the time is not far distant when both industries and nations will be governed by law rather than brute force." [59]

While outsiders hailed the wondrous Protocol, many within the industry nurtured resentment against it. Union members protested chiefly against bosses who fired workers without proper cause. Protocol procedure, however, stipulated that in cases of alleged unfair discharge the difficult burden of proof rested with the laborer. As workers lost case after case before the Grievance Board, their hostility toward the Protocol increased. Pressure steadily mounted; dissolution of the Protocol loomed imminent. Far from being a noble example of industrial peace, the garment industry by 1914 threatened to explode.[60]

6

An end to the Protocol would mean the collapse of America's most promising venture in industrial relations; its downfall preordained a general strike. What could deliver it from destruction? Cries for help from many sources reached the newly created Commission. All urged the federal body to hasten to New York. Brandeis consulted Mrs. Harriman. "He seemed to feel," she wrote, "that our going might save the Protocol from breaking down." Hurriedly,

Mrs. Harriman conferred with her fellow commissioners, Ballard, Lennon, and O'Connell—all agreed on the need for an inquiry. She then telegraphed Chairman Walsh and informed him of the acute situation in the garment industry. Walsh consented to her plan. An important trial prevented his appearance, but he exhorted as many of the commissioners as possible to attend. From the first day, angry witnesses and demonstrative spectators jammed into the hearing room. "My ideal for the hearings," Mrs. Harriman recalled, "may have been a very calm review of the causes, but what I had on my hands was heated and noisy dispute. I wielded my gavel like a pickax." [61]

What undermined the Protocol? Commission testimony reveals that the piece-price system, among other problems, still intruded as a major obstacle. Companies paid weekly workers regular wages, but 75 to 80 percent of all laborers operated on a piecework basis. According to the Protocol employees, price committees bargained with local management in each shop to fix the rate for a given job. Workers charged that employers discriminated against those men on committees who pushed for a higher scale. Manufacturers complained that evaluations for the same labor varied from shop to shop. Unethical owners, they declared, conspired with venal committee members to depress the prices. Frequent style and seasonal changes kept this bickering perpetually alive. One witness, Paul Abelson, portrayed "2,000 unions changing every week, bargaining every day . . . a condition of chaos and turmoil." [62]

Each party also accused the other of practices inimical to the letter and spirit of the Protocol. Some owners had evaded the entente when they contracted to ship large portions of their work to out-of-town shops with cheap labor. A Board of Arbitration decision, however, ruled that companies which made contracts with Protocol firms came under Protocol regulation. New York businessmen eluded this edict by a system of submanufacture. Instead of contracting for the performance of a service, they "sold" raw material to these outsiders and then repurchased the finished products. In earlier times submanufacture had played only a minimum role in the garment world, but by 1912 several hundred such firms dealt with Protocol members. For their part manufacturers decried work stoppages. From March, 1911, to July, 1913, a total of 304 suspensions hit 131 companies. On the average, two or three cessations occurred every week; these affected at least one out of every two firms during this period. Such a situation naturally annoyed owners who had agreed to the Protocol chiefly to avoid strikes.[63]

While these economic issues plagued the Protocol, internal dissensions erupted among workers. Three different union leaders had officiated as labor's chief clerk on the Grievance Board. As each tried to unravel problems posed by management, he ran into internecine warfare among his own people. Union men clashed over the effectiveness of arbitration as contrasted with conciliation and over the authority of the New York local as opposed to the International. Personality conflicts aggravated these schisms. Finally, they went outside their ranks and chose as chief clerk Dr. Isaac A. Hourwich, lawyer, government statistician, and economic expert on labor and immigration. Hourwich's energetic administration, however, only stirred up even greater discord. When the Commission opened its investigation, the Manufacturers' Association had threatened to abrogate the Protocol, the ILGWU had announced that it might withdraw its support from the pact, and civil war raged within the local.[64]

Hourwich believed that the Protocol overemphasized conciliation between disputants, when it should have stressed arbitration before impartial judges. "Now, I want, gentlemen, to make it perfectly clear," he declared to the Commission, "that I have not been, in fact, a conciliator at all. . . . The fact is that that was not my office." He saw himself as a "Secretary of War." "My duty is to fight. A lawyer who appears in court is not expected to conciliate." A union official, Perez Cotler, upheld the Doctor. On the Grievance Board, Cotler told the commissioners, "the manufacturer always votes for their [sic] side, and our people always vote for our side, and the situation remains the same as before." These unresolved questions, most of which emanated from the workers, then went to the Arbitration Board. But that body met only once or twice a year, and manufacturers greatly profited by the delay. "We have had mediation enough," Cotler announced. "We know we can never get justice." Hourwich concurred. Procrastination in grievance procedures demoralized workers and broke the spirit of unionism. As a remedy he proposed a permanent salaried Arbitration Board to sit in continuous session.[65]

Those who clashed with Hourwich defended Protocol machinery but charged that the Doctor had disrupted it. This concordat, L. E. Rosenfeld, president of the Garment Manufacturers' Association, assured the Commission, "is the greatest vehicle that capital and labor have ever had. . . . It is the dictatorial presentation of the grievances on the other side. That is something we cannot tolerate." Julius Henry Cohen branded Hourwich's policies as "syndicalism"—a "feeling on the part of the people in the shop that they were so powerful that they could make the boss do what they wanted him to do." Labor's present chief clerk, Cohen alleged, violated the entire spirit of Protocolism. "We endeavored to reform things not by fighting but by understanding," but "when he [Hourwich] came and substituted the Secretary of War idea, well, how could you conciliate? Shake your fist in my face, and I am not prone to help you to get what you want."

Some labor men joined the onslaught against the controversial economist—among them John Dyche, general secretary and treasurer of the International and former chief clerk. Long an advocate of cooperation, Dyche explained that Protocolism enhanced the best interests of both capital and labor. He staunchly promoted conciliation over arbitration. Hourwich's disparagement of his kind of unionism stung him badly. "If a demagogue comes and tells the people that those people who have been trying to maintain the Protocol are the friends of the bosses," Dyche asserted, "then, of course, the Protocol falls to pieces." [66]

Verbal debates during the investigation almost burst into physical brawls. Dyche and Hourwich once grew so wrathful that they rushed at each other. On another occasion Sam Stanhoffs, an unemployed worker, disgusted by Cohen's praise of conditions under the Protocol, leaped from his seat and broke into the testimony. "If Mr. Cohen would say that 50,000 people are satisfied," he shouted, "he should go on the East River Bridge and jump off." [67]

Mrs. Harriman's troubles did not always stem from garment people. A witness told of an incident in which workers in a shop struck because the foreman had grossly insulted a seventeen-year-old girl. Commissioner Thruston Ballard, described by Mrs. Harriman as "our . . . hot and gallant Southern gentleman," sprang to his feet and demanded to know why the male employees did not protect this young lady in a more chivalrous manner. In his home state of Kentucky, Ballard exclaimed, "we would have caught him by the throat and broken his head down there. Why didn't they get up and knock the brute down until he was nearly dead instead of merely remonstrating with him and threatening to call a strike?" Amid the shouts, denials, and gavel-pounding that followed, Ballard remained unsatisfied. "They don't do it that way in Kentucky," he concluded sadly.[68]

Although disorderly at times, the Commission's hearing clarified the issues. Soon afterward both principals agreed to retain the Protocol, Hourwich resigned, and Sidney Hillman, Chicago garment union leader, assumed the chief clerk's position. Over the next few years, officials tinkered further with Protocol machinery but left untouched the underlying causes of discontent. They narrowly averted a general strike in July, 1915, but by May, 1916, the pent-up pressures finally exploded. Clothing workers stormed out in one of the most bitter strikes in ILGWU history. After fourteen weeks the contestants wrote a collective agreement that abandoned the Protocol but retained many of its features. A unique experiment in industrial government had come to an end.[69]

7

For a short time cooperation and reason under the Protocol supplanted chaos in the garment industry. Some historians have suggested that recent immigrants, unfamiliar with American ways of compromise, tended to employ violence in labor disputes. Yet a majority of the garment workers who favored the Protocol had newly emigrated from European soil. In language, religion, and custom they formed a distinct group alien to the rest of the United States. Protocolism has also been viewed as an expression of Jewish communal life or of socialist collectivism. Whatever its nature, it certainly did not exemplify the triumph of any native American pragmatism.[70]

Protocolism failed to resolve its own contradictions and disintegrated. Hearings by the Commission disclosed that certain basic issues, inherent in all industrial relations, still defied solution. Could or should labor and capital really cooperate? Many manufacturers invented devices to evade a covenant they pledged to uphold.* Some workers quit their jobs, although they had promised to abandon the strike as a weapon. Cooperation implied settlement of disputes through conciliation, but constant deadlocks negated this process. An overreliance on arbitration, many contended, destroyed the desire of either party to seek adjustments through mutual effort. Commission testimony revealed union leaders sharply divided; they had no common philosophical approach to these problems.

In the garment world, as in many areas of the United States at this time, improper or inadequate civil authority, malevolence, and savagery dominated labor relations. Two bitter struggles led to a fragile temporary truce. Then, as in many other cases which fell under the Commission's jurisdiction, violence and turmoil returned to plague the industry.

* One writer has pointed out that many small non-unionized firms could still enter the industry at this time. The larger companies, out of fear of this new competition, failed to maintain Protocol standards. (See Lorwin, *The Women's Garment Workers*, p. 314.)

VI

CONTINENTAL BATTLEGROUND

1

> There can be no such thing as two irresistable forces meeting,
> yet this conflict approaches as near it as any that has ever been
> waged in the history of the labor movement. Every inch of ground
> is bitterly contested by both sides, and this, one of the greatest la-
> bor battles ever fought, has resolved itself into a matter of physi-
> cal endurance.[1]

THESE WORDS ACCURATELY DESCRIBE a struggle in the years 1911–
15, when unions from the West and Middle West united into one
federation and challenged two of the mightiest railroad empires in
America. Shopmen on all the sprawling Illinois Central and Harriman lines demanded the relatively new right of systemwide bargaining. Battle lines between the two foes extended halfway across the
nation. Property destruction, financial losses, and plant deterioration
afflicted the carriers; debt, broken homes, and physical assault
plagued the strikers. Neither side ever relented.

Disputes over wages, hours, and working conditions rarely drove
men to such extremes. Yet William Z. Foster, labor leader and later
American Communist Party chairman, ranked this strike as among
the most important in the annals of labor. Illinois Central vice-president and general manager W. L. Park damned it as "one of the most
uncalled for walkouts . . . in the history of this country." What lay beneath the surface? Had the Commission uncovered a far more significant issue—an issue so deeply embedded in the American social sys-

tem that it defied simple solution? The commissioners moved to investigate this meaningful and savage encounter.[2]

2

Half a century of incredible railroad expansion had preceded the conflict. After a period of cutthroat competition, the surviving companies consolidated, until six powerful systems controlled 95 percent of the high-grade mileage in the United States. A very few men, through interlocking directorates, ruled these empires. By the 1880s four great railroad brotherhoods had emerged as the dominant labor organizations; they represented engineers, firemen, trainmen, and conductors. Any interruption of the services of these highly skilled and hard-to-replace employees created tremendous hardships for the carriers. As a result, these workers attained most of their goals through peaceful collective bargaining and arbitration.

Thousands of other laborers, however, remained outside the brotherhoods. Shop craft employees (machinists, boilermakers, blacksmiths, electricians, etc.) formed unions within each craft and, unlike the brotherhoods, usually associated with the AFL. Loosely organized, the craft unions were an easy prey for the divisive tactics of management. In 1893 and again in 1898 they had formed federations for the purpose of centralization, but internal discord destroyed both organizations. Eugene Debs' attempt to build an industrial union among all railroad operatives also collapsed after the disastrous 1894 Pullman strike. Such failures temporarily settled any further efforts toward unification.[3]

Soon after the turn of the century, a number of railroads began to campaign for wage reductions and the introduction of piecework. In response, shop craft laborers formed federations on each of the several railroad systems. Systemwide negotiations forced management to bargain with a coalition instead of with every individual union; workers in each craft could fuse their demands and enforce uniform standards. In 1908 employees of the Southern Railway; the New York,

New Haven and Hartford; the Union Pacific, the Santa Fe; the Missouri Pacific; and the Canadian Pacific all fashioned similar alliances, and all smashed efforts to cut wages or to impose piecework. System federations soon sprang up all over America.[4]

AFL leaders feared that these new arrivals might eventually cut loose from the national. At their convention in 1908, therefore, AFL delegates established a Railway Employees' Department (RED) to coordinate all system federations in the United States. Officials of this new organization had the power to grant charters to any future amalgamations; two RED representatives served as lobbyists in Washington.[5]

3

A major test for RED arrived in 1911 in the great strike on the Illinois Central and the Harriman lines. Illinois Central stretched over 4,500 miles from Chicago to New Orleans, with a major branch that extended to Omaha. It served the commerce of the Mississippi Valley, which provided a rich carrying trade in bituminous coal, agricultural products, and livestock. Edward H. Harriman's empire encompassed a network of railroads from Texas to Oregon; it included the Union Pacific, the Southern Pacific, the Oregon Short Line, and the Santa Fe. Both systems maintained separate administrative staffs, but the Union Pacific possessed a controlling interest of Illinois Central stock.[6]

In June, 1911, shop crafts on both lines created their own system federation. They immediately notified the railroads and solicited recognition of their organization. In addition, workers wanted to discuss a minimum wage, standardization of hours, overtime rates, a seniority system, and the elimination of piecework. They also charged that a company program disguised as vocational training for high school students actually provided nonunion apprentices and that the roads deliberately hired cheap foreign and Negro labor.[7]

Company leaders expressed surprise and indignation over the

strike. Both W. L. Park, vice president and general manager of Illinois Central, and Julius Kruttschnitt, operating head of the Harriman lines, claimed that their roads paid the highest wages, hospital benefits, and pensions. In past years management had always negotiated with the unions in friendly bargaining sessions; seven out of the nine organizations in this new federation, they pointed out, possessed written contracts with their firms. All these agreements, rail officials stressed, stipulated that requests for changes must arrive 30 days prior to the expiration of the contract then in effect. In the present altercation, the unions had failed to observe this rule. President Charles H. Markham of Illinois Central denied that this insistence on the letter of the law denoted bickering over a technicality; he regarded this termination clause as a substantial feature of all compacts.[8]

Management stated a willingness to discuss economic issues with each individual union; it flatly refused to recognize or confer with the new federation. Railroad executives viewed this labor network as a plot to establish a dictatorship over both the workers and the companies. "The roads would be at their mercy," Park asserted. "It would have ten thousand times more power than the American Federation of Labor." *Railway Age Gazette,* a publication for management, supported this contention. "Victory for the strikers," it declared, "would mean unreasonable conditions of employment, unreasonable advances in wages, and a dangerous addition to the power of the leaders of the union." The Illinois Central, its directors concluded, "could not submit . . . and continue to perform the public functions for which it was created."[9]

Over the next few months, union chiefs and company administrators exchanged correspondence and held further parleys. Neither yielded on the question of recognition. When AFL officials asked all their members if they wished to walk out solely over this one issue, 97 percent of the operatives voted "Yes." After this ballot the labor leaders appealed to management for a last-minute conference but again met with rebuff.[10]

On September 30, 1911, the strike began. Illinois Central and Harriman employees, acting "like a trained disciplined army, threw down their tools and walked from the shops." Soon unionists were boasting that they had achieved "an almost complete tie up"; company spokesmen scorned this claim as a gross exaggeration. Nevertheless, the Illinois Central conceded that about 63 percent of its shopmen had struck, and Harriman's chief of operations admitted that he had lost half of his working force. From Chicago to New Orleans, from Memphis to Sacramento, workers marched out of their departments in a great strike that affected fifteen states and covered half the continent.[11]

Outside of union publications, almost the entire press expressed anger at the strikers. New Orleans' *Times-Picayune* branded the walkout an attempt on the part of a small cabal of labor "monarchs" to establish "an absolute despotism over every member" of the federation. Equally, the New Orleans *Item* found "nothing that would justify a strike at the present time." The Chicago *Inter-Ocean* believed that some of the demands of the workers seemed to have been formulated by socialistic theorists ignorant of railroad work. The entire business community, asserted the Chicago *Record-Herald*, regarded the strike as radical and unwise. "It is to be remembered," warned the New York *Tribune*, that the system federation "would be totally irresponsible. It would not be incorporated. It would not be governed by any of the public-service legislation." Even the sometimes reformist *Nation* averred that "it was manifest to every thinking man that the railways could not possibly concede." Only Socialist papers, such as the New York *Call*, defended the shopmen because "if federation . . . of weak competing lines into a strong system has been good for the Harriman roads, then the organization of small, weak and often warring unions into federation . . . will be good for the workers." [12]

President A. O. Wharton of the system federation explained this universal censure on the grounds that his organization did not command sufficient funds to buy publicity: "Our means of communication are practically nil so far as the public is concerned." [13] On the other hand, the railroad flooded the public with propaganda. Illinois Central President Markham testified that in addition to its own pamphlets the company periodically purchased space for strike statements in all leading newspapers from Chicago to New Orleans. He did not know if those who accepted the road's advertising also adopted an editorial policy favorable to the carriers.[14]

4

With the strike now a reality, both sides unleashed offensives. Pickets surrounded company property, and the railroads applied to detective agencies for replacements. Company officials found recruitment easy, although they admitted that they did not inquire into the character of their new employees. Management also hired special detectives to work with law-enforcement authorities and prepared court actions against the strikers.[15]

Violence erupted immediately. In New Orleans railroad workers stole company records, switched or destroyed identification cards on freight cars, and cut the air hoses of as many as fifteen to twenty cars a day. Mobs of varying size constantly bombarded nonstrikers with stones and gunfire. Once an assailant mistook an aide to the governor of Texas for a strikebreaker and beat him badly. When Illinois Central brought in a large platoon of replacements, a riot started which took the lives of six men and injured over 100. An observer described it as "one of the bloodiest on record in this section." Because of the unrest, New Orleans police summoned their entire reserve force to duty. U.S. deputy marshals and railroad detectives supplemented this staff.[16]

In Illinois periodic incursions damaged or destroyed company property. On one occasion, strike sympathizers in Carbondale turned loose a switch engine, which rammed into a freight train on the main line. In December, the Illinois Central offered a large reward for the arrest of persons responsible for the wreck of four suburban passenger trains in the vicinity of Grand Crossing and Parkside. Investigators also uncovered fourteen sticks of dynamite under the approach of a railway bridge that crossed the Mississippi River.[17]

Disorder swept through many parts of the state. Gangs in Centralia periodically harried car repairmen and forced them to abandon their work. Union mechanics in the same city frequently beset strikebreaking clerks and watchmen. On one occasion 800 furious strikers surrounded the Illinois Central depot. Newspapers carried stories of brutal physical assaults of both sides. In Carbondale workers subjected company roundhouses to gunfire, while in Mounds men sent volleys of bullets into passing trains. Under cover of darkness Illinois Central smuggled 200 strikebreakers into stockades at the railroad center of Burnside. A furious crowd rushed these buildings, stoned the occupants, and then advanced on them with clubs. Police issued a riot call in order to quell the battle. In Illinois, as in New Orleans, the company furnished shotguns to state and federal officials.[18]

Turbulence and bloodshed led to a complete breakdown of civil government in sections of Mississippi. On October 3, in McComb, hundreds of union men armed with clubs, razors, and pistols pounced on three newly arrived carloads of strikebreakers enroute to New Orleans. After a 20-minute gun battle, the strikers hurled brickbats on the heads of the company men. Hand-to-hand combat, which wrecked the three coaches and injured and killed several rioters, followed. When the train finally reached New Orleans, one reporter declared, "It looked as though it had been through the Boer War." As a result of this clash, authorities ordered the entire Third Regiment of the Mississippi National Guard to McComb.[19]

When these troops arrived, they found a city that verged on anarchy. A sudden dynamite explosion started a rumor that the strikers intended to blow up the whole $2-million complex of Illinois Central shops in McComb. A large crowd of union men surrounded the main company building and vociferously demanded the deportation of all scabs. They threatened to attack the structure and suggested the use of dynamite. In desperation the governor, the county sheriff, and the commander of the state National Guard appealed to the railroad to remove their employees in order to prevent a massacre. Reluctantly Illinois Central complied. Every striker and every striker's family witnessed the departure; only the loaded rifles of Guardsmen kept those onlookers under control. Soldiers assigned to protect the train received these instructions: "If any man aboard lifts a hand or makes a motion to hurl a missile, if any striker, strike sympathizer, or citizen makes a menacing demonstration . . . shoot, and shoot to kill." [20]

Soon McComb, a newsman reported, "took on the appearance of an armed camp." [21] Ten National Guard units, infantry and artillery, marched into the city. They enforced rigorous military discipline and even sent squads out to arrest guardsmen who failed to report for duty. Yet even with these extreme security measures, the Illinois Central feared for the safety of its president; his special train, scheduled to pass through McComb on the way to New Orleans, was re-routed across the entire state of Mississippi. When hardware stores quickly sold out their supply of revolvers, repeating rifles arrived from New Orleans in ominous quantities. "A human fence of half a thousand bayonets," one reporter noted, now surrounded company property. Even the outskirts of the town "resembled rural sections of Mexico before the recent insurrections. Everywhere there are men with guns." [22] Observers dubbed the city "Fort McComb."

With all these precautions, McComb's civilian officials still could not maintain order. His entire city in chaos, the mayor in a letter to the governor admitted total defeat: "In view of the intolerable conditions here, which seem to be growing worse instead of better, and in view of the complete failure of all civil powers to keep the peace, including the United States circuit court, I would request that martial law be temporarily invoked." Mississippi's chief executive assented and an emergency session of the state legislature appropriated the necessary funds.[23] McComb's troubles, the governor charged, emanated from "foreign agitators." He declared that authorities should hunt down those covert labor leaders who really inspired the violence. "Why don't you go after your own militia that commits all kinds of crime, even to murder?" a union vice president retorted. "Why don't you go after the railroad company that is bringing into the different towns men with criminal records?" [24]

But even military government did not end the violence. Outrages continued which included the murder of three Negro strikebreakers and the serious injury of two others. Police apprehended six men for the crime, but a jury refused to convict on purely circumstantial evidence. Alarmed by this unabated bloodletting, a special committee responsible to the state legislature journeyed to McComb. They interviewed strikers, businessmen, professional men, civil and military officials, and railroad executives. "After examining all those witnesses," this group attested, "none told us that it would be better to remove said troops, but many, on the other hand, advised us that it would be better to let them remain." In a unanimous report the investigators advised prolongation of martial law.[25]

This same pattern emerged in other parts of the state. In Jackson, striking clerks demolished company records and deliberately confused the routing of freight. One employee reported that seventy-five cars in the Jackson yard had suddenly lost their knuckle pins. On several occasions in Water Valley, mobs armed with revolvers and shotguns invaded Illinois Central offices and caused the employees to flee in panic. In Water Valley, as in McComb, local authorities could not cope with these upheavals. Even a high-level conference, attended by the governor, the mayor of Jackson, the president of the Illinois Central, a number of high union officials, and U.S. Senator John Sharp Williams, failed to restore peace. Hard experience gave Mississippi's governor an insight into the real nature of the problem: "Both the railroad men and the strikers are determined never to come together on the federation proposition, and that fact might as well be recognized." [26]

Accounts from other states on the Illinois Central's line only confirmed the familiar story of tumult. As a train that carried strikebreakers pulled into New Orleans, 500 unionists poured gunfire into their ranks. Then this angry mob closed in on the scabs and bashed them with clubs. Emergency police reserves finally put down the riot but not until several participants had sustained severe injuries. For two successive nights hordes swarmed through the streets of Central City, Kentucky. They set upon men in railroad cars and fired at employees lodged in temporary sleeping quarters. Paducah, according to a pro-labor attorney, F. E. Graves, "enjoyed the greatest carnival of crime this city has ever experienced." He blamed it on the desperate character of the strikebreakers. As soon as these men arrived, "all sorts of crime immediately made its appearance . . . and the emissaries of the railroad began an undercurrent of suspicion that the strikers were responsible for it." Altercations also broke out in Louisville and Princeton; the governor had to send troops into Fulton. In the neighboring state of Tennessee the strike bred a rash of mobbings, stonings, gun battles, and killings.[27]

Far-flung Harriman lines in the West, though not so badly crippled by the strike, enjoyed no immunity from violence. Reports from Portland, Oakland, and San Francisco described gang fights and severe assaults on civilians and policemen. Southern Pacific and Salt Lake Railroad chiefs at Los Angeles and Santa Barbara smuggled strikebreakers into well-provisioned stockades in expectation of sieges. Communiqués from Houston told of fatal stabbings and deaths from bullet wounds. Deputy sheriffs at Sherman, Texas, refused to protect company equipment and quit their jobs. Executives of the Missouri, Kansas and Texas Railroad begged state authorities to send troops to guard their property. Strikers in Denison, Texas, armed with clubs and beer bottles, ripped into a group of fifty-four scabs, beat them up, and drove them out of town.[28]

In order to frustrate these worker uprisings, management resorted to the law. A judge in Mississippi issued a sweeping statewide decree against every union member on strike against Illinois Central. He forbade them to congregate on or near railroad property, to intimidate nonstrikers or induce them to quit, or to interfere in any way with the Illinois Central's normal operations. Officers in Mississippi hauled hundreds into court for violation of edicts termed by labor leader John D. Buckalew as "the most severe" he had ever seen during a tour of strike-bound communities.[29] In Illinois, Louisiana, Texas, and Kentucky, comprehensive restraining orders overburdened court calendars and overloaded jails.[30] A judgment in Kentucky, grumbled the system federation president, prohibited strikers "from doing almost anything except breathing. They could not even speak to a man that was working for the Illinois Central Railroad." [31]

East St. Louis contributed a cogent example of this judicial hostility. When unionists challenged the validity of an injunction, Judge F. M. Wright denied their plea and told them, "It is a mistake to suppose you have a right to get together and conspire to induce these men to leave the employ of the company." Wright did not limit himself to legal matters but tendered advice on industrial relations. He blamed the ferment on familiar villains—those "outside agitators" who "want to break up the country." "I don't know what this strike is for. . . . I don't believe anybody else does. . . . Go back to work. There is no reason why you are out." [32]

The most dramatic case involved twenty-four-year-old system federation official and editor, Carl Person. "A battle royal is going on in Clinton, Illinois," wrote journalist Floyd Gibbons, "between a twentieth century David and an up-to-date Goliath of the Super-Dreadnought type. The David is Carl Person, the fighting editor of the *Strike Bulletin*. The all-powerful Goliath is the Illinois Central Railroad Company." [33]

When he began his drive to counteract the overwhelming anti-unionism of the press, Person owned only a second-hand typewriter and a mimeograph machine he had salvaged from a junk heap. Workers all along the Illinois Central, however, avidly took to the paper and many of them contributed to it. Soon the *Strike Bulletin* was appearing regularly in printed form.[34]

On November 13, 1911, Person published a special "Graveyard Edition." In it he charged that Illinois Central had hired incompetents as strikebreakers and had allowed its equipment to degenerate dangerously. As documentation, the editor presented thirty-two pages of photographs which featured blazing train wrecks, ambulances, wounded victims, coffins piled high, scalded children, and mangled bodies. This issue attracted nationwide attention, damaged the railroad's public image, and doubtless helped to drive down the price of its stock. Company detectives descended on Person's office and ransacked his files, desk drawers, and letter books.[35] Then railroad officials secured an indictment against the young publicist for "circulating through the U.S. mails, Matters Reflecting injuriously on the Conduct of the Illinois Central Railroad and its Officials"; the crime carried maximum penalties of $35,000 and thirty-five years. Released on bail, Person returned to work.[36]

Physical as well as judicial aggression now tormented the editor. In September, three men battered him so badly that they left him on the sidewalk for dead. Person recovered, but a month later a second assault produced more serious results. Tony Musser, a former police chief of Clinton, known as the "giant Portugee," attacked the slightly built writer on a street near the *Bulletin's* offices. Musser knocked his victim down, rained blows upon his face, and bashed his head repeatedly against the concrete sidewalk. When the former policeman grabbed Person's throat, a woman among the gathering crowd of onlookers screamed, "Take that big fellow off. He'll kill the boy!" With strenuous efforts, a group of spectators pulled the giant away, while others cast worried glances at Person. "Blood from gashes in his head streamed down his face and blinded his swollen eyes," Gibbons reported. "The scalp was torn from his skull in several places." [37]

Abnormally strong, the enraged Musser broke loose from his captors and lunged again at Person. "Damn you," he shouted, "I'll get you yet." Certain that his adversary intended murder, the youth, who had recovered slightly during this brief respite, drew a revolver and pumped its contents into Musser's body. The "giant Portugee" fell dead. Person then surrendered to police.[38]

Officers at the jail denied their prisoner access to his friends and rejected his request to allow a photographer to take pictures of his condition to use as evidence. They finally admitted one six weeks later, when almost every trace of the assault had disappeared from Person's body. Police also raided the *Bulletin's* offices, refused to accept bail for the captive, and confined him to his cell for five months. While the authorities thus held a fellow journalist virtually incommunicado, local newspapers denounced him as an anarchist agitator; they recommended that he hang for his crime.[39]

Union leaders created a Person Defense League, which received support from the Illinois and Chicago Federations of Labor. Person's attorney, chief counsel to the RED, grew convinced that his client could not obtain a fair trial in Clinton because the railroad completely dominated the city. In a bitter court battle, the lawyer successfully won a change of venue to Lincoln, Illinois. At the trial the jury, after twenty-three hours of deliberation and twenty-two ballots, returned a verdict of "Not guilty." After the trial, Person proclaimed: "The fight to crush organized labor is doomed." [40]

5

Although the carriers generally achieved legal victories, they suffered serious economic defeats. Illinois Central reacted vehemently to Person's exposé of its inefficiency because he had drawn blood. Soon many employee publications emphasized the public hazards of ill-trained workers, faulty maintenance, and decrepit machinery. They forcefully pointed out that government inspectors had condemned and ordered out of service vast numbers of Illinois Central engines. In only a few months since the start of the strike, they claimed, the total number of available Illinois Central locomotives decreased from 1,350 to about 500.[41]

A decline in equipment led to a stagnation of service. In New Orleans the postmaster complained about constant delays in mail delivery because almost all Illinois Central trains ran late. Dispatches from Illinois and Mississippi reported badly crippled service or complete tie-ups. Many freight schedules existed only on paper. Illinois Central could not deliver coal to Clinton, Illinois, and thereby forced the waterworks and the electric plants to shut down. For a time the whole community endured in darkness. Coal dealers in many parts of the country predicted a fuel shortage that would approach famine proportions unless the railroad furnished more motive power.[42]

Tragedy marked the Illinois road all during the strike. Much to the embarrassment of management, a disaster even struck down a former president of the railroad while he journeyed on his own line. A collision near Decatur, Illinois, wrecked the private car which carried the ex-official and his companion, an Illinois Central assistant vice-president. It killed both men and injured a number of trainmen. Investigation disclosed that the engineer of the train which hit the car had enjoyed a twenty-five-year record for perfect safety. He testified that excessive steam had blinded him. Leaking steampipes, one railroad publication observed, indicated a defective boiler, not a bad engineer. On November 11, 1912, in Louisiana, a fast freight crashed headlong into an excursion train on which a large number of women and children were traveling. Then the wreckage caught fire and added to the death toll. Those who inspected the scene noted many corpses, including those of babies, "mangled beyond description." In some instances this catastrophe wiped out entire families.[43]

In a public statement for the year that ended June 30, 1912, the Interstate Commerce Commission revealed that American railroads had sustained more than 180,000 casualties, over 10,000 of whom died. "This enormous slaughter of human life is not so much to be wondered at," the RED claimed, "when taking into consideration the conditions under which the Illinois Central and Harriman lines operated during that period." Many organizations and political figures flooded state legislatures, Congress, and the White House with petitions and resolutions which demanded an investigation of the line. They labored in vain.[44]

These deplorable consequences of the long strike hit the Illinois Central's financial structure severely. In its 1912 annual report, the company showed a loss in operating revenues of over $3 million, while its operating expenses rose by almost the same amount. Railroad officials candidly listed the strike as the chief cause for this setback; severe winter weather and floods also contributed to the decline. "The Illinois Central," commented the New York *Times*, "had about as hard a time last winter as any railroad could have without giving up the ghost." The shopmen's strike "cut into the earnings from above and below" because it decreased volume of business while it added to handling costs.[45]

On the exchange Illinois Central stock plunged ever downward. In June 18, 1913, it fell to 108½, its lowest since 1899. When in July the board of directors announced a slash in dividends, the price dropped to new depths. Since Union Pacific owned over $32 million worth of Illinois general stock, it stood to lose heavily on its investment. If "I.C. stock continues to tumble beautifully," declared a union magazine gleefully, "we may see it offered as premiums with smoking tobacco." [46]

6

Impaired machinery, debilitated finances, and frightful accidents did not swerve management from its adamant position toward the strikers. Many persons in public life, however, shocked by the violent course of the struggle, tried to attain a reconciliation. In November, 1911, governors of several states served by the Illinois

Central volunteered their services toward a mediation of the dispute. Illinois Central President Markham declined the offer. Seth Low suggested the intercession of the National Civic Federation, but the railroad administrator refused on the grounds that the principles involved transcended simple economic issues. Markham likewise rejected peacemaking proposals from the president of the New Orleans Cotton Exchange and the governor of Mississippi. Even President Taft could not obtain a conference between the antagonists.[47]

Early in 1913 the railroad and the unions reached their closest point of accord. Even this highly conditional rapprochement contained elements of cloak-and-dagger intrigue. In February a chief of the Machinists' Union managed through an intermediary to arrange an interview with the Illinois Central's general manager. By previous agreement, the negotiators used assumed names and met on neutral ground secretly in Chicago. They agreed upon tentative settlement terms, unsigned, unofficial, and subject to ratification by higher officials on both sides. Their pact called for a reinstatement of all employees, a restitution of the old contracts in effect prior to the walkout, and a company promise not to discriminate against any striker unless he had damaged railroad property. A final touch of mystery came when the railroad executive refused to initial the document but affixed his seal to it with a signet ring and wax as a token of good faith.

When system federation leaders examined this scheme, they recognized it as nothing but a restoration of the *status quo ante*—equivalent to total surrender. Nevertheless, they hoped to use it as a device for opening talks with management. At the first parley, however, company executives refused to discuss the possibility of additional concessions and quickly closed the meeting.[48]

Management obstinacy drove shop craft workers to demand more militant national leadership than that offered by RED. Although formed to coordinate and charter system federations, the AFL rail department functioned mainly as a propaganda and legislative agency. Its part-time officers received no remuneration and held no direct responsibility to rank-and-file railroad employees. On April 15, 1912, 200 delegates from south and west of Chicago convened for eight days in what one publication called "one of the most notable gatherings of railroad employes in the United States." They created a new association appropriately entitled the Federation of Federations. Its constitution provided for full-time, full-salaried executives elected directly in convention by system federation representatives. Power over all major policy decisions rested completely in the hands of the assembled delegates. "This meeting," declared the *Railway Clerk*, "marks a new epoch in the history of the railway employe, practically eliminating, as it does, all craft lines when it comes to dealing with the railroad corporations." [49]

Since Federation of Federations members represented the whole constituency of the RED, no jurisdictional fight developed. At its next convention the RED adopted, with only minor alterations, the Federation of Federations' constitution and elected the same officers. The AFL executive council then granted a new charter to the revitalized organization. This new body resembled Debs' old American Railway Union, with one significant modification. Debs tried to bring all railroad workers into one industrial union; RED preserved local distinctions yet supplied an effective agency for collective action. [50]

But the modernized RED arrived too late to aid the very strike which had led to its creation. When the Illinois Central System Federation had first voted to walk out, some of its chiefs had resisted because the fledgling group possessed no war chest. RED had collected a special strike fund, but almost four years of struggle had exhausted these resources. Even the machinists, among the strongest of all shop crafts, found it necessary to seek loans from their local lodges. A questionnaire sent to strikers revealed that the conflict compelled 10 percent of them to seek charity, 12 percent to sell their furniture, and 50 percent to borrow money. Over 90 percent of the workers and their families moved from already low-rent dwellings to even cheaper ones; 68 percent of the striker families broke up their homes. [51]

Financial attrition bred pessimism and division among the laborers. First the International Association of Car Workers, which had initially opposed the strike, defected from RED. In December, 1914, RED recognized the inevitable and completely terminated its

contributions; a few months later it officially called off the strike.*
Union officials estimated that it had cost all labor agencies combined
$2 million to $3 million. They had not achieved a single one of
their goals.[52]

7

Long before the strike ended, the AFL at its 1913 national convention deemed it important to secure a hearing before the Commission. After RED officials had conferred with Chairman Walsh,
they appointed a special committee to prepare a presentation of
their side. The Commission was listening to testimony just as the
strike entered its final month. It RED had acted more quickly and
grasped this opportunity one year earlier, Carl Person believed, the
public revelation of Illinois Central's collapsed finances and di-
lapidated rolling stock would have forced the company to come
to terms at that time.[53]

Workers' representatives at the hearing repeated their list of
economic requests. They particularly opposed the piecework speed-
up system, which, they protested, led to physical exhaustion. Company spokesmen issued a point-by-point refutation of these claims.
They termed them unreasonable, at variance with established practices, and contrary to scientific management. Once again both sides
clashed over whether the unions had fulfilled their obligation to
give 30 days' advance notice of desired contract changes.[54] Some
of the commissioners suspected that this bickering merely obscured
certain deeper issues. By persistent interrogation the panel finally
hit pay dirt. Illinois Central President Markham declared:

> The real cause was the fear of the combination. And we justified
> our refusal to these men by putting before them the fact they had
> not given the 30 days' notice, and demanded that they live up to their
> contract, just as they expected us to do. If you want me to be frank,
> the real cause was the fear of putting too much power into the
> hands of men who would not use it wisely.[55]

* Carl Person charged that the strikers lost because of a lack of unity
within the system federation. "The International Vice-Presidents assigned to
the strike zone were falling over each other. None of them knew where the
rest of them were, or where they were going." (*The Lizard's Trail*, p. 31.)

Union leaders might have attained a consideration of their other needs if they had abandoned the federation issue. Why, in view of management's inflexible attitude, had the shopmen so insisted on this point? Federation, argued a union advocate, induced standard wages, hours, and working conditions for all craft employees. Previously, the railroads had practiced a divide-and-conquer technique. They played one union off against another and pursued the same policy among the crafts. Management, they attested, deliberately prolonged negotiations in order to exhaust limited union treasuries, and then the bosses broke their contracts. No small union could stand up against a huge railroad; unless workers amalgamated, they remained at the mercy of corporate wealth.[56] What moral sanction, labor spokesmen asked, justified the carriers in their opposition to federation? "If we assume that the employer has the right to dictate to us the form of organization which we deem necessary to protect our interests," asserted A. O. Wharton, president of RED, "then, of course, we would assume that he had the right to say to us whom we should select to represent us." [57]

Why had capital battled so furiously? "This federation," asserted Julius Kruttschnitt, now board chairman of Southern Pacific, "was simply a plan to obtain absolute power over the operations of the carriers and to exert it to the utmost." [58] Individual system coalitions, another management witness explained, would inevitably combine into a superagency to cover the entire United States. This "National System Federation," declared Markham, "could order strikes on one road or on every road in North America. . . . The policy of a railroad would be absolutely under the dictation of such a powerful body." [59] Since men in shop crafts worked for many industries besides the railroads, their alliance, "becomes a weapon aimed . . . at the heart of practically every manufacturing enterprise in the country." [60] Appalled by such a prospect, he declared, "Illinois Central Railroad Co. felt that it owed a duty to its stockholders, to its patrons, and to the country to resist in every legitimate and proper way the beginning of such a monstrous system." [61]

Regardless of the strike's duration and expense, company executives stoutly defended their refusal even to discuss the issue with federation officers. "There has been absolutely nothing that we could mediate or arbitrate," protested Southern Pacific's Kruttschnitt.[62] "I take it," Chairman Walsh asked Markham, "that nothing has occurred since, either in the strike itself or in any experience that you have had, that has caused you to change your mind." Markham replied, "I am more strongly confirmed in it than ever, sir." [63]

These hearings disclosed that the shop craft workers had utterly failed to gain their immediate objectives. Their strike, however, made an important contribution to the future of railroad labor because it forced a reformation of the AFL Railway Employees' Department. Over the next few years this rejuvenated agency grew steadily stronger, until by 1916 forty-three system federations held RED charters. During World War I, when the national government operated the rails, federal officials recognized the RED as the sole collective bargaining agent for all railroad workers outside the train-service brotherhoods.[64]

The Illinois Central strike exemplified the fact that corporate collectivism had replaced rugged individualism in the business world. When labor formed its own combinations and tried to introduce systemwide bargaining, the two adversaries met head on in a struggle for power. Since no third force, public or private, provided effective machinery for the resolution of such disputes, the antagonists remained free to fight as they wished, restrained only by their own sense of social responsibility. As a result, the strike displayed characteristics similar to many others which the Commission studied; it wasted millions of dollars, weakened or shattered civil governments, devastated property, and obliterated human life.

VII

MASSACRE IN COLORADO

1

"WORSE THAN THE ORDER that sent the Light Brigade into the jaws of death, worse in its effect than the Black Hole of Calcutta." Thus the conservative New York *Times* described the "Ludlow Camp Horror." State troops in Colorado had machine-gunned a coalminers' tent colony that housed hundreds of women and children. Shortly afterward some of the inflammable canvas ignited. For fifteen hours, fire, aided by the soldiers, roared through the entire community. This terrible act climaxed a labor struggle in Colorado which erupted into a civil war all over the state.[1]

Demands for an investigation of the catastrophe soon reached the Commission. Journalist George Creel, who later headed Wilson's wartime Committee on Public Information, covered the story. When he saw the atrocities of the strike, the newsman was enraged. He called a mass meeting in front of the Colorado statehouse. There, in a driving rainstorm before 10,000 people, Creel denounced the governor, the lieutenant governor, and particularly the Rockefellers, who held a controlling interest in the state's largest mining company. "Traitors to the people," he called them, "accessories to the murder of babes." Then Creel reported to his old friend, Frank Walsh. He presented the Commission with material on the Colorado struggle and urged an immediate investigation.[2]

Humanitarian Jane Addams also pressed the Commission for action. Through her friend Mrs. Harriman, she persuaded the federal body to interrupt its normal schedule in order to hold an impromptu hearing on Ludlow. By special arrangement the investigators opened a short two-day session devoted to the disaster. Two miners' wives who had survived the fire, an officer of the state militia, and famous Judge Ben B. Lindsey of the Juvenile Court of Denver traveled to New York. Their stories, especially those of the women, so affected Commissioner Lennon that he wept openly during the testimony.[3]

Frank Walsh wanted to conduct an extensive inquiry during September. He postponed it, however, in deference to federal mediators whom President Wilson had recently dispatched to Colorado to effect a settlement. Nevertheless, members of the Commission's research staff went to the state in order to confer with these Presidential envoys. "They [the mediators] say the situation is as full of dynamite as ever," Commission investigator George P. West noted, "and that not the Lord Himself could come here and exert a spirit or influence that would soften the attitude of either side." Wilson's peacemakers told West that the operators became "wild men" when they discussed the strike. "They fly into a rage, curse the federal government, and froth at the mouth." Colorado "appalled" and "disgusted" both mediators. One of them, West wrote, "says the state ought to be disenfranchised." [4]

Commissioners Lennon and Ballard also traveled to the feud-ridden community. "The ranks of the operators, as well as those of the miners," they asserted, "are as solid as the day the contest opened." Hostile feelings infected every citizen and had divided the entire population into two warring camps. At one time, the United Mine Workers seriously considered calling out every miner in the United States. "There were several days," the commissioners declared, "when there was positive danger of a national revolution growing out of this Colorado strike." [5]

These reports convinced Walsh that this trouble spot demanded immediate attention. He ignored objections from both the governor and the governor-elect of Colorado that a probe would only "serve to inflame passion and endanger the peace." "This will be the most important and significant hearing that we will have," the Chairman told Ballard. "I am urging upon the full membership that they attend." Moreover, the Commission leader had recently enjoyed a "bully talk" with the President. Wilson evinced the "finest spirit toward our work," Walsh boasted, "in fact, has not only a hearty appreciation but a deep interest in the outcome of our endeavors." Everywhere in Washington, the Chairman found a rapt absorption in this Colorado venture. "If we have a good hearing there," he predicted, "it will stamp our commission all over with success." [6]

2

A strike at the Colorado Fuel and Iron Company (CFI) had started all the turmoil which the federal probers prepared to examine. This enterprise owned about 300,000 acres of mineral-rich territory in southern Colorado, located chiefly in Las Animas and Huerfano counties. As the largest coal firm in the state, CFI exerted a commanding influence over its smaller competitors. Behind the management stood the immense financial empire of the Rockefeller family, who controlled 40 percent of the company's stocks and bonds. [7]

Geographical isolation had allowed the CFI and its associated firms to impose medieval feudalism over some 30,000 workers. Most of the miners lived in camps situated from 10 to 30 miles from the principal towns. Rockefeller's firm owned the land and the laborers' dwellings; it deliberately discouraged independent home ownership and refused to sell building lots even to its oldest employees. These policies forced the miners to rent company houses, which the Rev. Eugene S. Gaddis, who was in charge of social work for the CFI, described as "hovels, shacks, and dugouts that are unfit for the habitation of human beings and are little removed from the pigsty make of dwellings." [8]

Within these settlements, unsanitary conditions easily spread disease. In 1912–13 alone, 151 persons contracted typhoid. Seepage water "with a distinctively dead-rat-essence," reported a physician quoted by Dr. Gaddis, was supplied to three camps "because it was cheaper than to tap the main pipe line." This doctor noted that for more than a year a cesspool a few feet from a company store overflowed into the main street. When he reported "this Stygian situation and others almost as offensive" to the firm's medical department, they warned him to take care, "or you will step on some one's toes." If a workman protested these conditions too vigorously, he risked the simultaneous loss of his job, his dwelling, and his right to remain in the community.[9]

This nonbenevolent despotism even extended to mundane commercial affairs. Until a law forbade the practice, CFI paid wages in a scrip valid only in company stores. Even at the time of the hearings, these establishments were still handing out change in this substitute currency. Employees courted the displeasure of management if they did not patronize such shops. Indeed, one tradesman threatened a miner's wife with her husband's dismissal unless he received her business. This compulsory patronage enabled the stores to charge prices high enough to earn them 20 percent per year on their capital.[10]

CFI also exercised strong control over education, religion, and intellectual freedom. Mine superintendents and company officers dictated the selection of school teachers and dismissed those to whom they objected. No one could erect a church building without CFI permission. J. F. Welborn, president of the company, considered it management's prerogative to fire ministers who opposed the firm or who exhibited "socialistic tendencies." A Commission inspector discovered that the firm censored movies, books, and magazines. It proscribed not only anti-capitalist literature but such works as Darwin's *Origin of the Species* and *The Rubaiyat of Omar Khayyam*. "We wish to protect our people from erroneous ideas," a company spokesman declared.[11]

Commission hearings also revealed the extent of CFI's political influence in Colorado. In a letter to Rockefeller's private secretary, quoted by Walsh, Executive Board Chairman L. M. Bowers had stated that in years past the company had been "a mighty power in the entire State." "When I came here," Bowers had written, "it was said that the C. F. & I. Co. voted every man and woman in the employ, without any regard to their being naturalized or not; and even their mules, it used to be remarked, were registered, if they were fortunate enough to possess names." Walsh also quoted from a speech delivered by Judge Jesse G. Northcutt, who had charged that management hand-picked delegates to state nominating conventions. These men then selected candidates, Northcutt had asserted, "not with a view to their fitness, not with a view to their ability to discharge their duties, not with a view to their integrity, but 'Are they satisfactory to the company?' " "If you don't like it," Northcutt had declared, "you will have to take it."

Both Bowers and Northcutt (now a CFI attorney) claimed that the company had since greatly curtailed its political activities. Northcutt told the Commission that in 1912 President Welborn had taken "some pretty drastic action in directing his superintendents and managing officers to be free from any inference of participation in politics." "Since I came here," Bowers had assured Rockefeller's secretary, "not a nickel has been paid to any politician or political party." [12]

Under cross-examination, however, Bowers admitted that in the 1914 gubernatorial campaign, the coal operators had dispatched 150 men into the wards to campaign for a Prohibition amendment to the state constitution. Had not management used "the prohibition sentiment that was strong in the State," Walsh asked, in order to gain acceptance of a "law and order platform" designed "to aid in the ruthless prosecution of the strikers and the union officers?" "It was all interlocked together," acknowledged Bowers.[13]

A Department of Labor study further revealed that in this same year CFI election precincts had been deliberately gerrymandered to coincide with company property. In addition, all polling places were located on CFI land, and registration lists were hidden in private offices in its buildings. Colorado's Supreme Court uncovered so much evidence of illegality and fraud that it threw all returns from these precincts out of the election count.[14]

A State Senate investigation in 1913 unveiled additional unorthodox electioneering practices. Republican leaders in Trinidad, Colorado, had forced some 100 prostitutes to donate $6 or $7 a month to the party in order to be permitted to practice their profession. On Election Day uniformed police hauled the women to polling places and "assisted them" in marking their ballots. The Colorado Senate concluded, "We express the hope that in no other place in the United States could be found a condition so degraded, so corrupt or so infamous as this." [15]

Under cross-examination Bowers also admitted that CFI dominated the election of judges and sheriffs and through them governed the selection of jurors. For years one man, regarded by workers as a corrupt political boss, had served as sheriff of Huerfano County. Many of his extensive realty and saloon holdings eventually connected with Colorado Fuel and Iron. This man conceded that on a number of occasions he had appointed jurors who could not even speak English. "I ask you, Mr. Bowers," Commissioner O'Connell inquired, "if you think a poor, humble miner . . . has any chance of getting justice in a situation of that kind?" Replied Bowers, "Why, no; no one need to ask me that." [16]

Political rule by management directly affected the safety and lives of workmen. A state inspector pointed out to the commissioners that Colorado had a mine death rate twice as high as any other state in the nation. Yet of 90 accident cases, during a ten-year period preceding this investigation, coroner's juries in Huerfano County blamed 89 on the mine laborers and only one on the operators. Company superintendents almost invariably worked with the coroner when he picked his jurors. In most instances no one ever took a deposition from either the injured man, if still alive, or his family.[17]

These intolerable conditions provoked union activity. Since 1900 UMW had sparked a series of membership campaigns and strikes, but each time management opposition smashed them. Now in 1913 the union opened up its biggest push in history. Crack national organizers Frank Hayes and John Lawson went to Colorado to spur a recruiting drive. By August enrollment had so expanded that the labor chiefs found it difficult to restrain their rank and file from an immediate walkout. UMW officials, however, first tried to win their goals at the bargaining table.[18]

The union demanded an eight-hour day, enforcement of safety regulations, removal of armed guards, and abolition of company scrip. Miners also asked for the right to elect their own checkweighmen to supervise the weighing of coal produced by each worker, the right to trade at stores of their own choosing, and the right to select their own boarding houses. Colorado statutes, unionists pointed out, already guaranteed all the foregoing rights, but the operators had persistently ignored or evaded the law. In addition, the union pressed for a 10 percent increase in wages and recognition of the United Mine Workers. Nine other coal-mining states had already recognized their organization, its officers pleaded. "Why oppose us here, spending millions of dollars in an industrial conflict for no good purpose?" [19]

Despite conciliation efforts by both UMW and Colorado's governor, the operators flatly refused to discuss the issues. Correspondence later unearthed by the Commission disclosed that CFI, whose lead the smaller companies followed, realized that just a single noncommittal conference could have averted a strike. Chairman Bowers, however, felt that even one such meeting would have allowed UMW to boast that it had gained recognition. Then, Bowers asserted, "disreputable agitators, socialists, and anarchists" would take over the company. John C. Osgood, head of the Victor-American Fuel Company, backed up these executives. An individual miner, he argued, did not need a union to guard his interests. If he did not like it in Colorado, he could always go elsewhere.[20]

At the end of September, 1913, with no compromise in sight, from 40 to 100 percent of the workers in each of the various mines left their jobs. Up to 10,000 laborers and their families packed their meager belongings onto carts and headed down the canyons during a drenching storm of snow and sleet. Striking employees could not remain in company-owned houses on company-owned property. In camps which the union provided, whole families now prepared to live in pits dug in the ground and covered only by canvas tents. "No more eloquent proof," the Commission's Colorado report noted, "could be given of the intense discontent of the miners and their families, and of their determination to endure any hardship rather than remain at work under existing conditions." [21]

3

Soon after the start of the strike, tension quickly mounted. Trinidad, a major mining center, bristled with armed men. CFI induced the sheriff to recruit large numbers of guards and deputies from outside the state; the company armed them and paid their salaries. At the hearings, a county sheriff admitted that he had made no attempt to check on the character or background of those whom he hired. For all he knew, some "may have been red-handed murderers fresh from the scenes of their crimes." A representative of the governor urged that the state disarm every guard and every man, woman, and child. "If something was not done and done quickly," he warned, "there would be an outbreak there that would be disastrous." [22]

Strike tactics soon resembled preparations for war. Colorado Fuel and Iron deployed its troops in trenches adjacent to mining properties and equipped them with huge searchlights and machine guns. The company also provided an armored automobile, which strikers quickly christened the "Death Special." Over a two-year span CFI brought more than $30,000 worth of arms and ammunition into the strike district. Many workmen had already obtained revolvers and shotguns clandestinely; now the union decided to buy weapons openly. Miners stored a good many of their armaments at spots where they knew strikebreakers would have to pass.[23]

Violence erupted almost immediately and grew in intensity. First a company detective and a union organizer lost their lives in separate shootings. Then, when mine guards and strikers clashed at Forbes tent colony, the "Death Special" roared into the crowd and opened fire. Its machine-gun spray killed one laborer and drove nine bullets into the leg of a small boy. He tried to scramble away, but every movement invited more missiles; the lad lay wounded on the ground for several hours during a rainstorm. A few days later, at Walsenburg, CFI troops broke up a strikers' mass meeting and killed three more workers. Vengeful miners then slew four company men at Laveta and evened up the score.[24]

A large tent colony at Ludlow quickly became a site of chronic disorder. When strikers attacked a detail of company police, the guards retreated to a canyon, where they awaited reinforcements. All during that night more than 100 strikers poured a deadly stream of bullets into the depression; on the next morning another battalion of laborers continued this onslaught. In order to rescue the trapped patrol, Trinidad's sheriff ordered a force of machine-gun-equipped men in steel boxcars to Ludlow. Terrified miners thought that this armored caravan intended to shoot up the entire colony.

They rushed to positions all along the tracks and blasted away at the oncoming vehicles. Their fire fatally wounded the engineer and compelled the train to reverse its course. Fighting ceased when the guards returned on foot to complete their mission.[25]

This savagery continued until Governor Ammons called out the National Guard. He enjoined them to protect all property and all those at work. In a highly important directive, Ammons specifically ordered that under no circumstances should National Guardsmen help to install strikebreakers. He further decreed the immediate disarmament of both sides. Under command of Adjutant General John Chase, the militia made ready to occupy a line about 120 miles long through Las Animas and Huerfano counties.[26]

On October 28, 1913, Colorado's National Guard executed the governor's orders. "I found . . . a condition of turmoil and terror," Chase reported, "each side welcoming the arrival of the troops." As the militia marched in, miners greeted them with cheers, brass bands, and parades. Chase's troops collected about 2,000 weapons and estimated that about three-fourths of them came from company guards. Later, militia leaders asserted that strikers had turned over only a small portion of their own arsenal.[27]

So long as Governor Ammons prevented the troops from aiding strikebreakers, the troubled community remained at peace. Then Ammons took a fateful step. He announced that in his original instructions he had gone beyond the law. A refusal to protect strikebreakers constituted, he explained, an interference with production. Colorado's chief executive, although he did not formally declare martial law, withdrew his initial orders and, in effect, placed the strike zone completely under the power of General Chase.[28]

This act destroyed the peace of Colorado. "From that time things went from bad to worse," former U.S. Senator Thomas M. Patterson, a Colorado Democrat, told the Commission. "Crimination and recrimination, the operators insisting that all violence was committed by the miners, and the miners insisting that there was ample provocation for whatever violence they resorted to." Many now suffered loss of their civil liberties. A congressional committee, appointed to investigate charges against the militia, discovered people "thrown into foul and miserable cells and kept there for days without any opportunity to prove their innocence." National Guard officers admitted that they apprehended men without warrants but claimed that they possessed this privilege, since civilian government had collapsed.[29]

A woman in her eighties, however, created the greatest stir over civil liberties. Mary Jones, affectionately known as "Mother Jones" throughout the labor world, decided to visit the miners. For many years she had participated as a UMW organizer in some of the nation's most bitter labor wars. "A little, trim, tight-waisted old lady with neat correct features, soft white hair and kind blue eyes," one writer observed, "she seemed a grandmotherly old person mild as a new born kitten." [30] But Mother Jones displayed "an element of eternal anger" in her eyes and "a quality adamant" in her close-set lips. "I have never had the ballot," she cried, "but I have raised hell anyhow, and I have made the nation know that I am alive and on the ground." Famous as an orator for over a generation, the "Joan of Arc of Labor," as one newspaper called her, now headed for Colorado.[31]

But Mother Jones' fame had preceded her. As soon as she arrived in Trinidad in January, 1914, militiamen deported her back to Denver. Undaunted, the elderly woman ventured forth again a week later. This time Guardsmen pulled her off the train and held Mother Jones incommunicado at a hospital for nine weeks. But the intrepid old lady would not give up; she tried again in March. This time troops invaded her railroad car, roused her from sleep, and dumped her in what George P. West's *Report on the Colorado Strike* described as "an insanitary and rat-infested cell." There she languished for twenty-six days.[32]

Not once during these apprehensions had the military fulfilled the usual requirements of civil law. Guardsmen never possessed a warrant for Mother Jones' arrest, nor was a writ of habeas corpus ever issued to release her from imprisonment. This elderly female apparently terrified a general who commanded hundreds of armed men. "She was a person who was dangerous to the peace of the community," claimed Chase, ". . . civil authorities, in my judgment, were not capable of handling the case." James H. Brewster, Professor of Law at the University of Colorado, took a different view: "The arrest of Mother Jones without warrant, without any suspicion of crime, was one of the greatest outrages upon civilized American jurisprudence that has been perpetrated." [33]

A special convention of the Colorado State Federation of Labor protested the National Guard's anti-striker tactics. In response to a suggestion by Governor Ammons, they assigned a committee, headed by Brewster, to study conditions under military rule. This group issued a blistering document. "Unprotected women," they charged, "have been roused from sleep by militiamen attempting to enter their homes at night." Many Guardsmen, their statement alleged, participated in robberies, lootings, and holdups. Troops not only shielded scabs but endeavored by deception and threat to induce strikers to return to work. The report demanded Chase's resignation as well as the discharge of a number of officers.[34]

Although this union account could not be accepted as impartial, later testimony before the Commission verified many of its accusations. A militia captain conceded that the Guard's personnel had degenerated badly. Most of the original members had completed their tour of duty, and their replacements sprang from less desirable elements of society. Local courts had convicted five Guardsmen of burglary. One of these men held a dishonorable discharge from the Army and had served time at Leavenworth; another had forged his military separation papers. Further Commission findings disclosed that a good number of these new troops had entered the state as company mine guards. President Welborn of CFI admitted that his firm billeted the troops on company property, furnished them company supplies from a company store, and advanced them up to $80,000 in certificates of indebtedness.[35]

4

All previous violence between laborers and militiamen seemed but a prelude to the horrors of the Ludlow massacre. A major tent colony, Ludlow stood at a point where the largest coal-producing mines in Colorado converged. Two roads led from the mines to the tracks of the Colorado Southern Railroad, the major artery between Trinidad and Denver. Scabs had to disembark at this junction close to the colony, which sheltered some 900 to 1,200 strike sympathizers. Militia had raided the camp four times; on each occasion worker resentment deepened.[36]

On April 20, 1914, the Ludlow volcano erupted. For many days laborers had been hearing rumors that the militia planned another attack, while National Guardsmen strongly suspected an onslaught by the miners. On the morning of April 20, Major Edward J. Boughton ordered a detachment of troops equipped with a machine gun to Water Tank Hill, which overlooked the entire colony and railway junction. Boughton informed the Commission that he had then spied a large contingent of Greek strikers, fully armed, dashing toward protected positions in a railroad cut. At the same time he noticed streams of women and children scurrying toward an arroyo about 10 to 20 feet deep at the rear of the colony. Convinced that these movements presaged an assault, Boughton detonated two bombs as a warning signal to his other troops at more distant posts. Strikers at the hearing claimed that they had not contemplated any aggression but that once they spotted the machine gun and heard the bombs, they prepared for a siege.[37]

No one agreed as to who triggered the first shot, but within a few moments both sides had opened fire. Boughton now determined to advance on the Greeks within the railroad cut. A rifle battle raged all afternoon, while militiamen also blasted the miners' stronghold with machine gun fire. Guardsmen charged the enemy lines four times and on one retreat had to leave behind a dying soldier in no man's land. Soon afterward strikers launched a counterattack, which reached the position of the injured man. When Boughton's troops finally dislodged the strikers late in the afternoon, they swore that the workers had brutally mutilated their comrade. "His face," an officer testified, was "beat in with the butts of guns." "One eye was out of his head; one of the men shoved it back in with his fingers. His body had been riddled with bullets." [38]

Colorado's militia captured a number of Greeks, including their leader, Louis Tikas.* A graduate of Athens University, Tikas had

---

* Laborers of Greek origin accounted for only a small fraction of the working population. A cross section of some 14,000 workers showed that the English and Italians predominated, with Slavs, Austrians, and Mexicans represented in smaller numbers. (George Creel, "Poisoners of Public Opinion," *Harper's Weekly*, LIX [Nov. 14, 1914], 465.)

earned the respect even of Major Boughton, who considered the immigrant "a restraining influence among his own people." But now this striker and Lieutenant Karl E. Linderfelt, who had led the final charge, engaged in a heated argument. "He called me a name that no man will take," Linderfelt attested. Enraged, the officer grabbed his Springfield rifle and smashed its butt over Tikas' head. Immediately afterward, according to this lieutenant, a wild confusion broke out and a number of prisoners tried to escape. Guardsmen quickly shot and killed them. When troops carted the bodies away on the "dead wagon," Linderfelt noted with astonishment that Tikas lay among them—a bullet in his back.[39]

Even before this incident, Lieutenant Linderfelt, a professional soldier of many campaigns, had acquired a reputation as the most hated of the National Guard officers. According to a witness, once while on horseback the Lieutenant had bellowed at some strikers, "I am Jesus Christ, and my men on horses are Jesus Christs, and we have got to be obeyed." From that time on workers generally referred to him as "Jesus Christ Linderfelt." At the hearing the officer emphasized his conviction that the miners were in armed rebellion against proper authority. Any man guilty of such "revolt," Linderfelt declared, should be "tried for treason or sedition and sent to the penitentiary." [40]

For the next twelve hours a battle raged across the whole community. Miners concealed themselves in the arroyo at the rear of the colony or behind mounds of earth that encircled the camp. Some women and children had already fled, but others remained huddled in pits beneath their tents. These noncombatants now found themselves trapped in a deadly crossfire. One miner's wife, who had served as a nurse, pinned red crosses on her arms and chest and tried to render first aid out in the open. Militiamen "took it for to be a good target," she attested, "and shot at me as hard as they could. I started to run for protection, and one of the bullets took the heel off my shoe." [41]

A twelve-year-old boy turned his back to the firing and endeavored to caress his little sister. Suddenly, according to a witness, "the top of his head was blown off, and his brains were spattered over all the little children in front of him." His frantic mother rushed out of her tent. "For God's sake, come and help me," she screamed, "I have a dead boy in here." An affidavit presented to the Commission by Judge Ben Lindsey affirmed that a National Guardsmen retorted, "It is a damned pity that all you damned red-necked bitches were not killed." [42]

Militiamen now launched a direct frontal attack on the arroyo; they charged the trench in full battle cry. All at once, recalled Lieutenant Linderfelt, "there rose up the most awful wail I ever heard in my life." Three of the largest tents burst into flames; the sparks, some of which shot 50 feet into the air, threatened to ignite other canvas tops. "My God," a captain shouted, "there are women and children in there!" Those who rushed to the rescue discovered that the victims feared the soldiers as much as the blaze. Some of them thought, Linderfelt declared, "they were going to be murdered by us." [43]

Fire now swept through the colony with catastrophic speed. One mother attempted to remove her three youngsters from a burning tent, but Guardsmen harassed her. "They hollered at me to get out of the way," she testified, "and they were shooting at me." With her children she jumped into another tent, but that too was ignited. Heavy black smoke choked and blinded her until she lost consciousness. The woman did not revive until the next morning. For nine days she was confined to bed, seized by pneumonia. Only when she regained strength could friends find the heart to tell her that all three of her children had burned to death. By the time the fire subsided, the charred corpses of two women and eleven young children lay beneath Ludlow's ruins.[44]

In a frank report, a military commission which investigated this disaster blamed the troops for spreading the blaze. "We find that the tents were not all of them destroyed by accidental fire," they declared. "Men and soldiers swarmed into the colony, and deliberately assisted the conflagration. . . . Beyond a doubt it was seen to intentionally that the fire should destroy the whole of the colony." Examination disclosed that "men and soldiers seized and took from the tents whatever appealed to their fancy . . . clothes, bedding, articles of jewelry, bicycles, tools, and utensils." "So deliberately [sic] was this burning and looting," the military commission stated, "that cans of oil found in the tents were poured upon them and the tents lit with matches." [45]

Such an admission seems remarkable in view of this board's methods. Only officers conducted the probe; they held all their hearings in secret and did not take testimony from a single striker or union member. Civilians who had recently joined the militia and were unaccustomed to military discipline committed this vandalism, they alleged, not National Guard regulars. They did not deny, however, that the military possessed complete jurisdiction over all these men. Cross-examination laid bare the fact that most of the troops at Ludlow had been employees of CFI. Even Major Boughton, who directly commanded these troops, enjoyed an annual retainer as legal adviser to the Colorado Mine Owners' Association.[46]

After Ludlow, one observer exclaimed, "the strikers went mad!" State Federation of Labor officials summoned every miner in Colorado to arms. "Organize the men in your community in companies of volunteers," they cried, "to protect the workers of Colorado against the murder and cremation of men, women, and children." Gather up all your weapons and ammunition, union chiefs exhorted, and keep all companies in readiness. "The State is furnishing us no protection and we must protect ourselves, our wives, and children from these murderous assassins." [47]

Bent on vengeance, the workers now waged open war. First they seized possession of Ludlow and Trinidad. Then they pounced upon mine after mine in rampaging assaults which ranged 250 miles from their base. One battalion stormed and captured Empire mine, killed three guards, and left the property in ashes. A few days later some 300 beseiged Walsen and McNally mines. After a fifty-hour gun battle, wrathful laborers dynamited the property. At Forbes, hundreds swarmed into hills and discharged terrific fusillades into the canyon below. They killed nine strikebreakers and policemen. Afterward these marauders set company buildings afire and laid waste CFI holdings 30 miles around. Similar armed bands burned, pillaged, and desolated company resources at Delagua, Aguilar, Hastings, and Black Hills.[48]

Anarchy ruled in Colorado. For ten days a workers' army which controlled vast areas of territory clashed with state and company forces. Exactly as in war, each belligerent issued communiqués, reported casualties, and boasted of victories. Newspapers discussed grand strategy, exulted in triumphs of their own side, and belittled claims of the enemy. Governor Ammons capitulated. He appealed to President Wilson for the U.S. Army to put down "open insurrection against the State." On April 28, 1914, several regiments of federal troops marched in to quell Colorado's civil war. If they had not arrived, a Commission researcher noted, "one side or the other would have been annihilated." [49]

5

Ludlow's horror jolted America and focused national attention on the Commission's hearings. For two weeks in Denver, the investigators queried those directly on the Colorado scene. Company executives, union leaders, politicians, and strikers unfolded their story of this war. Then the Commission traveled eastward to question the representative of Colorado's largest mining company—John D. Rockefeller, Jr.*

On January 27, 1915, the heir to America's greatest fortune arrived on time for his first encounter with the federal probers. He walked into a chamber that once had served as the Board of Estimate Room in the New York City Hall. Its airy colonial lines, crystal chandeliers, and pewlike seats spoke of an age far removed and quite indifferent to the harsh problems of the twentieth century. Yet high on a canopied dais sat the U.S. Commission on Industrial

---

* Originally the Commission had scheduled this New York hearing for a general investigation of large philanthropic institutions, but under Walsh's direction this quickly merged into a further study of the Colorado strike. Nevertheless, in the previous week commissioners had queried, among others, J. P. Morgan, Daniel Guggenheim, and Andrew Carnegie. During one session Carnegie distinguished himself as the only man ever to take control of a meeting away from Chairman Walsh. "Merry Andrew" turned his back on the commissioners and delivered a flamboyant address on his travels, women suffrage, and the superiority of the fair sex—all to the delight of a predominantly feminist audience. It was Carnegie's last public appearance. Although he lived for some time afterward, ill health prevented the industrialist from further sallies into the limelight. (*Testimony*, IX, 8286; Hendrick, *Life of Andrew Carnegie*, II, 359-62; Allen, "Suggestions Regarding Foundations. . . ," *Survey*, XXXIII [Feb. 27, 1915], 587.)

Relations. An audience chiefly of Single-Taxers, Socialists, anarchists, AFL members, and IWWs glared at the young millionaire. To peer into their eyes, one writer observed, "was like looking into the barrels of rows of guns." [50]

Apparently oblivious to this hostile atmosphere, Rockefeller maintained complete self-composure and calmly took his seat. Then he spotted Mother Jones. In a move which startled everyone, the millionaire stood up, reached across the table, and shook her hand. "I wish that you would come down to my office at your convenience," he said. "There are so many things on which you can enlighten me." Flustered, the elderly lady mumbled her acceptance. When she had regained her composure, Mother Jones also extended an invitation. "I want you to come out to Colorado with me and see the things I have seen," she told him. "I am sure what you see will make you do things which will make you one of the country's greatest men." Rockefeller smiled. "I am afraid you are inclined to throw compliments." "Oh, no," Mother Jones snapped, "I am more inclined to throw bricks." [51]

Rockefeller testified that in his capacity as a director of Colorado Fuel and Iron he enjoyed only limited responsibility. Directors did not shape a firm's managerial policies, he insisted; they concentrated almost exclusively on its financial affairs. For this reason he denied that he had influenced CFI's attitude toward labor. Charges that he exercised absolute control over Colorado's entire coal industry were, in his words, "abhorrent to me personally" and "contrary to the spirit of my whole purpose and training." [52]

Rockefeller insisted that he was not opposed to trade unions. Like capital, labor had a right to combine in order to advance its legitimate interests. If worker organizations promoted collective bargaining to obtain higher wages and better conditions, he announced, "I favor them most heartily." Colorado Fuel and Iron's refusal to recognize UMW represented only the judgment of the company's officials. They set their own course, he repeated, "without any consultation or communication with me. . . . I had no knowledge of their decision until after the strike had been declared." [53]

When Chairman Walsh endeavored to pin Rockefeller down to specific facts, the young man pleaded almost total ignorance. Although his family controlled 40 percent of the stock, the tycoon admitted that he had not visited the company in ten years. He did not know how many of the employees worked twelve hours a day or seven days a week, he could not tell whether such hours in a CFI steel mill constituted a hardship, and he possessed no knowledge about the character of blast furnace work or its physical effects on laborers. In addition, the millionaire disclaimed any familiarity with CFI's policies toward home ownership, rent charges, or company stores. Questioned if he knew that his firm retained a pool of armed men ready for transport across state borders and that it employed private detectives to pose as laborers, Rockefeller once more professed ignorance. "What are the names of the counties in which your mines are located?" Frank Walsh asked. "I could not tell you," replied the industrialist.[54]

Events in Colorado, however, had pricked the millionaire's conscience. He now realized that "there was something fundamentally wrong" in a situation which had spawned such bitterness and human suffering. "I have no desire to defend any conditions that are justly subject to criticism," he said. "I only ask that the responsibility for them be apportioned fairly." Rockefeller announced repentantly that his views on a director's moral duties had changed substantially. "You are like the church says, you are 'growing in grace,'" commented Commissioner Garretson. "I hope so," Rockefeller replied. As this poised and ostensibly sincere young man completed his testimony, even the predominantly radical audience broke out in applause.[55]

Rockefeller had scored a smash hit. "Mr. Rockefeller is not the kind of man the laboring men thought he was," observed Commissioner and Railroad Brotherhood Chief Garretson. The New York Times commended this youthful industrialist, who during the long hearing had "never wavered from his entire self-possession and courteous humor." Even the Socialist Masses sprinkled a few adjectives of praise among its barbs. It considered the heir "apparently frank," "gentle," and "Christianish," although a "master of evasion." For years Mrs. Harriman had considered Rockefeller "a psalm-singing, cold-blooded capitalist," but now she found him "intensely human."[56]

An alliance between Mother Jones and the millionaire seemed imminent. "I don't hold the boy responsible," she said. "When I have a good motherly talk with him I believe I can help him take another view of the situation among his miners out west." After their chat, Rockefeller announced, "I find we are in full accord upon most of the subjects in which we are mutually interested." He then invited other UMW officials to his office and praised them all as "clean cut fellows." Finally the young scion proclaimed that he had determined to visit Colorado in the near future. "We have been misrepresenting him terribly," lamented Mother Jones, "and I as much as anybody else." [57]

Rockefeller charmed almost everyone—except Frank Walsh. In speech after speech the Chairman tore into Rockefeller and his entire financial empire. Both men engaged in a running debate, which terminated when each called the other a liar. Newspapers, especially in New York, jumped on Walsh's back. A New York *Times* editorial blasted the Chairman's "illogical and absurd utterances," while the *Tribune* charged that he had debased the work of the Commission. "It is an oddity of our national system," exclaimed the *Sun*, "that any man whose notions are at once so loose and violent should hold a prominent place in government." [58] These attacks bothered Walsh not at all. "I am glad you understand how thoroughly I enjoyed my New York 'panning,'" he told a friend. "In fact I am busy at the present moment devising ways other than the old fashioned standard one for 'making the wildcat wild.'" [59]

Walsh had good reason for confidence. For some months Commission researchers had collected an ever-increasing file of letters from Rockefeller, Bowers, Welborn, and members of the millionaire's staff. Carefully and with mounting eagerness, Walsh and his assistants analyzed the contents. Each new batch of correspondence only increased their excitement. Finally they agreed that the sensational nature of some of this material cried out for additional hearings. Frank Walsh now prepared for the most dramatic session in the history of the Commission.[60]

If the previous hearing in New York closed in optimism, those now in Washington opened in tension. On a hot day, in a room crowded almost to suffocation, Rockefeller silently awaited his turn. He looked "rather lonesome," one newsman thought, "as most of those present were labor representatives." Dr. Constantin Dumba, the Ambassador from Austro-Hungary, on whose frontier Italian troops were massed, slipped into the chamber and attempted to engage the millionaire in conversation. Dumba wanted to persuade the industrialist to provide compensation for widows and orphans of Austro-Hungarian nationals killed at Ludlow. Rockefeller nodded to the diplomat but kept his eyes fixed on the witnesses. Walsh began the interrogation, according to one correspondent, "with apparent impetuosity," his manner "almost savage." "Mr. Walsh," he stated, "showed considerable feeling and gave the impression that he was personally hostile to Mr. Rockefeller. . . . Mr. Rockefeller appeared to realize that Chairman Walsh intended to handle him roughly." [61]

As in New York, the young heir once again proclaimed his ignorance of Colorado strike matters and professed his belief in collective bargaining. Now Walsh drew upon correspondence that his staffers had unearthed. At the very beginning of the strike, Walsh pointed out, Executive Board Chairman Bowers had written letters to Rockefeller and to the heir's attorney which outlined in detail the causes and major events of the altercation. Bowers told Rockefeller that the company refused to recognize UMW and would stick by its guns "until our bones were bleached as white as chalk in these Rocky Mountains." Then, Commissioner Walsh indicated, Rockefeller himself had responded, "We feel that what you have done is right and fair and that the position which you have taken in regard to the unionizing of the mines is in the interest of the employees of the company." "Whatever the outcome may be," the industrialist assured Bowers, "we will stand by you to the end." [62]

Rockefeller had insisted that he exerted no influence on his own or the other Colorado coal companies. Walsh now produced material to the contrary. "I want to express the appreciation of Mr. Welborn and myself," Bowers had informed Rockefeller, "together with that of several coal operators who have seen your letter, for the stand you have taken in supporting us in fighting this unjust, uncalled-for, and iniquitous strike." With no later objection from his director, Bowers decried mediation efforts by Secretary of Labor

William B. Wilson. Government had surely degenerated, the CFI president raged, when it permitted such men "together with the cheap college professors and still cheaper writers in muckraking magazines, supplemented by a lot of milk-and-water preachers" to defame America's businessmen. When asked by Walsh if he concurred with these sentiments, Rockefeller declined to comment except to describe Bowers' language as "rather picturesque." [63]

During the strike, Governor Ammons had rescinded his decree which had prevented militia from aiding strikebreakers. This crucial move signaled a renewal of bloodshed in Colorado. In public the state administrator explained his decision on grounds that he had to comply with requirements of the law. Walsh now disclosed that CFI with Rockefeller's complete sanction had forced the governor's hand. Bowers informed Rockefeller that he had mobilized all the bankers, the Chamber of Commerce, the real estate exchange, and fourteen editors of the most important state newspapers to intimidate "our little cowboy governor." "There probably has never been such pressure brought to bear upon any governor of this State," the Board Chairman wrote. "We used every possible weapon to drive him into action." In direct answer to this communication, Rockefeller expressed his own delight and that of his father, who "has followed the events of the past few months . . . with unusual interest and satisfaction." [64]

Nor had the younger Rockefeller limited himself to appraising the actions of his subordinates. On one occasion, Labor Secretary William B. Wilson had pleaded with the operators to hold at least one informal talk with the strike leaders. Rockefeller personally slammed the door. CFI's inflexible stand, he wired the Cabinet officer, "meets with our cordial approval, and we shall support them to the end." A jubilant Bowers reported to the tycoon that he had shown a copy of this telegram to every member of the company's executive board. Colorado management now felt quite free to spurn even a personal request from President Wilson, who had suggested arbitration. They had not misplaced their confidence. Blessings quickly flowed from New York. "You are fighting a good fight," Rockefeller proclaimed. [65]

As the strike progressed Rockefeller advanced ever more directly into the fray. Out of personal funds the young millionaire hired

Ivy L. Lee, public relations expert for the Pennsylvania Railroad, to conduct a nationwide pro-management publicity campaign. Under Rockefeller's guidance, Lee flooded the country with pamphlets and newspaper advertisements issued under the name of the Coal Mine Operators Committee. One of these bulletins insinuated that UMW had paid its leaders huge salaries for only a few weeks' activity. Months later Lee published a correction which acknowledged that the previous figures represented a yearly compensation. Company officials purposely kept the true author's name secret. Even at the Denver hearings, CFI Chairman Welborn flatly refused to reveal his identity.[66]

Rockefeller, the Commission divulged, not only sponsored Lee's activities but eagerly furnished him clippings, articles, and ideas to use as propaganda. A piece by a New York University professor, John J. Stevenson, particularly impressed the tycoon. "Unskilled labor is merely animated machinery for rough work and adds very little value to the final product," this economist maintained. "One E. H. Harriman is of more lasting service to a nation than would be 1,000,000 of unskilled laborers, without a Harriman they would be a menace." Then the Professor condemned all forms of organized labor. Union principles he damned as "no better than those of the India Thugs, who preached robbery and murder in the name of the Goddess Cali." The millionaire, who had endorsed collective bargaining while on a public witness stand, Walsh disclosed, had privately acclaimed this tract as "one of the soundest, clearest, most forcible pronouncements on this subject I have ever read." Indeed, Rockefeller zealously urged Lee to reprint the essay in its entirety.[67]

Walsh then laid bare evidence that he and his researchers had considered of "tremendous significance." Documents in the Chairman's possession clearly showed that Rockefeller personally collaborated with Lee in ghostwriting a letter for Governor Ammons to send to President Wilson. This communication presented a completely pro-company view of the struggle and damned the strikers. Rockefeller himself had instructed Lee on several points which he desired to include in the letter. Now the millionaire explained his action on the grounds that Major Boughton had first suggested the idea to Lee. Nevertheless, Walsh and his associates believed it of "national importance" that Rockefeller so ruled Colorado that he deemed it possible to use the governor as his mouthpiece in official correspondence with the President of the United States.[68]

Hour after hour, day after day, the Chairman kept up this relentless cross-examination. Walsh's voice barked and rasped as he tore into his witness. "Rockefeller's face grew whiter and whiter until it was ashy. His features seemed to sink back into the contours of his face," remarked one spectator. "The perspiration poured down his cheeks. . . . He looked wrung and writhing." "In spite of my bitterness," George Creel reflected, "I could not help feeling sorry for the man as he sweated under Frank's merciless questioning." [69]

Nothing could stop Walsh. Time and time again, the room rang with Rockefeller's protests: "I object to the form of the question," "I resent the imputation," "I repudiate utterly the implied motive." [70] In executive session, Mrs. Harriman and Weinstock issued a joint complaint against the Chairman's severity. But Frank Walsh refused to budge.* At the next public session, he announced that he would run this examination in his own way regardless of anyone's objections. Mrs. Harriman sat in her place, a newspaperman recorded, "with flushed cheeks and compressed lips and fanned herself with a vigor that was not altogether due to the weather." Frank Walsh "does not court the Truth," one writer quipped, "he goes after it with a rapid fire gun." [71]

6

Last of its public hearings, the Commission's sensational investigation of Rockefeller concluded in a blaze of publicity.† News-

---

* Although she strongly disagreed with Walsh's cross-examination methods, Mrs. Harriman felt that were it not for the Commission, Rockefeller "might never have gotten close to the terrible drama for which, because he was Capital, he was in the last analysis responsible." Probably with this hearing partly in mind, however, she and Commons later criticized the Walsh-Manly *Final Report* as "directed to making a few individuals scapegoats." (Harriman, *From Pinafores to Politics*, pp. 144-45, contains first quotation; USCIR, *Final Report*, p. 307, contains second quotation.)

†After the Rockefeller sessions the Commission met again for two days. It listened to testimony on labor conditions in Puerto Rico and heard from a few witnesses left over from an earlier investigation of labor and the law. (*Testimony*, XI, 10837-927, 11029-224.)

papers throughout the country covered the sessions extensively and commented upon them editorially. Even the outbreak of World War I in Europe could not drive the Commission off the front pages. Every publication, Walsh rejoiced, was "soaking it up." He brushed off adverse criticism so long as the factual story reached the public. "I believe, after all, " he asserted, "that the daily newspaper is the great avenue of information. The masses do not take time to read anything else." [72]

Most anti-Commission papers, chiefly conservative journals, heaped abuse on Walsh's head for his "bullying" tactics. In Detroit the *Free Press* speculated that "the Rockefellers will gain more than they will lose by the insensate perversion of office that has been displayed by their assailants." Walsh never tried to find the facts, complained the Colorado *News*. He never considered the possibility that miners might have caused the bloodshed but gleefully accepted all unsupported anticompany charges as fact. *Nation* reviled Walsh's methods as "offensive and absurd"; it found him guilty of "irresponsible and preposterous badgering." [73]

Many critics cried out for Walsh's scalp. The Philadelphia *Ledger* demanded the Chairman's removal because he had become a public scandal, who had made a "howling farce of the inquiries." "Can it be," asked the Washington *Post*, "Mr. Walsh feeds solely upon rancor and hate?" The "career of this commission," declared the *Free Press* of Philadelphia, "should be a warning to Congress" against the unthinking appointment of such bodies. "We hope Mr. Wilson will undo the great mistake he made," prayed the New York *Herald*, "in letting this man loose upon the country." If the Chairman had his way, it predicted, "he would set afoot influences that would lay waste the industrial centers." [74]

Aside from radical and labor publications, most of the Commission's support sprang from the Middle West and from reformist magazines. A writer in the Cincinnati *Post* hailed the Chairman as "magnificent." America needed more men like Walsh, the Kansas City *Star* and the Sioux City *Tribune* agreed, whom even the wealth and power of Rockefeller could not awe. Commission research, *Harper's Weekly* emphasized, proved that Rockefeller had "lied." In spite of his "smoothness" and "sly hypocrisy," the millionaire could no longer dodge his responsibility for Colorado's horrors. *Survey* maintained that Commission evidence conclusively demonstrated that the industrialist "was in constant receipt of information from the strike zone . . . that he acted on it spontaneously and vigorously . . . sponsoring without qualification all the acts of the Colorado officers." "They said he [Walsh] was too rough on Rockefeller," asserted the Denver *Express*. "If Rockefeller was roughed a bit he got less than his due." [75]

Labor and radical journals elevated Walsh to the status of a national idol. The *Machinists' Monthly Journal* commended the Chairman because he had subjected Rockefeller to "the most searching cross-examination that any millionaire in the United States has ever had to undergo." Samuel Gompers of AFL wrote an article titled "Walsh, a Great Tribune." *Solidarity*, an IWW organ, placed a picture of Walsh on its front page and carried an essay by the Chairman on "My Impressions of the Witnesses and Their Testimony." Not to be outdone, the *Christian Socialist* printed an entire Frank P. Walsh number. "Every indictment brought against the Rockefellers," it announced, "has been proven out of the mouth of John D. Rockefeller, Jr." New York's Socialist *Call* extolled the hearing as "The Exposure of the Century." "The facts were there, clean-cut, glaring, monstrous," declared *Masses*. "They reduced his [Rockefeller's] general statements to an absurdity and an impertinence." Chairman Walsh, it then proclaimed, "has made the year 1915 significant in our political history." [76]

A clamor for the Commission leader's dismissal soon reached the White House. "Chairman Walsh's methods have set all Washington talking," the New York *Sun* noted, "and it is understood President Wilson and those close to him are far from pleased." Indeed, the *Masses* remarked, "President Wilson is said to be outraged." [77] Protestations, chiefly from businessmen's associations, flooded the Chief Executive's desk. The Commission was not intended to afford a forum in which those who advocate murder, assassination and anarchy might air their views without rebuke," one writer complained, "while law abiding citizens testifying before it are browbeaten and insulted." Another group branded Walsh as "one-sided and unfair," a man who deliberately set out to "palliate acts of anarchy; to extol and extenuate lawlessness." One irate citizen, who signed himself Commander in Chief of the Patriotic Legion and Army of Peace, rebuked the Chairman for "conduct unbecoming an officer and gentleman in his treatment of witnesses . . . and particularly in the cases of John D. Rockefeller, jr., . . . a high-toned Christian gentleman." [78]

A fear that the businessmen might influence Wilson inspired labor organizations all over the United States to bombard the White House with pro-Commission sentiments. Walsh had turned a searchlight "into the dark and hidden recesses of corporate mendacity," one letter from Denver certified. The Chicago Federation of Labor expressed its "unbounded admiration for the fearless manner in which he [Walsh] exposed and thus helped to defeat this Rockefeller conspiracy." Frank Walsh had demonstrated, another document proclaimed "that Organized Labor is not composed of a group of fanatics, and that Organized Labor has a right to exist." [79]

Right in the center of this broiling controversy, Chairman Walsh remained as buoyant as ever. "I am sure you will not think it boastful when I say that I turned the young man [Rockefeller] inside out," he wrote, "and left him without a single justification for anything that took place in Colorado." "Of course, to get at the truth," Walsh confided, "I had to get a little rough at times, which I did not hesitate to do, and I notice that all the comment of a critical nature against me, up to this time, has been that I did so handle him." * He scoffed at the charge that he lacked "judicial poise." "I consider that commodity," he told a reporter, " as a great bar to human progress." [80]

At one time, Research Director Charles McCarthy conjectured that the Colorado investigation "might be the best thing that ever happened to John D. Rockefeller, Jr." Now the young heir con-

---

* In his favorable biography of John D. Rockefeller, Jr., Raymond B. Fosdick termed the Commission hearings "a carnival of sensationalism" led by "the merciless Walsh." Nevertheless, Fosdick did not deny the accuracy of the facts which Walsh uncovered with respect to Rockefeller's actions during the strike. According to Fosdick, a close friend and adviser of the millionaire who eventually headed the Rockefeller Foundation, Rockefeller's lack of experience in industrial relations led him to rely too heavily on the biased information supplied him by Bowers and Welborn. Later, Fosdick claims, the millionaire broadened his ideas about labor and management. CFI maintained its company union, however, and refused to recognize the UMW until 1933. (See Fosdick, *John D. Rockefeller, Jr.*, pp. 143-87.)

fessed that he regarded the hearing as one of the most significant events of his life. It had inspired in him a new conception of "the kinship of humanity" and marked a sharp change in his attitude toward labor.[81] In September the millionaire visited his Colorado holdings, inspected mines, chatted with laborers, danced with their wives, and bounced their children on his knee.[82]

Now the "new" Rockefeller announced a bold project for his workers—the Colorado Industrial Plan. * This scheme promised and indeed accomplished significant improvements in housing, schooling, and recreation. It eliminated compulsory company stores and loosened CFI's iron grip on state and local politics. Rockefeller's design called for freely elected worker representatives to serve with management on standing committees concerned with working conditions, sanitation, and safety; it also furnished efficient grievance machinery. But nowhere did the proposal provide for recognition of the union or assent to the principle of collective bargaining.[83]

Organized labor greeted this proposition with universal antagonism. UMW Vice President Frank Hayes stigmatized it as "pure paternalism" and "benevolent feudalism." At their annual convention the mine workers stressed that only a strong independent union could protect workers' interests. Under Rockefeller's system, employee delegates remained totally dependent upon company good will.[84] In his *Report on the Colorado Strike,* Commission researcher George B. West concluded that Rockefeller's company still retained absolute power. CFI had granted concessions "in the spirit of men who give as a charity or a favor that which they had denied when demanded as a right." Mother Jones quickly grew disenchanted with Rockefeller. "You can't fool my boys," she declared, "they know that this kind of scheme is a hypocritical and dishonest pretense." [85]

But Mother Jones' "boys" capitulated—they had no other choice. Although President Wilson had forbidden importation of strike-

---

* This plan derived in large measure from W. L. Mackenzie King, former Minister of Labor and later Prime Minister of Canada, whom Rockefeller hired as director of the industrial relations department of the Rockefeller Foundation. (*Testimony,* VIII, 8783-49; Charles W. Mills to Seth Low, Oct. 23, 1915, Rockefeller to Low, March 29, 1916, box marked "Arbitration, Colorado Coal Strike, President's Commission," Low Papers.)

breakers, CFI obtained sufficient scabs to stay in operation. In the meantime, company prosecution of UMW officials continued unabated. When management rejected all the Chief Executive's peace offers, UMW knew it faced disaster. At Denver the union policy committee voted to end the strike. After fifteen months of starvation, bloodshed, and death, Colorado's workers grasped at the only bone tossed to them—a company union.[86]

7

When Walsh brought the Colorado investigation to a close, he also signaled termination of the Commission's public hearings. Certainly, the probers completed their labors in sensational fashion; at that time few government inquiries had ever acquired quite so much notoriety. The praise or censure for this development rightly accrued to Frank Walsh, whose conduct of the Rockefeller examination dominated all the proceedings. In the public mind, the Chairman had stamped his own personality over the whole federal group. Indeed, most publications now generally referred to it as the Walsh Commission.

Yet the Chairman emerged from these sessions as an enigmatic figure. His behavior during the Rockefeller probe sharply designated him as the Commission's most vociferous radical. In previous investigations, however, the Kansas City lawyer usually appeared as an impartial overseer who exhibited that very judicial poise that he now scorned. Some New York newspapers, startled by his vehemence, wired Missouri to check on this "demagogue." Word flashed back to them, however, that "there was nothing the matter with Walsh out there." [87]

Actually, Walsh's background yielded ample evidence that he acted completely in character during the Rockefeller affair. As the son of a laboring family who had known poverty, Frank Walsh always retained a fierce loyalty to the cause of the workingman. Politically, he had invariably plunged into reform, first in Kansas City, then in the Missouri Progressive movement, and finally in the 1912 presidential campaign. A famous trial lawyer in his home state, Walsh had long practiced the art of rigorous cross-examination.

His entire life seemed to be preparation for his rendezvous with John D. Rockefeller, Jr.

More important for the nation than Walsh's personal traits, however, were the social and political forces that produced him and which he now symbolized. Many people in Walsh's part of the country had long felt that something had gone wrong with America. All their lives they had venerated the Jeffersonian ideal that the independent farmer and workingman constituted the basis of the republic. America promised, they believed, equality of opportunity. But inexplicable changes, they discovered, now threatened to saddle the small farmer with debt and reduce the laborer to a propertyless proletarian.

Walsh's contemporaries searched for answers. They scanned the pages of *Appeal to Reason* and devoured Edward Bellamy's *Looking Backward,* Henry George's *Progress and Poverty,* and Henry Demarest Lloyd's *Wealth Against Commonwealth.* On street corners and fairgrounds all across their land they listened and then cheered for "Bryan, Bryan Bryan!" They blamed the evils of their time on Wall Street, the "malefactors of great wealth," the trusts. Each of these vague epithets expressed a central idea of both the Populist and Progressive movements: somehow a very few men had accumulated such huge fortunes that they could control the destinies of millions of hitherto independent Americans.*

Walsh's social philosophy had developed to the point where it placed him within the most advanced faction of the Progressive movement.† Most reformers wanted to modify capitalism either

---

* Walsh, for example, remarked that Colorado miners lived under feudal conditions and the fault lay "in the fact that the controlling power was in the East" (Kansas City *Star,* Feb. 18, 1915).

For a discussion of the Populist antecedents of midwestern Progressivism see Nye, *Midwestern Progressive Politics,* pp. 169-90. Frank Walsh's intellectual development is examined in Meehan, "Frank Walsh and the American Labor Movement."

† Walsh's concern for economic reforms, his devotion to labor, and his interest in public power (he later served as chairman of the New York State Power Authority) suggest that he advocated a "New Deal" approach during the Progressive era.

For some studies concerned with the origins of the New Deal in the Progressive period see Scott, "The Progressive Era in Perspective," *Journal of Politics,* XXI (November, 1959), 685-701; Kirkendall, "The Great Depression:

by breaking up the trusts or by controlling them through government agencies. "The people must own the trusts in order to prevent the trusts from owning them," Walsh argued, "it is ridiculous to talk of regulating or destroying them by legislation." While many Progressives directed their primary efforts toward the achievement of greater political democracy, Walsh insisted that the major question of his age was "the material one, the economic one." He defined the modern rights of man as "the right to eat, the right to live decently, the right to work." Witnesses who appeared before the Commission, its Chairman declared, "should not have any doubt about my fundamental beliefs. That is among other things, that land should not be held away from the beneficial use of mankind; that I am strongly in favor of a graduated income tax; that I believe in the imposition of heavy inheritance taxes." [88]

In confronting Rockefeller, Frank Walsh acted as attorney for two generations of reformers.* Unlike his predecessors, he did not need to deal in economic abstractions. He did not need to coin rhetorical phrases. He believed that he held overwhelming, irrefutable, factual proof. Ultimate responsibility for the disaster in Colorado did not rest with company guards, state militiamen, nor local managers. It belonged to one man in an office thousands of miles away. He bore no personal animus toward the millionaire, said the Chairman, "it is the system that is under investigation." To Walsh, Rockefeller and the Colorado tragedy symbolized one of the major ills of America: too much private economic power in too few hands. As a climax to its career, reformer Walsh used the Commission to dramatize this situation before an audience of millions.[89] In a broader sense, the Colorado investigation, more than any other, exemplified the violence and social disruption in the Progressive era that the Commission had exposed in hearings across the nation.

Another Watershed in American History?" in Braeman, Bremner, Walters, eds., *Change and Continuity in Twentieth-Century America*, pp. 145-89; Braeman, "Seven Progressives: A Review Article," *Business History Review*, XXXV (Winter, 1961), 582.

* In reference to his work on the Commission, Walsh remarked, "For the past two years I have been merely a lawyer, with a struggling democracy for a client." (Kansas City *Post*, August 29, 1915.)

VIII

CLASS HARMONY—MYTH AND REALITY

1

WHILE MANY PROGRESSIVE LEADERS feared the possibility of violent social upheaval, some Americans cherished the notion that their society boasted a high degree of class harmony. Democracy had so blurred social distinctions, they believed, that relatively little class consciousness existed. Perlman and Taft found that the drive toward unionization sometimes foundered because of a "lack of class cohesiveness" among American workers. The anti-union Citizens' Industrial Alliance equated class amity with Americanism and claimed that capital and labor possessed an identity of interests. "The employee must realize," W. L. Park, Illinois Central general manager, argued, "that an attack upon his employer is an attack upon himself." Although NCF and NAM cordially disliked each other, they shared a common view of social concord in the United States. Ralph Easley of NCF found, especially in his own organization, increasing evidence that "capital and labor have met in friendly handclasp." "Ours is the most democratic of all countries in the world," concluded James W. Van Cleave, a chief of NAM; the government is "less affected by class spirit . . . than that of any other land." A number of citizens, of course, sharply disputed these sanguine views.* Class harmony nevertheless ranked as among those ideas current in circles important to the Commission's work.[1]

* Several examples of the more pessimistic view of classes in America appeared in Chapter II. Perlman and Taft, of course, recognize that class conflict did break out at times in America. They believe that factors such as the Western frontier and various immigrant groups accounted for much of this turbulence. (Perlman and Taft, *Labor Movements*, pp. 169-247, 262-86, 626-36.) An analysis of the work of the Commision reveals that during the period from 1910 to 1915, the incidence of violence was more general and widespread. See Chapter X of this book.

In addition to its major investigations, the Commission studied many other strife-torn communities. From coast to coast, by direct hearings and special research, they mapped American industrial relations. Agriculture as well as industry came under their jurisdiction. The Commissioners gained ample opportunity to explore the validity of this belief in the essential unity of class interests. Their findings displayed a startlingly different picture.

2

Social contentment certainly did not prevail in the Pacific North west. Commission hearings in this region resounded with cries of open class warfare. For many years IWW freedom-of-speech riots had rocked every major city on the coast. Although the commissioners did not investigate these disturbances specifically, they did attempt to discover their underlying causes.

In 1909 the direct-action IWW first launched its free-speech offensive. Forbidden to enter the isolated and closely guarded camps of lumber workers, the Wobblies took to the streets. From soapboxes on public corners in cities all along the coast, IWW orators whipped up the depressed and discontented. Spokane, Portland, and Seattle authorities retaliated by passing anti-street-speaking ordinances and throwing hundreds of speakers into jail. In order to dissuade their prisoners from future agitation, laborers asserted, police in Portland shut off all ventilation in the prisons and then turned up the steam full blast. In response to distress signals, additional armies of workers, traveling by boxcar, poured into these cities from all over the West. Municipal finances, under the double burden of augmented police forces and overcrowded jails, were strained to the breaking point.

This development stirred excitement far beyond the West Coast. It demonstrated the latent power of direct action. IWW leaders, by summoning their apparently inexhaustible supply of followers, upset urban economies and impeded civil administration because officials had violated their basic constitutional guarantees of free speech and assembly. These issues struck at the core of American society and aroused nationwide attention.[2]

Behind this labor turbulence lay economic conditions peculiar to the Northwest. Since the major demand for timber stemmed from the construction industry, the volume of lumber production varied as much as 50 percent in a single year. Prices, costs, and profits fluctuated violently. Irregular operations, frequent overproduction, and cut-throat competition plagued the entire business. This unstable situation in turn created an unusually high rate of labor turnover. Frequently, unscrupulous agencies deliberately supplied too many workers to a camp in order to split fees with an equally dishonest foreman. Some owners, economist Paul Douglas noted, favored this large turnover because it enabled them to exploit laborers at low wages.[3]

A hard life faced every lumberman. He usually toiled ten hours a day and earned 20 cents an hour. Conditions in the camps, according to the president of the International Union of Timber Workers, were the "worst in America." In isolated outposts, as many as fifty loggers might sleep in one unventilated room. They ate in unsanitary cookhouses, walked over filthy floors, slept on dirty mattresses, and grew ill because of inadequate garbage disposal. This situation discouraged family life and promoted a footloose restlessness. "Men are crowding before prostitution houses like before saloons," Peter A. Speek, a Commission investigator declared. "They call the prostitutes their common wives." [4]

This nomadic way of life militated against permanent union organization. Both AFL and IWW had met with failure. A series of disastrous strikes in 1914–15 almost destroyed the Federation's locals, and the national union withdrew its support from all branches of lumbering except shingle-weaving (packing). Success among agricultural hands had led IWW in 1910–11 to inaugurate a vigorous membership campaign; but except for its sporadic free-speech wars. lack of organizational discipline weakened its ability to withstand strike setbacks. By 1914 it too had declined in numbers and influence.[5]

Irregular and seasonal work created a chronic unemployment problem for all major cities along the Pacific. Every winter thousands of men, deprived of work in either lumbering or harvesting, poured into the cities. In Portland, for example, the secretary of the Oregon

Civic League told the Commission that men slept without blankets on the floors of basements, hallways, and stairways. Few ate more than one meal a day.[6]

Most cities resented these indigent armies. When a delegation representing 8,000 workers begged for aid from the city government and the labor unions in Portland, they met with rebuff. These officials, laborer Edward Gilbert told the Commission, were "more concerned in what the good people of Portland would think about a horde of hungry men walking through the streets than they were about the hungry men." Some private citizens organized the Gypsy Smith Tabernacle, which furnished lodging and food to destitute laborers. At times it served as many as 3,000 meals a day. Yet Portland authorities cried that the Tabernacle was a breeding place for disease. One cold and stormy night they closed this refuge and threw hundreds onto the street.[7]

Seattle's casual laborers fashioned what John Fitch described as one of the most unique institutions in labor history. Members of the West Coast branch of the International Hoboes of America contributed portions of their meager earnings to found "Hotel De Gink." This refuge functioned as both boarding house and employment agency. It housed and fed about 2,200 men at a time. De Gink's management stressed cleanliness and discipline; it insisted that all lodgers retire by 10:30 P.M. When auditors scrutinized the books, they found the hotel self-supporting without a penny misappropriated. In addition, 20,000 workers found jobs through the De Gink placement bureau.[8]

Itinerants had founded their union in order to escape mistreatment by ruthless placement agencies. "I wish to state," Henry Pauly, local union chairman, told the Commission, "that the majority of the men on the road are not there of their own free will. They are placed there through false representations by the employment office that ships them out to the different work." These bureaus jammed workers onto freight cars, and then "the men are not given water for days at a time. . . . They have to water hogs and cattle. . . . They don't do that for the men." When Commissioner O'Connell asked him why the workers did not insist on better treatment, Pauly replied, "We haven't the chance to demand anything." [9]

A bitter class feeling among laborers stoked IWW's fires. At a Commission hearing James P. Thompson, Wobbly organizer in Seattle, blatantly prophesied "that a revolution is rapidly approaching." Workingmen had no other choice but rebellion, he asserted. "They are being murdered on the installment plan. Now, they breathe bad air in the camps. That ruins their lungs. They eat bad food. That ruins their stomachs. The foul conditions shorten their lives and make their short lives miserable." He approved of the use of violence against strikebreakers and the destruction of property if it aided the cause. Thompson predicted a collapse of government in every state and a huge nationwide general strike. "To the capitalist class, I would say . . . "You are doomed. The best thing you can do is look for a soft place to fall.'" [10]

Portland executives showed relentless harshness toward labor. M. C. Banfield, a leader of the Pacific Coast Employer's Association, described his organization as a "clearing house . . . or a switchboard to notify quickly the industries along the coast of any one particular industry that might be attacked." A labor leader, he declared, was a "bloodsucker," a "leech," and a "man who never works" but "tries to make his living by his jawbone." Banfield condemned any attempt to restrict hours and improve conditions. Give the laborer individual liberty, he cried. "Don't tie him down to eight hours . . . keep the men at work; idle hands find mischief." This businessman damned the Commission as an undue interference in individual freedom: "This day and this hearing caused the greatest disturbance, the greatest dissatisfaction in the city among certain classes, of anything that has happened." "Men like Mr. Banfield," worker George H. Howell retorted, "are determined to crush labor. . . . They are absolutely merciless in their methods." [11]

In Seattle as well, employers assailed any form of unionization. If more than 40 percent of a plant was organized, Earl Constantine, manager of the Washington Employers' Association asserted, both owners and workers faced dictation by a third party. "I haven't been able to see where we as a firm could ever arbitrate or conciliate or agree with a union in any way whatsover," said George N. Skinner, president of the Employers' Association. He even fired off a letter of protest to Woodrow Wilson. This Commission, he complained, listened politely to labor agents, ministers, and professors but compelled businessmen to submit to "unwarranted sarcasm and badgering." Three prominent lumber executives flatly refused to hire union members; two of them advised the Commission to stop interfering with laissez-faire economics. "This commission will have to let labor hoe its own row," one witness announced. "You go to taking care of labor—put a man in the shade and fan him, and he will never develop, he will never create." There was no legitimate cause for discontent, another executive declared. A man who will not work, "gets just what is coming to him." [12]

J. V. Paterson, president of a ship construction company, delivered the most startling testimony. All unions, he insisted were "an absolute abomination." Congressmen who favored reform legislation, he condemned as "half-made utter failures of lawyers" and "infernal cowards." In equally vehement terms, the shipbuilder blasted modern education, liberal professors, the clergy, and President Wilson. Men of his kind would revolt, Paterson threatened. "We will fight you. We will rise with a counter revolution. . . . We have a right to do it. We have got the power. We certainly have the power. We will destroy you if it comes to that. . . . It is coming to a civil war, gentlemen, and we will fight."

For all of his hatreds, Paterson greatly admired Wobblies. "The I.W.W. appreciates the individual," he explained. "He has got something to offer above the sordid, rotten existence. He has got ideals. He is nearer to Almighty God than many other political propagandists that I know of." This apparent incongruity in Paterson's thought did not shock Carleton Parker. "It is accurate and also obvious," this economist observed, "that the upper reaches of business and society possess its I.W.W. The state of mind characterized by ruthlessness, high egotism, ignoring of the needs and helplessness of much of society breaks out at different social levels under different names, but the human elements and even much of the vocabulary remain the same." [13]

3

Unlike the roughhewn employers of the Pacific Northwest, a group of businessmen in Philadelphia, the Commission learned, had launched an equally aggressive but far more subtle attack on organized labor. These executives advanced the idea of a company union combined with "welfare capitalism."

This concept first emerged in 1909 on Philadelphia's streetcar lines. Through their local AFL, employees had set forth demands which, when refused by management, led to a brief but violent strike. Public pressure forced the company to yield, and the workers gained a wage hike and a ten-hour day. Soon afterward Philadelphia Rapid Transit established its own union, popularly known as the "Keystone Carmen." Management soon bestowed its choice jobs and promotions on members of this new organization.[14]

Early in January of 1910 AFL reopened negotiations. Its leaders charged that the public utility company had violated almost every one of its previous agreements. They particularly damned the obvious favoritism showered upon Keystone members. Officials of PRT literally forced a strike when they summarily fired 175 workers and imported an equal number of replacements from New York. Within an hour the strike was on.[15]

In vivid contrast to the case in many labor struggles, almost the entire community supported the workers. Most Philadelphians scorned the company as badly managed, politically corrupt, and financially bankrupt. Strikers also profited from the popularity of their leader, C. O. Pratt, national organizer of the Amalgamated Association of Street and Electric Railway Employees. A handsome Welshman fond of flaming red ties, Pratt radiated the "personal magnetism of a matinee actor." On the opening day of the strike, Pratt rode slowly through the city streets in an automobile and received the cheering adulation of crowds who lined the sidewalks. Children chanted a popular rhyme: "Who are we? Who are we? We are the strikers of the PRT." [16]

Despite its popularity, the strike threw Philadelphia into an uproar. All over the city, crowds smashed and burned streetcars and dragged company motormen out of their vehicles. Mobs and police clashed, with shooting on both sides. "Every obstacle imaginable," reported the New York *Times*, "was carried, trundled, or dragged in the centre of the tracks to stop cars." At one point strike sympathizers tore down the masonry from a half-constructed school building and piled the material on top of some tracks. When a trolley arrived, the marauders hid behind the debris and at a given sign bombarded the car with rocks and clubs. When policemen tried to stop the attack, the mob knocked them unconscious and moved on through the city, hooting and shouting. At an early date PRT released the following statistics: 2,608 windows shattered, 2 cars completely burned, and 297 others damaged or wrecked.[17]

Philadelphia's ordeal affected human beings as well as property. With the conflict only two days old, police had already arrested over 500 people; hundreds of others landed in hospitals. In Germantown, 10,000 strike sympathizers clashed with officers in a furious battle that raged for two hours. In another encounter, flying missiles hardly fractured the skull of an eight-year-old boy. In a different part of town, bullets felled a mother and her sixteen-year-old daughter. A streetcar and a wagon crushed an elderly man to death as he fled from a riot. One company motorman almost lost his life when a crowd dragged him from his car, placed a noose around his neck, and strung him up on a telephone pole. He escaped only when police dispersed the lynch mob.[18]

A bit of comic opera brightened this grim Philadelphia story. In an effort to augment his police force, Mayor Reyburn had called out the Pennsylvania Fencibles, a private military and social organization. Although these young men carried loaded rifles, they acted under strict instructions not to shoot unless ordered. Trim in their broad hats and glittering uniforms, the Fencibles soon attracted the attention of girls along the streets. "Oh, Mamie, ain't he pretty?" one exclaimed. "Do you suppose he knows which end of that gun to shoot with?" Laughter from onlookers brought blushes to the cheeks of these warriors, who were soon encircled by young women and boys. Urchins stole cartridges from Fencible belts, while girls snipped off their highly polished brass buttons.[19]

Some of the amateur soldiers could stand these indignities no longer and lashed out at the crowd with the butts of their guns. At this point, boys jumped upon the hapless Fencibles, tore off their coats, and scampered away with their weapons. Even if ordered to fire, hardly a Fencible retained a cartridge or a gun. Police finally rescued the musketeers, who retreated to their barracks to mend torn uniforms and dream of military balls. Pennsylvania's Humane Society will investigate these men of war, predicted the New York *Call*. "It is charged that the State Fencibles did cruelly and premeditatedly with malice aforethought tickle the sensibilities of Philadelphians until they almost laughed themselves to death." [20]

Aside from this one lighthearted incident, bloody combat continued in the City of Brotherly Love. On that same day, the New York *Times* reported "one of the fiercest riots of the strike." Employees of the Baldwin Locomotive Works pounced upon a streetcar, knocked the motorman senseless, and demolished the vehicle. When police rushed to the scene, a mob of several thousand hurled bricks at them. From inside the Baldwin factory, nuts, bolts, and wrenches rained down upon the officers. In retaliation, the lawmen opened fire. "The police attack was not an effort to terrify but an attack to kill," reported the New York *World*. "They fired their revolvers point blank through the windows of the shops. Pedestrians ran for safety and the entire neighborhood was in an uproar." Total damage of the strike by the end of this day mounted to 700 cars wrecked and 5,000 windows smashed.[21]

Convinced that his city verged on anarchy, Mayor Reyburn proceeded to inflame the city's prostrike population even more. He first appealed to the governor to place the entire state National Guard in readiness. Under Reyburn's direction, police then arrested the popular Amalgamated chief, C. O. Pratt, as well as John Murphy, head of Philadelphia's Central Labor Union. Authorities held both men on the questionable charges of inciting to riot and conspiracy. In protest, the chairman of a Citizens' Committee personally delivered a summons issued by the Court of Common Pleas to the mayor. Reyburn refused to obey it and slapped the man into jail for disorderly conduct. "It has always been known," maintained one newspaper, "that if Mayor Reyburn sees any possible chance to make an ass of himself he improves it." Finally, Reyburn summoned the state troopers. "Philadelphia today," growled Socialist *Call*, "is in the hands of the Cossacks." [22]

Even reinforced police power could not quell the violence. All day long on March 9, strikebreaking motormen on Frankfort Avenue had withstood a constant shower of missiles and jeers from crowds along the tracks. Exasperated beyond endurance, fifteen of these strikebreakers manned a single car and sent it hurtling at top speed down the city streets. As the trolley rumbled along, the men in the vehicle fired revolvers indiscriminately on combatants and noncombatants alike. When they reached the end of the line, the drivers reversed the motor and shot back up the same route.

Word spread down the line that these scabs had killed a fourteen-year-old girl. Bands of armed citizens sped like minutemen to ambush the returning streetcar. When those inside the streetcar perceived that they now faced a superior force, they ceased firing. Spoiling for a fight, the crowd challenged the embattled strikebreakers to resume shooting. But the motormen refused and instead raced into the carbarn, where a huge iron gate swung shut behind them. Thus ended perhaps the wildest trolley ride in history.[23]

When state policemen marched on Philadelphia, organized labor rushed into open rebellion. "If one man is shot," roared John Murphy, "there will follow a carnival of riot and bloodshed that will startle the entire country. There are men in the northeast who can shoot as straight as any trooper." At first the Philadelphia Central Labor Council had promised only financial support to the carmen—now they proclaimed a citywide general strike of all workers in all trades. Immediately, 60,000 men in sixty-five different occupations quit their jobs; the total, according to union statistics, had reached 146,000 a week later. Soon afterward the Pennsylvania AFL endorsed a statewide general strike if carmen failed to achieve a just settlement. This action marked an historic event in labor history, declared *Motorman and Conductor,* official organ of the transit employees. Workers everywhere were united because "they refused to stand idly by while members of their class were being slaughtered." [24]

These events greatly impressed the Socialists. They cited Philadelphia's ordeal as another example "of the absurdity of intrusting public functions to private corporations." Political corruption combined with captalism, they concluded, had now reached a point of disaster. Socialist presidential candidate Eugene Debs paid a special visit to the city, where he addressed overflow crowds. Debs stressed the fact that public sentiment had all inclined to the side of the workers. "The great middle class of Philadelphia," he proclaimed, "has entered the revolt with them [the workers], disgusted at the piratical methods of corrupt politicians. . . . It looks good for the Socialist party. . . . This strike is making people think." By March, Socialist writers hailed Philadelphia as the scene of the first general strike in America and whooped, "The War of the classes is on!" [25]

Efforts toward rapprochement finally gained ground after numerous failures. Philadelphia's Rapid Transit Company now faced bankruptcy. It estimated its losses at $20,000 per day and applied for a $2½-million loan from the city. Company officials also offered to increase wages at a rate of 1 cent per hour every six months until the minimum reached 25 cents. Rank-and-file workers, by a vote of 1,258–1,254, rejected these terms. Amalgamated's executive committee felt, however, that they could not continue the struggle when supported by so slim a majority; they accepted the proposal and ended the walkout. [26]

Soon after the cessation of this strike, a new transit company management inaugurated, with greater cunning, a new campaign against independent unionism. In December, 1910, Thomas E. Mitten, former president of the Chicago Street Railways, took over the bankrupt line. Mitten proposed that 22 percent of all passenger fares be placed aside exclusively for wages until the pay scale reached the level of 28 cents per hour. Both employees and the company, he suggested, should contribute to a welfare fund that would provide sickness, death, and pension benefits. His scheme also called for the adjudication of grievances through a series of joint labor-management committees. [27]

Mitten declared that he did not care whether his company dealt with the men as individuals or through the Amalgamated. A serious split, however, had occured in the ranks of the union. Mitten quickly took advantage of this schism and announced that he would recognize Amalgamated if two-thirds of its members agreed to his proposals. A referendum among the workers barely missed this needed majority. Management ignored the Amalgamated, and Mitten's welfare capitalism was proclaimed in operation. [28]

Those who testified in favor of the cooperative plan at the Commission's hearings boasted of the great improvements which had resulted from the idea. Now the line carried 20 percent more passengers in seventy-five new, well-serviced cars. New safety devices had cut accidents by 25 percent, while passenger complaints had dropped by 80 percent. Wages, Mitten asserted, had risen to a maximum of 30 cents an hour; almost half the employees enjoyed this rate. In addition, the welfare fund had already paid out substantial sickness and death benefits.[29]

Employee relations, company spokesmen maintained, had improved dramatically. In 1911 PRT had discharged one in every five workers; by 1914 that ratio decreased to one in every twenty. Resignations had also declined from 1,390 to only 337 during this same period. Every worker enjoyed ample opportunity to express his grievances, claimed management witnesses. No independent union, asserted the president of the Keystone Carmen, could ever obtain the benefits provided by this cooperative plan. Keystone, he stated, was "unalterably opposed to strikes." "If capital and labor as two men will push in one direction, they can accomplish something," Mitten believed. "We today here are pushing together for a common end." [30]

These soothing words clashed with the testimony of others who appeared before the Commission. Feelings ran so high, John Fitch noted, that "there were times when if shillalahs could have been used, instead of mere language, there might have been scenes reminiscent of an old-fashioned Donnybrook Fair." Amalgamated members scoffed at the increase in wages. Any rise from the previous depths, they insisted, would have seemed phenomenal. Mitten had deceived his employees by his apparent generosity in granting them 22 per cent of the gross receipts from passenger fares. After all, they declared, the company also garnered revenue from freight and mail and gave no part of it to labor.[31]

Critics leveled their most potent guns at the undemocratic character of the cooperative plan. Unionists scorned Mitten's committee system as a "cemetery for grievances." These agencies, they pointed out, met only at the company's pleasure. Their labor members, out of fear of dismissal, remained peaceful and submissive. While the company deluged its employees with constant propaganda, it prohibited independent union organizers on transit property. "I don't know of any cooperative plan," contended labor leader Pratt, "I don't know of any instance of cooperation; it is at dictation." [32]

Luke Grant, a special Commission investigator, considered Mitten's plan greatly overrated. Previous executives had run the line so inefficiently, Grant found, that Mitten seemed like a miracle-worker simply because he restored normal service. Orthodox business procedures, not the cooperative plan, had accounted for the apparently dramatic rise in wages and income. As soon as the transit firm attained its optimum point of operation, Grant predicted, both its profits and its pay scale would level off. At the same time, Mitten's scheme made independent unionism impossible. Capital completely controlled worker benefits. Welfare capitalism, which had emerged from a strike that possessed class-struggle overtones, merely represented management's latest weapon in its fight against organized labor. [33]

4

Another original Pennsylvania contribution to labor relations—the state police—now came under the Commission's scrutiny. Eventually this new system spread throughout the country, but when first inaugurated it faced bitter and violent opposition. During the investigation, the commissioners found themselves in the midst of a passionate controversy which had emerged directly from America's reaction to the industrial revolution.[34]

Pennsylvania had long wrestled with the problem of violence in labor disputes. Constant strikes in steel mills and coal mines created such turbulence that they had almost paralyzed local law agencies. In order to protect their property, mine and mill operators organized their own Coal and Iron Police. Although the state conferred commissions upon these men, they remained completely under the control of the corporations. Recruited at random and poorly disciplined, the Coal and Iron Police functioned as a private army on the side of capital. The state, Theodore Roosevelt remarked, had "sold her powers to one of the contending parties." During the great anthracite coal strike of 1902, so much disorder erupted because of mercenaries that leaders in Pennsylvania demanded a substitution of superior law-enforcement methods. Soon the legislature deliberately created a Department of State Police to eliminate further use of company battalions.[35]

A great strike at Bethlehem Steel in 1910 boldly challenged this new state constabulary. Under its president, Charles M. Schwab, this corporation loomed as the biggest independent producer of steel in the nation. Although not a part of U.S. Steel's immense combine, Bethlehem nevertheless pursued a similar policy of total opposition to labor unions. Over half of its employees worked twelve hours a day, one-third of them seven days a week. Management paid no higher rates for overtime, and more than 60 percent of the mill workers earned less than 18 cents an hour. Samuel Gompers attributed Bethlehem's abnormally high rate of injuries directly to overwork. "What state of health can laboring men be in," this labor chief inquired, "who work in a blast furnace twelve hours a day during seven days of a week?" "I have labored among my people in this community for nineteen years," Father Fretz, a South Bethlehem pastor declared, "and I know that the Bethlehem Steel Company is a human slaughterhouse." [36]

Sunday overtime ignited the 1910 rebellion. Government orders requiring precision work had placed added strain upon the men. Those engaged on this project had to toil Saturday and Sunday afternoons as well as until 8:30 P.M. every weekday. Bethlehem discharged anyone who did not appear on Sunday. When a committee of workers protested this rule, a superintendent fired them on the spot. Word spread throughout the factory, until some 800 walked off their jobs in protest. No union had guided Bethlehem's workers; their strike was entirely spontaneous.[37]

After a mass meeting, a worker delegation presented the company with a singularly simple list of demands. They pleaded for reinstatement of their committeemen and for an end to overtime, describing the latter as "a detriment to our health, our homes, and families." If Bethlehem would not abolish overtime, the laborers begged for time-and-a-half pay, "so as we may procure additional nutriment to give strength to our bodies to perform our tasks."

Schwab, who at first declined even to speak to his men, declared that he preferred to close down the plant rather than yield to these requests.[38]

Soon afterward AFL moved onto the scene; Gompers personally dispatched a special representative to Bethlehem. Through mass meetings, parades, and propaganda, the Federation induced workers to join its Amalgamated Machinists' Union. Within a week, striker ranks swelled, and union chiefs boasted of 3,500 recruits. A short time later, the Amalgamated proudly announced that its Bethlehem membership had surpassed all other chapters in the East. An executive committee now drew up a new schedule of demands, which included higher wages and improved conditions. For the first time in history, Bethlehem workers possessed a union of their own.[39]

At the outset of the strike, stories of turmoil varied according to the sympathies of the reporter. AFL officials and the pro-union Allentown *Democrat* found conditions remarkably peaceful; unfriendly newspapers, they charged, had falsely reported tales of disorder. A federal investigating team asserted that unionists had molested nonstrikers and hurled missiles at local policemen. "Hardware stores and pawnshops," said the Philadelphia *Inquirer*, "have virtually sold out their stocks of revolvers and dirks." One store alone, the Philadelphia *Ledger* reported, had sold 200 guns in one day. At the urging of Schwab, Bethlehem's sheriff telegraphed the governor that "serious riots and bloodshed occurred this morning and evening. . . . The whole town is in a lawless state and I must have help to preserve the peace." The governor then dispatched the state police.[40]

Once these troopers had entered Bethlehem, no one could deny the existence of violence. "Almost immediately upon their arrival," James Maurer, a labor leader and Socialist state legislator, claimed, "a regime of terror was inaugurated; men, women, and children were beaten, ridden down, and murder committed." Amalgamated's executive committee petitioned the governor to remove this state constabulary. They accused the officers of inaugurating "a campaign of slugging, arrests, murder, assaults and riot without cause, the viciousness of which beggars description." Police Chief Kelly of

Bethlehem agreed with the workers: "Whatever riot or troubles have occurred in our town since their arrival is due entirely to their high-handed and cowardly attacks upon innocent people." [41]

An obvious bias on the part of the state police in favor of the corporation stirred labor's wrath. Pennsylvania troopers established their headquarters on company property, ate in company buildings, and paid the company for their provisions. When state police officers made an arrest, they escorted their prisoners to the Bethlehem Corporation and tried them in the office of the firm's general manager. Charles Schwab himself attended some of these hearings as a spectator. Workmen further charged that troopers had forcibly smashed into the homes of foreign-born laborers and dragged them off to the mills under threat of imprisonment. One strike leader directed his followers to shoot to kill if these forced entries continued. Bethlehem, swore the *Amalgamated Journal*, is "the greatest monument of industrial despotism in the world." [42]

A killing touched off a series of dramatic events during the strike. When police used their clubs during a melee on the streets, someone hurled a brick with such force at a state patrolman that it crushed the bones in his face. Another trooper, James Maugham, thought he spied the culprit and jumped off his horse in pursuit. The man in question darted into a barroom and bolted the door. Trooper Maugham, however, battered down this partition with his rifle butt and burst into the cafe. Several revolver shots barked out. One bullet hit a bystander, Joseph Szambo, in the head; he died soon afterward without regaining consciousness. Another spectator miraculously escaped death as a bullet ripped through his cheeks but failed to strike his jaw. An infuriated crowd outside then trapped the troopers in a blistering crossfire. "Why more of our men were not killed I don't know," the state police superintendent, Major John C. Groome, exclaimed, "unless they were very bad shots." [43]

Workers elevated Szambo to martyrdom. During the night, reported the Philadelphia *Ledger*, foreign-born laborers, bent on revenge, prowled the streets in search of unsuspecting troopers. Austria-Hungary's consul demanded that authorities arrest and try the accused officer. Police Chief Kelly denounced the incident as an utterly inexcusable outrage. At the trial, however, investigation revealed that a bullet from a .45-caliber revolver felled Szambo; state troopers carried only .38s. The jury acquitted Maugham.[44]

A constant furor raged through Bethlehem for the next few weeks. Workers accused the state constabulary of making unnecessary and improper arrests and clubbing women and children. Once when a trooper ordered an elderly man to move on, he retorted, "I am an American citizen and a taxpayer and a citizen here for over 50 years, and I don't see why I should move on." The policeman leaped off his horse, seized the old man and beat him into insensibility, until, reported the Allentown *Democrat*, "the blood streamed from his head to the pavement." After this assault, labor chiefs urged "all men who had guns to strap them on their backs." [45]

Every attempt at compromise failed. "Under no circumstances," proclaimed Schwab, "will we deal with men on strike or a body of men representing organized labor." Although his company stood to lose $15 million in orders if the strike did not end quickly, the steel baron's only concession consisted of an offer to raise the pay of machinists 2 cents an hour; workers refused this boon because it did not aid those in other crafts. Schwab, according to labor testimony, threatened to vacate the town unless its businessmen backed him to the hilt. Soon afterward, Bethlehem merchants shut off credit to the strikers, and the workers hovered close to starvation. When the company promised to rehire all its men if they called off the strike, the broken laborers finally relented and trudged back to the mills. In the meantime, their union had disintegrated. Bethlehem Steel, like the rest of the industry, remained a bastion of nonunionized labor. "This is what your uniformed, legalized State strikebreakers have done," cried James Maurer, "broken the strike." [46]

Intense bitterness against Pennsylvania's state police permeated the entire Commission hearing. For a good part of his career Maurer had battled these "Cossacks." Now, he explained to the Walsh inquiry, he actually preferred the old Coal and Iron Police. In Maurer's opinion the former company guard was really a detective, or "gumshoe," who when not occupied with specific duties became at worst simply a local nuisance. But these new lawmen were former U.S. soldiers, many of them recruited, he swore, "from the

degenerate descendants of the middle classes." Their leader, Superintendent John C. Groome, had journeyed to Russia and Ireland to
study police methods. Pennsylvania's state police, Maurer insisted,
"are a cross between the Russian Cossacks and the Irish Constabulary," carefully drilled and specifically trained "in the art of
murder." [47]

Labor threatened a violent counterattack. Maurer had already
urged the Pennsylvania State Federation to train its members in
military science: "I am sick and tired of having our men constantly
stand up to be shot at. If we must fight, I would rather fight intelli-
gently than empty handed." Bethlehem had also driven this lesson
home to David Williams, editor of the Allentown *Labor Herald*.
"We are not going to see our people shot down by those official
strikebreakers and remain helpless," the journalist declared. "We
want peace, but if it comes to fighting, we won't go against a machine gun with a brick. . . . I want to tell you now, force to-day is the
most respected thing there is in this world." [48]

Pennsylvania troopers defended their organization. Deputy Superintendent George F. Lumb deplored the shafts aimed at his
superior, Major Groome. Five governors, Lumb pointed out, had
seen fit to reappoint Groome to his present position. Groome in
turn testified that the state police exercised the greatest of care in
the selection of personnel. Pennsylvania had subjected all applicants
to mental and physical examinations of far greater rigor than those
administered by the U.S. Army. No man, Groome asserted, could
enter the field until he had completed four months of intensive
training which included a thorough drilling in the laws of the state
and in the rights of citizens. He boasted that of the 230 officers in
his corps, all but five had received honorable discharges from the
Army; a majority of them had earned a character rating of "excellent." In nine years, Groome concluded, not a single trooper had
ever been convicted of an illegal killing. [49]

Representatives of the state police disclaimed any anti-labor bias
but protested that the hostility of workers had made their job
difficult. "The minute our men arrive on the scene in their uniforms," Lumb stated, "they are hissed at and jeered at and usually
meet with a shower of stones. To reason with them is an absolute

impossibility." Groome characterized *American Cossack*, a book against the state police written by Maurer, as "lame," "flabby," "untruthful," and "ridiculous." He questioned the validity of much of its evidence. In a perhaps unconscious commentary on America's industrial society, Groome confessed that he had fashioned the state police along the lines of Britain's Royal Irish Constabulary, not as an antilabor measure but because he felt that conditions in Pennsylvania resembled those of strife-torn Ireland.[50]

In its *Final Report*, the Commission granted that a state constabulary, properly employed, constituted an improvement over the former Coal and Iron Police. But these hearings amply disclosed that management had used this new agency as a weapon in their war against union labor. In place of its expensive quasi-legal private regiments, capital had gained an efficient military force, financed by taxes and invested with public authority. State policemen in the role of strikebreakers, the Commission declared, had acted as an incitement rather than a deterrent to violence.[51]

5

If class conflict characterized industrial Pennsylvania, equal violence plagued agrarian California. As in the Northwest, turbulence stirred up by migratory labor shook all of the state's major cities. Each year tens of thousands "hied up" for five to six months in urban districts. In December, 1913, there were 25,000 such migrants in Los Angeles and 40,000 in San Francisco; similar armies invaded Fresno, Sacramento, and Bakersfield. IWW dispatched hundreds of soapbox orators into these communities. When authorities responded with anti-free-speech ordinances, they only provoked further class hatred and brutality.

Open war exploded in San Diego. Local businessmen formed posses to oust the agitators by force. "Hanging is none too good for them [labor organizers]," cried the San Diego *Tribune*, "they are the waste material of creation and should be drained off into the sewer of oblivion there to rot in cold obstruction like any other excrement." Physician Ben L. Reitman, an anarchist, reported that six vigilantes had kidnapped, stripped, and tortured him: "With a lighted cigar they burned I.W.W. on my buttocks, then poured a can of tar over my head . . . twisted my testicles . . . and then commanded me tó run the gauntlet." Conservative unions united with the Socialists and IWW to combat employer belligerence. When Governor Hiram Johnson delegated Harris Weinstock to investigate San Diego's war, the future commissioner remarked that "it was hard for him to believe that he was not sojourning in Russia . . . instead of in this alleged 'land of the free and home of the brave.' " [52]

Even those who could find work suffered great hardships. In 1914, a California state commission examined over 800 agricultural labor camps. Of these camps, 96 percent maintained standards below minimums established by the state Board of Health; 25 percent possessed no garbage disposal units, 40 percent provided no bath facilities, and almost 70 percent operated toilets officially termed "filthy." Witnesses who appeared before the Commission also complained about inadequate medical facilities. One union representative presented documentary evidence of case after case where workers with lacerations and broken bones failed to obtain medical attention for hours after their original accidents. In rebuttal, businessmen claimed that their laborers would not bathe even if showers were available. Drunkenness, they contended, kept the worker poor. [53]

Some of California's migrants revolted with dramatic fury in August, 1913. Durst Ranch in Wheatland, largest single employer of agricultural labor in the state, had advertised for a huge force of hop pickers. It promised to pay the "going price" (about 90 cents) plus a bonus of 10 cents per 100 pounds. Actually, Californians had already pegged the "going price" at $1 per hundred, so Durst's "bonus" amounted to nothing. When labor proved plentiful, management lowered its base rate of pay. A state commission disclosed evidence that Durst had deliberately exaggerated his recruiting campaign in order to guarantee a surplus of pickers. [54]

From California, Oregon, and Nevada, almost 2,800 men, women, and children converged on the ranch within four days. Since management charged 75 cents a week for tent shelters, many people slept on piles of straw in the open fields. Durst provided only eleven toilets, which economist Carleton Parker described as "revoltingly filthy." Since this ranch possessed no waste disposal units, garbage was scattered behind tents and over pathways. "This disintegrating mass of refuse was not only a source of pollution for the drainage back into the well and a feeding-place for millions of blue flies," journalist George Bell noted, "but it also carried an unbearable stench throughout the camp." State investigators concluded that this unsanitary environment undoubtedly accounted for a dangerous epidemic of dysentery that swept through the entire population in a few days.[55]

Even worse conditions awaited the pickers in the fields. All during the first week, they slaved under a broiling sun in temperatures as high as 105 degrees. Children dropped from heat prostration; malaria and typhoid raged through the camp. Yet management refused to supply water to its field hands. A cousin of the owner, however, sold lemonade, made largely of citric acid, at 5 cents a glass. One mobile lunch wagon carried water, but the operator refused to serve it unless the worker first purchased some food. This concessionaire shared his profits with owner Durst.[56]

Grim resentment, which IWW soon fanned into open rebellion, smoldered among the field hands. Early in August, about 1,500 indignant workers—fathers, mothers, and single men—held a mass meeting. Led by "Blackie" Ford, a former Wobbly, they listened with mounting fervor to speeches of protest. At one point Ford lifted a sick baby from its mother's arms and held it aloft. "It's for the life of the kids we're doing this," he shouted. When Durst appeared in his automobile, the mob broke into a chorus of hisses.[57]

A workers' committee asked the owner for a regular pay scale of $1.25 per 100 pounds, free drinking water in the fields, and decent sanitation. Durst refused to increase wages but promised to consider the other requests. At this point, however, Ford and the owner became embroiled in a heated argument. Durst flicked Ford in the face with his glove and ordered him off the ranch.[58]

Soon afterward, the sheriff, at Durst's call, arrived with a posse. Armed with revolvers, the police burst into a workers' meeting to demand Ford's arrest. Without warning, a deputy fired a double-barreled shotgun, which wounded one of the pickers. This incident touched off a murderous riot. During the gunfight a deputy sheriff, the district attorney, and two farm laborers lost their lives. The rest of the posse fled in terror. All that night Wheatland remained unpoliced, while the roads teemed with workers escaping from the camp. Governor Johnson dispatched five or six companies of the state militia to Wheatland and placed the entire town under their control.[59]

Police during the next few months stretched a dragnet all over the Pacific Coast to catch the ringleaders of the riot. Authorities empowered a local detective agency to issue "John Doe" warrants and to make arrests at will. California officials jailed hundreds of suspects. In a number of instances they held prisoners incommunicado for long periods of time without lodging any formal charges. According to a state commission report, police dragged one victim from jail to jail for 75 days without allowing him an opportunity to appear before a judge. Officials recorded many of these arrests on a "secret blotter," which they later destroyed. "As far as the administrative end of the Wheatland case is concerned," one attorney exclaimed, "I consider it a scandal." [60]

Officers, the Commission learned, sometimes exerted undue brutality in the attempt to extort confessions by "third degree" or "sweating" methods. In one reported incident, detectives pointed a loaded revolver at their victim's head and threatened to shoot if he did not confess. When this unfortunate still refused, they pummeled him again. He suffered a two-inch cut on his head, bruises on his cheeks, a black eye, and black-and-blue marks all over his body. In one case a jury actually convicted a detective for cruelty and sentenced him to a year in prison.[61]

Alarmed by this reign of terror, many groups outside of the IWW rushed to insure fair trials for the Wheatland defendants. Resolutions of protest poured in from AFL labor councils all over California. Nonlabor and feminist organizations united to form an International Defense League. Neither "Blackie" Ford nor Herman Suhr stood trial for the actual crime of murder. Prosecuting attorneys charged Ford with "inciting" to murder and sought to convict Suhr on the basis of an alleged confession that he had fired two shots during the riot. On evidence regarded by many as flimsy, the court condemned both men to life imprisonment. When the trial ended, IWW tried unsuccessfully to stage a general strike all over California.[62]

Wheatland's riot and the facts revealed by the Commission cut sharply into American society. "For those who care to see," warned Professor Carleton Parker, who headed the state commission that investigated this affair, "there is abundant evidence that the Trade Union movement in the United States has become revolutionary. The much advertised split between the American Federation of Labor and the I.W.W. is bridged over with suggestive ease when the prosecution of an I.W.W. suggests the class struggle." These hearings demonstrated, John Fitch of *Survey* avowed, that "the scenes are changing in California." Men would hear more from the "unskilled, underpaid, disorganized seasonal workers. They will see to it that we hear." [63]

6

Only one Commission hearing on agricultural labor devoted itself exclusively to the landlord-tenant issue. A limited allotment for this subject forced the Commission to concentrate on a single geographical area. After a preliminary field study, they selected a region in the southwestern United States that extended in a 400-mile radius from Dallas. There, according to Commission expert Charles W. Holman, "the question of land ownership has become an imminent one and the landlord-tenant struggle has reached its most acute stage." In March, 1915, the commissioners opened the first public hearings on this problem ever conducted by representatives of the federal government.

Most witnesses agreed that concentration of property into fewer and fewer hands represented the major issue in Texas. Forty years before, the Commission learned, every Lone Star farmer had possessed his own land. Now more than half of them rented plots from landlords, many of whom were absentee owners. Steady increases in the population had intensified speculation and inflated real estate values. The larger farmers drove out the smaller ones, while high prices prevented tenants from buying their own homes.[64]

These economic processes pushed a significant proportion of the population into the status of permanent migratory sharecroppers. When a tenant rented land, he usually contracted to pay the owner one-third of the grain and one-fourth of the cotton produced. Landlords furnished only the premises; croppers had to supply all the necessary animals, tools, food, and seed. As land values rose, however, owners demanded an ever larger share of the crop, and some charged a flat cash rental. Merchants, distrusting the ability of tenants to raise sufficient money, tightened up on credit. Banks and moneylenders boosted interest charges to as high as 60 percent.[65]

Unmercifully squeezed, some of the sharecroppers helped to elect colorful James E. Ferguson governor. An unknown who had never held public office, Ferguson promised to restrict all rentals to the original ⅓–¼ basis. But Ferguson's law failed to aid the tenants. Landowners circumvented it through the device of a bonus system. They charged the cropper for a variety of additional items, such as partial payment of land taxes and rent for his house, and compelled him to purchase his tools and machinery from the owner.[66]

The Commission's hearings transformed these dry economic facts into human terms. A typical tenant-farm couple appeared before the federal body. A nondrinking, hard-working family man of forty-five, Levi Stewart loved his work. For eighteen years he had wandered from farm to farm in an attempt to support his family. In his best year Stewart had eked out a profit of $15; over most of this period he found himself unable to break even. After eighteen years of constant toil, Levi Stewart had nothing to show but a debt of $700.

Crushed financially, Stewart felt disinherited politically. He had voted a few times against those who he thought had oppressed him, but he had lost faith in the ballot because "it did not look like it done any good. It seemed like it went their way, anyway." Stewart never bothered to take a legal grievance to court, because he knew he could not obtain justice. "I was a poor man and the other fellow had the money." Nor did this unhappy man testify before the Commission voluntarily. It had to subpoena him because Stewart feared that owners would refuse to rent him land.[67]

An even more poignant story was told by this farmer's wife, Beulah Stewart, "a shrinking little woman with faded eyes and a broken body. Her figure was strained and quivered from nervous tension. The crowd stretched their necks to hear her thin little voice." Mrs. Harriman began the interrogation. Perhaps no two women who ever faced each other across a table ever stemmed from such different backgrounds. Yet, one observer noted, when Mrs. Stewart saw Chairman Walsh vacate his chair in favor of the lady commissioner, "a look of relief passed over the little woman's face, for already these two had become acquainted and had discussed matters that proved the universal sisterhood."

Beulah Stewart slowly related her tragic story. She had borne eleven children, three of whom had died. She had chopped wood and sowed cottonseed in addition to her housework and child-rearing. She had sometimes picked an average of 209 pounds of cotton a day. This little woman had toiled in the fields until the sixth month of each pregnancy. Worn by such a life, Mrs. Stewart contracted erysipelas, and then her health broke down completely. "I never have got a dress readymade for myself in my life since I have been a married woman," she told the amazed Mrs. Harriman. Now she could work no longer. "It is more than I can stand," she cried.[68]

Letters from Texas tenant farmers in circumstances similar to the Stewarts' filled several pages of the Commission's printed evidence. One woman, who like Mrs. Stewart had never owned a store-bought dress, declared angrily, "There are a few Socialists here and I wish that the whole State was Socialist." "We have a few clothes, but no shoes on our feet," wrote a farmer from Harleton, Texas. "Some renters have bread once a week, and they beg that." A preacher from Kerens emphatically proclaimed, "We must change the system from private to public property. . . . Jesus denounced the system under which rent, interest, and profit is taken as robbery, and this is why the common people heard Him gladly." "I am in a hard shape," a Cuthond farmer said in his communication, "and I don't know how I am going to make it through another year. If you can help us poor people out anyway, it will be highly appreciated." A letter from Blossom asserted, "Most all of the people in here are worse than barefooted and very near naked." "I want to tell you that I have lived honestly all my life," protested a sharecropper from Oakwood, "never committed a crime in my life; but I am ready to do something that will help my starving family; if it takes my life, let it be."

Testimony before the Commission abundantly disclosed the growing social tensions in Texas. Arthur Le Sueur, vice-president and dean of the Law School of the People's College, claimed that "the class spirit . . . is to-day permeating the entire agricultural world." An infinitesimal number of bankers, he contended, lived off the "niggardly, and slavish incomes" of millions of farmers. Populist Party Judge E. O. Meitzen asserted that absentee land-lordism made accommodation among the classes impossible. "If you try to harmonize the interest of exploiter and exploited," he proclaimed, "you are trying to harmonize the interests of a hawk and a dove." Farmers, Judge Meitzen noted, will endure privation more patiently than those wage-earners who now talk about a revolutionary class struggle. Nevertheless, he warned, when the agrarians rebel, "it will take more than all of the lawyers and bankers in the United States to stand between them and their goal . . . when they move . . . they will move so that institutions will go down like tenpins before them."

Witnesses who favored the established order blamed this unrest on demagoguery and ignorance. "There is no tragedy in the tenant situation here," claimed Judge M. M. Brooks, a landowner, "and there was none until the political Jack Cades stirred this thing up." These charlatans "go running around the country talking about the tragedy of the tenant farmers when we were in absolute harmony." Many sharecroppers wore "Stetson hats and fine shoes . . . and just as good clothes as you and I." Colonel E. W. Kirkpatrick, president of the Industrial Congress of Texas, blamed the state's plight on a lack of proper instruction in scientific farming. He blasted the newspapers for not stressing agricultural education:

"If they would keep all this baseball foolishness out of the papers, and put in a little of this home sense, it would be a good deal better." [69]

Reaction to the hearing varied. Conservative critics charged the Commission with inadequate coverage, bias, and needless agitation. Economist Charles W. Holman believed that the inquiry had at last bared the plight of the tenant farmers. For the first time, he asserted, Americans have learned about "a class that has not been generally recognized—a submerged class so low in the economic scale that they have no fixed abodes." Chairman Walsh considered these sessions "simply grand," but he and others complained that conservative newspapers had suppressed many of the inquiry's most significant features. Governor Ferguson praised the federal body as "one of the most patriotic and one of the most far-reaching movements on the part of the federal Government that it has undertaken in a long time." If such a commission had visited the state two decades before, Ferguson concluded, "Texas would be 20 years advanced." [70]

Texas shook Mrs. Harriman deeply. When Beulah Stewart testified, she recalled, "my own back seemed to ache. . . .The misery of the tenant farmers made me feel that the social scheme of things had gone wrong at the root." When the Commission rested for a few days, Florence Harriman could not bear to remain in Dallas: "All the delightful company there seemed curiously unsatisfying when one knew of the land problem that was the skeleton-in-the-Texas-closet." [71]

These hearings highlighted the growing class discontent which had erupted throughout much of the Southwest.* In a special report to the Commission, economist P. A. Speek noted that Socialist leaders in Texas rejoiced over their swelling numbers. In fact, they

* Other Commission activities included hearings which touched lightly on a variety of industries in New York, Chicago, and Philadelphia and on the West Coast. In addition, the commissioners listened to the testimony of experts on such broad topics as trade agreements and collective bargaining, efficiency systems, labor and the law, arbitration agencies, and employment bureaus. One session featured an oft-quoted debate between AFL President Samuel Gompers and Socialist leader Morris Hillquit. Some members of the Commission also conducted brief hearings on the smuggling of Asians and on labor conditions in Puerto Rico.

considered Texas the cornerstone of their movement. Nearby Oklahoma, in 1910, already boasted more paid-up Socialists than any other state in the union. In one year alone (1909–10), Party enrollment had more than quadrupled; in 1912 over 16 percent of Oklahoma's voters cast presidential ballots for Eugene Debs. Far from being a phenomenon limited only to industrial communities, militant class consciousness now threatened sweeping social change in one of the most exclusively agrarian regions of America.[72]

From the industrial East to the agrarian West, these nationwide hearings and reports indicated that many employers and workers possessed class consciouness. As in previous Commission studies, the evidence revealed a disposition on the part of a significant number of Americans to disregard the usual agencies of organized society and to resort to violence. This testimony lent little comfort to those who envisioned their nation as a community of harmonious classes.

IX

FINALE WITH FIREWORKS

1

"REJOICE!" CRIED *American Justice.* "Our Federal Commission on Industrial Relations is Now Dead". This Commission, declared the *Masses*, accomplished "probably the most interesting and significant investigation that the world has ever made." These two opinions reflected the raging controversy that broke over the nation when the Commission issued its *Final Report.* "Nothing would be more disheartening," Walter Lippmann once warned the federal probe, "than to do a good job and have nobody know about it." Now everybody knew about it.[1]

Discord also rent the Commission internally. A quarrel over the relative importance of research and public hearings flared into internecine war. When they wrote their *Report*, the investigators discovered no common ground and split three different ways. Created because of an act of violence, the Commission had lived in the midst of turbulence—now it left in an uproar.

2

A clash within the Commission first broke out over the function of the Research Division. In one capacity this section acted as an advance agent. Researchers studied specific strike areas, interviewed prospective witnesses, and supplied commissioners with background information. Other Division experts prepared special reports which analyzed a broad range of topics related to industrial affairs.

At the Division's helm stood Charles V. McCarthy, head of Wisconsin's famous Legislative Reference Bureau. A second-generation Irish-American, McCarthy had risen from the poverty of his Brockton, Massachusetts, boyhood to gain admission to Brown University. He won early fame as the first Brown halfback in history ever to score touchdowns against both Harvard and Yale. On the sidelines, the student assistant manager of the team, John D. Rockefeller, Jr., watched these exploits with unabashed hero worship. After a sojourn as football coach at the University of Georgia, McCarthy turned to more scholarly pursuits and earned his Ph.D. in American history at Wisconsin under the approving eye of Frederick Jackson Turner. But Turner seemed reluctant to send this brilliant but rough diamond to academic cloisters; instead, McCarthy accepted a position as a document clerk for the Wisconsin Free Library Commission.[2]

McCarthy arrived in the state capital just as Robert M. LaFollette assumed the governor's chair. With Progressivism in the air, the youthful scholar made the most of it. He persuaded the state government to establish a special Legislative Reference Library, the first of its kind. With this act he ushered his renowned "Wisconsin Idea" into the world. By use of telegraphic wires and a clipping service, McCarthy's new bureau furnished politicians with quick, complete, and reliable data on any subject under consideration. Staff librarians then drew up tentative drafts of proposals based on this information. McCarthy also dispatched copies of these prospective statutes to hundreds of experts, commissions, and attorneys for criticism and modification. Its enemies scoffed at Wisconsin's "bill factory," but this energetic scholar was trying to replace haphazard, lobbyist-dominated lawmaking with scientific disinterest.[3]

When McCarthy took command of the Research Division, he found it floundering badly. Economist W. Jett Lauck, its original director, had quit the post, although he stayed on the Commission staff as a researcher. A few months before, McCarthy had testified as a witness and so impressed the commissioners that they retained him as an *ad hoc* adviser. "I am dreadfully afraid," Walsh admitted to him, "that unless you give us the assistance personally we will be compelled to attempt to place somebody [else?] in charge of the work of Mr. Lauck, and one more mistake in that direction means irretrievable ruin." McCarthy embarked upon this task with a sense of high mission. There is "no greater problem any American can work at," he asserted, "than that of making a great statesmanlike program of social betterment. . . . It [the Commission] is of far greater significance than anything I know in this country today." [4]

Great improvement came with McCarthy. A remarkable team of brilliant young people, many of them former students of Professor Commons, now manned the Division. Despite a salary limitation ($3,000 maximum), the Research section also boasted at least nine persons already in *Who's Who in America*; twenty-four more appeared in later editions. Among those luminaries, the Division listed Robert F. Hoxie, Selig Perlman, David J. Saposs, Leo Wolman, and George Creel. One office memorandum disclosed intimations of future greatness: "The boy [Sumner] Slichter * . . . gets only $75.00 per month and is such a valuable worker that he should be kept on for a couple of months after this job is over." [5]

McCarthy expanded his number of research sections from four to nine. Under such major topics as "Labor and Collective Bargaining" and "Women in Industry," he developed subcategories, each one in the charge of an expert. In addition to daily and weekly statements, each unit furnished a full analysis of its subject every six weeks: "The groundwork was being laid," one observer noted, "for an extraordinary report on the underlying causes of industrial unrest and of proposals for industral cooperation." [6]

3

A streamlined investigative staff augured well for the Commission, but budgetary problems with a parsimonious Congress now darkened the horizon. In its *First Annual Report* to the legislative branch, the Commission sketched its achievements, presented a short preliminary analysis of testimony, and projected plans for the

* Sumner H. Slichter became one of the most influential economists in the nation. Author of several important books, he served as Lamont Professor of Economics at Harvard from 1940 until his death in 1959.

following fiscal year. Walsh, Commons, and McCarthy submitted a request to the President for an additional $250,000. As in all his dealings with the Commission, President Wilson quickly signed it.[7]

Congress handled the Commission with rougher hands. In the House, Representative Fitzgerald, a New York Democrat, Chairman of the Appropriations Committee, bluntly told Walsh that his probe could not expect more than a total of $350,000 for its entire program. Walsh scaled down his requisition to $200,000 and assured Fitzgerald that if the Commission obtained this amount immediately, it would not need further allotments. Although the lower chamber relented, Southern Democrats on the Senate Appropriations Committee slashed this sum to a mere $50,000. If successful, this amendment would spell death for the Commission. "There was a very general feeling in committee," explained Chairman Thomas B. Martin, a Virginia Democrat, in reference to the original House allocation, "that no good was being derived corresponding to that appropriation."[8]

When this question reached the floor, the Senators debated for several hours. In addition to Martin of Virginia and Lee S. Overman, a Democrat of North Carolina, the Commission's old bête noire, Hoke Smith, and Walsh's archrival, Senator James Reed, swung their axes. Since creation of this Commission, they argued, the Wilson administration had added both a Department of Labor and a Children's Bureau. These new agencies, Smith and Overman asserted, made the Commission superfluous. They particularly stressed the point that the new Bureau could conduct all necessary investigations with respect to child labor.

Senator William Borah, coauthor of the original Commission bill, defended his handiwork. He linked the opposition to powerful interests who had battled against child labor legislation and who feared revelations of fact on this subject. Then he scolded the entire upper chamber:

If the Senate ever has a spasm of economy, it is in relation to just this kind of proposition now before the Senate. Whenever there is a movement to investigate certain lines of industry and certain conditions in the industrial world and the relationship of capital and labor, if there is going to be a spasm of economy it will come upon us right at that time.

Borah spoke for most of the Senate. It voted 46–18 in favor of the $200,000 allotment. This overwhelming margin indicated that the probe never really faced any danger of defeat nor loss of its congressional support.[9]

Despite this victory, however, the federal investigators realized that highly placed Southern Democratic Senators had formed a cabal against the Commission. Indeed, of the eighteen who cast opposition ballots, fourteen bore that party's label and almost all hailed from below the Mason-Dixon line. An examination of Southern labor, including child labor, might have led to violent senatorial repercussions. Original Commission plans, now suddenly canceled, called for hearings in a number of cities in the South; researchers had already completed extensive surveys of Atlanta and Birmingham. An anxious but ominous telegram from Hoke Smith with respect to Atlanta may have further dampened the commissioners' spirits. Except for the Texas investigation, which covered a good part of the Southwest, the Commission never again ventured near Dixie.[10]

Budgetary difficulties worried Charles McCarthy. He had long dealt with tight-fisted legislators, and he scented danger. An ambitious program stretched before him, and he had already accomplished a prodigious amount of work. Walsh's optimism disturbed McCarthy, who strongly suspected that Congress would render no further aid. "I am certain that we haven't money enough to carry on this investigation along at the rate at which we are going," he told the Chairman, "unless we cut the hearings down or do away with them at present." But the Missourian waved away this and similar supplications with buoyant confidence. "You have always worried too much about the finances of this Commission," Walsh replied. "I feel almost as though I could do all I care to do without any financing from a public source. You stick to me . . . and we will come out all right." [11]

McCarthy viewed research as the Commission's most vital activity; he had always underestimated Frank Walsh's deep conviction about the importance of publicity. For this reason, the Wisconsin scholar, despite his forebodings of economic peril, remained totally unprepared for the shock which suddenly jolted him. In January, 1915, Walsh again trudged up Capitol Hill in search of additional sustenance. Even if Congress opened its purse, the Commission still lacked the means to support its full program. McCarthy moved that the Commission terminate its hearings and pour all its remaining funds into research. Frank Walsh decided to the contrary. He instructed the astounded Director to grant two weeks' notice to his staff and to close his office as soon as possible.[12]

This blow staggered McCarthy. "Just at the time of the fruition of all our hopes," he moaned, "and just at the time when opportunity comes knocking at his [Walsh's] door, he is throwing it all away." At this very moment, enemies in Wisconsin had mounted a political assault against McCarthy's "bill factory." Physically ill as well, the scholar headed back to Madison in a daze. "I was so sick with pain at the time," he said after his confrontation with Walsh, "that I did not notice I had been fired." Then McCarthy determined to launch an offensive. He accepted the counsel of his close associate on the Commission, economist William Leiserson, who declared, "The time has come when Walsh must be handled roughly in his own way. . . . Now it is a real fight to the finish."[13]

4

As he girded for battle, the director found a willing ally in John Commons, who had long admired McCarthy. Neither man fought simply to rescue the Research Division. Both passionately believed that the Wisconsin Idea of impartial legislative drafting represented the key to enlightened government. Through the Commission they hoped to project this technique onto the national scene.

Commons and McCarthy had already formulated their grand design. They planned to conduct nationwide employer-employee conferences at the highest levels. As these leaders threshed out their problems, the Research Division would supply factual data. Eventually, Commons trusted, these studies would produce specific legislative proposals. Then, prophesied McCarthy, the Commission could present "a great program to the President which all the progressives of America could get behind." [14]

Underlying this plan lay McCarthy's expectation that he could harness the power of manufacturers' associations and persuade them to cooperate with labor. He had already organized a Joint Committee of Associated Employers, comprised of NAM, the National Council for Industrial Defense, and the National Metal Trades and the National Erectors' Associations. All these agencies, their general counsel, Walter Drew, admitted, were "generally supposed to be the radical, aggressive, open shop employers of the country." But they cooperated with the Commission in order to publicize their viewpoint. [15]

Under Commons' guidance, this committee had already held the first of its parleys with union delegates nominated by Samuel Gompers. Commons introduced the least disputed problems first—vocational education, apprenticeship, unemployment, safety, and sanitation. "A great deal of good can be said to have come from this joint conference idea," Walter Drew remarked, "because it has demonstrated that there is a wide legislative field of practical, non-controversial character." It should, he predicted, "lead to future efforts along the same line." Professor Commons had scheduled further assemblies to discuss the more prickly issues. This sudden crisis within the Commission threatened to kill his dream. [16]

Frank Walsh contemplated the Wisconsin Idea with a wary eye. He considered the Commons-McCarthy approach one of "interminable bill-drafting [by] countless employees, experts and the like . . . the very thought of which should throw the legal profession into spasms of delight and the proletariat into hopeless despair. . . . While all this is going on, fundamentals remain practically untouched." Their faith in conferences with open-shop employers revolted him. This, he exclaimed, was "a little short of espionage over our work by the representatives of those forces in the country which a great majority of the workers, at least, believe to be the principal despoilers of their rights and the most notorious exploiters of their kind." [17]

Leiserson, McCarthy, and Commons plotted their strategy of rebellion. Walsh, confided McCarthy, expected a "big row." "I think the way to fool him is for me to make a dignified statement. We should not play the game the other fellow thinks we are going to play." First McCarthy compiled an elaborate brief crammed with facts, figures, and iron logic. Then he lobbied for support among the other commissioners. "Walsh knows I am in a desperate fight up here in Madison," McCarthy declared in anticipation of the Chairman's tactics. "He will try to prolong the hearing next week . . . and keep me away from Madison. Of course this would be fatal to me here, and he probably knows it." [18]

Their scheme perfected, the three conspirators moved to beard the lion in full executive session. Commons proposed that the commissioners reinstate McCarthy and approve a new version of the budget which would divert most of the remaining funds into research. He also offered a resolution that all future vouchers require the signatures not only of Walsh but of two other commissioners, one from each panel. In a final summation, McCarthy exhorted his audience to provide for a continuation of the Joint Committee project so that they could present President Wilson with a truly national reform policy.[19]

Resourceful Frank Walsh then unleashed his counterattack. First he accused the Research Division of dragging its feet: "I made them a blithe little speech which lasted four hours, going over every point of the Commission's work and refuting the criticism of McCarthy." On the spot, Walsh demanded that the commissioners read six to eight reports in order to examine the "grand piece of work" accomplished by this Division. "They threw up their hands," declared the Chairman, "and said that none would do for the Commission to sign." [20]

Walsh then hurled his biggest bombshell. He charged McCarthy with bad faith, duplicity, and reckless mishandling of the truth. In October, 1914, Walsh had first learned that the Rockefeller Foundation intended to invest a huge sum to study industrial relations. Suspicious that the millionaire schemed to use his enormous resources to drown out the Commission and subvert the truth about labor, Walsh ordered a full-scale investigation of Rockefeller's philanthropic activities. This probe, of course, coincided with and was overshadowed by the climactic hearings on Colorado.

McCarthy had prepared the questionnaires and background material for this exposé. Among Rockefeller Foundation correspondence subpoenaed by the Commission, Walsh unearthed a letter from McCarthy to Rockefeller, dated October 17, 1914, and marked "Personal and Confidential." This communication led to a further exchange of messages between the two friends. Now Walsh accused McCarthy of consorting with the enemy while on the Commission's payroll.[21]

As old college friends, McCarthy and the millionaire had retained their friendship over the years. When the Commission study loomed, McCarthy tried to persuade Rockefeller to drop his own industrial relations project. He urged the heir to channel these funds, without strings, to some totally independent agency. Rockefeller, the scholar insisted, possessed good intentions but was "surrounded by men who are simply wooden," some of whom exerted a "subtle and wrong influence" over him. "I want to again assure you of the same old personal relations," McCarthy promised the scion, "and behind all formalities which may come up, or red tape, you will find the same old Mac." [22]

John Commons sprang to the defense of his colleague. Walsh, Commons maintained, had once endeavored to use McCarthy's connection with Rockefeller to effect a joint Commission-Foundation arbitration of the Colorado trouble. Long before this present meeting, Commons insisted, the Chairman had known all about this correspondence. Walsh's "suppression or misinterpretation of these letters," the irate economist charged, "was a deliberate attempt to break down McCarthy's character by misleading the members of this Commission." [23]

Commons' accusation that the Chairman possessed previous knowledge of these letters was true, but the Missourian had already confronted McCarthy with this evidence in private. At that time Walsh expressed genuine anger at their contents; he felt betrayed and demanded satisfaction. "I did not think I ever would be called upon to make this explanation to you or that you would suspect me after all these years," McCarthy responded. "That I am a poor man at forty-one years of age, broke and in debt, is sufficient evidence to show you and every one else that I have never been hankering after money or opportunity and have been open and frank in everything I have done." [24]

After sifting evidence, the commissioners voted on Commons' resolutions. They defeated every one of them by seven to one. Even Mrs. Harriman, closest intellectually to Commons, cast her ballots with the majority. Thruston Ballard then moved approval of Walsh's budget and also resolved that they grant the Chairman additional fiscal powers. This time, again by a tally of seven to one, they passed the proposal. "It was the most complete cleaning out, I think, that the Wisconsin idea ever received in its tempestuous career," exulted Walsh, and "really the biggest intellectual victory that I ever won any place." [25]

Bitter disappointment moulded the two gentlemen from Wisconsin. McCarthy told the press that he resigned because of Walsh's "ridiculous and wasteful budget making" and blasted the Chairman as "thoroughly incompetent." Privately, the ill and overwrought former Director darkly intimated that Walsh was a "dangerous man" capable of "any kind of crooked work"; he suspected the attorney of disloyalty to President Wilson. Professor Commons licked his wounds and took little part in Commission business until the time of its *Final Report*. A letter to his friend Senator LaFollette seems to indicate that he may have considered resigning. With a victor's generosity, however, Walsh forgave them both. He still considered Commons "a fine well meaning man" and brushed off McCarthy's insinuation of wastefulness: "Of course, McCarthy is entitled to his opinion on that score. . . . It is shared by many others, one of whom, nevertheless, is not the undersigned." [26]

Walsh's conquest did not represent the triumph of an impatient radical over a skilled social scientist. As Chairman, he had always cooperated with the Research Division up to this time and indeed had installed McCarthy in order to strengthen its operation. But a financial emergency forced him to choose between two activities. He then clawed McCarthy badly but only in response to an open attack. As Director of Research, McCarthy had placed himself in an impossible position. He had tried to conduct an investigation of Rockefeller and at the same time maintain a close personal relationship with him. That the Commission endorsed Walsh with such impressive consistency argued strongly in the Chairman's favor. Nor did Walsh ever kill the Research Division once he ridded it of the Wisconsin Idea. Under its new chief, Basil Manly, this section continued to turn out weekly reports,* though with a greatly reduced staff.[27]

5

Their administrative quarrel resolved and their hearings completed, the commissioners turned to one last task—preparation of a *Final Report*. In June, 1915, they convened in Chicago and ratified a tentative draft drawn by Basil Manly. They all consented to an outline of major topics and seemingly reached accord on general conclusions. Professor Commons, who had missed this parley, secured a copy of its minutes and announced that he would compose his own text. Commons intended to fashion compromises on disputed issues in order that the Commission could publish a unanimous *Report*. "I missed you very much indeed, at the last meeting," Walsh informed him, "and am very glad to hear . . . that you can get to work at this point, where your ability will mean so much to the final result." [28]

Harmony in June yielded to acrimony in July. Bitter words shot across the conference table. Employer delegates charged the Walsh-Manly report with a bias toward labor. Garretson berated Commons for his failure to offer a substitute proposal as he had promised. They wrangled for weeks, finally gave up, and issued three separate statements: a staff report written by Manly and signed by Walsh and the three labor commissioners, a treatise by Commons and Mrs. Harriman, and an analysis by the employer representatives. A number of special individual dissents further fragmented the document. Symptomatic of the strife within their

* Edward A. Fitzpatrick, a Commission staffer and McCarthy's biographer, interpreted Walsh's victory as one of an "impatient crusader" over a "genuine social scientist." He described the Chairman's charges as "trumped up." Fitzpatrick, however, at the time of his work did not have access to the Walsh Papers. (Fitzpatrick, *McCarthy of Wisconsin*, p. 194.)

society, the U.S. Commission on Industrial Relations, on August 15, 1915, adjourned sine die "in a clash of discord." [29]

A majority if not a unanimous *Report* might have ensued if the two moderates, Commons and Mrs. Harriman, had initialed Manly's text. Both of these commissioners agreed with many conclusions in this statement with respect to the causes of industrial unrest and its remedies. Commons, however, saw the issue as "whether the labor movement should be directed toward politics or toward collective bargaining." The three labor commissioners, he claimed, "were being misled by the general unrest into throwing their movement into politics. I wanted them to avoid politics and to direct their energies toward . . . building up strong organizations of self governing unions." [30]

Mrs. Harriman censured Manly's essay as "a high handed Labor report and nothing more." She condemned its solutions as "idealistic and socialistic" and decried some of Walsh's language as "incendiary and revolutionary." Mother Jones pleaded with her by the hour. "She said I would be a traitor to the workers if I failed to sign Walsh's report," Mrs. Harriman explained. "What she could never understand was that the Employers were my own people, that all human beings were my own people." [31]

Management commissioners excoriated the staff's interpretation as "manifestly partisan." Their critique, Harris Weinstock complained, "laid all the blame for industrial unrest at the doors of the employer. This we regard as unfair and not warranted by the facts." Weinstock sought advice from Ralph Easley of NCF, and wrote the employer report for his colleagues. This California commissioner, Walsh swore, "gave me almost all my trouble. With all his palaver, he is preeminently the unremitting and autocratic employer." [32]

Manly's report appeared first in the volume and ranked in the public's mind as the "official" viewpoint. This study extended some 253 pages replete with documentation. First it examined the condition of American workers and the state of industrial relations in the country. It then named four major causes of unrest and suggested specific remedies under each topic:

1. American laborers had not received a fair share of their nation's wealth. Indeed, it found a great portion of our industrial population lived in dire poverty. Between one-fourth and one-third of families employed in manufacturing earned "less than enough to support them in anything like a comfortable decent condition." Like his urban cousin, the tenant farmer found himself "badly-housed, ill-nourished, uneducated and hopeless."

Corporate structure dominated the state of industrial relations. Yet neither stockholders nor directors really exerted any administrative control: "As far as operation and management are concerned, the executive officials are practically supreme." But even these managers depended upon second-hand information from foremen, superintendents, and straw bosses. This vast impersonal gulf between ownership-management and labor made unionization imperative. An individual worker could not bargain with a huge corporation.[33]

"Unjust distribution of wealth and income" was a major cause of discord. Only 2 percent of the nation's population owned 60 percent of its wealth; 65 percent of the people controlled but 5 percent. Enormous fortunes passed, through inheritance, to individuals who in no way shared in their production, yet almost a third of America's workers earned less than $10 a week. As an immediate remedy, in addition to others, the staff advocated a stiffly graded inheritance tax. These commissioners set $1,000,000 as the absolute maximum that any heir could receive.

2. "As a prime cause of a burning resentment and a rising feeling of unrest among the workers, unemployment and the denial of an opportunity to earn a living is on a parity with the unjust distribution of wealth." Most laborers in basic industries suffered joblessness for 20 percent of any twelve-month period. "At all times during any normal year there is an army of men who can be numbered only by hundreds of thousands, who are unable to find work." Inequality of income cut down mass purchasing power and led to periodic layoffs. The report also discovered a dangerous trend toward monopolization of land and mineral resources, which squeezed out independent farmers and threw them on the labor market. In addition to stringent inheritance taxes, these commissioners advo-

cated "vigorous and unrelenting prosecution" of fraudulent monop-
olists, revision of land laws, and a tax on all owners of nonproduc-
tive land.[34]

3. "No testimony presented to the Commission has left a deeper
impression than the evidence that there exists among the workers an
almost universal conviction that they, both as individuals and as a
class are denied justice." Authorities had deprived laborers of
constitutional guarantees and employed the agencies of government
to harass workmen while abetting the misdeeds of capital. "Relief
from these grave evils cannot be secured by petty reforms. . . . The
action must be drastic." This segment of the *Final Report* demanded
constitutional amendments to reinforce the Bill of Rights and included one to prohibit courts from invalidating legislative acts.
It requested severe restrictions on private detectives agencies and
further safeguards for trial by jury.

4. Denial of labor's right to organize constituted the final major
reason for unrest. "No group of workers can become free except by
combined action." The *Final Report* condemned the open shop as
synonymous with the anti-union shop. Without an independent
union, workers at best lived under a benevolent despotism where
justice hung "at the whim of the tyrant." In perhaps its most
historically significant passage, the report called for both constitutional amendments and new laws to protect and guarantee the
right of laborers to organize and bargain collectively. It further
asked that Congress empower the Federal Trade Commission to
investigate and prosecute all unfair labor practices.[35]

In a separate statement, Commons and Mrs. Harriman advocated
an extension of Common's joint labor-capital committees, in
conjunction with state and federal industrial commissions, to cen-
tralize and administer all labor laws. Concurrent with the national
commission, they suggested an advisory council comprised of the
Secretaries of Commerce and Labor and delegates from trade
associations and unions. Members of this second agency would
advise and criticize all policies of the industrial commission but
would have no actual power other than that of publicity and
persuasion.[36]

A good portion of the employer's report devoted itself to the evils of labor. It especially decried the secondary boycott as "unjust, inequitable and vicious." While these businessmen accepted collective bargaining in principle, they opposed sympathetic strikes, the closed shop, contract abrogation, restriction of output, and irresponsible labor union politics. Some Commons-Harriman mediation techniques appealed to them, but they feared any implied restrictions on the right to strike or lockout.

In one large area, all three reports attained harmony—their recognition of deep-rooted conflict and violence in American society. Each team, however, supplied a different explanation. "Where a people or group have been arbitrarily denied rights which they conceived to be theirs, reaction has been inevitable," Manly's analysis claimed. "Violence is a natural form of protest against injustice." It listed capital's arrogant refusal to negotiate and employment of strikebreakers as major incitements to disorder. Management had used law enforcement agencies in a "bitterly partisan" manner and had interfered with freedom of speech to "a degree of brutality which would be incredible if not vouched for by reliable witnesses." [37]

Commons and Mrs. Harriman both accepted the labor-management feud as a "permanent struggle no matter what legislation is adopted." Since 1877, they acknowledged, this clash "has frequently resulted in civil war. . . . It is claimed by some that this contest is irrepressible and will end in revolution." Both placed their faith in "a disinterested enforcement of law" by nonpolitical, nonpartisan industrial commissions. Whenever hostile economic forces collide, they argued, this kind of agency provided the best hope for peaceful arbitration.

An abundance of testimony forced the business commissioners to concede that some employers mocked democracy, exploited women, and hired gunmen who "assaulted innocent people and committed other crimes most reprehensible in character." They emphasized, however, that union members also perpetrated outrages and that some labor leaders openly advocated violence as a philosophical principle. This very Commission, they declared, sprang into existence as the result of a long series of atrocities by the Structural Iron Workers' Union. "We have found many sinners among the ranks of the employers," they acknowledged, but "unionists also cannot come into court with clean hands." [38]

6

"The evidence is in," proclaimed Frank Walsh when copies of the *Final Report* reached the public. "The case has gone to the great jury of the American people." Arguments over the document soon raged in publications all over the country. Most accepted Manly's discourse as the Commission's official statement. "The press of the nation," the Chairman remarked, "is absolutely soaking it up." [39]

Conservatives generally damned the report. With wishful thinking, perhaps, *American Industries* gave thanks that the Commission's ideas "were received with almost universal disfavor" by the nation's press. Congress, charged *American Justice*, "deserved to be indicted, convicted and severely punished for inflicting upon the country the Walsh Commission." The New York *Times* scourged the Chairman as a "passionate Red," and the New York *Sun* denounced him as a "Jacobin." "If the purpose of creating a Commission on Industrial Relations has been to foment unrest," growled *Iron Age*, "the scheme could hardly have been more successful." In Los Angeles, Harrison Gray Otis denigrated the reports as the spawn of "mangy politicians." Their statements, he thundered, "will live in political literature as rare specimens of envy, malice, and intellectual imbecility." [40]

Moderate unionists and radicals alike hailed the *Final Report* as a great manifesto. Gompers noted with satisfaction that even the employers' statement, "though it finds much fault with trade unions, accepts them as a necessary agency to secure . . . greater justice in industry." "The *Report* of the Commission," declared *Railway Federationist*, "will go down in history as the greatest contribution to labor literature of our time." In the *National Ripsaw*, Eugene Debs lauded the exposition as of "the most vital importance to the working people." "It peels the hide off capitalism," exulted *Appeal to Reason*. "Its circulation in sufficient number will put it on the fence to dry." The *Christian Socialist* compared this report to the Declaration of Independence and the Emancipation Proclamation. Such greatness, however, did not apply to the Commons-Harriman effort, which it spurned as "blatantly idiotic" and "comprehensively contemptible." The *Final Report*, proclaimed the *Masses*, is the "most remarkable official document ever published in this country. . . . It is the beginning of an indigenous American revolutionary movement." [41]

Other publications, less directly attached to either business or labor circles, expressed more temperate views. In *Survey*, John Fitch predicted that Manly's essay would occupy the center of the stage only temporarily. In the Commons-Harriman proposals, however, Fitch claimed, "we have a program that is broad and constructive, the product of clear-sighted statesmanship." A Denver *Post* cartoon depicted Walsh handing a sledgehammer to a worker who stood at the door of Congress. "Hammer on that door until you get what you are entitled to," admonished the caption, "a fair share of what you produced." *North American* found the statements faulty in spots but believed they constituted "an invaluable and imperishable record which should form the basis of real constructive work in eliminating some of the graver causes of that 'industrial unrest' which endangers this nation." "They Came Out Where They Went In," quipped the Binghamton *Press*. A perceptive editorial writer in the Springfield *Republican* commented that this fragmented document clearly reflected "the social and industrial upheaval of our time." [42]

With his report now abroad in the land, Walsh struck for action. Late in October, he and the labor commissioners formed a Committee on Industrial Relations. Various reformers and unionists, including Agnes Nestor of the Women's Trade Union League, journalist Frederic C. Howe, and Progressive politician Amos Pinchot enhanced their ranks. This committee pressed for immediate implementation of the *Final Report* by Congress. [43]

Trade organizations viewed this new group as an enemy lobby. In Ohio, the Manufacturers' Association, well-stocked with invectives, blasted the Committee as "notoriety seekers, dilettante [sic] reformers, anarchists, agitators, he-women and she-men" united for the purpose of "proclaiming, agitating, haranguing, and raising cain generally." "This fungus," protested *American Industries*, demanded funds "with an impudence that would make the shade of Captain Kidd smile." The *Iron Trade Review* also scorned these "Sociologists and Saloonists. . . . It is high time for the administration at Washington to suppress this mischief making coterie, which has no legal existence and ought to be driven from the national capital." [44]

At its first objective the Committee pushed for extensive publication of the *Final Report* by Congress. Enemies in the House succeeded in referring the motion to the Joint Committee on Printing instead of the more favorably inclined Labor Committee. Radical papers cried that reactionaries plotted to bury this document. "Don't Let Plutes Suppress Walsh's Valuable Report!" exclaimed *Appeal to Reason*. By spring of 1916, however, Congress had appropriated sufficient money to print 100,000 copies of the *Final Report* as well as 10,000 sets of the eleven-volume *Testimony*.[45]

Soon the Commission's work bore a few minor fruits. When former Governor Herbert S. Hadley of Missouri, a Republican, announced his candidacy for the U.S. Senate, he stressed industrial issues and quoted directly from Manly's study. In advertising its 1916 almanac, *Appeal to Reason* offered a summary of the "Walsh Commission Report." A Socialist school, the People's College, issued a "Vest Pocket Edition" of the discourse. "One of these books in your pocket," it counseled, "will cinch many an argument for you in the next few months. You can pull it on your opponent at a moment's notice." Cairoli Gigliotti, author of a book on the administration of justice in America, dedicated his work to Chairman Walsh, "who laid the rock-bottom foundation of equal rights to the humblest and equal duties to the mightiest." In Pittsburgh, where over 10,000 employees struck, the chief of the Employers' Association swore that Walsh deserved to be assassinated for stimulating their demands. An arbitration hearing in New York, concerned with the issue of an eight-hour day for railroad switchmen, listened to a reading of a portion of the staff's report.[46]

During the 1916 campaign, Walsh stumped for Wilson and

spread the gospel of the *Final Report* through several states. In Illinois one newspaper described how "tremendous applause" greeted the Chairman's "splendid presentation of the awful conditions revealed by the investigators." An upstate New York paper hailed the attorney for "one of the greatest speeches ever listened to by a Schenectady audience." "Thousands cheer Frank P. Walsh," headlined the Indiana *Forum*, "and Hear one of the Greatest Addresses of the Campaign." [47]

Walsh and his Committee lobbied in both major parties, in the Progressive Party, and in Congress. In 1916 many bills closely in line with Commission ideas filled the congressional hopper. For a variety of reasons, a Rural Credits Act and a Real Estate Tax, both of which resembled *Final Report* suggestions, passed both houses. Commission sentiments were certainly exemplified in the law that prohibited products of child labor from interstate commerce. After vigorous pressure from the Railroad Brotherhoods, led by Austin Garretson, legislators approved the Adamson Eight-Hour Act, a step toward the *Final Report's* ideal of a general eight-hour day.[48]

In one sense, World War I prevented further possible reforms on the home front. Both the government and the public turned away from peacetime domestic problems. War production and the manpower draft eventually tended to raise wages and create full employment. For the time, mass international violence replaced internal social conflict.

At the same time, hostilities furnished a unique opportunity to translate many of the Commission's ideas into reality. President Wilson nominated Frank Walsh as co-chairman of the War Labor Board with William Howard Taft. Taft, who considered Walsh a radical, donned this double harness with grave misgivings: "I would feel more confidence if they had not selected Walsh as their representative of the public, but perhaps good can come out of Nazareth again." But Walsh and W. Jett Lauck, now secretary of the WLB conference board, exerted a liberalizing influence over him. In one instance, when Lauck tried to tell the former Chief Executive about conditions in Southern textile mills, Taft ignored him. "Don't fill me with labor propaganda," he barked. "I know you're a

Socialist." After he had visited this area himself, Taft rebuked the economist for providing inadequate information. "Why I had no idea!" he exclaimed. "How can people live on such wages?" Later Walsh delightedly called Taft the WLB's "most radical member." Retorted Taft, "You're just a conservative." [49]

War Labor Board rulings enacted many principles similar to those outlined in the *Final Report*. Most significantly, it took a firm stand in favor of union representation and collective bargaining. In addition, the WLB sponsored the eight-hour day and equal compensation for women and recognized the right of all workers to a living wage. When the war ended, Taft realized the intensity of the social struggle. As a preventive measure, he submitted a proposal in line with the Commons-Harriman thesis. He suggested a permanent national board with equal capital-labor representation to act as a "safety valve through Government arbitration." This agency, he claimed, would reduce the "disastrous acuteness of the controversies between capital and labor which are likely to come." [50]

A final influence that stemmed from the Commission diffused itself over the years through the writings of Research Division staffers. Many of these experts published their reports, either under the Commission's auspices or independently. While George B. West's *Report on the Colorado Strike* and Luke Grant's study of violence and the Structural Iron Workers still stand as basic works in their fields, Robert F. Hoxie's *Scientific Management* ranks as by far the most important single book that emanated from the Research Division. Hoxie exposed the currently popular efficiency systems as both economically and socially irresponsible. Published under the guidance and encouragement of Professor Commons, this treatise rose to the status of a classic in modern economics.[51]

7

Their task completed, the Commissioners and their staff dispersed to pursue various individual careers. Most participated in public affairs either directly in government service or indirectly through business and academic life. A good number remained specifically in the area of industrial relations and played significant roles, especially during the New Deal.

Ill-fated Charles McCarthy died shortly after his service with the Commission, but most members of his Research Division moved on to important posts. W. Jett Lauck finished his term as WLB conference board secretary and in ensuing years acted as economic consultant to a number of labor unions and government agencies. Basil Manly succeeded Walsh as co-chairman of the WLB and during Franklin D. Roosevelt's administration acted as a member and finally as vice-chairman of the Federal Power Commission. Several Division experts developed into outstanding scholars and teachers: Sumner Slichter, Selig Perlman, Leo Wolman, Paul Brissenden, Edward A. Fitzpatrick, and David Saposs rank among the most noteworthy.[52]

Organized labor continued to benefit from the activities of the Commission's labor triumverate. In his few remaining years, John Lennon brought his experience to the federal Board of Mediators. During World War I, James O'Connell saw service on both the Executive Council of National Defense and the Washington Board of Trade. Until his death, in 1935, he remained chief of AFL's Metal Trades Department. Austin Garretson attained the peak of his fame when, as chairman of the Railroad Brotherhood Conference Committee, he directed the successful battle for the Adamson Eight-Hour Act. At the end of World War I he championed the Plumb Plan for public ownership of railroads.[53]

Those on the business panel expended their talents in a variety of new activities. Ebullient Thruston Ballard broke into politics and served as Lieutenant Governor of Kentucky. Among his many duties, Frederic Delano chaired the National Resources Planning Board in 1934 under appointment by his nephew Franklin D. Roosevelt. Richard Aishton rose to the presidency of the American Railway Association and performed further public service in 1924 as general chairman of the President's Conference Committee on Validation of Railroads. As California's state market director, Harris Weinstock still labored in the vineyard of his idol, Hiram Johnson. Always true to the strenuous life, Weinstock died at sixty-eight as the result of injuries sustained when he was thrown from a horse.[54]

One commissioner for the public, John Commons, emerged as the most important labor historian of his generation. History, Commons believed, fully justified his espousal of industrial commissions and labor-management committees: "What I proposed, in my report . . . was a collective bargaining national labor board." Acceptance of this idea, he implied, would have obviated the necessity for a War Labor Board in 1917 and an emergency National Labor Board during the 1933 depression. Eighteen years after his original proposal, Commons insisted, labor unions under the NRA found themselves compelled to formulate codes for collective bargaining under government administration. Adoption of his *Final Report* plan, this scholar contended, would have granted them almost two decades of experience in that field.[55]

Mrs. Harriman acted as a Democratic National Committeewoman for thirty-five years. In 1937, at President Roosevelt's behest, she traveled to Norway as the second woman in history ever to serve as a U.S. Ambassador. Only the Nazi invasion forced her to quit this post. Sometimes she speculated on how much her experience on the Commission changed her attitude toward labor, for she eventually broke with the National Civic Federation. "The Industrial Commission entirely changed you," Mrs. Ralph Easley told her. "It made you a radical." [56]

Mighty warhorse Frank Walsh battled for reformist causes the rest of his life. He championed De Valera's Sinn Fein movement at Versailles, acted as legal counsel for LaFollette's third party in 1924, and won a twenty-year crusade to free Tom Mooney from jail. In the 1930s he completed his career as chairman of the New York State Power Authority, under Governors Roosevelt and Lehman. At age seventy-five, a heart attack felled him in New York City as he strode toward a courthouse to challenge an injunction against a labor union. The New York *Times*, not always an admirer, now characterized him as "an able lawyer, a grim adversary, an untiring idealist." One of his daughters has applied the Sixth Beatitude to her father: "Blessed are they which do hunger and thirst after righteousness: for they shall be filled." [57]

After a turbulent career, the U.S. Commission on Industrial Relations receded into history. Its surviving records drifted into the dead files of various archives. Scholars occasionally picked at some portion of the voluminous published *Testimony* as an aid to their research on some special topic. In their entirety, these heavy tomes contain a tumultuous story. "Those eleven volumes may seem to be sharing the mouldy fate of most government print," a friend of Mrs. Harriman declared, "but they are the comedie humaine of America." [58]

X

AGE OF INDUSTRIAL VIOLENCE

DURING THE PROGRESSIVE ERA, the U.S. Commission on Industrial Relations accomplished the most sweeping study of American industrial life of its generation. It had traveled all over the continent to listen to the testimony of almost a thousand individuals from every stratum of society. Concentrating on labor-management strife from 1910 to 1915, the federal body explored some of the most volatile issues of its day. When it had completed its task, the Commission had contributed to a portrait of the American community as it crossed the threshold of the twentieth century.

Commission Research Division experts produced important economic studies, some of which proved remarkably perceptive and of lasting value. This section also provided a training school and workshop for a number of the nation's outstanding young economists. Later, as scholars and government advisers, particularly during the New Deal, they helped to reshape the country's labor policies.

Many ideas in the Commission's *Final Report* eventually found expression in law. During Wilson's administration, both Congress and the War Labor Board initiated programs similar to those advocated in the Commission document. New Deal policies such as a more steeply graduated tax structure, promotion of collective bargaining, minimum wage scales, and the eight-hour day moved toward fulfillment of *Final Report* goals.

Always in the midst of controversy and at times melodramatic, the Commission performed an invaluable agitational service. Organized labor, publicly disliked during much of this era, gained the chance "to tell its own story in its own way at its own length with the whole country for an audience." "For the first time in American history," Perlman and Taft later commented, "the employing class was arrayed as defendant before the bar of public opinion . . . the testimony tended to allay the notion that labor was an oppressive aggressor." [1]

In a broader sense the Commission exposed gaping fissures in the nation's social structure. Commission testimony indicated a growth of class consciousness among some segments of American labor. In eastern industrial centers, in western mining areas, and in agricultural regions of the Far West and Southwest, class lines hardened and class conflict sometimes erupted into violence. Syndicalism and socialism appealed to some farmers and lumbermen as well as to factory workers. With ample documentation, the *Final Report* unveiled the gross maldistribution of wealth that separated social groups and incited much of this unrest.

A dominant motif emerged from the numerous and apparently diverse strikes investigated by the Commission. In conflict after conflict, either one or both sides struck a posture of unyielding obduracy which produced open violence. Regardless of cause, geographic location, type of industry, or ethnic grouping, turbulence in industrial relations flared all over the United States. It rocked large cities and small towns, manufacturing areas and agrarian communities. On labor's side, native Americans as well as immigrants plunged into battle. Many management leaders of old American stock willingly employed the tactics of war. Industrialization had outdistanced American social attitudes and institutions. In many cases this led to a collapse of civil authority, to near-anarchy, and to military rule.

According to the image projected by the Commission, Americans on the eve of World War I lived in an age of industrial violence. This serious challenge to the entire basis of a free society deeply affected many progressive reformers. "They faced the twentieth century with mingled apprehension and hope," historian John Braeman has noted, "apprehension lest these disruptive forces [of modern industrialism] tear society to pieces; hope that men of intelligence and good will could harness these forces for the general welfare." [2] The Commission's work indicates the important role that industrial violence played in the shaping cf the Progressive era. Eventually American social concepts and law grew closer to the economic realities of the twentieth-century. During the period investigated by the Commission, labor, capital, and government groped for solutions in a new milieu for which history had provided few guideposts. In a real sense, the Commission disclosed, these Americans stood

> . . . as on a darkling plain
> Swept with confused alarms of struggle and flight,
> Where ignorant armies clash by night.[3]

NOTES

Chapter I. "The Crime of the Century"

1. Los Angeles *Times*, Oct. 2, 3, 1910; Woehlke, "Terrorism in America," *Outlook*, C (Feb. 17, 1912), 359-67; New York *Times*, Oct. 2, 1910, contains quotation.

2. *Ibid;* Los Angeles *Times*, Oct. 2, 1910; *ibid.*, Nov. 16, 1911, contains quotation.

3. Cross, *Labor Movement in California*, pp. 275-78; Palmer, "Otistown of the Open Shop," *Hampton's*, XXVI (January, 1911), 29-44.

4. Adamic, *Dynamite*, pp. 203-04; Connelly, "The Trial at Los Angeles," *Collier's*, XLVIII (Oct. 14, 1911), 32; Ray, P.O., "Harrison Gray Otis," *Dictionary of American Biography*, XIV (1934), 100-101.

5. Cross, *Labor Movement in California*, pp. 275-78; Palmer, *Hampton's*, XXVI (January, 1911), 29-44.

6. NAM, *Eighth Annual Convention*, pp. 50-62; Citizens' Industrial Association, *Bulletin No. 1*, pp. 1-23; Robbins, "Freeing San Francisco," *Public Policy*, XI (1904), 270-73; U.S. Senate, *Industrial Relations*, VI, 5494 (hereinafter referred to as *Testimony*); Stimson, *Rise of the Labor Movement in Los Angeles*, p. 258.

7. AFL, *27th Annual Convention*, p. 321; Stimson, *Rise of Labor Movement*, p. 277, contains quotation.

8. Adamic, *Dynamite*, pp. 201-09; Gallagher, "Something Doing in Los Angeles," *International Socialist Review*, XI (September, 1910), 166-67; Palmer, *Hampton's*, XXVI (January, 1911), 29-44. See also Bean, *Boss Ruef's San Francisco*.

9. Adamic, *Dynamite*, pp. 201-09; Gallagher, *International Socialist Review*, XI (September, 1910), 166-67; Palmer, *Hampton's*, XXVI (January, 1911), 29-44.

10. *Testimony*, VI, 5556-57; Gallagher, *International Socialist Review*, XI (September, 1910), 166-67; Stimson, *Rise of Labor Movement*, pp. 337-38; California State Federation of Labor, *Eleventh Annual Convention*, p. 53.

11. *Testimony,* VI, 5552-55, 5624-30; Woehlke, *Outlook,* C (Feb. 17, 1912), 359-67.

12. *Testimony,* VI, 5551-52, 5574; American Federation of Labor, *30th Annual Convention,* p. 208.

13. California State Federation of Labor, *Eleventh Annual Convention,* pp. 53-54; Palmer, *Hampton's,* XXVI (January, 1911), 38-39.

14. San Francisco *Call,* July 10, 1910, quoted in Stimson, *Rise of Labor Movement,* pp. 342-46.

15. Kipnis, *American Socialist Movement,* p. 349; *Testimony,* VI, 5515-17, 5798-800; Palmer, *Hampton's,* XXVI (January, 1911), 29-44; MacFarlane, "What Is the Matter with Los Angeles?" *Collier's,* XLVIII (Dec. 2, 1911), 28.

16. *Testimony,* VI, 5559, 5800-02, contains quotations; Los Angeles *Times,* Sept. 29, 1910; MacFarlane, *Collier's,* XLVIII (Dec. 2, 1911), 28; O'Higgins, "The Dynamiters, a Great Case of Detective William J. Burns," *McClure's,* XXXVII (August, 1911), 355.

17. Mayo, *Los Angeles,* pp. 151-53; Los Angeles *Times,* Oct. 26-28, 31, 1911; Stimson, *Rise of Labor Movement,* pp. 346-47, 353, 361-64; *Testimony,* VI, 5557-59.

18. Los Angeles *Times,* Oct. 2-4, 1910; New York *Times,* Oct. 2-6, 26, 1910.

19. *Ibid.*

20. New York *Times,* Oct. 2, 3, 1910, Oct. 2 contains quotation; Los Angeles *Times,* Dec. 25, 1910.

21. Los Angeles *Times,* Oct. 4, 6, 1910, Oct. 6, contains quotation.

22. "Los Angeles Conspiracy against Organized Labor," *International Socialist Review,* XI (November, 1910), 266.

23. *Appeal to Reason,* Oct. 15, 1910, contains first quotation; Gompers, "The McNamara Case," *American Federationist,* XVIII (June, 1911), 436, contains second quotation; New York *Times,* Oct. 2, 1910; Los Angeles *Times,* Oct. 2, 1910.

24. California State Federation of Labor, *Eleventh Annual Convention,* pp. 9, 36-37, 91-94, 98; New York *Times,* Oct. 2, 3, 1910.

25. Burns, *The Masked War,* pp. 44-49, 54-64; New York *Times,* Oct. 4, 1910; O'Higgins, *McClure's,* XXXVII (August, 1911), 357.

26. O'Higgins, *McClure's,* XXXVII (August, 1911), 347-57; Grant, *National Erectors' Association,* pp. 12-13 (one of a number of studies derived from the work of the Commission's Division of Research); Bonnett, *Employers' Associations,* pp. 139-44.

27. Grant, *National Erectors' Association,* pp. 105-06, 121-31; Adamic, *Dynamite,* pp. 191, 195-97; "Review of the World," *Current Literature,* L (June, 1911), 569; "The Common Welfare," *Survey,* XXVII (Dec. 30, 1911), 1407-12; New York *Times,* April 26, 1911.

28. O'Higgins, *McClure's*, XXXVII (August, 1911), 347-64; Burns, *The Masked War*, pp. 64-65, 98-127, 137-41; "How Burns Caught the Dynamiters," *McClure's*, XXXVIII (January, 1912), 328.

29. McManigal, *The National Dynamite Plot*, p. 89; *McClure's*, XXXVIII (January, 1912), 328; "Burns' Story on the Trail of the Men Higher Up," *McClure's*, XXXVIII (February, 1912), 363-71; Cohen and Chisholm, *"Take the Witness!"* p. 197; Burns, *The Masked War*, Chaps. XII, XIII, XXII.

30. New York *Times*, April 24, 27, 1911; O'Higgins, *McClure's*, XXXVII (August, 1911), 361-62; "Burns' Story on the Trail of the Men Higher Up," *McClure's*, XXXVIII (February, 1912), 363-71.

31. "Review of the World," *Current Literature*, L (June, 1911), 569-75, contains first quotation; *Appeal to Reason*, April 29, 1911, contains second quotation; "The Dynamiters," *Independent*, LXX (May 4, 1911), 923; "A Charge of Wholesale Murder," *Outlook*, XCVIII (May 6, 1911), 1-2; New York *Times*, April 24, 26, May 1, 1911.

32. Stone, *Clarence Darrow*, pp. 185-247; "History of the Case," *Current Literature*, XLII (June, 1907), 587-95; "Confession of Harry Orchard," *Current Literature*, XLIII (July, 1907), 1-5; "Mollie Maguires in the West," *Independent*, LX (March 8, 1906), 536; "The Confession and Autobiography of Harry Orchard," *McClure's*, XXIX (July, 1907), 294-306; "Acquittal of William D. Haywood," *Arena*, XXXVIII (September, 1907), 332-33; Jensen, *Heritage of Conflict*, pp. 197-218. See also Grover, *Debaters and Dynamiters*.

33. "A Call to Labor," *American Federationist*, XVIII (June, 1911), 451-52; Gompers, *American Federationist*, XVIII (June, 1911), 433-50; AFL, *31st Annual Convention*, pp. 72, 75; *American Federationist*, XVIII (September, 1911), 714, and (July, 1911), 536-38; "The Dynamiters," *Independent*, LXX (May 4, 1911), 923; New York *Times*, May 2, 1911; Gompers, *Seventy Years*, II, 187-88; Gompers to Seth Low, June 2, 1911, in box marked "Labor," Low Papers, contains quotation.

34. Harrison, *Clarence Darrow*, pp. 154-56.

35. "Trial by Jury," *Outlook*, XCIX (Dec. 2, 1911), 794-95; New York *Times*, July 12, Oct. 12-19, Nov. 1, 10, 1911; *ibid.*, Oct. 12, 1911, contains quotation; Commons *et al.*, *History of Labor*, IV, 322.

36. Cohen and Chisholm, *"Take the Witness!"* p. 204; New York *Times*, Nov. 29, Dec. 2, 1911.

37. Woehlke, "The End of the Dynamite Case—'Guilty,'" *Outlook*, XCIX (Dec. 16, 1911), 903, contains first quotation; New York *Times*, Dec. 2-4, 1911, contains second quotation.

38. Darrow, *Story of My Life*, p. 179; Steffens, *Autobiography*, pp. 646-66.

39. Harrison, *Clarence Darrow,* pp. 161-66; Steffens, *Autobiography,* pp. 666-72, 676.

40. Darrow, *Story of My Life,* pp. 181-83; Harrison, *Clarence Darrow,* pp. 163-66; Cohen and Chisholm, *"Take the Witness!"* p. 204; Steffens, *Autobiography,* pp. 672-80.

41. Darrow, *Story of My Life,* p. 183; Harrison, *Clarence Darrow,* pp. 161-70; Steffens, *Autobiography,* pp. 679-84; New York *Times,* Dec. 4, 1911; Lincoln Steffens–Edward Wyllis Scripps correspondence, 1907-10, Steffens Papers.

42. Steffens, *Autobiography,* pp. 686-88, contains quotation; New York *Times,* Dec. 4, 1911. (This edition of the *Times* contained some of the denunciatory sermons preached in New York.)

43. Steffens, *Autobiography,* pp. 688-90, contains quotation; New York *Times,* Dec. 6, 10, 1911.

44. New York *Times,* Dec. 4, 1911; Steffens, *Autobiography,* p. 690; Stimson, *Rise of Labor Movement,* pp. 408-09.

45. American Federation of Labor, *32nd Annual Convention,* p. 20; *Testimony,* pp. 5581-89; Stimson, *Rise of Labor Movement,* p. 422.

46. *Appeal to Reason,* Dec. 9, 1911, contains first quotation (with italics); Los Angeles *Citizen,* Feb. 2, 1912, quoted in Stimson, *Rise of Labor Movement,* p. 426; Darrow, *Story of My Life,* p. 183; Steffens, *Autobiography,* pp. 672-80; New York *Times,* Dec. 2, 5-7, 11, 1911; Adamic, *Dynamite,* p. 235.

47. Fine, *Labor and Farmer Parties,* pp. 286-89; Shannon, *Socialist Party,* pp. 72-79; Haywood, "Socialism the Hope of the Working Class," *International Socialist Review,* XII (February, 1912), 469; Debs, "Sound Socialist Tactics," *International Socialist Review,* XII (February, 1912), 481-86.

48. Woehlke, *Outlook,* XCIX (Dec. 16, 1911), 908, contains quotation.

49. New York *Times,* Dec. 2, 1911, contains quotation; *American Federationist,* XIX (March, 1912), 230, 250, XIX (July, 1912), 571; AFL, *32nd Annual Convention,* p. 20.

50. "Weekly News Letter," No. 36, McNamara Ways and Means Committee, box marked "Labor," Low Papers, contains first quotation; "Gompers Speaks for Labor," *McClure's,* XXXVIII (February, 1912), 371, 375; AFL, *32nd Annual Convention,* pp. 141-42; Taylor, "The McNamara Confessions," *Survey,* XXVII (Dec. 9, 1911), 1339-40, contains second quotation.

51. Debs, "The McNamara Case and the Labor Movement," *International Socialist Review,* XII (January, 1912), 397-401, contains first quotation; "Kind Words for the McNamaras," *Literary Digest,* XLIV (Jan. 6, 1912), 3-4, contains second quotation.

52. New York *Times,* Dec. 3, 1911, contains first quotation; *Wall Street Journal* (no date cited), as quoted in Adamic, *Dynamite,* p. 240 (italics in original), contains second quotation; *Nation,* XCIII (Dec. 7, 1911), 536, contains third quotation.

53. New York *Times,* Dec. 2, 4, 1911, contains quotation.

54. Los Angeles *Times,* Aug. 20, 23, 1914, Los Angeles *Tribune,* Sept. 8, 1914, in Walsh Scrapbooks, Walsh Papers, contain quotations.

55. Los Angeles *Herald,* Sept. 8, 1914; Los Angeles *Record,* Sept. 8–10, 1914, contains both quotations, in Walsh Scrapbooks, Walsh Papers.

56. *Testimony,* VI, 5503-07, contains Zeehandelaar quotations; 5513-14, 5523-26, contains Otis quotations; 5611, 5618.

57. *Ibid.,* VI, 5531, contains first Otis quotation; 5526, contains second Otis quotation; 5850-51, contains Los Angeles *Times* quotation; 5569-71, 5850-51.

58. *Ibid.,* VI, 5852-53 (brackets in original).

59. *Ibid.,* VI, 5811-15.

60. *Ibid.,* VI, 5687-88, 5721, 5732.

Chapter II. Taft Proposes, the Senate Disposes

1. Steffens, "An Experiment in Good Will," Kansas City *Star,* New York *Globe, et al.,* reprinted in *Survey,* XXVII (Dec. 30, 1911), 1434, contains quotation.

2. "The Commission on Industrial Relations," *Outlook,* CIV (July 5, 1913), 492, contains quotation.

3. Kellogg, "Statement Prepared for the New York Hearings," *Survey,* XXXIII (Feb. 20, 1915), 561-64; Devine, *Organized Charity,* pp. 2-4; New York *Times,* Nov. 2, 1958, contains quotation; Jane Addams–Paul U. Kellogg Correspondence, 1916-18, in folder "Jane Addams 1918," file "Editorial 1, AB–AZ," and Paul U. Kellogg to Edward T. Devine, Aug. 13, 1909, in folder, "Dr. Edward T. Devine 1912-38," file "Paul U. Kellogg No. 1," Kellogg Papers.

4. New York *Times,* Feb. 28, June 17, 1959; Devine, *Misery,* p. 12, contains quotations; *Social Service Review,* XXII (June, 1948), 260; *Wilson Library Bulletin,* XXII (May, 1948), 650.

5. New York *Times,* Nov. 2, 1958, contains quotations; *Social Service Review,* XXXII (December, 1958), 425; see Kellogg to Devine, Aug. 13, 1909, folder, "Dr. Edward T. Devine," file "Paul U. Kellogg No. 1," Kellogg Papers.

6. Kellogg, "Conservation and Industrial War," *Survey,* XXVII (Dec. 30, 1911), 1412.

7. "Larger Bearings of the McNamara Case," *Survey*, XXVII (Dec. 30, 1911), 1419-29, contains quotations.

8. *Ibid.* 9. *Ibid.* 10. *Ibid.* 11. *Ibid.*

12. Letter from Committee on Industrial Relations to Secure Appointment of a Federal Commission on Industrial Relations to Seth Low, Dec. 26, 1911 (unsigned), Box No. 88, "Labor," Low Papers; Washington *Times*, Dec. 31, 1911; "A Communication to the Hon. William Howard Taft, President of the United States, Urging the Creation of a Federal Commission on Industrial Relations" (copy), Box 78, Labor Department Files 21/20–23/20; Devine, *Organized Charity*, pp. 2-4; Wise, *Challenging Years*, p. 58; "The Constructive Work before the Industrial Relations Commission," *Survey*, XXX (Aug. 2, 1913), 571-88; "Petition to the President for a Federal Commission on Industrial Relations," *Survey*, XXVII (Dec. 30, 1911), 1430-31, contains quotations.

13. *Ibid.*, p. 1431, contains quotation.

14. Washington *Post*, Dec. 27, 1911; Washington *Times*, Dec. 30, 1911.

15. Taft, "Address," *American Economic Review*, II, No. 1, Supplement (March, 1912), 42-47; Washington *Times*, Dec. 30, 1911; New York *Times*, Dec. 27, 1911.

16. New York *Times*, Dec. 30, 1911; Washington *Times*, Dec. 30, 1911, and Washington *Post*, Dec. 30, 1911. (The Committee tendered the actual petition on Dec. 29, although later reprints used the date of Dec. 30.)

17. New York *Times*, Dec. 30, 1911; *Report of the Industrial Commission* (1900–01), Vols. I–XVIII; *Final Report* (1902), Vol. XIX.

18. Pringle, *William Howard Taft*, II, 756-61; "The Constructive Work," *Survey*, XXX (Aug. 2, 1913), 571-88; Theodore Marburg to Edward T. Devine, Feb. 10, 1912, Devine to Marburg, Feb. 17, 1912, Taft Papers; Rapport, "The United States Commission on Industrial Relations," pp. 10-14.

19. *Congressional Record*, XLVIII (1912), 1661-62, contains quotation; New York *Times*, Feb. 3, 1912.

20. *Congressional Record*, XLVIII (1912), 1661-62, contains quotation.

21. *Nation*, XCIV (Feb. 8, 1912), 123; *Independent*, LXXII (Feb. 22, 1912), 426-27; *Outlook*, C (Jan. 13, 1912), 67-68; *Literary Digest*, XLIV (Feb. 17, 1912), 319–20, contains all other quotations.

22. Devine, *Organized Charity*, p. 215; "The Constructive Work," *Survey*, XXX (Aug. 2, 1913), pp. 571-88; Committee to Secure . . . Relations to Seth Low, Feb. 8, 1912, Box 88, "Labor," Low Papers; Hilles to Taft, Oct. 26, 1912, Taft Papers. See also Davis, "Campaign for the Industrial Relations Commission," *Mid-America*, XLV (Octo-

ber, 1963), 211-27, which concentrates on the social workers' part in the fight for a commission.

23. Kellogg, *Work Relationships and the Democracy*, Pocket Pamphlet No. 1 (New York, Committee on Industrial Relations, n.d.), pp. 3-15, contains first quotation; Roosevelt, *President Taft's Message on Industrial Relations*, Pocket Pamphlet No. 2 (New York, Committee on Industrial Relations, n.d.) contains second quotation; Weyl, *It Is Time to Know*, Pocket Pamphlet No. 8 (New York, Committee on Industrial Relations, n.d.), contains third quotation. Other pamphlets published by the Committee at this same time included Edward T. Devine, *The Terms of Industry*; John B. Clark, *A Commission on Industrial Relations, Why It Is Needed*; Shelby M. Harrison, *The Hap-Hazard Public Agencies for Settling Industrial Disputes*. Examples of some Committee propaganda broadsides are in Low Papers.

24. Gompers, *Seventy Years*, II, 210-13; *ibid.*, pp. 183, 192, contain quotations; New York *Times*, Dec. 27, 1911; Washington *Times*, Dec. 3, 1911; Low to Taft (copy), Dec. 7, 1911, Low Papers; Ralph Easley to Charles D. Hilles, Feb. 11, 1912, Taft Papers; Philip Taft, *A.F. of L. in Time of Gompers*, pp. 268-69.

25. *Seventy Years*, I, 444, 447; *ibid.*, II, 123.

26. *Ibid.*, I, 447, contains quotation; Gompers to Henry Moscowitz, Jan. 18, 1912, Gompers to Devine, March 1, 1912, Gompers to Frank Morrison, Sept. 5, 1912, Gompers Papers.

27. "History of the National Civic Federation" (rough draft probably prepared by Ralph Easley for presentation before the Commission but not delivered, unsigned, *ca.* 1914), NCF Papers; Croly, *Marcus Alonzo Hanna*, pp. 217-19.

28. Easley to Taft, Sept. 17, 1912, Taft Papers, contains first and third quotations; Easley to Gompers, July 2, 1912, NCF Papers, as quoted in Green, *National Civic Federation*, p. 184, contains second quotation; memorandum (copy), "Concerning the Policy to be Pursued by the Department of Industrial Economics of the National Civic Federation," NCF Papers; NCF, *Twelfth Annual Meeting*, pp. 19-93; "Social Survey Enlists Nationwide Support," *National Civic Federation Review*, IV (March, 1914), 1, 21-24.

29. NAM, *Seventeenth Annual Convention*, pp. 75-93. Two lengthy congressional investigations amply demonstrated the power of the NAM: U.S. Senate, *Maintenance of a Lobby to Influence Legislation* (hereinafter referred to as *Maintenance of a Lobby*); U.S. House of Representatives, *Charges against . . . National Association of Manufacturers* (hereinafter referred to as *Charges Against NAM*).

30. NAM, *Seventeenth Annual Convention*, pp. 75-93, contains quotations; *American Industries*, XII–XIV (1911–13).

31. NAM, *Seventeenth Annual Convention,* pp. 75-93, contains first two quotations; "Th' Doins Av th' Civic Fideration," *American Industries,* XIII (May, 1912), 28-30, contains third quotation; *American Industries,* XII (August, 1911), 10; XII (November, 1911), 6; XIII (February, 1912), 6; XIII (March, 1912), 8; XIII (May, 1912), 6, contains remaining quotations. (During this period the magazine usually prefaced its issues with a cartoon against Gompers which often included an unsympathetic figure representing NCF.)

32. *Congressional Record,* XLVIII (1912), 2595, 2646; U.S. House of Representatives, *Industrial Commission Hearings,* pp. 3-30; Lombardi, *Labor's Voice,* p. 63.

33. U.S. House of Representatives, *Industrial Commission Hearings,* pp. 3-30, contains all quotations.

34. U.S. House of Representatives, *Report 726,* pp. 1-2; Gompers, *Seventy Years,* I, 216-17; *ibid.,* II, 170-71.

35. U.S. House of Representatives, *Report 1233,* pp. 2-4; *Survey,* XXVIII (July 27, 1912), 583; *Congressional Record,* LI (1914), 11692, contains quotation.

36. *Ibid.,* XLVIII (1912), 9191-207, contains quotations.

37. *Ibid.,* pp. 9191-207; 9201, 9196, contains quotations.

38. *Ibid.,* pp. 9191-207; 9196, 9197, contains quotations.

39. *Ibid.,* pp. 9191-207; *ibid.,* LI (1914), 11692, contains quotation.

40. *Ibid.,* XLVIII (1912), 11608; U.S. Congress, *U.S. Statutes at Large,* XXXVII (1913), 415-16, contains quotation.

41. Taft to Nagel, Aug. 23, 1912, Taft Papers, contains first quotation; *Nation,* XCIV (Feb. 8, 1912), 123, contains final quotation; *Literary Digest,* XLIV (Feb. 17, 1912), 319-20, contains all other quotations.

42. Gompers to Lennon, Aug. 27, 1912, Gompers to Morrison, Sept. 5, 1912 (copy) contains first quotation, Gompers Papers; Taft to Nagel, Aug. 26, 1912 (copy), Taft Papers; Gompers to Taft, Sept. 9, 1912, Gompers to Morrison, Sept. 5, 1912 (copy), contains second quotation, Gompers Papers; *Seventy Years,* I, 447-48.

43. AFL Executive Council Meeting, *American Federationist,* XIX (October, 1912), 850, 853, and AFL, *32nd Annual Convention,* pp. 136-37, 348; Order of Railway Conductors, *Proceedings of the Grand Division,* pp. 111-14; Gompers to Morrison, Sept. 5, 1912 (copy), Gompers Papers.

44. Emery to Kirby, Aug. 20, 1912, in *Charges Against NAM,* I, 90-91, contains quotation; Emery to Taft, Dec. 9, 1912, Taft Papers.

45. Letter (unsigned) to Schwedtman, Aug. 29, 1912, in *Maintenance of a Lobby,* Appendix IV, p. 4108, contains first quotation; Kirby to Taft, Sept. 6, 1912, Emery to Taft, Dec. 9, 1912, Taft Papers; Emery [? (unsigned)] to Kirby, Aug. 27, 1912, in *Maintenance of a Lobby,* p.

4108; Emery to Taft, Nov. 25, 1912, in *Charges Against NAM*, p. 103; NAM letter to Nagel (?), *ibid.*, p. 92, contains second and third quotations; Emery to Taft, Sept. 28, 1912, Taft Papers; Kirby to Schwedtman, Aug. 29, 1912, in *Maintenance of a Lobby*, p. 4107, contains final quotation.

46. Schwedtman (unsigned) to Kirby, Aug. 30, 1912, in *Maintenance of a Lobby*, p. 4109, contains quotation; *Charges Against NAM*, p. 92.

47. Easley to August Belmont, Aug. 30, 1912, NCF Papers, as quoted in Green, *National Civic Federation*, p. 316; Easley to John Hays Hammond, Sept. 5, 1912, as quoted in Green, *ibid.;* Easley to Mrs. John Hays Hammond, Sept. 11, 1912, Easley to Taft, Sept. 17, 1912, Taft Papers, contains quotations; Easley to Gompers, Sept. 13, 1912, Easley to Charles P. Neill, August 30, 1912, as cited in Green, *National Civic Federation*, p. 346.

48. Taft to Adolph Lewisohn, Sept. 10, 1912 (copy), Nagel to Taft, Sept. 12, 1912, Penrose to Taft, Aug. 27, 1912, Emery to Taft, Dec. 9, 1912, Taft Papers.

49. Neill to Nagel, Nagel to Neill, Dec. 2, 1912 [telegrams (copies)], Commerce and Labor File 68117/15; Gompers, *Seventy Years*, I, 447-48; New York *Times*, Dec. 18, 1912.

50. Taft to Adolph Lewisohn, Sept. 10, 1912 (copy), Hilles to Taft, Oct. 26, 1912, Aug. 22, 1912, Taft Papers, contains first quotation; New York *Times*, Dec. 18, 1912; *Who's Who in America*, VII (1912), 616; Nagel to Taft, Dec. 14, 1912, contains second quotation; Delano to Nagel, Dec. 16, 1912 (telegram), Taft Papers; *American Industries*, XIV (January, 1913), 19.

51. Paschal, *Mr. Justice Sutherland*, pp. 91-92; letter to Schwedtman, Aug. 29, 1912, in *Maintenance of a Lobby*, p. 4108; *American Industries*, XIV (January, 1913), 19; Nagel to Borah, Jan. 8, 1913 (copy), Commerce and Labor File 68117/15.

52. New York *Times*, Dec. 18, 1912; Nagel to Borah, Jan. 8, 1913 (copy), Commerce and Labor File 68117/15; Nagel to Taft, Dec. 14, 1912, Taft Papers; Grantham, *Hoke Smith*, p. 300.

53. Taft to Senator George P. McLean, Aug. 22, 1912, Taft to Senator Frank B. Brandegee, Aug. 22, 1912, White House Files memorandum by Senator McLean, Sept. 10, 1912, Taft to McLean, Sept. 11, 1912 (copy), Taft Papers; New York *Times*, Dec. 18, 1912.

54. Easley to Nagel, Dec. 17, 1912 (telegram), Commerce and Labor File 68117/15, contains first quotation; Easley to Sutherland, Dec. 18, 1912, Sutherland to Easley, Dec. 18, 1912, NCF Papers, as cited in Green, *National Civic Federation*, pp. 346-47.

55. Easley to Hilles, Dec. 17, 1912 [telegram (copy)], Taft Papers; Easley to Nagel, Dec. 17, 1912 (telegram), Commerce and Labor File

68117/15; *American Industries*, XIV (January, 1913), 19, contains first quotation; Emery to Kirby, Dec. 18, 1912, in *Maintenance of a Lobby*, pp. 4135-36, contains other quotations.

56. New York *Globe*, Dec. 20, 1912, contains first quotation; *Survey*, XXIX (Dec. 28, 1912), 381-82; *Survey* to Nagel, Dec. 18, 1912, Commerce and Labor File 68117/15, contains second quotation.

57. Kellogg, "The Industrial Relations Commission," *Survey*, XXIX (Dec. 28, 1912), 385-86, contains all quotations; New York *Globe*, Dec. 23, 1912.

58. Healy to Lindsay and Kellogg, Dec. 27, 1912 (copy), NCF Papers, contains Healy quotations; New York *Globe*, Dec. 23, 1912, contains anti-AFL nominees quotations.

59. Healy to Lindsay, Jan. 13, 1913 (copy), NCF Papers, contains quotation.

60. Holmes, Lindsay, Wald, and Kingsbury to Healy, quoted in "To Friends of Organized Labor! " Box 88, Low Papers.

61. Gompers, *Seventy Years*, I, 447, contains quotation.

62. Gompers, "They Don't Suit the 'Intellectuals,' " *American Federationist*, XX (February, 1913), 128-32.

63. Gompers to the Committee, *American Federationist*, XX (February, 1913), 132, contains quotation.

64. Easley to Nagel, Dec. 24, 1912, Taft Papers; Washington *Post*, Jan. 28, 1913.

65. Emery to Kirby, Feb. 5, 1913, in *Charges Against NAM*, I, 103-04, contains quotation; Senator Hoke Smith to Woodrow Wilson, May 21, 1913, USCIR File 21A; Washington *Post*, Jan. 28, 1913.

Chapter III. Mr. Wilson Makes His Choice

1. Lippmann, "The Greatest Question," *Everybody's*, XXX (April, 1914), 502.

2. New York *Times*, Sept. 27, 1913.

3. Lindsay to Woodrow Wilson, March 28, 1913 (copy), USCIR File 21, Labor Department Papers, contains quotation; John M. Glenn, Russell Sage Foundation to William B. Wilson, May 24, 1913, Devine to Woodrow Wilson, May 27, 1913, USCIR File 21A; Lindsay to Woodrow Wilson, June 6, 1913 (telegram), Lindsay to Woodrow Wilson, March 5, 1913, Wilson Papers.

4. Mary E. Dreir, President, National Women's Trade Union League of New York, to Woodrow Wilson, June 16, 1913, Mrs. S. M. Franklin, Secretary, National Women's Trade Union League, to Woodrow Wilson, June 13, 1913, USCIR File 21B; Lindsay to Woodrow Wilson, March 28, 1913 (copy), USCIR File 21.

5. Gompers, *Seventy Years*, I, 544, contains first quotation; Link,

Wilson, I, 470-71; Gompers to W. B. Wilson, April 7, 1913, USCIR File 21A, contains second quotation.

6. Easley to Tumulty, June 17, 1913, USCIR File 21B, contains first quotation; Easley to W. B. Wilson, June 18, 1913, USCIR File 21A; Easley to Gompers, March 7, 1913 (copy), NCF Papers, contains second quotation.

7. *Ibid.;* Easley to Commons, July 1, 1913, as cited in Green, *National Civic Federation,* p. 350, contains quotation.

8. Kirby and Emery to Woodrow Wilson, March 20, 1913, USCIR File 21-9; F. D. Underwood, President, Erie Railroad, to W. B. Wilson, April 11, 1913, USCIR File 21A.

9. W. B. Wilson to Woodrow Wilson, April 7, 1913, USCIR File 21, and "Memorandum for the President," April 22, 24, 1913, USCIR File 21A.

10. *Ibid.*

11. House to McAdoo, March 11, 1913, Wilson Papers.

12. *Ibid.*   13. *Ibid.*   14. *Ibid.*

15. New York *Times,* June 27, 1913; Woodrow Wilson to Brandeis, May 22, 1913, Brandeis to Woodrow Wilson, May 26, 1913, Wilson Papers.

16. Louisville *Courier-Journal,* June 27, 1913.

17. Senator Smith to Woodrow Wilson, May 21, 1913, Lindsay to Woodrow Wilson, June 6, 1913 [telegram (copy)], Woodrow Wilson to Lindsay, June 10, 1913 [telegram (copy)], Wilson Papers.

18. Harriman, *From Pinafores to Politics,* pp. 98-116; House to McAdoo, March 11, 1913, Wilson Papers.

19. Baker, *Woodrow Wilson,* III, 450-51, 455-56; Woodrow Wilson to Brandeis, April 24, 1913, Wilson Papers, contains quotation.

20. Brandeis to Woodrow Wilson, April 29, 1913, Woodrow Wilson to Brandeis, May 22, 1913, contains quotation, Brandeis to Woodrow Wilson, May 26, 1913, Brandeis to McAdoo, May 22, 1913, Wilson Papers.

21. Harriman, *From Pinafores to Politics,* p. 132, contains quotation. Newspaperman identified only as "Ferguson."

22. McAdoo to Woodrow Wilson, May 30, 1913, Wilson Papers.

23. *Nation's Business,* I (Sept. 15, 1913), 2.

24. Easley to Gompers, July 3, 1913 (copy), NCF Papers, contains first quotation; Easley to Gompers, Oct. 17, 1913, AFL Files, Washington, D.C.; "To Study Causes of Industrial Discord," *National Civic Federation Review,* IV (Dec. 1, 1913), 13, contains second quotation.

25. Easley to Gompers, Oct. 17, 1913, contains quotation, Easley to Gompers, July 3, 1913, NCF Papers.

26. New York *Times,* Sept. 11, 1913, contains first quotation; Kansas City *Journal,* Sept. 10, 1913; Melinda Scott, Vice-President, National

Women's Trade Union League, to Woodrow Wilson, June 24, 1913, Mrs. S. M. Franklin, Secretary, NWTUL, to W. B. Wilson, June 25, 1913, USCIR File 21B; "Industrial Relations," *Survey*, XXX (July 5, 1913), 452-53, contains second quotation.

27. Woodrow Wilson to John J. Fitzgerald, April 10, 1913, Wilson Papers.

28. Boyd Fisher to Woodrow Wilson, June 27, 1913, contains first quotation; Walsh to Bert St. Clair, Sept. 8, 1913, Walsh Papers, contains second quotation.

29. Stone to Shannon, Aug. 19, 1913, Walsh Papers; New York *Commercial*, Sept. 11, 1913; Kansas City *Star*, Sept. 10, 1913; New York *Times*, Sept. 10, 11, 1913; *Congressional Record*, L (1913), 4637.

30. Brewer, *History of Linn County*, II, 96-97; Philip Taft, "Austin Bruce Garretson," in *Dictionary of American Biography* (New York, Scribner, 1944), Supplement 1, XXI, 333-34; Green, *National Civic Federation*, p. 347.

31. Kellogg, "The Industrial Relations Commission," *Survey*, XXIX (Dec. 28, 1912), 386; P. Taft, "Garretson," in *Dictionary of American Biography*, XXI, 333-34; *Railway Conductor*, XLVIII (March, 1931), 129.

32. *Ibid.;* Brewer, *History of Linn County*, II, 96-97; Kellogg, *Survey*, XXIX (Dec. 28, 1912), 386.

33. Gompers, *Seventy Years*, I, 336, 389; *ibid.*, II, 54, contains quotation; *Who's Who in America*, VIII (1914), 1751; Rhea, "Organized Labor a Business?" *New Review*, III (Sept. 1, 1915), 205-06; Perlman, *The Machinists*, pp. 13-38.

34. Rhea, *New Review*, III (Sept. 1, 1915), 206, contains quotation; Kellogg, "The Government, the People and the Labor Problem," *Review of Reviews*, XLVIII (September, 1913), 343, contains second quotation; *America*, V (Sept. 16, 1911), 542-43; "Nominations for the Industrial Commission," *American Industries*, XIII (January, 1913), 19; Charles Hilles to William Howard Taft, Oct. 26, 1912, Taft Papers; Harriman, *From Pinafores to Politics*, pp. 137-38, contains third quotation.

35. Lennon to Mitchell, Dec. 18, 1912, contains first quotation; Lennon to Mitchell, Sept. 20, 1912, contains second quotation; Lennon to Mitchell, Aug. 26, Sept. 1, 9, 11, 1912, March 5, 21, 22, April 24, 28, 1913, Mitchell Papers.

36. John R. Commons, "John Brown Lennon," in *Dictionary of American Biography* (New York, Scribner, 1933), XI, 170-71; Lennon to Mitchell, Dec. 21, 1909, contains quotations; Lennon to Mitchell, April 3, 1912, Mitchell Papers; "Biographical Sketch—John B. Lennon" (manuscript), AFL Files; Rapport, "The United States Commission on Industrial Relations," p. 64.

37. Rhea, *New Review*, III (Sept. 1, 1915), 205-06, contains first quotation; Harriman, *From Pinafores to Politics*, p. 137, contains second quotation; Walsh to Woodrow Wilson, Nov. 17, 1914, Wilson Papers, contains third quotation.

38. "Frederic A. Delano," in *National Cyclopedia of American Biography* (New York, J. T. White, 1940), XL, 564-65; Kellogg, *Review of Reviews*, XLVIII (September, 1913), 344; *Survey*, XXIX (Dec. 28, 1912), 336.

39. Walsh to Tumulty, Aug. 8, 1914, Wilson Papers, contains first quotation; Harriman, *From Pinafores to Politics*, p. 137, contains second quotation; "Delano," in *National Cyclopedia*, XL, 464-65.

40. *Who's Who in America*, VIII (1914), 21; Walsh to Garretson, Nov. 16, 1914, Walsh Papers.

41. *Union Labor Bulletin*, Dec. 12, 1914, Walsh Scrapbooks, Walsh Papers, contains first quotation; "Harris Weinstock," in *National Cyclopedia of American Biography* (New York, J. T. White, 1926), XIX, 440-41; Weinstock, *Jesus the Jew*.

42. *National Cyclopedia*, XIX, 440-41; Harriman, *From Pinafores to Politics*, p. 136; Bean, *Boss Ruef's San Francisco*, pp. 259-63.

43. Weinstock, *Disturbances in the City of San Diego; National Cyclopedia*, XIX, 440-41; Weinstock, "The German Courts for the Arbitration of Industrial Disputes," *Annals of the American Academy of Political Science*, XXXVI (September, 1910), 197, contains quotation.

44. Louisville (?) *Evening Post*, USCIR File 21-20; "Samuel Thruston Ballard," in *National Cyclopedia*, XX (1929), 132-33; Ballard, "Eight-Hour Shifts in the Milling Industry," *American Labor Legislation Review*, IV (1914), 117-19.

45. W. B. Wilson to Woodrow Wilson (memorandum), May 3, 1913, USCIR File 21A; John B. Pirtle to Woodrow Wilson, June 1, 1913, USCIR File 21-20; Ballard to Woodrow Wilson (invitation), Sept. 5, 1914, Wilson Papers.

46. Personal interview with Sister Frances Marie Walsh, Aug. 7, 1950; *National Cyclopedia*, XX, 132-33; Harriman, *From Pinafores to Politics*, p. 137, contains quotation.

47. "Industrial Relations," *Masses*, VII (November, 1915), 21.

48. Harriman, *From Pinafores to Politics*, pp. 2-10.

49. *Ibid.*, pp. 11-61.

50. Harriman, "Is the 'Society Woman' a Useless Person?" *Harper's Bazaar*, XLVII (March, 1913), 118; Kellogg, *Review of Reviews*, XLVIII (September, 1913), 343; Harriman, *From Pinafores to Politics*, pp. 72-87; *ibid.*, p. 35, contains quotation.

51. Harriman, "Some Phases of the Southern Cotton Industry," *Harper's Weekly*, LV (July 1, 1911), 12; Harriman, *From Pinafores to Politics*, p. 77; *ibid.*, p. 90, contains quotation; Easley to Gompers,

March 7, 1913, NCF Papers, as cited in Green, *National Civic Federation*, p. 348; NCF, *Welfare Workers' Fourth Conference* (Jan. 11, 1911), pp. 378-85.

52. *From Pinafores to Politics*, pp. 109-11.

53. *Ibid.*, pp. 111-14.

54. *Union Labor Bulletin*, Dec. 12, 1914, Walsh Scrapbooks, Walsh Papers, contains first quotation; *From Pinafores to Politics*, pp. 68, 133, contains other quotation.

55. Commons, *Myself*, pp. 8-26.

56. *Ibid.*, pp. 38-53; "John Rogers Commons," in *National Cyclopedia*, XIII (1906), 511.

57. Kellogg, *Review of Reviews*, XLVIII (September, 1913), 343; Commons, *Myself*, pp. 53-58.

58. *Ibid.*, pp. 65-67, 82-89, contains quotations; *National Cyclopedia*, XIII, 511; Kellogg, *Review of Reviews*, XLVIII (September, 1913), 342-44; Dorfman, *Economic Mind*, III, 288-89.

59. Kellogg, *Review of Reviews*, XLVIII (September, 1913), 342-44; Commons, *Myself*, pp. 95-111, 119, 128, 140-41, contains quotations; Commons et al., *History of Labor*, Vols. I–IV; Dorfman, *Economic Mind*, III, 290; Commons, "How the Wisconsin Industrial Commission Works," *American Labor Legislation Review*, III (February, 1913), 9-14.

60. *Union Labor Bulletin*, Dec. 12, 1914, Walsh Scrapbooks, Walsh Papers, contains first quotation; *Roosevelt-Lodge Correspondence*, II, 406, contains second quotation; New York *Times*, June 30, 1913, contains third quotation.

61. Creel, *Rebel at Large*, p. 48, contains quotation; Graham Adams, Jr., "Frank P. Walsh," in *Dictionary of American Biography* (New York, Scribner, 1958), Supplement 2, XXII, 690-91; personal interview with Sister Frances Marie Walsh, Aug. 7, 1950, and letters from Celia Walsh Bradley (Mrs. Harold S. Bradley), Oct. 26, 27, 1955.

62. "Walsh a Real Investigator," *Typographical Journal*, XLVII (August, 1915), 189-90, contains first quotation; Garwood, *Crossroads of America*, pp. 196-98, contains second quotation; Reddig, *Tom's Town*, p. 54; Kansas City *Times*, Kansas City *Star*, Sept. 4, 1906, Kansas City *Journal*, Sept. 1, 1906, Walsh Scrapbooks, Walsh Papers.

63. Reddig, *Tom's Town*, pp. 63-64; Garwood, *Crossroads of America*, pp. 192-96, contains quotation.

64. *Typographical Journal*, XLVII (August, 1915), 189-90; Garwood, *Crossroads of America*, pp. 248-55; Reddig, *Tom's Town*, pp. 72-76.

65. Barton, "Frank P. Walsh," *Harper's Weekly*, LVIII (Sept. 27, 1913), 24; *Catholic Citizen* (Milwaukee), Sept. 27, 1913, Walsh Scrapbooks, Walsh Papers; Reddig, *Tom's Town*, p. 54, contains quotation; Creel, "Why Industrial War?" *Collier's*, LII (Oct. 18, 1913), 5, 6, 31; Kansas City *Star*, Aug. 20, 21, 24, Sept. 1, 1906, Kansas City *Times*,

Aug. 21, 1906, Kansas City *Journal,* Sept. 19, Oct. 17, 1906, Walsh Scrapbooks, Walsh Papers.

66. Barton, *Harper's Weekly,* LVIII (Sept. 27, 1913), 24; Reddig, *Tom's Town,* pp. 57, 60-61; St. Louis *Post-Dispatch,* Nov. 14, 1906, Kansas City *Star,* Oct. 15, 1906, Walsh Scrapbooks, Walsh Papers; Creel, *Collier's,* LII (Oct. 18, 1913), 5, 6, 31, contains quotation; Blackmore, "Joseph B. Shannon," pp. 124-30; Walsh to the Rev. Irvin St. John Tucker, Sept. 16, 1915, Walsh Papers.

67. Creel, *Collier's,* LII (Oct. 18, 1913), 5-6, contains first quotation; letters from Celia Walsh Bradley, Oct. 26, 27, 1955, contain second quotation; Barton, *Harper's Weekly,* LVIII (Sept. 27, 1913), 24; *Catholic Citizen,* Sept. 27, 1913; Kellogg, "The Government, the People and the Labor Problem," *Review of Reviews,* XLVIII (September, 1913), 342, contains last quotation.

68. Woodrow Wilson to Walsh, June 20, 1913 (telegram), Walsh to Woodrow Wilson, June 20, 1913 (telegram), Wilson Papers; Commons to LaFollette, June 20, 21, 1913, LaFollette Papers (by special permission of Miss Fola LaFollette); Barton, *Harper's Weekly,* LVIII (Sept. 27, 1913), 24, contains quotation; Kansas City *Star,* Sept. 11, 1913, Walsh Scrapbooks, Walsh Papers.

69. Kansas City *Post,* Sept. 11, 1913, Kansas City *Star,* Sept. 12, 1913, Walsh Scrapbooks, Walsh Papers; AFL Executive Council Minutes Sept. 27, 1913, p. 81, Mitchell Papers; Walsh to F. S. Monroe, Sept. 26, 1913, Walsh Papers.

70. USCIR, *First Annual Report,* pp. 5-8, contains first quotation; Boston *Transcript,* Oct. 30, 1913, USCIR File 21A; Creel, *Collier's,* LII (Oct. 18, 1913), 6, contains second quotation (italics are Creel's); New York *Times,* Oct. 26, 1913, March 8, 1914.

71. New York *Evening Post,* Nov. 1, 1913; Creel, *Collier's,* LII (Oct. 18, 1913), 6, contains first quotation; *Testimony,* XI, 10574, contains second quotation; "To Study Causes of Industrial Discord," *National Civic Federation Review,* IV (Dec. 1, 1913), 13, contains final quotation.

Chapter IV. War in Paterson

1. John Reed, "War in Paterson," *Masses,* IV (June, 1913), 13-17, contains first quotation; *Testimony,* III, 2563-64, contains second quotation (italics added).

2. "A Possible Paterson," *Outlook,* CIV (June 14, 1913), 318-21.

3. New Jersey, *36th Annual Report of the Bureau of Statistics of Labor and Industries* (1913), pp. 179-80, hereinafter referred to as *Statistics.* (All citations refer to the 1913 report unless otherwise indicated.)

4. *Ibid.*, pp. 187-88; Paterson *Press*, Jan. 27, 1913.

5. *Survey*, XXX (April 19, 1913), 81-82. (The last figures available prior to the strike reveal that about 90 percent of Paterson's workers received a bare subsistence wage.) *Statistics*, pp. 188-89; Haywood, "The Rip in the Silk Industry," *International Socialist Review*, XIII (May, 1913), 783-88; New York *Press*, June 16, 1914, Walsh Scrapbooks, Walsh Papers.

6. "Report of the Socialist Labor Party to the International Socialist Congress, August 23-29, 1914," *Weekly People*, Aug. 22, 1914; Brissenden, *The I.W.W.*, pp. 213-41; *Testimony*, III, 2472-88; New Jersey, *35th Annual Report of the Bureau of Statistics of Labor and Industry* (1912), pp. 229-35; Sumner, "The Broad-Silk Weavers of Paterson," *Survey*, XXVIII (March 16, 1912), 1932-34; New York *Globe*, June 15, 1914, Walsh Scrapbooks, Walsh Papers.

7. *Statistics*, pp. 200-91; Paterson *Press*, Jan. 27, March 7, 1913; New York *Times*, Feb. 26, March 3, 1913; New York *Globe*, June 15, 1914, Walsh Scrapbooks, Walsh Papers; *Testimony*, III, 2417.

8. New York *Call*, March 1, 1913; Paterson *Press*, March 7, 1913; *Statistics*, p. 200; *Testimony*, III, 2452-72; *General Strike Call*, reprinted in *Solidarity*, IV (March 1, 1913), contains quotation.

9. New York *Times*, Feb. 26, 1913; *Testimony*, III, 2452-72, 2585-607.

10. *Testimony*, III, 2585-607; Weed and Carey, "I Make Cheap Silk," *Masses*, V (November, 1913), 7, contains quotation.

11. *Testimony*, III, 2573-76.

12. Newman, "The I.W.W. in New Jersey 1912–1913"; Paterson *Press*, Feb. 25, 1913; New York *Times*, March 4, 1913; *Statistics*, pp. 183-201.

13. New York *World*, Feb. 26, 1913; *Statistics*, pp. 178, 202; Mason, "Industrial War in Paterson," *Outlook*, CIV (June 7, 1913), 283-87, contains quotation.

14. Poole, *The Bridge*, p. 199, contains first quotation; Flynn, *Debs, Haywood, Ruthenberg*, p. 26, contains second quotation; W. J. Ghent, "William Dudley Haywood," in *Dictionary of American Biography* (New York, Scribner, 1932), VIII, 467-69; *Testimony*, XI, 10569-99; Haywood, "Socialism the Hope of the Working Class," *International Socialist Review*, XII (February, 1912), 469; New York *Times*, Feb. 27, 1913; "Report of the Socialist Labor Party," *Weekly People*, Aug. 22, 1914.

15. *Testimony*, XI, 10569-99.

16. Flynn, *Sabotage* (n.p.); New York *Times*, July 1, 1913, contains first quotation; Flynn, *I Speak My Own Piece*, pp. 42-57, contains other quotation; Orth, *Armies of Labor*, pp. 207-09.

17. Eastman, *Heroes I Have Known*, pp. 17-43.

18. St. Louis *Mirror*, cited in *Current Opinion*, LV (August, 1913),

80-81; Flynn, *I Speak My Own Piece*, p. 140, contains quotation; Orth, *Armies of Labor*, pp. 207-09; Eastman, *Heroes I Have Known*, p. 37.

19. Paterson *Press*, Feb. 25, 1913; New York *Times*, Feb. 26, 27, 1913, contains quotation; New York *Globe*, Feb. 26, 1913.

20. Paterson *Press*, Feb. 27, 1913; *Testimony*, III, 2629-31; New York *Globe*, Feb. 27, 1913; *Statistics*, p. 200; New York *World*, March 1, 1913.

21. *Testimony*, III, 2629-31; Paterson *Press*, Feb. 28, March 1, 2, 1913; New York *Times*, March 4, 1913; New York *Globe*, Feb. 28, March 1, 1913.

22. Paterson *Press*, March 31, 1913; *Testimony*, III, 2529-72; New York *Globe*, March 31, 1913.

23. Paterson *Press*, March 31, April 1, 5, 1913; New York *Times*, April 8, Nov. 11, 1913; New York *Globe*, April 1, 1913; "Haywood's Release," *Appeal to Reason*, April 26, 1913; Haywood, *Bill Haywood's Book*, pp. 267-68, contains quotation; *Testimony*, III, 2502-00, 2031-32.

24. New York *Times*, Feb. 26, 1913; Paterson *Evening News*, April 11, 1913; *Testimony*, III, 2526, 2558-72; *ibid.*, p. 2566, contains quotation.

25. Fitch, "The I.W.W., an Outlaw Organization," *Survey*, XXX (June 7, 1913), 358.

26. New York *World*, Feb. 26, 1913; New York *Call*, March 1, April 4, 1913; *Syndicalist*, III (Sept. 1–15, 1913), 53; *Solidarity*, IV (April 19, 1913), contains final quotation.

27. New York *Times*, April 26, 27, 1913; New York *Globe*, April 26, 28, 1913; Paterson *Evening News*, April 26-28, 30, May 1, 1913.

28. New York *Times*, May 8, 1913.

29. Paterson *Evening News*, May 10–15, 1913; New York *Times*, May 10, 14, 15, 1913; New York *Globe*, May 10, 15, 1913; New York *Call*, May 12, 1913; *Testimony*, III, 2529-44.

30. New York *Times*, June 4, 1913.

31. Paterson *Evening News*, May 14, 15, 1913; New York *Times*, May 14, 15, 17, 1913, contains quotations.

32. *Weekly People*, May 31, 1913; New York *Call*, May 12, 1913; *Appeal to Reason*, July 26, 1913; New York *Times*, May 26, 1913, June 6, 20, 1914; Orth, *Armies of Labor*, pp. 207-09.

33. Paterson *Evening News*, May 23, 1913; New York *Times*, May 23, 24, 1913.

34. Paterson *Press*, June 30, 1913; Paterson *Evening News*, June 20, 1913; New York *Times*, July 1–4, 1913; Paterson *Guardian*, July 1–3, 1913.

35. New York *Times*, Nov. 27, Dec. 2, 1915; Paterson *Evening News*, Dec. 1, 1915, quoted in Flynn, *I Speak My Own Piece*, pp. 158-59.

36. *Testimony*, III, 2542; Flynn, *I Speak My Own Piece*, p. 158; New

York *Evening Journal,* July 3, 1914 (unsigned editorial, attributed by Miss Flynn to Arthur Brisbane).

37. Passaic *Weekly Issue,* Feb. 28, 1913, as quoted in New York *Times,* June 29, 1913; *Testimony,* III, 2541, 2544-53.

38. New York *World,* June 7, 1913; *Testimony,* III, 2541; Boston *Transcript,* Kansas City *Star,* quoted in *Literary Digest,* XLVI (June 21, 1913), 1366-67; New York *Times,* April 20, 1913; *International Socialist Review,* XIV (July, 1913), 10.

39. *Testimony,* III, 2544-52.

40. Paterson *Evening News,* April 18, 1913; New York *Times,* April 18, 1913; New York *Globe,* April 18, 1913; *Testimony,* III, 2544-55.

41. *Testimony,* III, 2529-53; *Statistics,* p. 209; *Pageant of the Paterson Strike,* pp. 16-18.

42. *Testimony,* III, 2529-44.

43. John Reed, "Sheriff Radcliff's Hotel," *Metropolitan,* XXXVIII (September, 1913), 15-16, 59-60; New York *Globe,* April 28, 1913; John Reed, *Masses,* IV (June, 1913), 14-17, contains quotation.

44. *Ibid.* (italics in original).

45. *Testimony,* III, 2544-53, 2558-72, 2585-697; New York *Times,* April–July, 1913; New York *Globe,* April–July, 1913; "The End of the Paterson Strike," *Outlook,* CIV (Aug. 9, 1913), 780.

46. New York *Times,* May 25, 1913; New York *Call,* March 5, 1913.

47. *Statistics,* pp. 201-02.   48. *Ibid.,* p. 202.

49. Paterson *Evening News,* April 11, 12, 14, 1913; New York *Times,* April 11, 13, contains quotation; New York *Globe,* April 14, 1913; New York *Call,* April 11, 1913; *Testimony,* III, 2576-78, 2617.

50. New York *World,* April 21, 1913; New York *Evening Post,* quoted in *Literary Digest,* XLVI (May 10, 1913), 1043-44; *Statistics,* pp. 219-21; Paterson *Evening News,* April 21-24, 1913; New York *Times,* April 20, 22, May 18, 1913; New York *Globe,* April 21, 1913; *Testimony,* III, 2413-32; Gordon, "A Labor Man's Story of the Paterson Strike," *National Civic Federation Review,* IV (Dec. 1, 1913), 16-17.

51. New York *Times,* May 28, 1913; *Statistics,* pp. 217-18; Fitch, *Survey,* XXX (June 7, 1913), 357-62.

52. *Statistics,* p. 222, contains quotation; New York *Times,* June 7, 1913.

53. Mannheimer, "Darkest New Jersey," *Independent,* LXXIV (May 29, 1913), 1192.

54. Steiger, *Memoirs of a Silk Striker,* pp. 36-42; Paterson *Evening News,* May 1, 1913; New York *Times,* April 30, 1913; New York *Globe,* April 30, May 1, 1913; *Statistics,* pp. 191-92, 212.

55. Sinclair, *American Outpost,* pp. 262-63; Luhan, *Intimate Memories,* III, 188-89, 204, contains quotations (italics in original).

56. Granville Hicks, *John Reed,* p. 102, contains first quotation; Luhan, *Intimate Memories,* III, 203, contains second quotation.

57. Paterson *Press,* June 7, 9, 1913; Paterson *Evening News,* June 7, 9, 1913; Luhan, *Intimate Memories,* III, 203, contains first quotation; New York *World,* June 8, 1913; New York *Times,* June 8, 1913, contains second quotation.

58. Haywood, *Bill Haywood's Book,* pp. 261-77; New York *Times,* June 8, 1913, contains quotation.

59. New York *World,* June 8, 1913; Paterson *Press,* June 7, 9, 1913; New York *Times,* June 8, 1913, contains quotation; Paterson *Evening News,* June 7, 9, 1913; Luhan, *Intimate Memories,* III, 203.

60. *Pageant of the Paterson Strike,* pp. 16-18; Paterson *Evening News,* June 9, 1913; Haywood, *Bill Haywood's Book,* pp. 261-77; New York *World,* June 8, 1913.

61. Paterson *Press,* June 25, 1913; Paterson *Evening News,* June 25, 1010, New York *Times,* June 9, 23, 25, 1913; *Mother Earth,* VII (June, 1913), 102; New York *World* and New York *Tribune,* quoted in "The Pageant as a Form of Propaganda," *Current Opinion,* LV (July, 1913), 32; "The Paterson Strike Pageant," *Independent,* LXXIV (June 19, 1913), 1406-07; "Pageant of the Paterson Strike," *Survey,* XXX (June 28, 1913), 428; New York *Call,* June 9, 1913.

62. Poole, *The Bridge,* pp. 198-99; *The Education of John Reed,* p. 18, contains quotation; New York *Times,* May 19, 1913; Draper, *Roots of American Communism,* pp. 44, 118; Paterson *Evening News,* May 19, 1913; Steiger, *Memoirs of a Silk Striker,* pp. 58-70.

63. *Miners' Magazine,* XIV (July 24, 1913), 5-6, contains quotation; New York *Times,* June 23–25, 27, 1913; Flynn, *I Speak My Own Piece,* p. 56; Paterson *Press,* June 25, 1913; Paterson *Evening News,* June 25, 1913.

64. Gompers, "The I.W.W. Strikes," *American Federationist,* XX (August, 1913), 622-24; New York *Times,* July 25, 1913.

65. *Statistics,* pp. 225-27; New York *Times,* July 6, 7, 21-23, 1913.

66. "The End of the Paterson Strike," *Outlook,* CIV (Aug. 9, 1913), 780; New York *Times,* Nov. 22, 1913; *Statistics,* p. 238.

67. New York *Times,* July 25, 1913; Philadelphia *Inquirer,* New York *Herald, Journal of Commerce,* quoted in *Literary Digest,* XLVII (Aug. 9, 1913), 197-98.

68. New York *Call,* July 21, 1913; *Weekly People,* Aug. 21, 1913; *Miners' Magazine,* XIV (July 21, 1913), 6 (italics in original); Gompers, *American Federationist,* XX (August, 1913), 622-24; Stokes, "Paterson," *Masses,* V (November, 1913), 13.

69. *Testimony,* XI, 10574-82.

70. *Labor World* (1914), Walsh Scrapbooks, Walsh Papers; *Testimony,* II, 1451; *ibid.,* III, 2439.

71. *Testimony,* III, 2578-83, contains quotation; New York *Call,* New York *Tribune,* Paterson *Evening News,* Paterson *Morning Call,* Paterson *Press,* June 18, 1914, Walsh Scrapbooks, Walsh Papers.

72. *Testimony,* III, 2607-11; New York *Evening Post,* New York *Globe,* Paterson *Guardian,* Paterson *Evening News,* June 18, 1914, Walsh Scrapbooks, Walsh Papers.

73. Paterson *Press,* March 10, April 23, 24, 1913, quoted in *Testimony,* III, 2583-84; Paterson *Evening News,* Paterson *Press,* June 17, 1914, Walsh Scrapbooks, Walsh Papers.

74. Paterson *Evening News,* Paterson *Morning Call,* Paterson *Press,* June 18, 1914, *Journal of Commerce* (New York), June 19, 1914, Walsh Scrapbooks, Walsh Papers.

75. New York *World,* May 22, 1914, New York *Evening Sun,* June 19, 1914, Walsh Scrapbooks, Walsh Papers; Fitch, "The Paterson Silk Mill Strike a Year After," *Survey,* XXXII (June 27, 1914), 339-40.

Chapter V. Revolt in New York

1. New York *Times,* June 30, 1910, contains quotation.

2. *U.S. Census: 1900,* IX, *Manufactures,* Part III, p. 285; *U.S. Census: 1910,* VIII, *Manufactures,* p. 125; *ibid.,* IX, 188-89; Magee, *Trends in the Location of the Women's Clothing Industry,* p. 39; Price, "General Survey of Sanitary Conditions of the Shops in the Cloak Industry," *First Annual Report of the Joint Board,* p. 39.

3. Lorwin, *Women's Garment Workers,* pp. 99-100.

4. Dickinson and Kolchin, *Governor's Advisory Commission,* pp. 7, 12, 13; New York State, *Annual Report of the Bureau of Statistics and Labor,* III (1885), 23-25, contains quotation.

5. Eaton, "Receipts and Expenditures of Certain Wage-Earners in the Garment Trades," *American Statistical Association,* IV (June, 1895), 135-80; New York State, *Report of Factory Inspector,* 1894, pp. 788-89, cited in Lorwin, *Women's Garment Workers,* p. 22.

6. ILGWU, *Report of General Secretary-Treasurer, 1900–01;* ILGWU, *Reports and Proceedings, 1903–09;* New York State, *Department of Labor Bulletin,* IX (1907), 164-65; Lorwin, *Women's Garment Workers,* pp. 102-03, 120-26; Seidman, *Needle Trades,* pp. 99-102.

7. *Outlook,* XCIII (Dec. 11, 1909), 799-801; Women's Trade Union League, *Annual Aeport, 1909–10,* pp. 11-14; Boone, *Women's Trade Union Leagues,* p. 77.

8. Goodman and Ueland, "The Shirtwaist Trade," *Journal of Political Economy,* XVIII (December, 1910), 817-20; New York State Department of Labor, *Annual Report,* I (1910), 481-91; Hutchinson,

"Hygienic Aspects of the Shirtwaist Strike," *Survey*, XXIII (Jan. 22, 1910), 541-50.

9. *Ibid.*, pp. 547-50, contains first quotation; Sumner, "The Spirit of the Strikers," *Survey*, XXIII (Jan. 22, 1910), 554, contains second quotation.

10. Mailly, "The Working Girls' Strike," *Independent*, LXVII (Dec. 23, 1909), 1416-20; *Survey*, XXIII (Nov. 13, 1909), 228; New York *Times*, Dec. 16, 1909; Lorwin, *Women's Garment Workers*, p. 151; *Jewish Daily Forward*, Aug. 12, Sept. 11, 17, Oct. 3, 1909, cited in H. Berman, "The Era of the Protocol," p. 76; Clark and Wyatt, "Working Girls' Budgets," *McClure's*, XXXVI (November, 1910), 80.

11. *Ibid.*, pp. 70-86; *Survey*, XXIII (Jan. 8, 1910), 489-90; Mailly, *Independent*, LXVII (Dec. 23, 1909), 1416-20; New York *Times*, Jan. 4, 1910; *Outlook*, XCIII (Dec. 11, 1909), 800.

12. Sumner, *Survey*, XXIII (Jan. 22, 1910), 554; Mailly, *Independent*, LXVII (Dec. 23, 1909), 1417, contains quotation.

13. Clark and Wyatt, *McClure's*, XXXVI (November, 1910), 81.

14. Leupp, "The Shirtwaist Makers' Strike," *Survey*, XXIII (Dec. 18, 1909), 383.

15. Comstock, "The Uprising of the Girls," *Collier's*, XLIV (Dec. 25, 1909), 14-16, 20; Mailly, *Independent*, LXVII (Dec. 23, 1909), 1417-18; *Hampton's*, XXIV (March, 1910), 423-25; *Outlook*, XCIII (Dec. 11, 1909), 799; Lorwin, *Women's Garment Workers*, pp. 158-59.

16. Mailly, *Independent*, LXVII (Dec. 23, 1909), 1419; New York *World*, Nov. 26, 28, 1909; New York *Herald*, Nov. 26, 28, 1909; New York *Times*, Dec. 28, 1909, contains quotation.

17. New York *Times*, Dec. 24, 1909; Barnes, "The Strike of the Shirtwaist Makers," *World Today*, XVIII (March, 1910), 265-70; Clark and Wyatt, *McClure's*, XXXVI (November, 1910), 80-86.

18. New York *Times*, Dec. 24, 1909; Barnes, "The Strike of the Shirtwaist Makers," *World Today*, XVIII (March, 1910), 265-70.

19. *Survey*, XXIII (Jan. 8, 1910), 489.

20. Clark and Wyatt, *McClure's*, XXXVI (November, 1910), 82; Barnes, *World Today*, XVIII (March, 1910), 267, contains quotation.

21. New York *Call*, Dec. 29, 1909, contains first quotation; New York *Times*, Jan. 6, 1910, contains second quotation.

22. *Survey*, XXIII (Jan. 8, 1910), 489-90; Clark and Wyatt, *McClure's*, XXXVI (November, 1910), 82; New York *Times*, Jan. 3, 1910; Barnes, *World Today*, XVIII (March, 1910), 266-67, contains quotation.

23. *Century*, LXXIX (March, 1910), 791.

24. New York *World*, Dec. 4, 1909; New York *Times*, Dec. 4, 20, 21, 24, 1909, contains quotation; Comstock, *Collier's*, XLIV (Dec. 25, 1909), 16.

25. Malkiel, *Diary of a Shirtwaist Striker,* p. 24; *Hampton's,* XXIV (March, 1910), 423-25; New York *World,* Dec. 6, 1909, contains quotation.

26. New York *Times,* Dec. 10, 16, 1909; Sumner, *Survey,* XXIII (Jan. 22, 1910), 550-55, contains quotation; *Hampton's,* XXIV (March, 1910), 423-25.

27. *Ibid.;* New York *Times,* Dec. 16, 1909, Jan. 8, 1910.

28. New York *Times,* Dec. 19, 21, 30, 1909.

29. New York *Times,* Jan. 16, 1910.

30. *Survey,* XXIII (Jan. 8, 1910), 489; New York *Times,* Jan. 3, 1910, contains all quotations.

31. "Philadelphia Shirtwaist Strike," *Survey,* XXIII (Feb. 5, 1910), 595-96; New York State, *Department of Labor Bulletin,* XII (1910), 34-43; Boone, *Women's Trade Union League,* pp. 81-82; New York *Times,* Dec. 12, 1912, contains quotation; New York *Times,* Dec. 8, 24, 30, 1912.

32. Scott, "What the Women Strikers Won," *Outlook,* XCV (July 2, 1910), 480-81; Boone, *Women's Trade Union League,* pp. 81-82; Bernheimer, *The Shirtwaist Strike,* pp. 4-5; Clark and Wyatt, *McClure's,* XXXVI (November, 1910), 85.

33. Barnes, *World Today,* XVIII (March, 1910), 267-68; AFL, *Thirtieth Annual Convention,* p. 25; Clark and Wyatt, *McClure's,* XXXVI (November, 1910), 85-86; Scott, *Outlook,* XCV (July 2, 1910), 480-81.

34. Riis, *How the Other Half Lives,* pp. 120-35, 234-42; Lorwin, *Women's Garment Workers,* pp. 164-70, contains quotations.

35. *Testimony,* II, 1030, 1038; Joint Board of Sanitary Control, *Third Annual Report* (1913), pp. 19-20, quotations from a survey of the industry completed under its auspices.

36. "Men Who Make Women's Clothes," *Survey,* XXIV (Aug. 13, 1910), 701-03; Wyatt, "New York Cloak-Makers' Strike," *McClure's,* XXXVI (April, 1911), 708; "The Cloakmakers' Strike," *Outlook,* XCV (July 23, 1910), 596-97; Lorwin, *Women's Garment Workers,* p. 175; *Testimony,* II, 1030.

37. ILGWU, *Tenth Annual Convention* (1910), *Eleventh Annual Convention* (1911), *Twelfth Annual Convention* (1912); New York *Times,* July 10, 1910; Berman, "The Era of the Protocol," pp. 178-79.

38. ILGWU, *Eleventh Annual Convention* (1911), pp. 10-11; *Ladies' Garment Worker,* I (July, 1910); New York *Times,* June 30, 1910.

39. McPherson, "The New York Cloakmakers' Strike," *Journal of Political Economy,* XIX (March, 1911), 154-56; New York *Times,* July 8, 1910.

40. *Ibid.;* Lorwin, *Women's Garment Workers,* p. 182, contains first quotation; Abraham Rosenberg, *Memoirs of a Cloakmaker* (New York, 1920, original in Yiddish), cited in *ibid.,* contains second quotation.

41. New York *Times*, July 14, 1910, contains quotation; New York *Times*, July 8, 1910; McPherson, *Journal of Political Economy*, XIX (March, 1911), 154-56; Cloak, Suit, and Skirt Manufacturers Protective Association, "Memorandum of Agreement," in *The Cloakmakers' Strike*, pp. 2-4.

42. New York *World*, Aug. 9, 1910; New York *Times*, Aug. 6, 8–10, 1910.

43. New York *Times*, Aug. 9, 1910.

44. New York *Times*, Aug. 17–20, 1910.

45. New York *Times*, Aug. 12–14, 1910; New York *Times*, Aug. 7, 1910, contains quotation.

46. McPherson, *Journal of Political Economy*, XIX (March, 1911), 182-83; New York *Times*, Aug. 28, 1910, contains quotation.

47. New York *World*, Aug. 28, 29, 31; New York *Times*, Aug. 28, 1910, contains quotation; New York *Times*, Aug. 29-31, Sept. 2, 1910.

48. New York *Times*, Aug. 19, 1910, contains quotation; New York *Times*, Aug. 20, Sept. 2, 1910.

49. New York *Globe*, July 28, 1910; New York *World*, July 28, 1910; New York *Call*, July 20, 1910; Cloak, Suit, and Skirt Manufacturers Protective Association, "Minutes of Joint Conference," in *The Cloakmakers' Strike*, pp. 127-47; Wyatt, *McClure's*, XXXVI (April, 1911), 710-11; McPherson, *Journal of Political Economy*, XIX (March, 1911), 166-67.

50. New York *Call*, July 30, 1910; New York *Times*, July 30, Aug. 2, 4, 5, 1910; "Minutes of Joint Conference," pp. 1-145; "The Cloakmakers' Strike," *Outlook*, XCV (Aug. 20, 1910), 855-56; Wyatt, *McClure's*, XXXVI (April, 1911), 710-12.

51. *Ibid.*, p. 712, contains both quotations.

52. New York *World*, Aug. 23, 26, 1910; New York *World*, Aug. 27, 1910, contains quotations; New York *Times*, Aug. 26, 28, 30, Dec. 28, 1910.

53. "The Outcome of the Cloakmakers' Strike," *Outlook*, XCVI (Sept. 17, 1910), 100; *Ladies' Garment Worker*, II (February, 1911); New York *Times*, Sept. 3, 1910; Wyatt, *McClure's*, XXXVI (April, 1911), 714.

54. "Text of Protocol Agreement, Sept. 2, 1910, for the Cloak, Suit and Skirt Industry of New York City," reprinted in Winslow, *Industrial Court*, pp. 56-58; *Testimony*, II, 1031, 1062.

55. Winslow, *Industrial Court*, pp. 56-58.

56. Brandeis, "The Preferential Shop," *Human Engineering*, II (August, 1912), 179-81; J. H. Cohen, *Law and Order in Industry*, pp. 15-16, 42.

57. ILGWU, *Twelfth Annual Convention*, pp. 54-55, contains first

quotation; *Testimony*, II, 1045; *ibid.*, p. 1041, contains second quotation.

58. Winslow, *Industrial Court*, pp. 8, 19; Lorwin, *Women's Garment Workers*, pp. 203-05; *Survey*, XXIX (Jan. 18, 1913), 491.

59. "Economic Statesmanship," *New Republic*, II (Feb. 6, 1915), 11-12; New York *Times*, April 7, 1912, March 31, 1913, Jan. 6, 1914; Moscowitz, "An Experiment in Democratic Industrial Control," *LaFollette's*, V (April 19, 1913), 5, 13, 14; Weed, "Instead of Strikes," *Everybody's*, XXIX (July, 1913), 131-32; Barnum, "How Industrial Peace Has Been Brought About in the Clothing Trade," *Independent*, LXXIII (Oct. 3, 1912), 777, contains first quotation; Marcosson, "A Truce in the Trades," *Munsey's*, XLIX (July, 1913), 527; *Cloak and Suit Review*, III (June, 1912), 128, contains second quotation; *Ladies' Garment Worker*, II (October, 1911), 11-16; Barnum, *Independent*, LXXIII (Oct. 3, 1912), 777, contains third quotation.

60. "Report of the General Secretary," in ILGWU, *Twelfth Annual Convention*, pp. 52-59; Winslow, *Industrial Court*, pp. 20, 24-26, 29-31; *Testimony*, II, 1037.

61. New York *Times*, Jan. 5, 8, 10, 1914; Harriman, "Hither and Yon," *Century*, CVII (December, 1923), 299, contains first quotation; Harriman to Walsh, Jan. 12, 1914 (telegram), Walsh to Harriman, Jan. 12, 1914, Walsh Papers; *Testimony*, II, 1042, 1151-56; New York *World*, Jan. 17, 18, 1914; New York *Call*, Jan. 16, 17, 1914; New York *Times*, Jan. 17, 1914; Harriman, *Century*, CVII (December, 1923), 300, contains second quotation.

62. *Testimony*, II, 1034-35, 1046, 1053-54, 1113, 1140-41; *ibid.*, p. 1075, contains quotation.

63. *Ibid.*, pp. 1034-35; Lorwin, *Women's Garment Workers*, pp. 241-43; Winslow, *Industrial Court*, pp. 5-55.

64. *Ladies' Garment Worker*, III (November, 1912), 9-11; IV (January, 1913), 13-16, (July, 1913), 11-14; Kennan, "How Russia Loses Good Citizens," *Outlook*, CIV (July 26, 1913), 714-17; New York *Times*, Jan. 5, 8, 10, 19, 1914; Selig Perlman, "Recent Developments in the Cloak and Suit Protocol Situation, March 1914" (manuscript in USCIR Papers, Records Group 174).

65. *Testimony*, II, 1094-142, 1147, 1157; *ibid.*, pp. 1096-97, 1105, 1048-49, contain quotations.

66. *Ibid.*, pp. 1040, 1041, 1082, 1116, 1119.

67. New York *Herald*, Jan. 17, 1914; New York *World*, Jan. 17, 1914; Harriman, *Century*, CVII (December, 1923), 140; *Testimony*, II, 1132-33, contains quotation.

68. New York *World*, Jan. 17, 1914; Harriman, *Century*, CVII (December, 1923), 300, contains first quotation; *Testimony*, II, 1112-13, contains other quotations.

69. New York *Times,* Feb. 4, 10, 1914, July–August, 1915, April–August, 1916; *Survey,* XXXIV (July 31, 1915), 390; *Outlook,* CX (July 14, 1915), 591; *Independent,* XXCVI (May 15, 1916), 233-34, (June 19, 1916), 464-65.

70. *Testimony,* II, 1132.

Chapter VI. Continental Battleground

1. *Railway Clerk,* XI (February, 1912), 33.

2. Foster, *The Railroader's Next Step,* p. 22; St. Louis *Globe-Democrat,* Oct. 4, 1911, contains quotation.

3. Faulkner, *Quest for Social Justice,* pp. 32-35; Kirkland, *History of American Economic Life,* pp. 339-78; Sharfman, *American Railroad Problem,* pp. 319-21; Barnett, "Growth of Labor Organizations in the United States, 1897–1914, *Quarterly Journal of Economics,* XXX (August, 1916), 780-85; Trachtenberg, ed., *American Labor Yearbook, 1914–1920,* pp. 147-99; *Locomotive Firemen's Magazine,* XVII (June, 1893), 511; Kirk, *National Labor Federations,* p. 87; *Testimony,* X, 9761; Moody, *Masters of Capital,* pp. 19-34, 89-108; Tarbell, *Nationalizing of Business,* pp. 91-112.

4. *American Federationist,* XXIV (February, 1917), 116-19; Brotherhood of Railway Carmen, *Eleventh Biennial Convention,* pp. 10-12; Conlon, "Memories of the Past," *Machinists' Monthly Journal,* XXXIV (November, 1922), 729; *Machinists' Monthly Journal,* XX (April, 1908), 295, (May, 1908), 420-21; XXI (April, 1909), 342; *Testimony,* X, 9761.

5. AFL, *28th Annual Convention* (1908), p. 242; *Railway Clerk,* VIII (February, 1909), 50-52; *American Federationist,* XXIV (February, 1917), 116-19.

6. *Illinois Central System,* pp. 1-8; Illinois Central Railroad Co., *61st Annual Report* (1911), p. 5; *The Union Pacific System,* p. 5; Kirkland, *History of American Economic Life,* pp. 353-55.

7. *Machinists' Monthly Journal,* XXIII (August, 1911), 789; *Railway Carmen's Journal,* XVIII (February, 1913), 87-88, (May, 1913), 265-66; *American Engineer,* XXCVII (May, 1913), 249-56; *Testimony,* X, 9703-04, 9782.

8. Park, *Facts about the Shopmen's Strike; Railway Age Gazette,* LI (Oct. 6, 1911), 680; *Testimony,* X, 9701-05; St. Louis *Globe-Democrat,* Oct. 1, 1911.

9. Park, *Facts about the Shopmen's Strike,* p. 9, contains first quotation; *Railway Age Gazette,* LI (Oct. 6, 1911), 626; Illinois Central Railroad, *62nd Annual Report* (1912), pp. 1-6, contains final quotation.

10. *Boilermakers' Journal*, XXIII (Nov. 1, 1911), 867, (Dec. 1, 1911), 976; *Railway Carmen's Journal*, XVIII (February, 1913), 87-88; New York *Tribune*, Sept. 1, 2, 5, 1911; Vicksburg *Herald*, Sept. 1, 2, 1911; *Testimony*, X, 9701-05; Memphis *Commercial Appeal*, Sept. 26, 1911, in *Railway Clerk*, X (October, 1911), 372-76; St. Louis *Globe-Democrat*, Oct. 1, 1911; New Orleans *Times-Picayune*, Sept. 30, Oct. 1, 1911; Chicago *Record-Herald*, Oct. 1, 1911.

11. Chicago *Record-Herald*, Oct. 1, 3, 1911, contains quotations; St. Louis *Globe-Democrat*, Oct. 1, 3, 1911.

12. New Orleans *Times-Picayune*, Oct. 1, 1911; Chicago *Record-Herald*, Oct. 1, 1911; New Orleans *Item*, Sept. 10, 1911; Chicago *Inter-Ocean*, Oct. 3, 1911, in *Testimony*, X, 9708-09; New York *Tribune*, Sept. 7, 1911; *Nation*, XCIII (Sept. 7, 1911), 228-29; New York *Call*, Oct. 2, 1911.

13. *Testimony*, X, 9799.

14. *Ibid.*, pp. 9734-35; St. Louis *Globe-Democrat*, Oct. 1, 4, 5, 1911.

15. *Testimony*, X, 9710-11, 9732, 9736, 9754; *Deseret Evening News*, Oct. 2–11, 1911; New York *Call*, Oct. 4, 1911; St. Louis *Globe-Democrat*, Oct. 4, 1911.

16. *Testimony*, X, 9723-24; *Railway Age Gazette*, LI (Oct. 6, 1911), 681; New York *Call*, Oct. 6, 1911, contains quotation; *Deseret Evening News*, Oct. 6, 1911; St. Louis *Globe-Democrat*, Oct. 3, 1911; Chicago *Record-Herald*, Oct. 3, 1911; Vicksburg *Herald*, Oct. 6, 1911.

17. Chicago *Daily Socialist*, Oct. 2, 1911; *Testimony*, X, 9711-12; *Railway Age Gazette*, LII (Jan. 5, 1912), 26.

18. St. Louis *Globe-Democrat*, Oct. 3, 4, 1911; *Deseret Evening News*, Oct. 3, 1911; New Orleans *Times-Picayune*, Oct. 4, 1911; *Testimony*, X, 9711.

19. Chicago *Record-Herald*, Oct. 4, 1911; New York *Call*, Oct. 4, 1911; New Orleans *Times-Picayune*, Oct. 4, 1911, contains quotation; *Railway Age Gazette*, LI (Oct. 6, 1911), 681; St. Louis *Globe-Democrat*, Oct. 4, 5, 1911.

20. Vicksburg *Herald*, Oct. 5, 1911; New York *Call*, Oct. 5, 6, 1911, contains quotation; St. Louis *Globe-Democrat*, Oct. 5, 1911; *Testimony*, X, 9714-15; *Railway Age Gazette*, LI (Oct. 6, 1911), 681; New Orleans *Times-Picayune*, Oct. 9, 1911.

21. New York *Call*, Oct. 6, 1911, contains quotation; St. Louis *Globe-Democrat*, Oct. 6, 7, 1911; New Orleans *Times-Picayune*, Oct. 6, 1911.

22. *Railway Clerk*, X (December, 1911), 456-58; St. Louis *Globe-Democrat*, Oct. 7, 1911, contains first and third quotations; New York *Call*, Oct. 5, 1911, contains second quotation; Vicksburg *Herald*, Oct. 6, 7, 1911.

23. *Testimony*, X, 9719.

24. *Machinists' Monthly Journal,* XXIII (December, 1911), 1232; XXIV (March, 1912), 226, contains quotation.

25. *Testimony,* X, 9715-20, contains quotation.

26. New Orleans *Times-Picayune,* Oct. 2, 1911; *Testimony,* X, 9715-18, contains quotation; St. Louis *Globe-Democrat,* Oct. 6, 1911.

27. St. Louis *Globe-Democrat,* Oct. 6, 1911; *Testimony,* X, 9720-23, 9830, contains quotations.

28. New Orleans *Times-Picayune,* Oct. 2-4, 7, 1911; St. Louis *Globe-Democrat,* Oct. 4, 6, 1911; *Deseret Evening News,* Oct. 2, 3, 5, 10, 1911; New York *Call,* Oct. 3, 4, 10, 1911; Chicago *Record-Herald,* Oct. 7, 8, 1911.

29. St. Louis *Post-Dispatch,* Oct. 4, 1911; St. Louis *Globe-Democrat,* Oct. 3-5, 1911; *Deseret Evening News,* Oct. 2, 1911; New York *Call,* Oct. 3, 1911; *Machinists' Monthly Journal,* XXIII (December, 1911), 1232, contains quotation.

30. *Railway Age Gazette,* LI (Oct. 6, 1911), 681, *Testimony,* X, 9711-12; St. Louis *Globe-Democrat,* Oct. 5, 6, 1911; *Deseret Evening News,* Oct. 11, 1911; St. Louis *Post-Dispatch,* Oct. 2, 1911; St. Louis *Globe-Democrat,* Oct. 5, 6, 1911; Chicago *Daily Socialist,* Oct. 2, 1911.

31. *Testimony,* X, 9830; Chicago *Record-Herald,* Oct. 3, 6, 1911.

32. St. Louis *Post-Dispatch,* Oct. 4, 1911; *Testimony,* X, 9713, contains quotation.

33. Gibbons, "A Fight to a Finish," *International Socialist Review,* XV (August, 1914), 72-78.

34. *Ibid.;* "War! War! War!" *Blacksmith's Journal,* XVI (October, 1914), 1-6.

35. *Ibid.;* Gibbons, *International Socialist Review,* XV (August, 1914), 72-78.

36. "War! War! War!" *Blacksmith's Journal,* XVI (October, 1914), 1-6; Gibbons, *International Socialist Review,* XV (August, 1914), 72-78.

37. *Ibid.,* p. 76.

38. New York *Call,* Oct. 1, 1914; Gibbons, *International Socialist Review,* XV (August, 1914), 72-78.

39. *Ibid.;* "War! War! War!" *Blacksmith's Journal,* XVI (October, 1914), 1-6.

40. Railway Employees' Department, AFL, *Second Biennial Convention* (1914), pp. 23-24; "War! War! War!" *Blacksmith's Journal,* XVI (October, 1914), 1-6; New York *Call,* Oct. 6, 1914, contains quotation.

41. *Railway Clerk,* XI (February, 1912), 34.

42. New Orleans *Times-Picayune,* Oct. 2, 1911; St. Louis *Globe-Democrat,* Oct. 4, 1911; *Railway Clerk,* XI (March, 1912), 74; *Deseret Evening News,* Oct. 9, 20, 27, 1911.

43. *Railway Clerk,* XI (February, 1912), 34; Chicago *Examiner,* Feb. 23, 1912, cited in "Now Who Is to Blame?" *Blacksmith's Journal,* XIV (March, 1912), 11; *Railway Clerk,* XI (December, 1912), 401-02, contains quotation.

44. Comerford, "Organized Labor Demands to Be Heard," *Railway Carmen's Journal,* XVIII (July, 1913), 417-20; "Twelve Months of Train Wrecks," *Literary Digest,* XLV (Dec. 28, 1912), 1209-10; Railway Employees' Department, AFL, *Second Biennial Convention,* pp. 24-25, contains quotation; Interstate Commerce Commission, *Railway Accidents, Extracts from the 25th Annual Report* (1912), p. 5.

45. Illinois Central Railroad Company, *61st Annual Report* (1911), p. 5, *62nd Annual Report* (1912), pp. 5-6; New York *Times,* Jan. 25, 1913.

46. New York *Times,* June 19, July 31, 1913; *Railway Clerk,* XI (June, 1912), 191-94.

47. Chicago *Daily Socialist,* Nov. 21, 1911; Helbing, *Departments of the A.F. of L.,* p. 80; *Machinists' Monthly Journal,* XXIV (April, 1912), 325; Conlon, "Memories of the Past," *Machinists' Monthly Journal,* XXXV (January, 1923), 21-22; Chicago *Record-Herald,* Oct. 7, 1911; *Testimony,* X, 9735.

48. Conlon, *Machinists' Monthly Journal,* XXXV (January, 1923), 21-22. Carl Person claimed that these union officials tried to sell out the AFL. The latter denied this accusation. See Person, *The Lizard's Trail,* pp. 174-78; Conlon, *Machinists' Monthly Journal,* XXXV (January, 1923), 21-22.

49. "Federation of Federations, Official Proceedings," *Blacksmith's Journal,* XIV (May, 1912), 1-38; *Machinists' Monthly Journal,* XXVII (April, 1915), 362-63; Conlon, *Machinists' Monthly Journal,* XXXV (January, 1923), 17-23; *Railway Clerk,* XI (May, 1912), 159-60, includes both quotations. See also Perlman, *The Machinists,* pp. 40-42.

50. *American Federationist,* XXIV (February, 1917), 116-19; *Machinists' Monthly Journal,* XXV (January, 1913), 37.

51. *Railway Carmen's Journal,* XXVIII (April, 1913), 252-53; Conlon, *Machinists' Monthly Journal,* XXXV (January, 1923), 19; Helbing, *Departments of the A.F. of L.,* p. 90; *Testimony,* X, 9832, 9938-39.

52. AFL, *32nd Annual Convention* (1912), pp. 378-79; Railway Employees' Department, AFL, *Second Biennial Convention* (1914), pp. 13-15; *Machinists' Monthly Journal,* XXVII (January, 1915), 44; XXVII (July, 1915), 648-49.

53. AFL, *33rd Annual Convention* (1913), pp. 382-83; Railway Employees' Department, AFL, *Second Biennial Convention* (1914), pp. 16-19, and *Third Biennial Convention* (1916), p. 7, cited in Helbing,

Departments of the A.F. of L., p. 81; Person, *The Lizard's Trail*, pp. 246-47.

54. *Testimony*, X, 9738-39, 9759-80, 9742, 9799, 9822-27, 9913-16, 9925; New York *Call*, April 9, 1915.

55. *Testimony*, X, 9742.   56. *Ibid.*, pp. 9315-25, 9781-99.

57. *Ibid.*, p. 9798; New York *Times*, April 10, 1915.

58. *Testimony*, X, 9900.   59. *Ibid.*, p. 9706.   60. *Ibid.*, p. 9707.

61. *Ibid.*   62. *Ibid.*, p. 9895.   63. *Ibid.*, p. 9740.

64. Railway Employees' Department, AFL, *Second Biennial Convention* (1914), pp. 4, 57-58, and *Third Biennial Convention* (1916), pp. 1-2, cited in Helbing, *Departments of the A.F. of L.*, p. 81; Perlman and Taft, *Labor Movements*, p. 373.

Chapter VII. Massacre in Colorado

1. New York *Times*, April 23, 1914.

2. Creel, *Rebel at Large*, pp. 127-28, contains quotation; Lauck to Walsh, Walsh to Lauck (telegrams), Jan. 10, 1914, Lauck to Walsh, Jan. 12, 1914, Walsh to Lauck, Jan. 15, 22, 1914 (copies), Walsh Papers.

3. Harriman to Addams, May 7, 1914, Papers of Mrs. J. Borden Harriman, Library of Congress; Walsh to West, May 4, 1914 (two telegrams, copies), Walsh Papers; New York *Mail*, New York *Herald*, May 27, 1914, Walsh Scrapbooks, Walsh Papers; New York *Times*, May 28, 1914; Fitch, 'The Colorado War Interrupts Inquiry into Jurisdictional Disputes," *Survey*, XXXII (June 6, 1914), 252.

4. West to Walsh, June 26, 27, 1914, USCIR Papers, Department of Labor Files, contains quotations; U.S. Department of Labor, *Second Annual Report* (1914), pp. 40-41; Ralph Easley to E. R. A. Seligman, Nov. 7, 1914, Seligman Papers.

5. Lennon and Ballard, "Report on Situation in Colorado Strike Zone," May 14, 1914 (unpublished, copy), USCIR Papers, Labor Department Files.

6. Elias M. Ammons and George A. Carlson to Walsh, May 24, 1914 (telegrams), contains first quotation; Walsh to Creel, Nov. 27, 1914 (copy); Denver *Times*, Nov. 24, 1914; Walsh to Ballard, Garretson, Weinstock, Nov. 16, 1914 (three letters, copies), contains other quotations; *Rocky Mountain News*, Nov. 26, 1914, Denver *Times*, Denver *Post*, Nov. 25, 1914, Walsh Scrapbooks, Walsh Papers.

7. Yellen, *American Labor Struggles*, pp. 205, 210, 220; West, *Report on the Colorado Strike*, p. 139.

8. *Ibid.*, p. 54; W. T. Davis, "The Strike War in Colorado," *Outlook*, CVII (May 9, 1914), 70; U.S. House, *Report on the Colorado*

Strike Investigation, p. 39, hereinafter referred to as *Congressional Report; Testimony*, IX, 8492, contains quotation.

9. Davis, *Outlook*, CVII (May 9, 1914), 70; Yellen, *American Labor Struggles*, p. 206; *Testimony*, IX, 8492-93, 8499, contains quotations.

10. *Testimony*, VII, 6356-60, 6554-55, 6566; West, *Report on the Colorado Strike*, pp. 68-71; *Congressional Report*, p. 5.

11. *Testimony*, IX, 8496-98, 8557-58, contains first quotation; M. McCusker, "Report on the Colorado Situation" (unpublished), USCIR Papers, Labor Department Files, contains second quotation.

12. *Testimony*, IX, 8503, contains Bowers quotations; *ibid.*, VIII, 7135-39, contains Northcutt quotations; *Congressional Report*, pp. 26-30.

13. *Testimony*, IX, 8773, contains quotations.

14. Mote, *Industrial Arbitration*, pp. 297-98; *Testimony*, VII, 6500; U.S. Department of Labor, Bureau of Labor Statistics, *Monthly Review*, III (August, 1916), 35-37.

15. Colorado Senate, *Testimony Taken before the Committee on Privileges and Elections of the Nineteenth General Assembly*, February 5, 1913, pp. 843-44, as cited in George S. McGovern, "The Colorado Coal Strike, 1913–1914," p. 58.

16. *Congressional Report*, p. 22; Mote, *Industrial Arbitration*, pp. 293, 297; *Testimony*, IX, 8781-82, contains quotations.

17. McCusker, "Report on the Colorado Situation"; *Testimony*, VII, 6463, 6471, 6780, VIII, 7193; *Congressional Report*, pp. 4-5, 24.

18. Colorado Bureau of Labor Statistics, *Ninth Biennial Report* (1903–04), pp. 193-98; United Mine Workers of America, *Proceedings of the 25th Consecutive and Second Biennial Convention*, I (1916), 100; *UMW Journal*, XXIV (Sept. 11, 1913), 1; McGovern, "The Colorado Coal Strike," pp. 115-21; "Report on Colorado," USCIR Papers, Labor Department Files.

19. *UMW Journal*, XXIV (Sept. 18, 25, 1913), 1; *Testimony*, VII, 6515, contains quotation; *Congressional Report*, p. 5; West, *Report on the Colorado Strike*, pp. 62-63, 33.

20. Report on Colorado by two investigators, USCIR Papers, Labor Department Files; *Testimony*, IX, 8415-16, contains quotation; *ibid.*, VII, 6454-56; VIII, 7117; Mote, *Industrial Arbitration*, pp. 290-91; New York *Times*, Dec. 3, 1914.

21. *Testimony*, VII, 6518; New York *Call*, Sept. 24, 25, 1913; *Rocky Mountain News*, Sept. 18, 1913, as cited in McGovern, "The Colorado Coal Strike," p. 161; West, *Report on the Colorado Strike*, pp. 31-32, contains quotation.

22. *Military Occupation*, pp. 20-24; *Testimony*, VII, 6800-02, *ibid.*, VIII, 7234-35, contains quotations; New York *Globe*, Oct. 28, 1913; *Congressional Report*, pp. 6, 37.

23. *UMW Journal*, XXIV (Aug. 21, 1913), 1, 2, 7, 8, (Aug. 28, 1913), 1, 2, 8; West, *Report on the Colorado Strike*, pp. 102-06.

24. *Military Occupation*, pp. 18-20; *UMW Journal*, XXIV (Oct. 30, 1913), 1, XXIV (Nov. 13, 1913), 1; Fitch, "Law and Order: The Issue in Colorado," *Survey*, XXXIII (Dec. 5, 1914), 252; *Congressional Report*, p. 17.

25. New York *Times*, Oct. 27, 1913; New York *Call*, Oct. 28, 1913; *Testimony*, VII, 6867-70; West, *Report on the Colorado Strike*, pp. 104-05.

26. *Military Occupation*, pp. 8-9; *Testimony*, VII, 6362, 6488-89; New York *Globe*, Oct. 28, 1913; Ammons to Chase, Oct. 28, 1913, Ammons Papers, as cited in McGovern, "The Colorado Coal Strike," p. 208.

27. *UMW Journal*, XXIV (Nov. 6, 1913), 1; *Military Occupation*, pp. 13-15, 37-38; *Testimony*, VII, 6362, 6412-13, 6488-89, 6826-27, contains quotation; New York *Globe*, Oct. 00, 1913; New York *Times*, Oct. 30, 31, 1913.

28. Eastman, "Class War in Colorado," *Masses*, V (June, 1914), 6; Bowden, "New Developments in the Colorado Strike Situation," *Survey*, XXXI (Feb. 14, 1914), 613-14; New York *Times*, Dec. 3, 1914; *Testimony*, VIII, 7170-71.

29. Mote, *Industrial Arbitration*, p. 294; Bowden, *Survey*, XXXI (Feb. 14, 1914), 614; *Testimony*, VII, 6484-89, contains first quotation; *Congressional Report*, p. 16, contains second quotation; New York *Times*, Dec. 5, 1914.

30. Gilmore, "Shadows of Revolt," *Masses*, VI (July, 1915), 8, contains quotations; *UMW Journal*, XXIV (Nov. 6, 1913), 1, 2.

31. Harriman, *From Pinafores to Politics*, p. 143, contains first quotation; Kansas City *Star*, Feb. 7, 1915, Walsh Scrapbooks, Walsh Papers, contains second quotation.

32. West, *Report on the Colorado Strike*, p. 122, contains quotation; *Testimony*, VII, 6833; *Christian Socialist*, Jan. 15, 1915, p. 13; *UMW Journal*, XXV (Jan. 8, 1914), 1; *Military Occupation*, pp. 27, 31-32, 47.

33. Bowden, *Survey*, XXXI (Feb. 14, 1914), 614; *UMW Journal*, XXV (Dec. 17, 1914), 13; *Testimony*, VII, 6648, 6833, contains quotations; *Military Occupation*, pp. 31-32, 45-47; Colorado Federation of Labor, *Militarism in Colorado*, p. 12.

34. *Ibid.*, contains quotation; *Congressional Report*, pp. 3-16.

35. Fitch, *Survey*, XXXIII (Dec. 5, 1914), 256; *Testimony*, VII, 6642, 6707, 6810.

36. Eastman, *Masses*, V (June, 1914), 6; West, *Report on the Colorado Strike*, pp. 125-26; *Testimony*, VII, 6363-64; New York *Times*, April 21, 1914.

37. New York *Times,* April 21-22, 1914; Fitch, *Survey,* XXXIII (Dec. 5, 1914), 257; Eastman, *Masses,* V (June, 1914), 6; *Testimony,* VII, 6364-66, 6816, 6886-96; New York *Globe,* May 28, 1914, Walsh Scrapbooks, Walsh Papers.

38. Davis, *Outlook,* CVII (May 9, 1914), 68-70; *Testimony,* VII, 6891, contains quotation, 6316, 6364-66, 6888-96; New York *Globe,* May 28, 1914; New York *Mail,* May 28, 1914, Walsh Scrapbooks, Walsh Papers; New York *Times,* April 21, 22, 1914.

39. New York *Times,* April 21, 22, Dec. 12, 1914; New York *Evening Sun,* May 28, 1914, Walsh Scrapbooks, Walsh Papers; Eastman, *Masses,* V (June, 1914), 8; *Testimony,* VII, 6886-96; *ibid.,* pp. 6364-66, contains first quotation; *ibid.,* p. 6895, contains second quotation.

40. *Testimony,* VII, 6646, 6887, contains quotations; Fitch, *Survey,* XXXIII (Dec. 5, 1914), 252; West, *Report on the Colorado Strike,* p. 125; New York *Times,* Dec. 12, 1914; *Christian Socialist,* May 15, 1914.

41. New York *Evening World,* May 27, 28, New York *Evening Journal,* May 28, New York *Evening Post,* May 27, 1914, Walsh Scrapbooks, Walsh Papers; *Testimony,* VII, 6347-51, 6366-67, contains quotation, *ibid.,* IX, 8190-98; Fitch, *Survey,* XXXII (June 6, 1914), 252.

42. *Testimony,* VII, 6351; *ibid.,* VIII, 7101, 7378, contains quotations; Fitch, *Survey,* XXXII (June 6, 1914), 252; *Christian Socialist,* May 15, 1914, pp. 3-5; New York *American,* New York *Tribune,* New York *Times,* May 28, 1914, Walsh Scrapbooks, Walsh Papers; New York *Times,* April 22, 1914.

43. *Testimony,* VII, 6894.

44. New York *Globe,* April 21, 1914; New York *Times,* April 21, 22, May 29, 1914; *UMW Journal,* XXIV (May 7, 1914), 1, 2, 3; Davis, *Outlook,* CVII (May 9, 1914), 69-69; Fitch, *Survey,* XXXIII (Dec. 5, 1914), 252; *Testimony,* IX, 8190-98, contains quotation; *ibid.,* VII, 6353-67, 6371; G. J. Stowell, "Chronology of the Colorado Strike" (unpublished); George P. West, "Report on Ludlow," May 19, 1914 (unpublished), USCIR Papers, Labor Department Files. These papers also contain many photographs and affidavits relevant to Ludlow.

45. Military Commission Report, cited in *Testimony,* IX, 8626, contains quotations; New York *Call,* New York *Sun,* May 29, 1914, Walsh Scrapbooks, Walsh Papers; Mote, *Industrial Arbitration,* pp. 294-95.

46. Fitch, *Survey,* XXXIII (Dec. 5, 1914), 252-55; *Testimony,* VII, 6368, 6371-72, 6389, contains all quotations; New York *Call,* New York *Sun,* May 29, 1914, Walsh Scrapbooks, Walsh Papers.

47. Fitch, *Survey,* XXXIII (Dec. 5, 1914), 254, contains first quotation; John R. Lawson, President of Colorado State Federation of La-

bor, and UMW officials, "A Call to Rebellion," reprinted in *Testimony*, VII, 6983, contains other quotations; New York *Times*, April 24, 1914; *Congressional Report*, p. 37; Davis, *Outlook*, CVII (May 9, 1914), 69.

48. Chicago *Record-Herald*, April 26, 29, 1914; Denver *News*, April 23, 30, 1914, as cited in Perlman and Taft, *Labor Movements*, pp. 339-40; New York *Times*, April 23, 24, 30, 1914; New York *Globe*, April 22, 1914; Davis, *Outlook*, CVII (May 9, 1914), 68-69; *Testimony*, VII, 6984, VIII, 7005-07.

49. *Christian Socialist*, May 15, 1914, p. 3; Chicago *Record-Herald*, April 26, 1914; New York *Times*, April 27, May 1, 1914; *Survey*, XXXII (May 23, 1914), 211-13; *Testimony*, VII, 6416-17; "Report on Colorado Strike" (unpublished), USCIR Papers, Labor Department Files; Link, *Wilson: The New Freedom*, p. 459.

50. Gilmore, *Masses*, VI (March, 1915), 8-9, contains quotations; New York *Times*, June 20, 1915.

51. Kansas City *Star*, Jan. 26, 27, 1915, Walsh Scrapbooks, Walsh Papers, contains quotations; Kansas City *Post*, Jan. 25, 26, 1915, Walsh Scrapbooks; New York *Times*, Jan. 26, 1915; Gilmore, *Masses*, VI (March, 1915), 8-9.

52. *Testimony*, VIII, 7764, contains quotations; Fitch, "The Rockefeller Interests in Industry and Philanthropy," *Survey*, XXXIII (Feb. 6, 1915), 519-20; New York *Call*, New York *Times*, Jan. 26, 1915; Kansas City *Post*, Jan. 25, 1915, Walsh Scrapbooks, Walsh Papers.

53. New York *Call*, New York *Times*, Jan. 26, 1915; Kansas City *Post*, Jan. 25, 1915, Walsh Scrapbooks, Walsh Papers; Fitch, *Survey*, XXXIII (Feb. 6, 1915), 519-20; *Testimony*, VIII, 7764-65, contains quotations.

54. Kansas City *Post*, Jan. 26, 1915, Walsh Scrapbooks, Walsh Papers; New York *Times*, New York *Call*, Jan. 27, 1915; *Testimony*, VIII, 7801-05, 7822; *ibid.*, p. 7819, contains quotations.

55. *Testimony*, VIII, 7766, 7886, contains quotations; New York *Times*, Jan. 28, 1915; Kansas City *Star*, Kansas City *Post*, Jan. 28, 1915, Walsh Scrapbooks, Walsh Papers.

56. New York *Times*, Jan. 28, 26, 1915; Gilmore, *Masses*, VI (March, 1915), 8; Harriman, *From Pinafores to Politics*, pp. 144, 145.

57. Kansas City *Post*, Jan. 26, 28, 1915, Walsh Scrapbooks, Walsh Papers, contains first two quotations; New York *Times*, Jan. 28, 1915, contains all other quotations.

58. New York *Times*, New York *Tribune*, New York *Sun*, Jan. 19, 1915.

59. Kansas City *Times*, April 26, 1915, Kansas City *Star*, Feb. 15, 1915, Chicago *Tribune*, April 24, 1915, Chicago *Record-Herald*, April

24, 1915, Walsh Scrapbooks, Walsh Papers; New York *Times,* Feb. 18, April 24–26, 30, May 3, 1915; Walsh to William Marion Reedy, March 3, 1915 (copy), Walsh Papers, contains quotation.

60. Manly to Walsh, April 20, 1915, USCIR Papers, Labor Department Files; Manly to Walsh, April 23, 1915, West to Walsh, April 20, 1915, Walsh to Manly, Walsh to West, April 22, 1915 (copies), Walsh Papers.

61. New York *Times,* May 19, 21, 1915, contains quotations; Dumba, *Memoirs of a Diplomat,* p. 172; New York *Sun,* May 22, 1915.

62. *Testimony,* IX, 8418-20, 8659, contains quotations; *ibid.,* pp. 8421, 8620, 8676; Fitch, "What Rockefeller Knew and What He Did," *Survey,* XXXIV (Aug. 21, 1915), 468-69; New York *Call,* May 22, 1915.

63. New York *Call,* May 21, 1915; *Testimony,* IX, 8664, 8420, contains quotations; Baker, *Woodrow Wilson,* IV, 386-87.

64. Fitch, *Survey,* XXXIV (Aug. 21, 1915), 462-64; *Testimony,* IX, 8421-22, 8427, contains quotations; New York *Times,* May 22, 1915; New York *Sun,* May 22, 1915.

65. Weyl, "Three Years' Truce for the Colorado Coal Strike," *Survey,* XXXII (Sept. 19, 1914), 608; *Testimony,* IX, 8422-26, contains quotations; U.S. Department of Labor, *Second Annual Report,* pp. 41-42; United Mine Workers, *25th Convention,* p. 101; Ralph Easley to E. R. A. Seligman, Nov. 7, 1914, Seligman Papers; Low correspondence with Governor Carlson, W. B. Wilson, Rockefeller, Jr., et al., Dec. 22, 1914–Jan. 28, 1916, box marked "Arbitration Colorado Coal Strike, President's Commission," Low Papers.

66. Creel, "Poisoners of Public Opinion," *Harper's Weekly,* LIX (Nov. 7, 1914), 436-38, (Nov. 14, 1914) 465-66; *Testimony,* VIII, 7772-76, 7882-83, 7897, 7900-05; *The Struggle in Colorado for Industrial Freedom* (Committee of Coal Mine Operators), almost complete set of these bulletins in Department of Commerce Files; Denver *Post,* Nov. 8, 1913, *Evening Chronicle* (Leadville, Colo.), Oct. 27, 1913, Pueblo *Star Journal,* Oct. 30, 1913, Department of Commerce Files.

67. Stevenson, "Labor and Capital," *Popular Science Monthly,* LXXXIV (May, 1914), 459-70; *Testimony,* IX, 8720, 8881; *ibid.,* pp. 8635-38, contains Rockefeller quotation; *ibid.,* pp. 8866-92, contains complete set of Rockefeller-Lee correspondence; New York *Call,* May 22, 1915.

68. Manly to Walsh, April 20, 1915, USCIR Papers, Labor Department Files, contains quotation; *Testimony,* IX, 8609-10, 8869, 8875, 8882-83, 8895-96; Seligman, "A Skilled Publicity Man," *Masses,* VI (August, 1915), 14; New York *Times,* May 21, 23, 1915; New York *Sun,* May 21, 1915.

69. Gilmore, *Masses,* VI (July, 1915), 7-8, contains first quotation;

Creel, *Rebel at Large,* p. 129, contains second quotation; New York *Call,* Jan. 27, 1914.

70. New York *Sun,* May 22, 1915.

71. *Ibid.* contains first quotation; "Who Is This Man Walsh?" *Current Opinion,* LIX (August, 1915), 90, contains second quotation; *Testimony,* IX, 8638; "Try to 'Gag' Walsh," *Appeal to Reason,* May 29, 1915; Walsh to Barton, May 24, 1915, Walsh Papers.

72. Walsh to West, April 22, 1915 (copy), Walsh Papers.

73. Detroit *Free Press,* quoted in Chicago *Record-Herald,* June 6, 1915; *Colorado News,* June 6, 1915, Walsh Scrapbooks, Walsh Papers; *Nation,* C (May 27, 1915), 586.

74. Philadelphia *Ledger,* quoted in *Journal* (probably Kansas City), June 3, 1915, Washington *Post,* Sept. 25, 1915, Walsh Scrapbooks, Walsh Papers; Philadelphia *Free Press,* quoted in Chicago *Record-Herald,* June 6, 1915; New York *Herald,* May 30, 1915. Adverse criticism of the Commission also appeared in the Philadelphia *Inquirer,* the Pittsburgh *Gazette,* the New York *Sun,* and the Buffalo *Express,* all as cited in Chicago *Record-Herald,* June 6, 1915.

75. Cincinnati *Post,* July 12, 1915, Denver *Express,* n.d., Walsh Scrapbooks, Walsh Papers; Kansas City *Star,* Sioux City *Tribune,* as cited in Chicago *Record-Herald,* June 6, 1915; Hapgood, "Smooth," *Masses,* VI (June 12, 1915), 551-54; Fitch, *Survey,* XXXIV (Aug. 21, 1915), 468-69.

76. *Machinists' Monthly Journal,* XXVII (July, 1915), 581; Gompers, "Walsh, a Great Tribune," *American Federationist,* XXII (July, 1915), 514-15; *Solidarity,* July 31, 1915; *Christian Socialist,* July, 1915, pp. 1, 3; Gilmore, *Masses,* VI (July, 1915), 7-8; "Chairman Walsh," *Masses,* VI (September, 1915), 10. Ralph Easley of the National Civic Federation sent Gompers a copy of the "FPW" issue of *Christian Socialist* with the comment that it was "as radical and irresponsible in its utterances as 'Solidarity' or 'Appeal to Reason'" (Easley to Gompers, July 7, 1915, AFL Archives).

77. New York *Sun,* May 22, 1915; Brubaker, "The Spotlight," *Masses,* VI (June, 1915), 7. Wilson's papers offer no evidence of the President's alleged displeasure.

78. Employers' Association of Washington to Woodrow Wilson, May 25, 1915, Merchants and Manufacturers' Association of Sacramento to Wilson, May 28, 1915 [telegram (copy)], Brainerd H. Warner to Wilson, May 25, 1915, Wilson Papers. Wilson Papers contain many other similar demands for Walsh's ouster. See also Chicago *Tribune,* June 5, 1915, Walsh Scrapbooks, Walsh Papers.

79. Justice League of Denver to Wilson, June 1, 1915, Wilson Papers; Chicago Federation of Labor to Wilson, June 28, 1915 (copy), Walsh Papers; Kansas City Printing Press Assistants' Union, Aug. 1,

1915, to Wilson. Wilson Papers contain many of these pro-Commission petitions from every section of the country.

80. Walsh to Barton, May 24, 1915 (copy), Walsh Papers, contains first quotation; New York *Times*, Feb. 7, 1915, Walsh Scrapbooks, Walsh Papers, contains second quotation.

81. McCarthy to J. S. Murdock, Jan. 14, 1915, McCarthy Papers, contains first quotation; Fosdick, *John D. Rockefeller, Jr.*, pp. 144, 167, contains second quotation.

82. New York *Tribune*, Sept. 27, 1915, Washington *Post*, Sept. 25, 1915, Walsh Scrapbooks, Walsh Papers; New York *Times*, Sept. 21, 27, 1915; Rockefeller, Jr.–Seth Low correspondence, December, 1914, January, October, 1915, box marked "Arbitration of Colorado Coal Strike, President's Commission," Low Papers.

83. Rockefeller, *The Colorado Industrial Plan*, and "Labor and Capital—Partners," *Atlantic Monthly*, XCVII (January, 1916), 12-21; Selekman and Van Kleeck, *Employees' Representation in Coal Mines*, pp. 27, 80, 188.

84. United Mine Workers, *25th Convention*, p. 107, contains quotations.

85. West, *Report on the Colorado Strike*, p. 156, contains first quotation; Kansas City *Star*, Jan. 28, 1915, Walsh Scrapbooks, Walsh Papers, contains second quotation; New York *Times*, Jan. 29, 1915.

86. *UMW Journal*, XXV (Dec. 17, 1914), 13; United Mine Workers, *25th Convention*, p. 102; Fitch, *Survey*, XXXIII (Dec. 5, 1914), 241-43; New York *Times*, Dec. 9, 1914; West, *Report on the Colorado Strike*, p. 242; *United Labor Bulletin* (Denver), Dec. 12, 1914, Walsh Scrapbooks, Walsh Papers.

87. New York *Times*, Feb. 7, 1915.

88. Kansas City *Star*, October (n.d.), 1906, Walsh Scrapbooks, Walsh Papers, contains first quotation; Reddig, *Tom's Town*, p. 54, contains second and third quotations; Charles H. Grasty, New York *Times*, Feb. 7, 1915, contains final quotation.

89. "Who Is This Man Walsh?" *Current Opinion*, LIX (August, 1915), 90; Kansas City *Post*, Feb. 18, 1915, Walsh Scrapbooks, Walsh Papers; Walsh to McCarthy, Dec. 20, 1914, McCarthy Papers; "Let There Be Light," *Christian Socialist*, July, 1915, p. 2, contains quotation.

Chapter VIII. Class Harmony—Myth and Reality

1. Perlman and Taft, *Labor Movements*, pp. 129-37; *ibid.*, p. 7, contains first quotation; Park, *Concern of the Railroad Employee*, p. 16; Easley, *National Civic Federation Review*, III (Feb. 15, 1912), 18;

Van Cleave, *Americanism the True Solution of the Labor Problem*, pp. 3-4.

2. *Industrial Worker*, Feb. 12, 19, March 19, 1910; New York *Call*, Nov. 12, 18, 24, Dec. 1, 2, 1909; *Testimony*, II, 1460, 1461; Flynn, "Free Speech Fight at Spokane," *International Socialist Review*, X (December, 1909), 485-87; *Congressional Record*, L (1913), 2900-03, 4400, 4410, 4411-13, 5980-83.

3. *U.S. Census: 1920*, Vol. X, *Manufactures*, 1919, *Reports for Selected Industries*, 423, 426; Howd, "Industrial Relations in the West Coast Lumber Industry," *Bulletin of U.S. Bureau of Labor Statistics*, No. 349 (December, 1923), pp. 17-27; Peter A. Speek, "Some General Observations . . . in the State of Washington" (unpublished), Division of Research, USCIR Papers, Department of Labor Files; *Final Report of the Commission on Industrial Relations*, p. 167; *Testimony*, V, 4575-89, 4605-23, 4768, 4939; *Timber Worker*, Feb. 1, 1913; Douglas, "The Problem of Labor Turnover," *American Economic Review*, VIII (June, 1918), 308-16.

4. *U.S. Census: 1920*, X, 426; Howd, *Bulletin of U.S. Bureau of Labor Statistics*, No. 349, pp. 40, 47-53; Washington State, *Ninth Biennial Report of the Bureau of Labor Statistics and Factory Inspection*, p. 34 ff.; *Testimony*, V, 4207-25, 4381-90, contains quotations; Seattle *Sun*, Aug. 12, 1914, Seattle *Daily Times*, Aug. 12, 15, 1914, in Walsh Scrapbooks, 1914, Walsh Papers; Speek, "Some General Observations . . . ," USCIR Papers contains quotation.

5. *Shingle Weaver*, Jan. 27, 1912, Feb. 1, 22, 1913; *Solidarity*, Sept. 16, 1911, July 15, 1911, as cited in Howd, *Bulletin of U.S. Bureau of Labor Statistics*, No. 349, pp. 40, 47-53.

6. P. A. Speek, "Notes on Investigation in Spokane, Washington, Aug. 10–13, 1914" (unpublished), Division of Research and Investigation, USCIR Papers, Department of Labor Files; *Testimony*, V, 4595-605; *Oregon Daily Journal*, Aug. 20, 1914; Portland *Evening Telegram*, Aug. 20, 1914, in Walsh Scrapbooks, 1914, Walsh Papers.

7. P. A. Speek, Report to Commission on Portland, Ed Gilbert to P. A. Speek, Sept. 17, 1914, "The Unemployed League" (broadside regarding Gypsy Smith Tabernacle), Division of Research and Investigation, USCIR Papers, Department of Labor Files; *Testimony*, V, 4595-605, 4721-24, contains quotation; Portland *Evening Telegram*, Aug. 20, 1914, *Oregon Daily Journal*, Aug. 20, 1914, Walsh Scrapbooks, Walsh Papers; Fitch, "Unemployment, Charity and the Minimum Wage in Process," *Survey*, XXXII (Sept. 12, 1914), 593-94.

8. Fitch, "Class Fighters and a Hobo Who Solved a Problem," *Survey*, XXXII (Sept. 5, 1914), 558; *Testimony*, V, 4242-49, 4405, 4374-77.

9. *Testimony*, V, 4242-49; P. A. Speek, "Notes on Investigation of

Private Employment Agencies in City of Seattle" (unpublished), Division of Research and Investigation, USCIR Papers, Department of Labor Files.

10. Fitch, *Survey*, XXXII (Sept. 5, 1914), 558; *Testimony*, V, 4233-42, contains all quotations; Seattle *Post-Intelligencer*, Aug. 12, 1914, Walsh Scrapbooks, 1914, Walsh Papers.

11. Fitch, *Survey*, XXXII (Sept. 12, 1914), 593-94; *Testimony*, V, 4589-95, 4643-54, 4697, 4729; Portland *Evening Telegram*, Aug. 20, 21, 1914, *Oregon Daily Journal*, Aug. 20, 21, 1914, Portland *News*, Aug. 21, 1914, *Morning Oregonian* (Portland), Aug. 22, 1914, in Walsh Scrapbooks, Walsh Papers.

12. G. U. Skinner, President of the Employers' Association of Washington, to Woodrow Wilson, Sept. 17, 1914, Wilson Papers, contains second quotation; *Testimony*, V, 4136-57, 4236-336, 4249-311, contain other quotations; Seattle *Post-Intelligencer*, Aug. 11, 14, 1914, Seattle *Sun*, Aug. 11, 14, 15, 1914, Seattle *Star*, Aug. 11, 14, 15, 1914, Seattle *Daily Times*, Aug. 12, 14, 15, 1914, in Walsh Scrapbooks, Walsh Papers.

13. *Testimony*, V, 4311-25, contains first quotation; Parker, *The Casual Laborer*, p. 97.

14. "Philadelphia Strike and Settlement," *Motorman and Conductor*, XVII (June, 1909), 4-6; New York *Call*, May 29, 31, June 1-5, 1909; *Current Literature*, XLVIII (April, 1910), 362-64; Philadelphia *Public Ledger*, June 3, 4, 1909.

15. Howland, "The War in Philadelphia," *Outlook*, XCIV (March 5, 1910), 523-25; *Current Literature*, XLVIII (April, 1910), 362-64; New York *Times*, Feb. 21, 1910.

16. "Brickbats in the City of Brotherly Love," *Collier's*, XLIV (March 12, 1910), 11-13; New York *Times*, Feb. 24, 1910, contains second quotation.

17. New York *Times*, Feb. 21, 1910; Philadelphia *Inquirer*, Philadelphia *Public Ledger*, Feb. 21, 1910.

18. New York *Call*, Feb. 23, 1910; New York *Times*, Feb. 20–23, 1910; Howland, *Outlook*, XCIV (March 5, 1910), 523-25; Philadelphia *Inquirer*, Feb. 20–23, 1910; Philadelphia *Public Ledger*, Feb. 20–24, 1910.

19. New York *Call*, Feb. 23, 1910; New York *Times*, Feb. 20–23, 1910; K. Mayo, *Justice to All*, pp. 172-74; New York *World*, Feb. 23, 1910, contains all quotations; Philadelphia *Inquirer*, Philadelphia *Public Ledger*, Feb. 23, 1910.

20. New York *Call*, Feb. 23, 25, 1910; Philadelphia *Public Ledger*, Philadelphia *Inquirer*, Feb. 23, 1910.

21. New York *Times*, Feb. 24, 1910, contains first quotation; New York *World*, Feb. 23, 1910, contains second quotation; New York *Call*,

Feb. 24, 1910; Philadelphia *Public Ledger*, Philadelphia *Inquirer*, Feb. 24, 1910.

22. "The Arrest of Chairman Pratt," *Motorman and Conductor*, XVIII (March, 1910), 18-19; New York *Times*, Feb. 23-25, 1910; *Current Literature*, XLVIII (April, 1910), 364; New York *Call*, Feb. 23, 1910, contains first quotation; New York *Call*, Feb. 25, 1910, contains second quotation; Philadelphia *Inquirer*, Feb. 23, 1910.

23. New York *Times*, March 9, 1910; New York *Call*, March 9, 1910; Philadelphia *Public Ledger*, March 9, 1910.

24. *Motorman and Conductor*, XVIII (March, 1910), 18-19, contains first quotation; New York *Times*, Feb. 21, 25, 28, March 5, 12, 18, 1910; *Amalgamated Journal*, March 17, 1910, contains second quotation; New York *Call*, March 10, 1910; *Outlook*, XCIV (March 12, 1910), 559-60; *American Federationist*, XVII (April, 1910), 330; Philadelphia *Public Ledger*, March 5, 6, 1910.

25. New York *Call*, Feb. 20, 24, March 3, 5, 6, 8, 1910; Feb. 24, March 8, contain quotations.

26. Philadelphia *Public Ledger*, March 20, 21, April 18, 1910; New York *Call*, March 18, 22, 23, 24, 28, April 7-9, 18, 1910; *Current Literature*, XLVIII (April, 1910), 361-65; New York *Times*, March 21, 24, 1910.

27. Philadelphia Rapid Transit Company, "A Plan for Collective Bargaining and Cooperative Welfare," reprinted in Commons, ed., *Trade Unionism and Labor Problems*, pp. 270-87; *Testimony*, III, 2731-35; Luke Grant, "Co-operative Plan of Philadelphia Rapid Transit Company" (unpublished report), Division of Research and Investigation, USCIR Papers, Department of Labor Files.

28. *Testimony*, III, 2735, 2810-11; Philadelphia *Morning Press*, June 24, 1914, Philadelphia *Public Ledger*, June 24, 1914; Philadelphia *North American*, June 24, 1914, in Walsh Scrapbooks, Walsh Papers.

29. *Testimony*, III, 2736-37; Philadelphia *Inquirer*, June 24, 1914, Philadelphia *New Post*, June 24, 1914, Philadelphia *Evening Star*, June 24, 1914, Philadelphia *Evening Bulletin*, June 24, 1914, Philadelphia *Evening Telegraph*, June 24, 1914, in Walsh Scrapbooks, Walsh Papers.

30. *Testimony*, III, 2740-41, 2768-71, contains first quotation; *ibid.*, p. 2747, contains second quotation; Fitch, "Collective Bargaining and Industrial Unrest," *Survey*, XXXII (July 11, 1914), 398; Philadelphia *Record*, June 25, 1914, Philadelphia *Press*, June 25, 1914, Philadelphia *Public Ledger*, June 25, 1914, in Walsh Scrapbooks, Walsh Papers.

31. Fitch, *Survey*, XXXII (July 11, 1914), 397-98 contains quotations; *Testimony*, III, 2762, 2765, 2782, 2794.

32. *Ibid.*, pp. 2758, 2763-65, 2784-85, 2798, contains quotations; Philadelphia *Evening Telegraph, Evening Star, Public Ledger,* all June 24, 1914; Philadelphia *North American, Inquirer, Record, Press, Public Ledger, Evening Star,* all June 25, 1914, in Walsh Scrapbooks, Walsh Papers.

33. Luke Grant, "Co-operative Plan of Philadelphia Rapid Transit Company" (unpublished report), Division of Research, USCIR Papers, Department of Labor Files.

34. Smith, *The State Police,* p. 49.

35. *Ibid.*, pp. 40, 33-34; K. Mayo, *Justice to All,* pp. 1-10; *ibid.*, p. xxv, contains quotation; *Testimony,* XI, 10932.

36. U.S. Senate, Document 521, pp. 7-17, contains first quotation (hereinafter referred to as *Senate Report*); *Amalgamated Journal,* May, 1910; *ibid.*, June 9, 1910, contains second quotation.

37. *Senate Report,* p. 17; *Testimony,* XI, 10943; New York *Call,* Feb. 7, 1910.

38. *Testimony,* XI, 10944-45; Allentown *Call,* Feb. 7, 1910, quoted in *Testimony,* XI, 10945; New York *Call,* Feb. 5, 1910; *Senate Report,* pp. 18-19; Philadelphia *Inquirer* and *Public Ledger,* both Feb. 5, 1910.

39. New York *Call,* Feb. 7, March 7, 1910; *Amalgamated Journal,* March, 1910; *Senate Report,* pp. 18-20; Allentown *Democrat,* March 7, 1910, cited in *Amalgamated Journal,* March 10, 1910; South Bethlehem *Globe,* Feb. 25, 1910, cited in *Testimony,* XI, 10946-47; Philadelphia *Inquirer,* Feb. 7–13, 1910; Philadelphia *Public Ledger,* Feb. 7, 9, 11, 12, 1910.

40. *Testimony,* XI, 10934; *Senate Report,* p. 21; *ibid.*, p. 56, contains second quotation; Allentown *Democrat,* Feb. 11, 1910, as cited in *Testimony,* XI, 10945; Philadelphia *Public Ledger,* Feb. 27, 1910, Philadelphia *Inquirer,* Feb. 28, 1910, in K. Mayo, *Justice to All,* p. 191; Philadelphia *Inquirer,* Feb. 26, 28, 1910.

41. *Senate Report,* p. 134, contains second quotation; *Testimony,* XI, 10955, contains third quotation; Philadelphia *Inquirer,* Feb. 26, 27, 1910; Philadelphia *Public Ledger,* Feb. 26, 27, 1910.

42. *Testimony,* XI, 10979, 10947-49; Allentown *Call,* March 1, 1910, Allentown *Democrat,* March 4, 5, 1910, cited in *Testimony,* XI, 10950-51, contains first quotation; *Amalgamated Journal,* March 10, 1910, contains second quotation.

43. New York *Times,* Feb. 28, 1910; K. Mayo, *Justice for All,* pp. 191-99; *Testimony,* XI, 10948, 10974, contains quotation; Philadelphia *Inquirer,* Feb. 27, 28, 1910; Philadelphia *Public Ledger,* Feb. 27, 28, 1910.

44. New York *Times*, March 1, 1910; Philadelphia *Public Ledger,* n.d., cited in K. Mayo, *Justice for All,* pp. 192-93; *Senate Report,* p. 49; *Testimony,* XI, 10974; New York *Call,* Philadelphia *Inquirer,* both Feb. 28, 1910; Philadelphia *Public Ledger,* Feb. 27, 28, 1910.

45. Philadelphia *Inquirer,* Feb. 10, 1910; Allentown *Democrat,* March 17, 1910, cited in *Testimony,* XI, 10952, contains first quotation; *Testimony,* XI, 10951-52, contains second quotation.

46. *Senate Report,* p. 134; *ibid.,* pp. 18-20, contains quotation; New York *Call,* March 5, 7, 16, 17, April 8, 1910; *Testimony,* XI, 10934, 10956-60. In his book, *American Cossack,* Maurer presented his documentary evidence of police brutality all over Pennsylvania.

47. *Testimony,* XI, 10932-36, contains first two quotations; Maurer, *American Cossack,* p. 6, contains last quotation.

48. Maurer, *American Cossack,* pp. 10-20, 79-80; *Testimony,* XI, 10937, 10960-62, contains quotation.

49. *Ibid.,* pp. 10965-68, 10972, 10999.

50. *Ibid.,* pp. 10937, 10976, 10999, contains quotations; *ibid.,* pp. 10968-69.

51. USCIR, *Final Report,* pp. 149-50.

52. Flynn, "Free Speech Fight at Spokane," *International Socialist Review,* X (December, 1909), 483-87; New York *Call,* Nov. 12, 15, 17–19, 24, Dec. 1, 2, 1909; Shippey, "Shame of San Diego," *International Socialist Review,* XII (May, 1912), 720-21; Goldman, "The Outrage in San Diego," *Mother Earth,* VII (June, 1912), 116-18; Reitman, "The Respectable Mob," *Mother Earth,* VII (June, 1912), 119-23; Daniel O'Regan (unpublished report), USCIR Division of Research, USCIR Papers, Department of Labor Files; Weinstock, *Disturbances in the City of San Diego.*

53. Parker, *The Casual Laborer,* pp. 74-75; *Testimony,* V, 4932-36; *ibid.,* VI, 5089-168, 5218-24; San Francisco *Chronicle,* Aug. 30, 1914, San Francisco *Examiner,* Aug. 30, 1914, San Francisco *Call,* Aug. 31, 1914, San Francisco *Daily News,* Aug. 31, 1914, San Francisco *Bulletin,* Sept. 1, 1914, in Walsh Scrapbooks, 1914, Walsh Papers; "A Report to His Excellency Hiram W. Johnson, Governor of California, by the Commission of Immigration and Housing of California on the Causes and All Matters Pertaining to the So-Called Wheatland Hop Fields' Riot . . ." (hereinafter referred to as *Wheatland Report*), reprinted in Parker, *The Casual Laborer,* pp. 171-99; Fitch, "The Way of the Transgressor in a Closed Shop City," *Survey,* XXXII (Sept. 26, 1914), 632-33.

54. *Wheatland Report,* pp. 176, 178; Parker, *The Casual Laborer,*

pp. 62-63; Bell, "The Wheatland Hop-Fields' Riot," *Outlook*, CVII (May 16, 1914), 120; Parker, "The Wheatland Riot and What Lay Back of It," *Survey*, XXXI (March 21, 1914), 768-69.

55. Bell, *Outlook*, CVII (May 16, 1914), 119-20, contains second quotation; Parker, *The Casual Laborer*, p. 62, contains first quotation; Parker, *Survey*, XXXI (March 21, 1914), 768-69.

56. Bell, *Outlook*, CVII (May 16, 1914), 120; Parker, *The Casual Laborer*, p. 62.

57. *Wheatland Report*, p. 192; Bell, *Outlook*, CVII (May 16, 1914), 121; Whitten, "The Wheatland Episode," *Pacific Historical Review*, XVII (February, 1948), 37-42.

58. Los Angeles *Citizen*, Nov. 7, 1913, cited in Perlman and Taft, *Labor Movements*, p. 243; Bell, *Outlook*, CVII (May 16, 1914), 121; Parker, *Survey*, XXXI (March 21, 1914), 770; *Wheatland Report*, p. 192; Los Angeles *Times*, Aug. 4, 1913.

59. Los Angeles *Herald*, Aug. 4, 1913, cited in Perlman and Taft, *Labor Movements*, p. 244; New York *Times*, Aug. 4, 5, 1913; Bell, *Outlook*, CVII (May 16, 1914), 121; *Wheatland Report*, p. 172; Los Angeles *Times*, Aug. 4, 5, 1913.

60. *Testimony*, V, 4979-5001, 5019-25; *ibid.*, p. 5001, contains quotation; Bell, *Outlook*, CVII (May 16, 1914), 121; *Wheatland Report*, p. 197; San Francisco *Examiner*, Aug. 28, 1914, San Francisco *Call*, Aug. 28, 1914, San Francisco *Bulletin*, Aug. 28, 1914, San Francisco *Chronicle*, Aug. 29, 1914, San Francisco *Call*, Aug. 29, 1914, in Walsh Scrapbooks, Walsh Papers.

61. Fitch, "Old and New Labor Problems in California," *Survey*, XXXII (Sept. 19, 1914), 609-10; Bell, *Outlook*, CVII (May 16, 1914), 121; *Testimony*, V, 4994-97; San Francisco *Chronicle*, Aug. 29, 1914, in Walsh Scrapbooks, Walsh Papers.

62. Whitten, *Pacific Historical Review*, XVII (February, 1948), 37-42; Los Angeles *Citizen*, Nov. 14, 1913, Feb. 6, 1914, as cited in Perlman and Taft, *Labor Movements*, p. 244; Bell, *Outlook*, CVII (May 16, 1914), 121.

63. Parker, *The Casual Laborer*, p. 139; Fitch, *Survey*, XXXII (Sept. 19, 1914), 610.

64. Holman, "The Tenant Farmer," *Survey*, XXXIV (April 17, 1915), 62-64; *Testimony*, IX, 8951-58, contains quotation.

65. *Ibid.*, IX, 8959-61, 9004-05, 9050; *ibid.*, X, 9095-97.

66. Holman, *Survey*, XXXIV (April 17, 1915), 63-64; *Testimony*, IX, 8966, 8981, 8957, 8934, 9050; *ibid.*, X, 9193.

67. *Ibid.*, IX, 9006-36; Holman, *Survey*, XXXIV (April 17, 1915), 62.

68. *Ibid.*, pp. 62-64; *Testimony*, IX, 9038-44.

69. *Ibid.*, X, 9146, 9206-86; *ibid.*, IX, 8974-89.

70. Holman, *Survey*, XXXIV (April 17, 1915), 62, contains first quotation; Walsh to William Marion Reedy, April 17, 1915 (copy), contains second quotation; Walsh to Editor of Dallas *Dispatch*, March 31, 1915 (copy), Walsh Papers; *Testimony*, IX, 8970, contains third quotation.

71. Harriman, *From Pinafores to Politics*, pp. 172-76.

72. Socialist State Convention of Oklahoma, *Proceedings*, 1914, Oklahoma City, pp. 20-24; Kipnis, *American Socialist Movement*, p. 364; Shannon, *Socialist Party of America*, pp. 34-36; P. A. Speek, "Notes on . . . Texas," Oct. 17-19, 1914 (unpublished), USCIR Division of Research, USCIR Papers, Department of Labor Files.

Chapter IX Finale with Fireworks

1. *American Justice*, September, 1915, pp. 13-14, in Walsh Scrapbooks, Walsh Papers; Gilmore, "Shadows of Revolt," *Masses*, VI (July, 1915), 8; Lippmann, "The Greatest Question," *Everybody's*, XXX (April, 1914), 504.

2. Fitzpatrick, *McCarthy of Wisconsin*, pp. 12-27.

3. *Ibid.*, pp. 40-61; McCarthy, *The Wisconsin Idea*; Commons, *Myself*, pp. 107-11; McCarthy to Walsh, June 25, 1914, McCarthy Papers.

4. McCarthy to Walsh, Walsh to McCarthy, June 3, 1914, contains first quotation, Walsh to McCarthy, June 6, 1914, McCarthy to M. S. Dudgeon, Dec. 9, 1914, McCarthy to Walsh, May 29, 1914, contains second quotation, McCarthy Papers.

5. "Investigation and Research, Payments made to employees . . . from organization to January 31, 1915 inclusive," McCarthy to Walsh, Sept. 8, 1914, contains quotation, McCarthy Papers. (A list of published reports that originated in the Research Division appears under a special heading in the Bibliography. This work, in previous chapters, has cited a number of unpublished studies. For a complete roster of the Division's staff, see the above-cited "Payments." The Commission's *Final Report* carries the names of most of these experts. See *Who's Who in America*, 1912–35, for their biographies.)

6. "Organization, Subject of Investigation and Progress of Work to September," USCIR, Division of Research, McCarthy Papers; Fitzpatrick, *McCarthy of Wisconsin*, p. 192, contains quotation.

7. *First Annual Report;* "The White House Files Memorandum," Nov. 1, 1913, Wilson Papers.

8. U.S. House of Representatives, *Estimates of Appropriations Re-*

quired for the Service of the Fiscal Year Ending June 30, 1915,
House Document 398, 63d Congress, 2d Session, p. 543; *Congressional Record,* LI (1914), Part 12, 11677-701, contains quotation.

9. *Ibid.,* contains quotation; W. B. Wilson to Walsh, Oct. 10, 1914, USCIR File 21/18, Department of Labor Files.

10. Research reports on Atlanta and other Georgia communities, USCIR, Research Division, Department of Labor Files; Manly to Walsh, March 12, 1915 (telegram), Walsh Papers; Walsh to McCarthy, July 13, 1914, Lewis Brown to Walsh, Walsh to Brown, July 14, 24, 1914 (telegram), McCarthy Papers.

11. McCarthy to Walsh, June 25, 1914, contains first quotation, Walsh to McCarthy, Dec. 23, 1914, McCarthy Papers.

12. "Memorandum of a Meeting Sunday, Feb. 28 [1915]," Walsh to McCarthy, March 2, 1915, McCarthy Papers.

13. McCarthy to Redmond S. Brennan, March 1, 1915, contains first quotation, McCarthy to Walsh, March 1, 1915, contains second quotation, Leiserson to McCarthy, March 2, 1915, McCarthy Papers.

14. McCarthy to Brennan, March 1, 1915, contains quotation, McCarthy to Commons, March 1, 1915, McCarthy Papers.

15. Drew to Tumulty, Oct. 16, 1914, Wilson Papers; Commons, *Myself,* pp. 175-76.

16. Walter Drew, "Federal Commission on Industrial Relations," in NAM, *Twentieth Annual Convention,* p. 37.

17. Walsh to William Marion Reedy, April 17, 1915 (copy), Walsh Papers.

18. McCarthy to Leiserson, March 3, 1915, contains first quotation, McCarthy to Leiserson, March 4, 8, 1915, contains second quotation, McCarthy Papers.

19. Leiserson to McCarthy, March 4, 8, 12, 1915, McCarthy to Fitch, March 9, 1915, McCarthy Papers; Commons to Helen M. Sumner, May 5, 1914, File 6007, Children's Bureau Files; Walsh to George Creel, March 14, 1915, Walsh Papers.

20. Walsh to Creel, March 14, 1915, Walsh Papers.

21. McCarthy to Rockefeller, Oct. 17, 1914, McCarthy to Rockefeller, Oct. 29, 1914, McCarthy Papers; Creel, "How 'Tainted Money' Taints," *Pearson's,* XXXIII (March, 1915), 296.

22. McCarthy to Lefferts Dashiel, Feb. 18, 1915, McCarthy to J. S. Murdock, Jan. 14, 1915, contains first quotation; McCarthy to Rockefeller, Oct. 17, 1914, contains second quotation, McCarthy to Rockefeller, Aug. 7, Oct. 17, 29, 1914, McCarthy Papers.

23. "To the Members of the Commission. . ." (undated), enclosed in letter, Commons to McCarthy, March 26, 1915, McCarthy Papers.

24. McCarthy to Walsh, Feb. 15, 1915, McCarthy Papers.

25. Walsh to Creel, March 14, 1915, contains quotation, Walsh to William Marion Reedy, April 17, 1915 (copy), Walsh Papers.

26. New York *Times*, March 31, 1915, contains quotation; Commons, *Myself*, p. 177; Commons to La Follette, n.d., Folder 1915, La Follette Papers, as verified in interview with Miss Fola La Follette, *ca.* July, 1961. McCarthy to Walter Rogers, March 30, 1915, McCarthy Papers, contains quotation; Walsh to Reedy, April 17, 1915 (copy), contains final quotation.

27. For evidence of work accomplished under Basil Manly, see Research Division Reports, Walsh Papers.

28. Minutes of a meeting of Commission, Chicago, June 15, 1915, Brown to Walsh, June 17, 1915, Manly to Walsh, June 19, 1915, Walsh to Commons, June 24, 1915 (copy), contains quotation, Walsh Papers.

29. Notes taken at meeting of full Commission, July 31, 1915, five memos dated June 14, 1915, *Reedy's Mirror*, April 23, 1915, Walsh Papers; Kansas City *Star*, August 15, 1915, contains quotation.

30. Commons, *Myself*, pp. 167-68.

31. Harriman, *From Pinafores to Politics*, pp. 173-75.

32. *Final Report*, p. 411, contains first quotation; Weinstock to Easley, August 9, 1915, File 177373, Justice Department Files, contains second quotation; Walsh to Sarah Bard Field, August 20, 1915, Walsh Papers, contains last quotation.

33. *Final Report*, pp. 16-21.   34. *Ibid.*, pp. 23-79.

35. *Ibid.*, pp. 33-91.   36. *Ibid.*, pp. 307-404.

37. *Ibid.*, pp. 407-39, 139-51.   38. *Ibid.*, pp. 309-31, 407-36.

39. Kansas City *Post*, August 29, 1915, contains first quotation; Walsh to West, August 27, 1915, Walsh Papers.

40. *Iron Age*, XCVI (Aug. 26, 1915), 474; *American Justice* (September, 1915), 13-14, in Walsh Scrapbooks, Walsh Papers; New York *Times*, New York *Sun*, quoted in "Some Second Thoughts on the Work of the Industrial Commission," *Current Opinion*, LIX (October, 1915), 225-27; Los Angeles *Times*, Aug. 25, 1915; *American Industries*, XVI (September, 1915), p. 13.

41. Gompers, "Industrial Commission's Report," *American Federationist*, XXII (October, 1915) 862; *Railway Federationist*, September, 1915, *National Ripsaw*, October, 1915, *Christian Socialist*, September, 1915, in Walsh Scrapbooks, Walsh Papers; *Appeal to Reason*, Sept. 11, 1915; "The Industrial Committee," *Masses*, VIII (January, 1916), 8.

42. *North American*, Springfield *Republican*, quoted in *Current Opinion*, LIX (October, 1915), 225-27; Binghamton *Press*, Aug. 24, 1915, Denver *Post*, Nov. 9, 1915, in Walsh Scrapbooks, Walsh Papers; "The Commons Report," *Survey*, XXXV (Jan. 1, 1916), 402.

43. "A Follow-Up Committee on Industrial Relations," *Survey*, XXXV (Nov. 13, 1915), 155.

44. Ohio Manufacturers' Association, Bulletin No. 32, typed copy enclosed in letter, O'Connell to Walsh, Dec. 14, 1915, Walsh Papers; *American Industries*, XVI (February, 1916), 16; *Iron Trade Review*, XCII (January, 1916), 214-15.

45. U.S. Senate, Public Resolution No. 15, Senate Document No. 415, 64th Congress, 1st Session; New York *Call*, May 5, 1916; *Appeal to Reason*, Jan. 23, 1916.

46. "Committee on Industrial Relations," press release, Nov. 29, 1915, Walsh Papers; *Appeal to Reason*, Jan. 30, 1916; *People's College News*, April, 1916; Barton, "The Pittsburgh Strike," *Masses*, VII (July, 1916), 17; Gigliotti, *Toward the Danger Mark*.

47. Galesburg *Labor News*, Sept. 8, 1916, Schenectady *Gazette*, Oct. 18, 1916, *Indiana Forum*, Nov. 4, 1916, in Walsh Scrapbooks, Walsh Papers.

48. Kansas City *Post*, Sept. 1, 1916; James A. Reed to Tumulty, Sept. 9, 1915, Wilson Papers; *Congressional Record*, 64th Congress, 1st Session, LII (1915–16), Part 16, Index and History of Bills.

49. Taft to Emery, March 4, 1918, Taft Papers; Pringle, *William Howard Taft*, II, 916, contains quotations.

50. *Ibid.*, p. 918; Perlman and Taft, *Labor Movements*, pp. 408-10; Taft to William D. Disston (copy), Dec. 18, 1918, Taft Papers, contains quotation.

51. Commons, *Myself*, pp. 178-80 (see list of research publications in Bibliography).

52. *Who Was Who in America*, III (1960), 550; Lauck Papers.

53. John R. Commons, "John Brown Lennon," in *Dictionary of American Biography*, XI (1933), 170-71; Philip Taft, "Austin Bruce Garretson," *ibid.*, XXI (1944), 333-34; *Who Was Who in America*, I (1942), 910.

54. *Ibid.*, II (1950), 19; *National Cyclopedia of American Biography*, XIX (1926), 440-41; *ibid.*, XL (1940), 564-65; *ibid.*, XX (1929), 132-33; *Who's Who in America, 1914–1915*, VIII (1914), 21.

55. Commons, *Myself*, pp. 173-75.

56. Harriman, *From Pinafores to Politics*, p. 91; *Current Biography*, I (1940), pp. 365-66.

57. New York *Times*, May 31, 1939; letter to author from Mrs. Celia Walsh Bradley, Oct. 25, 1955; Matthew 5:6.

58. Harriman, *From Pinafores to Politics*, p. 139 (friend is not identified).

Chapter X. Age of Industrial Violence

1. Gilmore, "Shadows of Revolt," *Masses,* VI (July, 1915), 8, contains first quotation; Perlman and Taft, *Labor Movements,* p. 164.

2. Braeman, "Seven Progressives, a Review Article," *Business History Review,* XXXV (Winter, 1961), 583.

3. Matthew Arnold, "Dover Beach."

BIBLIOGRAPHY

Published Work Derived from the Division of Research of the U.S. Commission on Industrial Relations

Barnett, George E. "Growth of Labor Organization in the United States 1897–1914," *Quarterly Journal of Economics*, XXX (August, 1916), 780-93.

—— and David A. McCabe. *Mediation, Investigation and Arbitration in Industrial Disputes*. New York, Appleton, 1916.

Curry, Nelle B. *Investigation of the Wages and Conditions of Telephone Operating*. Washington, D.C., U.S. Commission on Industrial Relations, 1915.

Grant, Luke. *The National Erectors' Association and the International Association of Bridge and Structural Ironworkers*. Washington, D.C., 1915.

Hoagland, Henry E. *Collective Bargaining in the Lithographic Industry*. Studies in History, Economics, and Public Law, No. 176. New York, Columbia University Press, 1917.

—— "Trade Unionism in the Iron Industry: A Decadent Organization," *Quarterly Journal of Economics*, XXXI (August, 1917), 674-89.

Hoxie, Robert F. *Scientific Management and Labor*. New York, Appleton, 1915.

Lauck, W. Jett. *Political and Industrial Democracy, 1776–1926*. New York, Funk and Wagnalls, 1926.

Leiserson, William M. *Adjusting Immigrant and Industry*. New York, Harper, 1924.

McCabe, David A. *National Collective Bargaining in the Pottery Industry*. Baltimore, Johns Hopkins Press, 1932.

Obenauer, Marie L., and Bertha Von Der Nienburg. *Effect of Minimum-Wage Determinations in Oregon*. Bulletin of the U.S. Bureau of Labor Statistics No. 176. Washington, D.C., 1915.

—— and Frances W. Valentine. *Hours, Earnings, and Conditions of Labor of Women in Indiana Mercantile Establishments and*

Garment Factories. Bulletin of the U.S. Bureau of Labor Statistics No. 160. Washington, D.C., 1914.

Parker, Carleton H. "The Wheatland Riot and What Lay Back of It," *Survey,* XXXI (March 21, 1914), 768-70.

Speek, Peter A. "The Psychology of Floating Workers," *Annals of the American Academy of Political and Social Science,* LXIX (January, 1917), 72-78.

Sydenstricker, Edgar. *Collective Bargaining in the Anthracite Coal Industry.* Bulletin of the U.S. Bureau of Labor Statistics No. 191. Washington, D.C., 1916.

—— *Unemployment among Women in Department and Other Retail Stores of Boston.* Bulletin of the U.S. Bureau of Labor Statistics No. 182. Washington, D.C., 1914.

—— and B. S. Warren, *Health Insurance: Its Relation to the Public Health.* Bulletin of the U.S. Public Health Service No. 76. Washington, D.C., 1916.

U.S. Bureau of Labor Statistics. *Regularity of Employment in the Women's Ready-to-Wear Garment Industry.* Bulletin No. 183. Washington, D.C., 1915.

West, George P. *Report on the Colorado Strike.* Washington, D.C., 1915.

Witte, Edwin E. *The Government in Labor Disputes.* New York, McGraw-Hill, 1932.

Wolman, Leo. "Collective Bargaining in the Glass Bottle Industry," *American Economic Review,* VI (September, 1916), 549-67.

—— "The Extent of Labor Organization in the United States in 1910," *Quarterly Journal of Economics,* XXX (May, 1916), 486-518.

Special Manuscript Collections

Jane Addams Papers, Peace Collection, Swarthmore College, Swarthmore, Pa.

American Federation of Labor, General Files, AFL Archives, Washington, D.C.

Mrs. Emmons Blaine Papers, McCormick Collection, Wisconsin State Historical Society, Madison.

William E. Borah Papers, Library of Congress, Washington, D.C.

Sophonisba P. Breckinridge Papers, Library of Congress, Washington, D.C.

Children's Bureau Central Files, National Archives, Washington, D.C.

Commerce and Labor Department Files, National Archives, Washington, D.C.

Justice Department Central Files, National Archives, Washington, D.C.

Samuel Gompers Papers, AFL Archives, Washington, D.C.

Florence Jaffray Harriman (Mrs. J. Borden Harriman) Papers, Library of Congress, Washington, D.C.

Paul U. Kellogg Papers, New York School of Social Research, New York.

Labor Department Files, National Archives, Washington, D.C.

Robert M. La Follette Papers, Library of Congress, Washington, D.C.

William Jett Lauck Papers, Alderman Library, University of Virginia, Charlottesville.

Seth Low Papers, Columbia University, New York.

Charles V. McCarthy Papers, State Historical Society of Wisconsin, Madison.

John Mitchell Papers, Catholic University, Washington, D.C.

National Civic Federation Papers, New York Public Library, New York.

Raymond Robins Papers, Wisconsin State Historical Society, Madison.

William Howard Taft Papers, Library of Congress, Washington, D.C.

Graham Taylor Papers, Newberry Library, Chicago.

E. R. A. Seligman Papers, Columbia University, New York.

Lincoln Steffens Papers, Columbia University, New York.

U.S. Commission on Industrial Relations Papers, General Records of Department of Labor, National Archives, Washington, D.C.

Lillian Wald Papers, New York Public Library, New York.

Frank P. Walsh Papers, New York Public Library, New York.

Woodrow Wilson Papers, Library of Congress, Washington, D.C.

Books and Articles

"The Acquittal of William D. Haywood," *Arena*, XXXVIII (September, 1907), 332-33.

Adamic, Louis. *Dynamite: The Story of Class Violence in America.* New York, Viking, 1931. (Rev. ed., 1954; reprinted, Gloucester, Mass., Peter Smith, 1963.)

Adams, Graham, Jr., "Frank P. Walsh," *Dictionary of American Biography.* New York, Scribner, 1958, Supplement 2, XXII, 690-91.

Addams, Jane. *The Second Twenty Years at Hull House, September 1909 to September 1929: With a Record of a Growing World Conciousness.* New York, Macmillan, 1930.

Allen, William H. "Suggestions Regarding Foundations Operating in More Than One State," *Survey*, XXXIII (Feb. 27, 1915), 587.

Altmeyer, Arthur J. *The Industrial Commission of Wisconsin: A Case Study in Labor Law Administration.* Studies in the Social Sciences and History, No. 17. Madison, University of Wisconsin Press, 1932.

America, V (Sept. 16, 1911), 542-43.

American Engineer, XXCVII (May, 1913), 249-56.

American Federation of Labor. *Report of Proceedings of 27th Annual Convention* (1907).

—— *Report of Proceedings of 28th Annual Convention* (1908).

—— *Report of Proceedings of 30th Annual Convention* (1910).

—— *Report of Proceedings of 31st Annual Convention* (1911).

—— *Report of Proceedings of 32nd Annual Convention* (1912).

—— *Report of Proceedings of 33rd Annual Convention* (1913).

AFL Executive Council Meeting, Atlantic City, N.J., Aug. 12–19, 1912, abstracts, *American Federationist,* XIX (October, 1912), 850-53.

American Federationist, XVII (April, 1910), 330; XVIII (June, 1911), 431-32; (July, 1911), 536-38; (September, 1911), 714; XIX (January, 1912), 17-23; (March, 1912), 230, 250; (July, 1912), 571; XXIV (February, 1917), 116-19.

American Industries, XII–XIV (1911–16).

American Justice, II (September, 1915), 13-14.

Anderson, Nels. *The Hobo: The Sociology of the Homeless Man.* Chicago, University of Chicago Press, 1923.

"The Arrest of Chairman Pratt," *Motorman and Conductor,* XVIII (March, 1910), 18-19.

Baker, Ray Stannard. *Woodrow Wilson, Life and Letters.* Vol. III: *Governor, 1910–1913.* New York, Doubleday, 1931.

Ballard, S. Thruston. "Eight-Hour Shifts in the Milling Industry," *American Labor Legislation Review,* IV (1914), 117-19.

Barnes, Mary Clark. "The Strike of the Shirtwaist Makers," *World Today,* XVIII (March, 1910), 266-67.

Barnum, Gertrude. "How Industrial Peace Has Been Brought About in the Clothing Trade," *Independent,* LXXIII (Oct. 3, 1912), 777.

Barton, Dante. "Frank P. Walsh," *Harper's Weekly,* LVIII (Sept. 27, 1913), 24.

—— "The Pittsburgh Strike," *Masses,* VII (July, 1916), 17.

Bean, Walton. *Boss Ruef's San Francisco: The Story of the Union Labor Party, Big Business, and the Graft Prosecution.* Berkeley, University of California Press, 1952.

Bell, George L. "The Wheatland Hop-Fields' Riot," *Outlook,* CVII (May 16, 1914), 119-21.

Berman, Edward A. *Labor Disputes and the President of the United States.* Studies in History, Economics, and Public Law, No. 249. New York, Columbia University Press, 1924.

Berman, Hyman. "The Era of the Protocol: A Chapter in the History of the International Ladies' Garment Workers' Union, 1910–1916." Ph.D. dissertation, Department of History, Columbia University, 1956.

Bernheimer, Charles S. *The Shirtwaist Strike.* New York, University Settlement Studies, 1910.

Blackmore, Charles P. "Joseph B. Shannon." Ph.D. dissertation, Department of History, Columbia University, 1951.

Boilermakers' Journal, XXIII (Nov. 1, 1911), 867; (Dec. 1, 1911), 976.

Bonnett, Clarence E. *Employers' Associations in the United States: A Study of Typical Associations.* New York, Macmillan, 1922.

Boone, Gladys. *The Women's Trade Union Leagues in Great Britain and the United States of America.* Studies in History, Economics, and Public Law, No. 489. New York, Columbia University Press, 1942.

Bowden, Whitt. "New Developments in the Colorado Strike Situation," *Survey,* XXXI (Feb. 14, 1914), 613-14.

Brandeis, Louis D. "The Preferential Shop," *Human Engineering,* II (August, 1912), 179-81.

Bremner, Robert H. *American Philanthropy.* Chicago, University of Chicago Press, 1960.

—— *From the Depths: The Discovery of Poverty in the United States.* New York, New York University Press, 1956.

Brewer, Luther. *History of Linn County, Iowa.* Chicago, Pioneer, 1911.

"Brickbats in the City of Brotherly Love," *Collier's,* XLIV (March 12, 1910), 11-13.

Brissenden, Paul F. *The I.W.W., a Study of American Syndicalism.* Studies in History, Economics, and Public Law, No. 193. New York, Columbia University Press, 1919.

Brotherhood of Railway Carmen of America. *Eleventh Biennial Convention* (1909).

Brubaker, Howard. "The Spotlight," *Masses,* VI (June, 1915), 7.

Burns, William J. *The Masked War.* New York, George H. Doran, 1913.

"Burns' Story on the Trail of the Men Higher Up," *McClure's,* XXXVIII (February, 1912), 363-71.

California State Federation of Labor. *Proceedings of Eleventh Annual Convention* (1910).

"A Call to Labor," *American Federationist,* XVIII (June, 1911), 451-52.

Century, LXXIX (March, 1910), 791.

"Chairman Walsh," *Masses,* VI (September, 1915), 10.

Chaplin, Ralph. *Wobbly: The Rough-and-Tumble Story of an American Radical.* Chicago, University of Chicago Press, 1948.

"A Charge of Wholesale Murder," *Outlook*, XCVIII (May 6, 1911), 1-2.

Christian Socialist, XI (September, 1915).

Citizens' Industrial Association of America. *Bulletin No. 1.* Indianapolis, 1903.

Clark, Marjorie R., and S. Fanny Simon. *The Labor Movement in America.* New York, Norton, 1938.

Clark, Sue Ainslie, and Edith Wyatt. *Making Both Ends Meet.* New York, Macmillan, 1911.

—— and —— "Working-Girls' Budgets," *McClure's*, XXXVI (November, 1910), 80-86.

Cloak and Suit Review, III (June, 1912), 128.

"The Cloakmakers' Strike," *Outlook*, XCV (July 23, 1910), 596-97; (Aug. 20, 1910), 855-56.

Cloak, Suit, and Skirt Manufacturers' Protective Association. "Memorandum of Agreement," [from] Alexander Bloch, Chairman of Settlement Committee to Cloak Manufacturers, July 5, 1910, in *The Cloakmakers' Strike.* New York, 1910.

Cohen, A., and Joe Chisholm. *"Take the Witness!"* New York, Stokes, 1934.

Cohen, Julius Henry. *Law and Order in Industry: Five Years' Experience.* New York, Macmillan, 1916.

Cohen, Sanford. *Labor in the United States.* Columbus, Ohio, Charles E. Merrill, 1960.

Colorado Bureau of Labor Statistics. *Ninth Biennial Report, 1903–1904.* Denver, 1904.

Colorado State Federation of Labor. *Militarism in Colorado.* Report of the Committee Appointed at the Suggestion of the Governor of Colorado. Denver, 1914.

Comerford, Frank. "Organized Labor Demands to Be Heard," *Railway Carmen's Journal*, XVIII (July, 1913), 417-20.

"Commission on Industrial Relations," *American Labor Legislation Review*, II (October, 1912), 465-66.

"The Commission on Industrial Relations," *Outlook*, CIV (July 5, 1913), 492.

Committee of Coal Mine Operators. *The Struggle in Colorado for Industrial Freedom.* [Bulletins.]

Committee on Industrial Relations. *Pocket Pamphlets Nos. 1–9.* New York, n.d.

Commons, John R. *The Economics of Collective Action.* New York, Macmillan, 1930.

—— "How the Wisconsin Industrial Commission Works," *American Labor Legislation Review*, III (Feb. 1, 1913), 9-14.

—— "John Brown Lennon," in *Dictionary of American Biography*. New York, Scribner, 1933, XI, 170-71.

—— *Myself*. New York, Macmillan, 1934.

—— et al. *History of Labor in the United States, 1896–1932*. New York, Macmillan, 1918–35. 4 vols.

——, ed. *Trade Unionism and Labor Problems*. Boston, Ginn, 1921. Second series.

"The Commons Report," *Survey*, XXXV (Jan. 1, 1916), 402.

"The Common Welfare," *Survey*, XXVII (Dec. 30, 1911), 1407-12.

Comstock, Sarah. "The Uprising of the Girls," *Collier's*, XLIV (Dec. 25, 1909), 14, 16.

"The Confession and Autobiography of Harry Orchard," *McClure's*, XXIX (July, 1907), 294-306.

"Confession of Harry Orchard," *Current Literature*, XLIII (July, 1907), 1-5.

Congressional Record, 62nd Congress, 2nd Session, XLVIII (1912), Parts 2, 3, 9, 11.

—— 63rd Congress, 1st Session, L (1913), Parts 3, 5, 6.

—— 63rd Congress, 2nd Session, LI (1914), Part 12.

—— 64th Congress, 1st Session, LIII (1915-16), Parts 1, 14, 15, 16.

Conlon, P. J. "Memories of the Past," *Machinists' Monthly Journal*, XXXIV (November, 1922), 729; XXXV (January, 1923), 17-23.

Connelly, Christopher P. "The Trial at Los Angeles," *Collier's*, XLVIII (Oct. 14, 1911), 32.

"The Constructive Work before the Industrial Relations Commission," *Survey*, XXX (Aug. 2, 1913), 571-89.

Creel, George. "How 'Tainted Money' Taints," *Pearson's Magazine*, XXXIII (March, 1915), 296.

—— "Poisoners of Public Opinion," *Harper's Weekly*, LIX (Nov. 7, 1914), 436-38; (Nov. 14, 1914), 465-66.

—— *Rebel at Large: Recollections of Fifty Crowded Years*. New York, Putnam, 1947.

—— "Why Industrial War?" *Collier's*, LII (Oct. 18, 1913), 5-6, 31.

Croly, Herbert. *Marcus Alonzo Hanna: His Life and His Works*. New York, Macmillan, 1912.

Cross, Ira B. *A History of the Labor Movement in California*. University of California Publications in Economics, Vol. XIV. Berkeley, University of California Press, 1935.

Current Literature, XLII (June, 1907), 587-95; XLVIII (April, 1910), 361-65.

Current Opinion, LV (August, 1913), 80-81.

Danish, Max D. *The World of David Dubinsky*. Cleveland, World Publishing, 1957.

Darrow, Clarence. *The Story of My Life*. New York, Scribner, 1932.

Davis, Allen F. "The Campaign for the Industrial Relations Commission, 1911–13," *Mid-America*, XLV (October, 1963) 211-27.

—— "The Social Workers and the Progressive Party, 1912–1916," *American Historical Review*, LXIX (April, 1964), 671-88.

—— "The Women's Trade Union League: Origins and Organization," *Labor History*, V (Winter, 1964), 3-17.

Davis, W. T. "The Strike War in Colorado," *Outlook*, CVII (May 9, 1914), 70.

Debs, Eugene V. "The McNamara Case and the Labor Movement," *International Socialist Review*, XII (January, 1912), 397-401.

—— "Sound Socialist Tactics," *International Socialist Review*, XII (February, 1912), 481-86.

Devine, Edward T. *Misery and Its Causes*. New York, Macmillan, 1909.

—— *Organized Charity and Industry: A Chapter from the History of the Charity Organization of the City of New York*. New York, New York School of Philanthropy [1915].

—— *When Social Work Was Young*. New York, Macmillan, 1939.

Dickinson, John, and Morris Kolchin. *Governor's Advisory Commission. Report of an Investigation. New York State. Cloak, Suit and Skirt Industry, New York City*. New York, 1928.

"Th' Doins Av th' Civic Fideration," *American Industries*, XIII (May, 1912), 28-30.

Dorfman, Joseph. *The Economic Mind in American Civilization*. Vol. III: *1865–1918*. New York, Viking, 1949.

Douglas, Paul H. "The Problem of Labor Turnover," *American Economic Review*, VIII (June, 1918), 308-16.

—— *Real Wages in the United States: 1890–1926*. Pollak Foundation for Economic Research. Research Publication No. 9. Boston, Houghton Mifflin, 1930.

Draper, Theodore. *The Roots of American Communism*. New York, Viking, 1957.

Dreier, Mary E. *Margaret Dreier Robins: Her Life, Letters, and Work*. New York, Island Press Cooperative, 1950.

Drew, Walter. "Federal Commission on Industrial Relations," in National Association of Manufacturers, *Proceedings of Twentieth Annual Convention* (1915).

Dubofsky, Melvyn. "Organized Labor and the Immigrant in New York City, 1900–1918," *Labor History*, II (Spring, 1961), 182-201.

Dulles, Foster Rhea. *Labor in America: A History*. New York, Crowell, 1949.

Dumba, Konstantin T. *Memoirs of a Diplomat.* Translated by Ian F. D. Morrow. Boston, Little, Brown, 1932.

"The Dynamiters," *Independent,* LXX (May 4, 1911), 923.

Easley, Ralph. *National Civic Federation Review,* III (Feb. 15, 1912), 18.

Eastman, Max. "Class War in Colorado," *Masses,* V (June, 1914), 6.

―― *Heroes I Have Known: Twelve Who Lived Great Lives.* New York, Simon and Schuster, 1942.

Eaton, Isabel. "Receipts and Expenditures of Certain Wage-Earners in the Garment Trades," *American Statistical Association,* IV (June, 1895), 135-80.

"Economic Statesmanship," *New Republic,* II (Feb. 6, 1915), 11-12.

Egbert, Donald D., and Stow Persons, eds. *Socialism and American Life.* Princeton, N.J., Princeton University Press, 1952. 2 vols.

"The End of the Paterson Strike," *Outlook,* CIV (Aug. 9, 1913), 780.

Epstein, Melech. *Jewish Labor in U.S.A.: An Industrial, Political, and Cultural History of the Jewish Labor Movement, 1882-1914.* New York, Trade Union Sponsoring Committee, 1950.

―― *Jewish Labor in the U.S.A., 1914-1952.* New York, Trade Union Sponsoring Committee, 1953.

Faulkner, Harold U. *The Quest for Social Justice, 1898-1914.* History of American Life, Vol. XI. New York, Macmillan, 1931.

―― and Mark Starr. *Labor in America.* New York, Oxford Book Co., 1957. Revised edition.

"Federation of Federations, Official Proceedings," *Blacksmith's Journal,* XIV (May, 1912), 1-38.

Filler, Louis. *Crusaders for American Liberalism.* New York, Harcourt, Brace, 1939.

Fine, Nathan. *Labor and Farmer Parties in the United States, 1828-1928.* New York, Rand School, 1928.

Fitch, John A. *The Causes of Industrial Unrest.* New York, Harper, 1924.

―― "Class Fighters and a Hobo Who Solved a Problem," *Survey,* XXXII (Sept. 5, 1914), 558.

―― "Collective Bargaining and Industrial Unrest," *Survey,* XXXII (July 11, 1914), 397-398.

―― "The Colorado War Interrupts Inquiry into Jurisdictional Disputes," *Survey,* XXXII (June 6, 1914), 252.

―― "The I.W.W., an Outlaw Organization," *Survey,* XXX (June 7, 1913), 357-362.

―― "Law and Order: The Issue in Colorado," *Survey,* XXXIII (Dec. 5, 1914), 241-58.

―― "Old and New Labor Problems in California," *Survey,* XXXII (Sept. 19, 1914), 609-10.

Fitch, John A. "The Paterson Silk Mill Strike a Year After," *Survey*, XXXII (June 27, 1914), 339-40.

—— "The Rockefeller Interests in Industry and Philanthropy," *Survey*, XXXIII (Feb. 6, 1915), 519-20.

—— "The Way of the Transgressor in a Closed Shop City," *Survey*, XXXII (Sept. 26, 1914), 632-33.

—— "Unemployment, Charity and the Minimum Wage in Process," *Survey*, XXXII (Sept. 12, 1914), 593-94.

—— "What Rockefeller Knew and What He Did," *Survey*, XXXIV, (Aug. 21, 1915), 462-69.

Fitzpatrick, Edward A. *McCarthy of Wisconsin*. New York, Columbia University Press, 1944.

Flynn, Elizabeth Gurley. *Debs, Haywood, Ruthenberg*. New York, Workers Library, 1939.

—— "The Free Speech Fight at Spokane," *International Socialist Review*, X (December, 1909), 483-88.

—— *I Speak My Own Piece: Autobiography of the Rebel Girl*. New York, Masses and Mainstream, 1955.

—— *Sabotage*. Chicago, Industrial Workers of the World, *ca.* 1913.

"A Follow-Up Committee on Industrial Relations," *Survey*, XXXV (Nov. 13, 1915), 155.

Foner, Philip S. *History of the Labor Movement in the United States*. Vol I: *From Colonial Times to the Founding of the American Federation of Labor*. Vol. IV; *The Industrial Workers of the World, 1905–1917*. New York, International, 1947, 1965.

Fosdick, Raymond B. *John D. Rockefeller, Jr.: A Portrait*. New York, Harper, 1956.

Foster, William Z. *The Railroader's Next Step*. Labor Herald Pamphlet No. 1. Chicago, Trade Union Educational League, 1921.

Gallagher, Andrew J. "Something Doing in Los Angeles," *International Socialist Review*, XI (September, 1910), 166-67.

Gambs, John S. *The Decline of the I.W.W.* Studies in History, Economics, and Public Law, No. 361. New York, Columbia University Press, 1932.

Garwood, Darrell. *Crossroads of America: The Story of Kansas City*. New York, Norton, 1948.

Ghent, W. J. "William Dudley Haywood," in *Dictionary of American Biography*. New York, Scribner, 1932, VIII, 467-69.

Gibbons, Edward J. "Frank Walsh and the United States Commission on Industrial Relations." Master's thesis, Department of History, University of Notre Dame, South Bend, Ind., 1958.

Gibbons, Floyd. "A Fight to a Finish: The Carl Person Case," *International Socialist Review*, XV (August, 1914), 72-78.

Gigliotti, Cairoli. *Toward the Danger Mark*. Chicago, 1916.

Gilmore, Inez Haynes. "At the Industrial Hearing," *Masses*, VI (March, 1915), 8-9.

——— "Shadows of Revolt," *Masses,* VI (July, 1915), 8.

Ginger, Raymond. *The Bending Cross: A Biography of Eugene Victor Debs.* New Brunswick, N.J., Rutgers University Press, 1949.

Goldman, Emma. "The Outrage in San Diego," *Mother Earth,* VII (June, 1912), 116-18.

Goldmark, Josephine C. *Impatient Crusader: Florence Kelley's Life Story.* Urbana, University of Illinois Press, 1953.

Gompers, Samuel. "Industrial Relations Commission's Report," *American Federationist,* XXII (October, 1915), 862.

——— "The 'I.W.W. Strikes,'" *American Federationist,* XX (August, 1913), 622-24.

——— "The McNamara Case," *American Federationist,* XVIII (June, 1911), 433-50.

——— "Gompers Speaks for Labor," *McClure's,* XXXVIII (February, 1912), 371, 375.

——— *Seventy Years of Life and Labor: An Autobiography.* New York, Dutton, 1925. 2 vols.

——— "They Don't Suit the 'Intellectuals,'" *American Federationist,* XX (February, 1913), 128-32.

——— "Walsh, a Great Tribune," *American Federationist,* XXII (July, 1915), 514-15.

Goodman, Pearl, and Elsa Ueland. "The Shirtwaist Trade," *Journal of Political Economy,* XVIII (December, 1910), 817-20.

Gordon, F. G. R. "A Labor Man's Story of the Paterson Strike," *National Civic Federation Review,* IV (Dec. 1, 1913), 16-17.

Grantham, Dewey W. *Hoke Smith and the Politics of the New South.* Baton Rouge, Louisiana State University Press, 1958.

Green, Marguerite. *The National Civic Federation and the American Labor Movement, 1900–1925.* Washington, D.C., Catholic University Press, 1956.

Grover, David H. *Debaters and Dynamiters: The Story of the Haywood Trial.* Oregon State Monographs: Studies in History, No. 4. Corvallis, Oregon State University Press, 1964.

Gulick, Charles A., and Melvin K. Bers. "Insight and Illusion in Perlman's Theory of the Labor Movement," *Industrial and Labor Relations Review,* VI (July, 1953), 510-31.

Haber, Samuel. *Efficiency and Uplift: Scientific Management in the Progressive Era, 1890–1920.* Chicago, University of Chicago Press, 1964.

Haferbecker, Gordon M. *Wisconsin Labor Laws.* Madison, University of Wisconsin Press, 1958.

Hampton's, XXIV (March, 1910), 423-25.

Hapgood, Norman. "Smooth," *Masses,* VI (June 12, 1915), 551-54.

Harbaugh, William Henry. *Power and Responsibility: The Life and Times of Theodore Roosevelt.* New York, Farrar, Straus and Cudahy, 1961.

Hardman J. B. S. "The Needle-Trades Unions: A Labor Movement at Fifty," *Social Research,* XXVII (Autumn, 1960), 321-58.

Harriman, Florence J. *From Pinafores to Politics.* New York, Holt, 1923.

—— "Hither and Yon," *Century,* CVII (December, 1923), 299-300.

—— "Is the 'Society Woman' a Useless Person?" *Harper's Bazaar,* XLVII (March, 1913), 118.

—— "Some Phases of the Southern Cotton Industry," *Harper's Weekly,* LV (July 1, 1911), 12.

Harrison, Charles Yale. *Clarence Darrow, Man of the People.* New York, Cape and Smith, 1931.

Harter, Lafayette G., Jr. *John R. Commons: His Assault on Laissez-Faire.* Oregon State Monographs: Studies in Economics, No. 5. Corvallis, Oregon State University Press, 1962.

Harvey, Rowland H. *Samuel Gompers, Champion of the Toiling Masses.* Stanford, Calif., Stanford University Press, 1935.

Haywood, William D. *Bill Haywood's Book: The Autobiography of William D. Haywood.* New York, International, 1929.

—— "The Rip in the Silk Industry," *International Socialist Review,* XIII (May, 1913), 783-88.

—— "Socialism the Hope of the Working Class," *International Socialist Review,* XII (February, 1912), 469.

Helbing, Albert T. *The Departments of the American Federation of Labor.* Johns Hopkins University Studies in Historical and Political Science, Vol. XLIX. Baltimore, Johns Hopkins Press, 1931.

Helfgott, Roy B. "Trade Unionism among the Jewish Garment Workers of Britain and the United States," *Labor History,* II (Spring, 1961), 202-14.

Hendrick, Burton J. *The Life of Andrew Carnegie.* New York, Doubleday, 1932. 2 vols.

Hicks, Clarence J. *My Life in Industrial Relations: Fifty Years in the Growth of a Profession.* New York, Harper, 1941.

Hicks, Granville. *John Reed: The Making of a Revolutionary.* New York, Macmillan, 1936.

Hillquit, Morris. *History of Socialism in the United States.* New York, Funk and Wagnalls, 1906.

"History of the Case," *Current Literature,* XLII (June, 1907), 587-95.

Holman, Charles W. "The Tenant Farmer: Country Brother of the Casual Worker," *Survey,* XXXIV (April 17, 1915), 62-64.

"How Burns Caught the Dynamiters," *McClure's*, XXXVIII (January, 1912), 328.

Howd, Cloice R. *Industrial Relations in the West Coast Lumber Industry*. Bulletin of the U.S. Bureau of Labor Statistics No. 349. Washington, D.C., 1923.

Howland, Harold J. "The War in Philadelphia," *Outlook*, XCIV (March 5, 1910), 523-25.

Hutchinson, Woods. "The Hygienic Aspects of the Shirtwaist Strike," *Survey*, XXIII (Jan. 22, 1910), 541-50.

Illinois Central Railroad Company. *61st Annual Report* (1911).

—— *62nd Annual Report* (1912).

Illinois Central System. New York, Wood Struthers, 1926.

Independent, LXXII (Feb. 22, 1912), 426-27; XXCVI (May 15, 1916), 233-34; XXCVI (June 19, 1916), 464-65.

"The Industrial Commission," *Masses*, VIII (January, 1916), 8.

"Industrial Relations," *Masses*, VII (November, 1915), 21.

"Industrial Relations," *Survey*, XXX (July 5, 1913), 452-53.

International Ladies' Garment Workers' Union. *Report of General Secretary-Treasurer*, June 3, 1900–June 1, 1901.

—— *Reports and Proceedings of ILGWU*, 1903–09, 1910–15.

ILGWU News-History, 1900–1950. Atlantic City, N.J., ILGWU, 1950.

International Socialist Review, XIV (July, 1913), 10.

Interstate Commerce Commission. *Railway Accidents. Extracts from the 25th Annual Report* (1912), 5-6.

Iron Age, XCVI (Aug. 26, 1915), 474.

Iron Trade Review, XCII (January, 1916), 214-15.

Jensen, Vernon H. *Heritage of Conflict: Labor Relations in the Nonferrous Metals Industry up to 1930*. Cornell Studies in Industrial and Labor Relations, Vol. I. Ithaca, N.Y., Cornell University Press, 1950.

Joint Board of Sanitary Control [New York]. *Third Annual Report* (December, 1913) [I.L.G.W.U.].

Jones, Dallas Lee. "The Wilson Administration and Organized Labor, 1912–1919." Ph.D. dissertation, Cornell University, Ithaca, N.Y., 1954.

Jones, Mary H. *Autobiography of Mother Jones*. Ed. by Mary Field Parton. Chicago, Charles H. Kerr, 1925.

Karson, Marc. *American Labor Unions and Politics, 1900–1918*, Vol. I. Carbondale, Southern Illinois University Press, 1958.

Kellogg, Paul U. "Conservation and Industrial War," *Survey*, XXVII (Dec. 30, 1911), 1412.

—— "The Government, the People and the Labor Problem," *Review of Reviews*, XLVIII (September, 1913), 339-46.

Kellogg, Paul U. "The Industrial Relations Commission," *Survey*, XXIX (Dec. 28, 1912), 385-86.

—— "Statement Prepared for the New York Hearings of the United States Commission on Industrial Relations," *Survey*, XXXIII (Feb. 20, 1915), 561-64.

Kellor, Frances A. *Out of Work*. New York, Putnam, 1915.

Kennan, George. "How Russia Loses Good Citizens," *Outlook*, CIV (July 26, 1913), 714-17.

"Kind Words for the M'Namaras," *Literary Digest*, XLIV (Jan. 6, 1912), 3-4.

Kipnis, Ira. *The American Socialist Movement, 1897–1912*. New York, Columbia University Press, 1952.

Kirk, William. *National Labor Federations in the United States*. Baltimore, Johns Hopkins Press, 1906.

Kirkendall, Richard S. "The Great Depression: Another Watershed in American History?" in *Change and Continuity in Twentieth-Century America*. Ed. by John Braeman, Robert H. Bremner, and Everett Walters. Columbus, Ohio State University Press, 1964, pp. 145-89.

Kirkland, Edward C. *A History of American Economic Life*. 3d ed. New York, Appleton-Century-Crofts, 1951.

—— *Industry Comes of Age: Business, Labor, and Public Policy, 1860–1897*. The Economic History of the United States, Vol. VI. New York, Holt, Rinehart, and Winston, 1961.

Knight, Robert E. L. *Industrial Relations in the San Francisco Bay Area, 1900–1918*. Berkeley, University of California Press, 1960.

Kornbluh, Joyce L. ed. *Rebel Voices, An I.W.W. Anthology*. Ann Arbor, University of Michigan Press, 1964.

Ladies' Garment Worker, I (July, 1910); II (October, 1911), 11-16; III (November, 1912), 9-11; IV (January, 1913), 13-16; IV (July, 1913), 11-14.

Laidler, Harry W. *Social-Economic Movements: An Historical and Comparative Survey of Socialism, Communism, Co-operation, Uto-pianism, and Other Systems of Reform and Reconstruction*. New York, Crowell, 1944.

"Larger Bearings of the McNamara Case," *Survey*, XXVII (Dec. 30, 1911), 1419-29.

Laslett, John. "Reflections on the Failure of Socialism in the American Federation of Labor," *Mississippi Valley Historical Review*, L (March, 1964), 634-51.

Lauck, W. Jett, and Edgar Sydenstricker. *Conditions of Labor in American Industries*. New York, Funk and Wagnalls, 1917.

Leupp, Constance D. "The Shirtwaist Makers' Strike," *Survey*, XXIII (Dec. 18, 1909), 383.

Levine, Louis. *See* Lorwin, Louis.

Lindsay, Samuel M. "A Colossal Inquiry Completed," *American Monthly Review of Reviews,* XXIV (December, 1901), 711-18.

Link, Arthur S. *Wilson: The Road to the White House.* Princeton, N.J., Princeton University Press, 1947.

—— *Wilson: The New Freedom.* Princeton, N.J., Princeton University Press, 1956.

Lippmann, Walter. "The Greatest Question," *Everybody's,* XXX (April, 1914), 502, 504.

Literary Digest, XLIV (Feb. 17, 1912), 319-20; XLVI (May 10, 1913), 1043-44; XLVI (June 21, 1913), 1366-67; XLVII (Aug. 9, 1913), 197-98.

Locomotive Firemen's Magazine, XVII (June, 1893), 511.

Lodge, Henry Cabot. *See* Roosevelt, Theodore.

Lombardi, John. *Labor's Voice in the Cabinet: A History of the Department of Labor from Its Origin to 1921.* Studies in History, Economics, and Public Law, No. 468. New York, Columbia University Press, 1942.

Lorwin, Louis [Louis Levine]. *The Women's Garment Workers: A History of the International Ladies' Garment Workers' Union.* New York, Huebsch, 1924.

—— and J. A. Flexner. *The American Federation of Labor: History, Policies, and Prospects.* Institute of Economics Publication No. 50. Washington, D.C., The Brookings Institution, 1933.

"The Los Angeles Conspiracy against Organized Labor," *International Socialist Review,* XI (November, 1910), 266.

Luhan, Mabel Dodge. *Intimate Memories.* Vol. III: *Movers and Shakers.* New York, Harcourt, Brace, 1936.

McCarthy, Charles V. *The Wisconsin Idea.* New York, Macmillan, 1912.

MacFarlane, Peter Clark. "What Is the Matter with Los Angeles?" *Collier's,* XLVIII (Dec. 2, 1911), 28, 30-31.

McGovern, George S. "The Colorado Coal Strike, 1913–1914." Ph.D. dissertation, Department of History, Northwestern University, Evanston, Ill., 1953.

Machinists' Monthly Journal, XX (April, 1908), 295; (May, 1908), 420-21; XXI (April, 1909), 342; XXIII (August, 1911), 789; (December, 1911), 1232; XXIV (March, 1912), 226; (April, 1912), 325; XXV (January, 1913), 37; XXVII (January, 1915), 44; (April, 1915), 362-63; (July, 1915), 581, 648-49.

McKenna, Marian C. *Borah.* Ann Arbor, University of Michigan Press, 1961.

McManigal, Ortie E. *The National Dynamite Plot.* Los Angeles, Neal, 1913.

McNamara Ways and Means Committee. *Weekly Newsletter No. 36*, n.d.

McPherson, John B. "The New York Cloakmakers' Strike," *Journal of Political Economy*, XIX (March, 1911), 154-183.

Magee, Mabel A. *Trends in Location of the Women's Clothing Industry*. Chicago, University of Chicago Press, 1930.

Mailly, William. "The Working Girls' Strike," *Independent*, LXVII (Dec. 23, 1909), 1416-20.

Malkiel, Theresa S. *The Diary of a Shirtwaist Striker*. New York, Cooperative Press, 1910.

Mandel, Bernard. *Samuel Gompers: A Biography*. Yellow Springs, Ohio, Antioch Press, 1963.

Mann, Arthur. "Gompers and the Irony of Racism," *Antioch Review*, XIII (June, 1953), 203-14.

Mannheimer, Rabbi Leo. "Darkest New Jersey: How the Paterson Strike Looks to One in the Thick of the Conflict," *Independent*, LXXIV (May 29, 1913), 1192.

Marcosson, Isaac F. "A Truce in the Trades," *Munsey's*, XLIX (July, 1913), 527.

Mason, Gregory. "Industrial War in Paterson," *Outlook*, CIV (June 7, 1913), 283-87.

Maurer, James. *American Cossack*. Reading, Pennsylvania State Federation of Labor, n.d.

Mayo, Katherine. *Justice to All: The Story of the Pennsylvania State Police*. 5th ed. Boston, Houghton Mifflin, 1920.

Mayo, Morrow. *Los Angeles*. New York, Knopf, 1933.

Meehan, Sister Maria Eucharia. "Frank Walsh and the American Labor Movement." Ph.D. dissertation, New York University, 1962.

"Men Who Make Women's Clothes," *Survey*, XXIV (Aug. 13, 1910), 701-03.

The Military Occupation of the Coal Strike Zone of Colorado by the National Guard, 1913–1914. Report of the Commanding General to the Governor.

Millis, Harry A., and Royal E. Montgomery. *Organized Labor*. Economics of Labor Series, Vol. III. New York, McGraw-Hill, 1945.

Miners' Magazine, XIV (July 21, 1913), 6; XIV (July 24, 1913), 5-6.

"Mollie Maguires in the West," *Independent*, LX (March 8, 1906), 536.

Moody, John. *The Masters of Capital*. New Haven, Yale University Press, 1921.

Morris, James O. *Conflict within the AFL: A Study of Craft versus Industrial Unionism, 1901–1938*. Cornell Studies in Industrial and

Labor Relations, Vol. X. Ithaca, New York State School of Industrial and Labor Relations, 1958.

Moskowitz, Henry. "An Experiment in Democratic Industrial Control," *LaFollette's Weekly*, V (April 19, 1913), 5, 13, 14.

Mote, Carl H. *Industrial Arbitration*. Indianapolis, Bobbs-Merrill, 1916.

Mother Earth, VII (June, 1913), 102.

Nadworny, Milton J. *Scientific Management and the Unions, 1900–1932: A Historical Analysis*. Cambridge, Mass., Harvard University Press, 1955.

Nation, XCIII (Sept. 7, 1911), 228-29; (Dec. 7, 1911), 536; XCIV (Feb. 8, 1912), 123; C (May 27, 1915), 586.

National Association of Manufacturers of the U.S.A. *Proceedings of the Eighth Annual Convention* (1903).

—— *Proceedings of the Seventeenth Annual Convention* (1912).

National Civic Federation. *Twelfth Annual Meeting* (1912).

—— Employers Welfare Department. *Welfare Workers' Fourth Conference* (1911).

National Ripsaw, II (October, 1915).

"A National Stock-Taking of Social Assets and Liabilities," *National Civic Federation Review*, IV (Dec. 1, 1913), 2-3.

Nation's Business, I (Sept. 15, 1913), 2.

New Jersey. *35th Annual Report of the Bureau of Statistics of Labor and Industries for the Year Ending October 31st, 1912*.

—— *36th Annual Report of the Bureau of Statistics of Labor and Industries of New Jersey for the Year Ending October 31st, 1913*.

Newman, Charles Philip. "The I.W.W. in New Jersey, 1912–1913." Master's thesis, Department of History, Columbia University, 1940.

New York State. *Department of Labor Bulletin*, Vol. IX (1907); Vol. XII (1910).

—— Department of Labor. *Annual Reports of Department Bureaus, 1910*. Vol. I, Part III, Bureau of Mediation and Arbitration.

—— *Third Annual Report of the Bureau of Statistics and Labor for the Year 1885*. New York State Senate Documents, Jan. 21, 1886, Vol. III.

"Nominations for the Industrial Commission," *American Industries*, XIII (January, 1913), 19.

"Now Who Is to Blame?" *Blacksmith's Journal*, XIV (March, 1912), 11.

Nye, Russel B. *Midwestern Progressive Politics*. East Lansing, Michigan State University Press, 1959.

O'Higgins, Harvey J. "The Dynamiters, a Great Case of Detective William J. Burns," *McClure's*, XXXVII (August, 1911), 347-64.

Order of Railway Conductors. *Proceedings of the Grand Division, 34th Session* (1913).

Orth, Samuel P. *Armies of Labor: A Chronicle of the Organized Wage-Earners*. The Chronicles of America Series, Vol. XL, Abraham Lincoln Edition. New Haven, Yale University Press, 1919.

"The Outcome of the Cloakmakers' Strike," *Outlook*, XCVI (Sept. 17, 1910), 99-100.

Outlook, XCIII (Dec. 11, 1909), 799-801; XCIV (March 12, 1910), 559-60; (August 20, 1910), 555-56; C (Jan. 13, 1912), 67-68; CX (July 14, 1915), 591.

"The Pageant as a Form of Propaganda," *Current Opinion*, LV (July, 1913), 32.

The Pageant of the Paterson Strike [official program]. New York, Success Press, 1913.

"Pageant of the Paterson Strike," *Survey*, XXX (June 28, 1913), 428.

Palmer, Frederick. "Otistown of the Open Shop," *Hampton's*, XXVI (January, 1911), 29-44.

Park, W. L. *The Concern of the Railroad Employee in the Existing Situation*. Chicago, Illinois Central Railroad, *ca.* 1910.

—— *The Facts about the Shopmen's Strike*. Chicago, Illinois Central Railroad, 1911.

Parker, Carleton H. *The Casual Laborer and Other Essays*. New York, Harcourt, Brace and Howe, 1920.

Paschal, Joel F. *Mr. Justice Sutherland: A Man Against the State*. Princeton, N.J., Princeton University Press, 1951.

"The Paterson Strike Pageant," *Independent*, LXXIV (June 19, 1913), 1406-07.

Pelling, Henry M. *American Labor*. Chicago, University of Chicago Press, 1960.

Perlman, Mark. *Labor Union Theories in America: Background and Development*. Evanston, Ill., Row, Peterson, 1958.

—— *The Machinists: A New Study in American Trade Unionism*. Cambridge, Mass., Harvard University Press, 1961.

Perlman, Selig, and Philip Taft. *Labor Movements*. Vol. IV of J. R. Commons, ed., *History of Labor in the United States, 1896–1932*. New York, Macmillan, 1935.

Person, Carl E. *The Lizard's Trail*. Chicago, Lake Publishing, 1918.

"Petition to the President for a Federal Commission on Industrial Relations," *Survey*, XXVII (Dec. 30, 1911), 1430-31.

"The Philadelphia Shirtwaist Strike," *Survey*, XXIII (Feb. 5, 1910), 595-96.

"Philadelphia Strike and Settlement," *Motorman and Conductor*, XVII (June, 1909), 4-6.

Pollack, Norman. *The Populist Response to Industrial America: Midwestern Populist Thought*. Cambridge, Mass., Harvard University Press, 1962.

Poole, Ernest. *The Bridge, My Own Story.* New York, Macmillan, 1940.

"A Possible Paterson," *Outlook,* CIV (June 14, 1913), 318-321.

Price, George. "A General Survey of the Sanitary Conditions of the Shops in the Cloak Industry," in *First Annual Report of the Joint Board of Sanitary Conditions in the Cloak, Suit and Skirt Industry.* New York, I.L.G.W.U. Joint Board of Sanitary Control, 1911.

Pringle, Henry F. *The Life and Times of William Howard Taft: A Biography.* New York, Farrar and Rinehart, 1939. 2 vols.

Quint, Howard H. *The Forging of American Socialism: Origins of the Modern Movement.* Columbia, University of South Carolina Press, 1953.

Railway Age Gazette, LI (Oct. 6, 1911), 626, 680-681; LII (Jan. 5, 1912), 26.

Railway Carmen's Journal, XVIII (February, 1913), 87-88; XVIII (May, 1913), 265-66; XVIII (April, 1913), 259 60.

Railway Clerk, VIII (February, 1009), 50-52; X (October, 1911), 372-76; (December, 1911), 456-58; XI (February, 1912), 33, 34; (March, 1912), 74; (May, 1912), 159-60; (June, 1912), 191-94; (December, 1912), 401-02.

Railway Conductor, XLVIII (March, 1931), 129.

Railway Employees' Department, AFL. *Official Proceedings, Second Biennial Convention* (1914).

Railway Federationist, VI (Sept. 2, 1915), 34.

Rapport, Leonard. "The United States Commission on Industrial Relations." Master's thesis, Department of History, George Washington University, Washington, D.C., 1957.

Ray, P. O. "Harrison Gray Otis," in *Dictionary of American Biography.* New York. Scribner, 1934, XIV, 100-101.

Rayback, Joseph G. *A History of American Labor.* New York, Macmillan, 1959.

Reddig, William M. *Tom's Town: Kansas City and the Pendergast Legend.* New York, Lippincott, 1947.

Reed, John. *The Education of John Reed: Selected Writings.* Ed. by John Stuart. New York, International, 1955.

—— "Sheriff Radcliff's Hotel," *Metropolitan,* XXXVIII (September, 1913), 15-16, 59-60.

—— "War in Paterson," *Masses,* IV (June, 1913), 13-17.

Reed, Louis S. *The Labor Philosophy of Samuel Gompers.* Studies in History, Economics, and Public Law, No. 327. New York, Columbia University Press, 1930.

Regional Plan Committee. "The Women's Garment Industry," in *Regional Plan of New York and Its Environs.* New York, 1924.

Reitman, Ben. "The Respectable Mob," *Mother Earth*, VII (June, 1912), 119-23.

"Review of the World," *Current Literature*, L (June, 1911), 569-75.

Rhea, M. "Organized Labor a Business?" *New Review*, III (Sept. 1, 1915), 205-06.

Riis, Jacob A. *How the Other Half Lives: Studies among the Tenements of New York*. New York, Scribner, 1900. (Reprinted, New York, Sagamore Press, 1957.)

Rischin, Moses. "From Gompers to Hillman: Labor Goes Middle Class," *Antioch Review*, XIII (June, 1953), 191-201.

—— "The Jewish Labor Movement in America," *Labor History*, IV (Fall, 1963), 227-47.

Robbins, Hayes. "Freeing San Francisco," *Public Policy*, XI (1904), 270-73. (Originally printed in Boston *Evening Transcript*.)

Rockefeller, John D., Jr. "Brotherhood of Men and Nations." Address delivered before the Civic and Commercial Club of Denver, June 13, 1918.

—— *The Colorado Industrial Plan*. New York, 1916.

—— "Labor and Capital—Partners," *Atlantic Monthly*, CXVII (January, 1916), 12-21.

Roosevelt, Theodore, and Henry Cabot Lodge. *Selections from the Correspondence of Theodore Roosevelt and Henry Cabot Lodge, 1884–1918*. New York, Scribner, 1925. 2 vols.

Sandburg, Carl S. "The Two Mr. Rockefellers—and Mr. Walsh," *International Socialist Review*, XVI (July, 1915), 18-25.

Saposs, David J. *Left Wing Unionism: A Study of Radical Policies and Tactics*. New York, International, 1926.

Schumpeter, Joseph A. *Capitalism, Socialism, and Democracy*. New York, Harper, 1942.

Scott, Andrew M. "The Progressive Era in Perspective," *Journal of Politics*, XXI (November, 1959), 685-701.

Scott, Miriam Finn. "What the Women Strikers Won," *Outlook*, XCV (July 2, 1910), 480-81.

Seidman, Joel I. *The Needle Trades*. New York, Farrar and Rinehart, 1942.

Selekman, Benjamin M. *A Moral Philosophy for Management*. New York, McGraw-Hill, 1959.

—— and Mary Van Kleeck. *Employes' Representation in Coal Mines: A Study of the Industrial Representation Plan of the Colorado Fuel and Iron Company*. New York, Russell Sage, 1924.

Selekman, Sylvia K., and Benjamin M. Selekman. *Power and Morality in a Business Society*. New York, McGraw-Hill, 1956.

Seligman, Herbert J. "A Skilled Publicity Man," *Masses*, VI (August, 1915), 14.

Shannon, David A. *The Socialist Party of America: A History.* New York, Macmillan, 1955.

Sharfman, I. Leo. *The American Railroad Problem: A Study in War and Reconstruction.* New York, Century, 1921.

Shippey, Hartwell S. "Shame of San Diego," *International Socialist Review,* XII (May, 1912), 720-21.

Sinclair, Upton. *American Outpost: A Book of Reminiscences.* New York, Farrar and Rinehart, 1932.

—— *The Autobiography of Upton Sinclair.* New York, Harcourt, Brace and World, 1962.

Smith, Bruce. *The State Police: Organization and Administration.* New York, Macmillan, 1925.

Smith, John S. "Organized Labor and Government in the Wilson Era; 1913–1921: Some Conclusions," *Labor History,* III (Fall, 1962), 265-86.

Socialist State Convention of Oklahoma. *Proceedings.* Oklahoma City, 1914.

Social Service Review, XXII (June, 1948), 260; XXXII (Dec., 1958), 425.

"Social Survey Enlists Nation-wide Support," *National Civic Federation Review,* IV (March, 1914), 1, 21-24.

Solidarity, IV (March 1, April 1, 19, 1913).

"Some Second Thoughts on the Work of the Industrial Relations Commission," *Current Opinion,* LIX (October, 1915), 225-27.

Spargo, John. *Syndicalism, Industrial Unionism and Socialism.* New York, B. W. Huebsch, 1913.

Steffens, Lincoln. *The Autobiography of Lincoln Steffens.* New York, Harcourt, Brace, 1931.

—— "An Experiment in Good Will," *Survey,* XXVII (Dec. 30, 1911), 1434-36.

Steiger, John H. *The Memoirs of a Silk Striker.* Privately printed, 1914.

Steigerwalt, Albert K. *The National Association of Manufacturers, 1895–1914.* Michigan Business Studies, Vol. XVI. Ann Arbor, University of Michigan Press, 1964.

Stevenson, John J. "Labor and Capital," *Popular Science,* LXXXIV (May, 1914), 459-70.

Stimson, Grace H. *Rise of the Labor Movement in Los Angeles.* Institute of Industrial Relations, University of California, Berkeley, University of California Press, 1955.

Stokes, Rose Pastor. "Paterson," *Masses,* V (November, 1913), 13.

Stone, Irving. *Clarence Darrow for the Defense: A Biography.* New York, Doubleday, 1941.

Sumner, Mary Brown. "The Broad Silk Weavers of Paterson," *Survey*, XXVII (March 16, 1912), 1932-34.

―― "The Spirit of the Strikers," *Survey*, XXIII (Jan. 22, 1910), 550-55.

Survey, XXIII (Nov. 13, 1909), 228; (Jan. 8, 1910), 489; XXVIII (July 27, 1912), 583; XXIX (Dec. 28, 1912), 336, 381-82; XXIX (Jan. 18, 1913), 491; XXX (April 19, 1913), 81-83; XXXII (May 23, 1914), 81-82; XXXIV (July 31, 1915), 390.

Syndicalist, III (Sept. 1, 15, 1913), 53.

Taft, Philip. "Austin Bruce Garretson," in *Dictionary of American Biography*. New York, Scribner, 1944, Supplement 1, XXI, 333-34.

―― *The A.F. of L. in the Time of Gompers*. New York, Harper, 1957.

―― "Commons-Perlman Theory: A Summary," in *Proceedings of Third Annual Meeting of the Industrial Relations Research Bureau* (1950), pp. 140-45. Madison, Wis., 1951.

―― "The I.W.W. in the Grain Belt," *Labor History*, I (Winter, 1960), 53-67.

―― "A Rereading of Selig Perlman's 'A Theory of the Labor Movement,' " *Industrial and Labor Relations Review*, IV (October, 1950), 70-77.

Taft, William Howard. "Address of President Taft at the Luncheon of the American Economic Association," *American Economic Review*, II, Supplement (March, 1912), 42-47.

Tarbell, Ida M. *Nationalizing of Business, 1878–1898*. History of American Life Series, Vol. IX. New York, Macmillan, 1936.

―― *New Ideals in Business: An Account of Their Practice and Their Effects Upon Men and Profits*. New York, Macmillan, 1916.

Taylor, Albion G. *Labor Policies of the National Association of Manufacturers*. Studies in the Social Sciences, Vol. 15, No. 1. Urbana, University of Illinois Press, 1928.

Taylor, Graham. "The McNamara Confessions," *Survey*, XXVII (Dec. 9, 1911), 1339-40.

―― *Pioneering on Social Frontiers*. Chicago, University of Chicago Press, 1930.

Teper, Lazare. *The Women's Garment Industry*. New York, International Ladies' Garment Workers' Union, 1937.

Todes, Charlotte. *Labor and Lumber*. New York, International, 1931.

"To Study Causes of Industrial Discord," *National Civic Federation Review*, IV (Dec. 1, 1913), 13.

Trachtenberg, Alexander, ed. *American Labor Yearbook, 1914–1920*. New York, Rand School, 1921.

"Trial by Jury on Trial," *Outlook*, XCIX (Dec. 2, 1911), 794-95.

"Twelve Months of Train Wrecks," *Literary Digest*, XLV (Dec. 28, 1912), 1209-10.

Ulman, Lloyd. *The Rise of the National Trade Union: The Development and Significance of Its Structure, Governing Institutions, and Economic Policies.* Cambridge, Mass., Harvard University Press, 1955.

The Union Pacific System. New York, Wood, Struther, 1925.

United Mine Workers of America. *Proceedings of the 25th Consecutive and Second Biennial Convention* (1916), Vol. I.

United Mine Workers' Journal, XXIV (Aug. 21, 28, Sept. 11, 18, 25, Oct. 30, Nov. 6, Nov. 30, 1913); XXV (Jan. 8, May 7, Dec. 17, 1914).

U.S. Census. *Twelfth Census of the United States* (1900). Vol. IX: *Manufactures*, Part III.

—— *Thirteenth Census of the United States* (1910). Vols. VIII and IX: *Manufactures.*

—— *Fourteenth Census of the United States* (1920). Vol. X: *Manufactures, Reports for Selected Industries.*

U.S. Commission on Industrial Relations. *First Annual Report of the Commission on Industrial Relations.* Washington, D.C., 1914.

—— *Final Report of the U.S. Commission on Industrial Relations.* Washington, D.C., 1915. (Barnard & Miller Print., Chicago.)

U.S. Congress. "An Act to Create a Commission on Industrial Relations, August 23, 1912." H.R. 21094, Public Law No. 300, Public Acts and Resolutions. *U.S. Statutes at Large.* 62nd Congress (1911–12), Vol. XXXVII, Part 1.

U.S. Department of Labor. *Second Annual Report of the Secretary of Labor* (1914).

—— Bureau of Labor Statistics. *Monthly Review*, Vol. III (August, 1916).

U.S. House of Representatives. *Charges against Members of the House and Lobby Activities of the National Association of Manufacturers of the United States and Others.* Select Committee on Lobby Investigations, 1913.

—— *Commission on Industrial Relations Report to Accompany H.R. 21094.* Report No. 726, 62nd Congress, 2nd Session (1912).

—— *Commission on Industrial Relations, Conference Report to Accompany H.R. 21094.* Report No. 1233, 62nd Congress, 2nd Session (1912).

—— *Estimates of Appropriations Required for the Service of the Fiscal Year Ending June 30, 1915.* House Document No. 398, 63rd Congress, 2nd Session (1914).

—— *Industrial Commission Hearings.* Committee on Labor of the House of Representatives, H.R. 20109 to Create a Commission on Industrial Relations, March 22, 1912. 62nd Congress, 2nd Session (1912).

U.S. House of Representatives. *Report on the Colorado Strike Investigation Made under House Resolution 387*. Document No. 1630, 63rd Congress, 3rd Session (1915).

U.S. Senate. *Industrial Relations: Final Report and Testimony Submitted to Congress by the Commission on Industrial Relations Created by the Act of August 23, 1912*. Document No. 415, 64th Congress, 1st Session (1916). 11 Vols.

—— *Maintenance of a Lobby to Influence Legislation*. U.S. Judiciary Committee Hearings, 63rd Congress, 1st Session (1913). 4 Vols., 4 appendixes.

—— *Public Resolution No. 15*. Document No. 415, 64th Congress, 1st Session (1916).

—— *Report on Strike at Bethlehem Steel Works*. Senate Document No. 521, 61st Congress, 2nd Session (1910).

Van Cleave, James W. *Americanism the True Solution of the Labor Problem*. New York, National Association of Manufacturers, *ca.* 1912.

Walsh, Frank P. "The Federal Industrial Relations Commission," *American Labor Legislation Review*, IV (March, 1914), 9-12.

—— "My Impressions of the Witnesses and Their Testimony," *Solidarity*, VIII (July 31, 1915).

"Walsh a Real Investigator," *Typographical Journal*, XLVII (August, 1915), 189-90.

"War! War! War!" *Blacksmith's Journal*, XVI (October, 1914), 1-6.

Ware, Norman J. *Labor in Modern Industrial Society*. New York, Heath, 1935.

—— *The Labor Movement in the United States, 1860–1895: A Study in Democracy*. New York, Appleton, 1929.

Washington State. *Ninth Biennial Report of the Bureau of Labor Statistics and Factory Inspection* (1914).

Weed, Iris. "Instead of Strikes," *Everybody's*, XXIX (July, 1913), 131-132.

—— and Louise Carey. "I Make Cheap Silk," *Masses*, V (November, 1913), 7.

Weinstock, Harris. "The German Courts for the Arbitration of Industrial Disputes," *Annals of the American Academy of Political Science*, XXXVI (September, 1910), 197.

—— *Disturbances in the City of San Diego*. Report to Hiram W. Johnson, Governor of California. Sacramento, 1912.

Weyl, Walter E. "Three Years' Truce for the Colorado Coal Strike," *Survey*, XXXII (Sept. 19, 1914), 608.

Whitten, Woodrow C. "The Wheatland Episode," *Pacific Historical Review*, XVII (February, 1948), 37-42.

"Who Is This Man Walsh?" *Current Opinion,* LIX (August, 1915), 90.

Winslow, Charles. *Industrial Court of the Cloak, Suit and Skirt Industry of New York City.* Bulletin of the U.S. Bureau of Labor Statistics No. 144. Conciliation and Arbitration Series 4. Washington, D.C., 1914.

Wise, Stephen S. *Challenging Years: Autobiography.* Ed. by James W. Wise. New York, Putnam, 1949.

—— *Personal Letters.* Ed. by Justine Wise Polier and James W. Wise. Boston, Beacon Press, 1956.

Woehlke, Walter V. "The End of the Dynamite Case—'Guilty,'" *Outlook,* XCIX (Dec. 16, 1911), 903-08.

—— "Terrorism in America," *Outlook,* C (Feb. 17, 1912), 359-67.

Wolman, Leo. *Ebb and Flow in Trade Unionism.* Publication No. 30. New York, National Bureau of Economic Research, 1936.

—— *The Growth of American Trade Unions, 1880-1923.* Publication No. 6. New York, National Bureau of Economic Research, 1924.

Women's Trade Union League. *Annual Report, 1909–1910.* New York, 1910.

Wyatt, Edith. "The New York Cloak-Makers' Strike," *McClure's,* XXXVI (April, 1911), 710-14.

Yellen, Samuel. *American Labor Struggles.* New York, Russell and Russell, 1956.

Newspapers

Amalgamated Journal (Pittsburgh), 1910.
Appeal to Reason (Girard, Kan.), 1910, 1911, 1913, 1915, 1916.
Boston *Transcript,* 1913.
Catholic Citizen (Milwaukee), 1913.
Chicago *Daily Socialist,* 1911.
Chicago *Record-Herald,* 1911, 1914, 1915.
Chicago *Tribune,* 1915.
Cincinnati *Post,* 1915.
Denver *Times,* 1914.
Denver *Post,* 1913, 1914, 1915.
Deseret Evening News (Salt Lake City), 1911.
Evening Chronicle (Leadville, Colo.), 1913.
Galesburg (Ohio) *Labor News,* 1916.
Indiana Forum (Indianapolis), 1916.
Industrial Worker (Spokane and Seattle), 1910.
Kansas City *Journal,* 1906, 1913, 1915.

Kansas City *Post,* 1913, 1915, 1916.
Kansas City *Star,* 1906, 1913, 1915.
Kansas City *Times,* 1906, 1915.
Labor World (Spokane), 1914.
Louisville *Courier-Journal,* 1913.
Los Angeles *Herald,* 1914.
Los Angeles *Record,* 1914.
Los Angeles *Times,* 1909, 1910, 1911, 1913, 1914, 1915, 1939.
Los Angeles *Tribune,* 1914.
Morning Oregonian (Portland), 1914.
New Orleans *Item,* 1911.
New Orleans *Times-Picayune,* 1911.
New York *American,* 1914.
New York *Call,* 1909-1915.
New York *Commercial,* 1913.
New York *Herald,* 1909, 1914, 1915.
New York *Evening Journal,* 1914.
New York *Evening Post,* 1913, 1914.
New York *Globe and Commercial Advertiser,* 1910, 1912, 1913, 1914.
New York *Journal of Commerce,* 1914.
New York *Mail,* 1914.
New York *Press,* 1914.
New York *Sun,* 1914, 1915.
New York *Times,* 1909–16, 1939, 1958, 1959.
New York *Tribune,* 1911, 1914, 1915.
New York *World,* 1909, 1910, 1913, 1914.
Oregon Daily Journal, (Portland), 1914.
Paterson (N.J.) *Evening News,* 1913–15.
Paterson (N.J.) *Guardian,* 1913–14, 1927.
Paterson (N.J.) *Morning Call,* 1914.
Paterson (N.J.) *Press,* 1913–14, 1927.
Philadelphia *Evening Bulletin,* 1914.
Philadelphia *Evening Star,* 1914.
Philadelphia *Evening Telegraph,* 1914.
Philadelphia *Inquirer,* 1910, 1914.
Philadelphia *Morning Press,* 1914.
Philadelphia *New Post,* 1914.
Philadelphia *North American,* 1914.
Philadelphia *Press,* 1914.
Philadelphia *Public Ledger,* 1909–10, 1914.
Philadelphia *Record,* 1914.
Portland (Ore.) *Evening Telegram,* 1914.
Portland (Ore.) *News,* 1914.

Pueblo (Colo.) *Star-Journal,* 1913.
Rocky Mountain News (Denver), 1914.
Reedy's Mirror (Kansas City, Mo.), 1915.
St. Louis *Globe-Democrat,* 1911.
St. Louis *Post-Dispatch,* 1906, 1911.
San Francisco *Bulletin,* 1914.
San Francisco *Call,* 1914.
San Francisco *Chronicle,* 1914.
San Francisco *Daily News,* 1914.
San Francisco *Examiner,* 1914.
Schenectady (N.Y.) *Gazette,* 1916.
Seattle *Daily Times,* 1914.
Seattle *Post-Intelligencer,* 1914.
Seattle *Star,* 1914.
Seattle *Sun,* 1914.
Shingle Weaver (Everett, Wash.), 1912, 1913.
Timber Worker (Portland, Ore., Seattle), 1913,
United Labor Bulletin (Denver), 1914.
Vicksburg *Herald,* 1911.
Washington *Post,* 1911, 1913, 1915.
Washington *Times,* 1911.
Weekly People (New York), 1913, 1914.

INDEX